GRETA GARBO

Divine Star

DAVID BRET

The Robson Press

First published in Great Britain in 2012 by
The Robson Press (an imprint of Biteback Publishing Ltd)
Westminster Tower
3 Albert Embankment
London SE1 7SP
Copyright © David Bret 2012

ISBN 978-1-84954-251-7

10 9 8 7 6 5 4 3 2 1

A CIP catalogue record for this book is available from the British Library.

Set in Edition and Adobe Garamond Pro

Printed and bound in Great Britain by
CPI Group (UK) Ltd, Croydon CR0 4YY

N'oublie pas
La vie sans amis c'est comme
un jardin sans fleurs

Twenty years after her passing, this book is
dedicated to my great friend, Marlene Dietrich.

ACKNOWLEDGEMENTS

Writing this book would not have been possible were it not for the inspiration, criticism and love of that select group of individuals who, whether they be in this world or the next, I will always regard as my true family and *autre coeur*: Barbara, Irene Bevan, Marlene Dietrich, René Chevalier, Axel Dotti, Dorothy Squires, Anne Taylor and Roger Normand, *que vous dormez en paix*. Lucette Chevalier, Jacqueline Danno, Hélène Delavault, Tony Griffin, Betty and Gérard Garmain, Annick Roux, John Taylor, Terry Sanderson, Charley Marouani, David Bolt. Also a very special mention for Amália Rodrigues, Joey Stefano, those *hiboux, fadistas* and *amis de foutre* who happened along the way and *mes enfants perdus*.

Very many thanks to Jeremy Robson and the munificent team at The Robson Press. Likewise my agent, Guy Rose, and his lovely wife. Also to my wife, Jeanne, for putting up with my bad moods and for still being the keeper of my soul.

And finally a *grand chapeau bas* to Garbo, for having lived it.

CONTENTS

INTRODUCTION

Greta Garbo was an enigma. She appeared as if from nowhere, taking Hollywood – and the world – by storm at a time when the movies were ruled by the likes of 'America's Sweetheart', Mary Pickford, and a clutch of now-forgotten vamps. She was one of the few to survive the transition from silents to talkies – not only this, but to reach such unprecedented heights of success as to leave her contemporaries gasping in amazement.

Because she was a foreigner from a country where attitudes towards life – and sex – were much more relaxed than in 1920s America, myths and rumours sprang up about her upon her arrival Stateside, as had happened with Valentino. Here was no ordinary girl-next-door, but a sophisticated, worldly woman who had probably seen and done more in her twenty years than most of them would in a dozen lifetimes. MGM, headed by the tetchy Louis B. Mayer, had no way of knowing how to handle her or her irrational behaviour, yet they complied with her every whim and submitted to demands other stars would never have got away with because, as a creature of great mystery as well as one of great beauty, the general public – the ones who put money in their pockets – could not get enough of her. No one would ever tell Garbo how to dress, how to conduct herself, and most importantly what to say. Unlike the other stars on their roster, she also refused to submit to a largely fabricated biography penned by a studio publicist. Until she stopped giving interviews, very early in her career, she replied to each question she wanted to reply to with stark honesty. If the subject was too personal, she would tell the interviewer to mind their own business and if she disliked a journalist, she would tell them so to their face and walk away.

In the male-orientated studio system, Garbo afforded herself the kind of power no other actress had ever possessed. She was never less than her own woman, the pawn of no man – not even when it came to love affairs. If things ever seemed like they were getting a little too tough and she might be disciplined – fired, even – she would pronounce the stock statement, 'Fine. Then I will go home to Sweden!'

Garbo was a minor star in Sweden when her Svengali, Mauritz Stiller, took her to America. There she was treated like some kind of freak, though it was not long before she put her most formidable weapons to good use: her ice-queen beauty, sharp wit and abrasive tongue, her indifference towards her surroundings, money, and her peers. Soon she was taking lovers of her choice, caring little if they belonged to someone else. When MGM warned her to steer clear of a man – or woman – she ran towards them with open arms.

Garbo appeared with most of the great stars of the day, and eclipsed them all in every scene they shared: Clark Gable, Wallace Beery, Marie Dressler, the Barrymores, Robert Taylor, Joan Crawford, and most importantly, John Gilbert, with whom she had a massively publicised affair. She very rarely granted interviews – when she did, they were heavily edited and censored by MGM's publicity department. Here, they are drawn from their original uncensored sources and give a clear insight into Garbo's mystique, and *why* she always wanted to be alone. On and off the screen, Garbo never ceased being an actress, keeping herself constantly in check, like a great military strategist planning her every move – so terrified was she of letting slip that infamous mask of cool reserve.

Garbo's films are masterpieces. Though she portrayed great heroines from literature and world history – Anna Karenina, Marie Walewska, The Lady of the Camellias, Queen Christina – each role was specifically adapted to match her complex persona, which, as this represented a myriad of contrasting moods, expressions and emotions, proved a nightmare for scriptwriters and directors alike. Garbo *lived* these roles, and with her innate talent for climbing inside her character's skin, refused to play a scene other than *her* way. If her way was not accepted, the set would be closed down until her wishes could be carried out to the letter.

Like her nearest counterpart, fellow 'exile' Marlene Dietrich, Garbo knew more about lighting and stagecraft than the most experienced technician. She very rarely rehearsed with any of her co-stars, even for complicated dance-routines, preparing her role in the privacy of her home and always getting it right. She could change her facial expression ten times within the space of a few seconds: from joy to melancholy, from laughter to tears, from passion to 'Pity me!' This pathos is most evident in her three most celebrated films, *Camille*, *Anna Karenina* and *Queen Christina*.

Garbo left the movies in 1941, following what she considered unfair criticism of her yet to be released film, *Two-Faced Woman*. Despite numerous phenomenal offers, she never faced another movie camera and for half a century lived as an 'open recluse' – rarely confined to her apartment for long, travelling the world and mixing with the social set, yet always on the lookout for 'that accursed photographer', with friends sworn to the strictest secrecy regarding her movements. Garbo always kept a magazine or hat in her hand, which would be brought up to her face whenever she felt in danger of being photographed.

Garbo's major relationships during her post-Hollywood years were conducted outside the acting fraternity. She had an affinity with gay men and Sapphic women: socialite Mercedes de Acosta, musician Leopold Stokowski, nutritionist Gayelord Hauser, and tetchy snapper Cecil Beaton all boasted passionate love affairs with her, but these are now known to have been platonic. Alistair Cooke called her, 'Every man's fantasy mistress. She gave you the impression that, if your imagination had to sin, it could at least congratulate itself on its impeccable taste.'

Garbo said more with her eyes than most of her contemporaries would ever dare put into words. An involuntary gesture from her – a frown, the slightest shrug of the shoulder – would have acted every one of today's so-called superstars off the screen.

This is her story.

CHAPTER ONE

GRETA GUSTAFFSON: SAPPHO RISING

'I can't remember being young, really young like other children. I always had my opinions, but never told my mind. No one ever seemed to think I was young!'

She was born Greta Lovisa Gustaffson[1] at 7.30 p.m. on 8 September 1905, at the Gamla Sodra BB Maternity Hospital in Södermalm, on Stockholm's south side, at that time little more than a slum. Records show that she was a healthy, seven-and-a-half-pound baby, though this did not prevent her parents from insisting she should be baptised into the Lutheran faith (then technically Sweden's only legal religion). For the first ten years of her life, almost everyone addressed her as 'Kata', the way she mispronounced her name.

Greta's father, Karl Alfred, was born in Frinnaryd, a small farming community in the south of the country, on 11 May 1871. The few surviving photographs of him reveal a strong resemblance to his daughter: tall – around 6′ 3″ – but not heavily built, with fair hair, angular cheekbones, an aquiline nose, full, almost feminine lips, deep-set eyes, and unusually broad shoulders. Karl Alfred preferred frowning to smiling – another Garbo trait – and enjoyed singing, but only when no one was listening.

Her mother was Anna Lovisa Karlsson, a plump, rosy-cheeked peasant's daughter of Lapp stock – she was born in Högsby, a village in Värmland, central Sweden, on 10 September 1872. Garbo is alleged to have once remarked how fortunate she had been *not* to have inherited any of her mother's traits other than her long, thick eyelashes and drooping eyelids – exquisite characteristics which would set her apart from just about every other Hollywood star. Karl Alfred and Anna Lovisa met in Högsby, where he was working on a local farm. They married on 8 May 1898, just ten weeks before the birth of their only son, Sven Alfred. Their other daughter, Alva Maria, was born on 20 September 1903, almost two years to the day before her more celebrated sister.

Covering the large island formerly known as Ason, Södermalm was one of the most densely populated areas of Scandinavia, and one of the poorest – a catastrophe of dilapidated buildings and narrow backstreets festooned with rubbish, the type of scenario which would not have been amiss in a penurious Brecht and Weill drama.

Home for the Gustaffsons was a shabby, three-room apartment, without its own facilities, in a tawdry tenement building at Blekingegaten 32 – on the third or fourth floor, depending on which account one reads (the block was demolished in 1972). The apartment was connected to an equally unbecoming courtyard by a series of stone staircases with rickety handrails. All five members of the family slept in the same room – Greta on a truckle bed in the middle, where there were fewer draughts blowing through the broken window frame.

Karl Alfred, not a healthy man despite his size, supported his family as best he could by taking on ad-hoc jobs, mostly helping out the local butcher or abattoir, evidence of which is supported by surviving photographs. In one, he and another employee wear butcher's aprons. One holds a slaughter-hammer, while there is an entrails bucket in the foreground. Behind them stands a cow, about to be led into the abattoir – hanging from the wall are meat carcasses.[2] Anna worked most days as a cleaner, skivvying for houses in a more opulent part of town. Alva, when she was old enough, did most of the shopping and cooking, while Greta was assigned to menial duties: washing dishes, sweeping the stairs and cleaning the outside toilet. This left her with a lifelong resentment of housework.

Garbo rarely spoke of her childhood. Indeed, the subject was broached with such reticence that one might be excused for thinking it might never have occurred! 'I was born. I grew up. I have lived like every other person,' she once said, 'That's all there is to anyone's life story, isn't it?'[3] She also recalled her 'games of pretence', and her belief that children should be given as much freedom as possible to think for themselves and develop their young minds, a process which she was convinced would shape their future lives:

When just a baby, I was always figuring, wondering what it was all about, just why we were living. Children should be allowed to think when they please, should not be molested! 'Go and play now,' their mothers and fathers tell them. They shouldn't do that. Thinking means so much, even to small children ... I didn't play much. Except skating and skiing and throwing snowballs. I did most of my playing by thinking. I played a little with my brother and sister, pretending we were in shows. Like other children. But usually I did my own pretending. I was up and down. Happy one moment. The next moment, there was nothing left for me.[4]

Over the years, nothing would change. In 1931 she told a Swedish journalist friend, Lars Saxon (1900–50), 'I found my greatest pleasure in my childhood dreams. Unfortunately, as a grown woman I am still the same, finding it hard to adjust to other people.'[5] Saxon knew more about Garbo's childhood than most, but never betrayed her confidence, and therefore always had her respect. Not so *Screen Book*'s Peter Joel, a Los Angeles-based Swedish reporter who in 1933 earned her enmity after visiting Stockholm, and Blekingegaten 32, where, with the help of a few of the locals, he pieced together a scenario involving the young Greta Gustaffson *before* fame had beckoned, when she and her family had struggled to survive:

In a small courtyard, in the rear of an apartment house, a small girl plays with her dolls. She talks to them, admonishing, cajoling, threatening. She walks back and forth. Her hands move. Her mood changes. Her voice is soft, then high-pitched then laughing. She lives through various emotions. Pretending. Always pretending. The courtyard is no different than hundreds of others in Stockholm. A patch of green grass, worn to the soil in some places. A place where the sunlight comes filtering down with its cheer and warmth. A sheltered little place, especially in the sweet coolness of a summer evening. But the girl who plays with the dolls adds distinction to the courtyard. The girl is Greta Gustafsson.[6]

Joel might have been describing the Garbo of the future, in a downbeat scene from *Susan Lenox: Her Fall And Rise*, or *Anna*

Christie. It was certainly not a scenario that she wanted the world to know had happened for real. Joel interviewed the Gustaffsons' next-door neighbour, Mrs Emanuel Lonn, who recalled an amiable but somewhat bossy child who knew back then that she was going somewhere in life:

> She was always so happy and full of life. She spent many hours here in my apartment, and I liked her very much. Everybody liked her ... She used to get all the children together out there [in the courtyard]. And how the children loved her! They came from all around to have Greta teach them how to play games. You could tell then that she was a born actress ... She mentioned it to me many times. She was so fond of pretending in her games ... You couldn't help but love her. And she was *so* pretty!

Another neighbour and friend, Agnes Lind, ran the tobacconists store which Greta visited every day to pick up her father's cigarettes and study the dozens of photographs lining the walls: all the famous Scandinavian theatrical stars of the day. Her favourites, Mrs Lind said, were the actor Kalle Pedersen, with whom she would one day become involved, and the operetta singer Naima Wifstrand.[7]

Some years later, Garbo opened up – but only briefly – to another friend of sorts, Swedish writer and journalist Sven Broman, whom she befriended in 1985, five years before her death. To Broman, she recalled her fondness for the Salvation Army, and for selling copies of *Stridsropet* (the Swedish equivalent of Britain's *War Cry*) in the streets of Stockholm. In later years, Garbo would drop in frequently at the Salvation Army Mission near her New York apartment.

In August 1912, unusually a month shy of her seventh birthday, Greta was enrolled at the Katarina Elementary School and barely tolerated the establishment:

> I hated school and I hated the restrictions it imposed on me. There were so many things to do *away* from school! History I liked, though the subject filled me with all manner of dreams. My fantasies led me to shortening the life of a cruel king and replacing him with a romantic knight, or reawakening an unhappy queen centuries after

her death. But I was *afraid* of the map – geography, you call it? I could never understand how anyone could be interested in faraway places, or in trying to solve ridiculous problems – such as how many litres of water could pass through a tap so-and-so wide in one hour and fifteen minutes. But I had to go to school like the other children![8]

In school photographs, Greta is by far the biggest girl in her class and, as if aware of this, stands slightly hunched forwards, with her long hair reaching her shoulders. Indeed, *because* of her size she was always given the job of cleaning the blackboard – a task which delighted her because, she said, nothing pleased her more than obliterating the 'rubbish' the teachers had been trying to drill into her. That said, she appears to have been an able, but at times lazy pupil. Her school records and reports, dating from this time until June 1919, have survived. Her teachers deemed her well above average in most subjects – awarding her straight As in behavioural application, discipline, concentration, religious studies, reading, writing and arithmetic. On the other hand she received Bs (the lowest grades) for art and gymnastics.

The dolls phase was short-lived as Greta took possession of her brother Sven's collection of tin soldiers. She was also the local marbles champion. Very much the tomboy, when not ruling her 'courtyard mob' she roamed the streets of Södermalm with her gang, frequently getting up to no good. She began wearing Sven's clothes – because the family were so poor, hand-me-downs were obligatory, and Greta was too big to wear her sister's cast-offs. One nosey, complaining elderly local lady who took on the 'Gustaffson boy' was rewarded by regularly having a bucket of sand and water flung at her window. Yet in direct contrast to this bravado there were reports of incredible shyness – bolting under the table, or hiding behind the drapes whenever a stranger visited the Gustaffson apartment. Also, the young Greta appears to have been always hungry and not averse to dropping in at the local soup kitchen whenever her father took sick, which was often, and there was no money to put food on the table.

The acting bug, Garbo said, bit when she was around six or seven. In 1927, in a very rare interview she told Ruth Biery of *Photoplay* how she had stumbled upon two theatres in Stockholm, the Soder and the Mosebacke, opposite each other in the same street. Because she had no money to buy a ticket, she lingered around the stage door – occasionally, if no one was around she would sneak inside and watch from the wings, but always make herself scarce the moment the curtain came down:

> I would smell the greasepaint. There is no smell in the world like the smell of a backyard of a theatre. No smell that will mean that much to me – ever! ... When I was just a little thing I had some watercolours, just as other children have watercolours. Only I drew pictures on myself rather than on paper. I used to paint my lips, my cheeks, paint pictures on me. I thought that was the way actresses painted![9]

Greta's best friend at the time, who sometimes accompanied her on her theatrical adventures, was Elizabeth Malcolm, with whom she stayed in touch after relocating to Hollywood – until Malcolm 'betrayed' her by revealing details of her childhood, albeit innocuous ones, to *Motion Picture*. According to Malcolm, on warm days she and the budding actress would scramble on to the roof of the row of outside lavatories in the courtyard of Blekingegaten 32 and, mindless of the obvious stench – these were earth toilets, shovelled out and emptied once a week by local workmen – pretend they were relaxing in some exotic location:

> 'We are on a sandy beach,' Greta would say, 'Can't you see the waves breaking on the shore? How clear the sky is! And do you hear how sweetly the orchestra at the Casino is playing? Look at that girl in the funny green bathing suit! It's fun to be here and look at the bathers, isn't it?' Greta's vivid imagination had no difficulty in transferring the tin roof into a glistening beach, the backyard with its clothes lines and ash cans into a windswept ocean, the raspy gramophone music floating through some neighbour's open window into some sweet melodies from a fashionable casino orchestra. The children shouting in the yard were, of course, the bathers.[10]

Greta was well-versed in the lives of all the big American movie stars – so far as she could glean from their frequently faked (by studio publicity departments) biographies in the movie magazines. Her first glimpse of these stars in the flesh occurred in 1913 when Karl Alfred took her to Stockholm's Bromma Airport, where she saw Mary Pickford and her husband, Douglas Fairbanks, arriving for a Scandinavian tour. Not much more than a decade later, she would have eclipsed them both.

In 1914, war broke out, with Sweden opting to remain officially neutral. No one knew for sure how long the conflict would last, if or when the government would change its mind. Rationing was imposed and the country – particularly the poorer classes – suffered the same as elsewhere. Karl Alfred had an allotment on the outskirts of the city, close to the shore of Lake Arsta, and once a week he packed a picnic basket and treated the family to an 'outing' to tend the tiny plot of land. While their parents worked, the children swam in the lake – Greta was a powerful swimmer, and swam regularly, often in the ocean, until she was almost eighty – picked whatever produce was ready to be eaten, sold it locally, and used the money to buy household essentials. With the outbreak of war, these outings stopped: Karl Alfred could no longer afford the fare for the trolley-bus.

Greta was a big girl (by the age of thirteen she would have reached her full height of 5′ 7″) and was eating almost as much as the rest of her family put together. The now daily diet of potatoes and bread – butter was expensive, and consumed only on Sundays – never affected her. Throughout her life, even when wealthy, she never ate extravagantly. She was a robust and healthy child, while everyone about her suffered from a variety of ailments: Anna and Alva were prone to chest infections, while her father and Sven were frequently stricken with intestinal problems attributed to their high-starch diet.

For the Gustaffsons, these were anxious times, as Garbo explained to Lars Saxon:

> My father would be sitting in a corner, scribbling figures on a newspaper. On the other side of the room, my mother would be repairing old clothes. We [children] would talk in low voices, or remain silent, filled with anxiety as if danger was in the air. Such evenings are unforgettable for a sensitive girl.[11]

Greta coped with her hunger pangs by making more visits to the soup kitchens, though her intentions were far from selfish. To ease the boredom of those standing in line she and her *frangine*, Elizabeth Malcolm, put on little 'street-cabaret' performances, doubling as anti-war protests, which they believed earned them the right to the gratis meal on offer – forward thinking for nine-year-olds, though it was Greta who scripted and choreographed each piece. Draped in a white bed sheet, she appeared as the Goddess of Peace – her friend, the handmaiden who crouched subserviently at her feet – and delivered pacifist speeches and poems, decrying the shedding of blood and the needless loss of life which was happening in every country in the world (she believed) but Sweden. And on the rare occasions when someone threw a few coppers at her feet, she collected these not for herself but to buy food for her elderly neighbours on Blekingegaten.

Sometimes, these propaganda trips took Greta as far as Fjallgratan, in Stockholm's Italian quarter, where the mind boggles to think of a clumsy-looking but pretty girl stumbling among all manner of low life and poverty to remind them, in no uncertain terms, of the horrors of a war they were not interested in. She wagged school to embark on these escapades, and was so wrapped up in her 'work' that her father and brother had to go looking for her. Her parents never punished her for going walkabout, though she once received a spanking from her teacher for playing truant. One of her childhood friends, Kaj Gynt (of whom more later) held this incident responsible for her frequently crippling shyness later in life:

> Before the whole class, the future queen of the screen had her small panties unbuttoned, was turned across the teacher's knee, and while we all looked on was soundly spanked. The humiliation of that public chastisement wounded her beyond anything. From that day she shrank more and more into herself. It was the end of her childhood.[12]

To Ruth Biery, Garbo recalled a childhood incident when *she* had rescued her father. Karl Alfred had been out with friends, and when he failed to return home for his supper, Anna sent out a search party. Greta was apparently the only one who could handle him when inebriated:

> I saw two men fighting. They were drunk. I can't *stand* people who are drunk! One was big and the other little. The big man was hurting the little one. I went up and pulled on the big man's sleeve. Asked him why he was doing it ... The big man said to the little man, 'You can go now. Here's your little daughter!' I ran away. I wasn't his 'little daughter' anymore.[13]

Garbo almost certainly is being facetious here. Her father was one of the biggest men in the neighbourhood, but in her eyes, now that he had humiliated her by getting into a scrap – and coming off worst – she had demoted him to the 'little man' whom she would never see in the same light again. The episode also appears to have provided her with an almost pathological loathing of arguments and violence. 'It's just the same today,' she told Ruth Biery, 'If I see an accident or hear two people fighting, I am just sick all over. I *never* fight, and I *won't* be doing any fighting in my pictures!'

In common with many of the poorer European communities, the one Garbo grew up in frequently staved off hunger pangs with an over-indulgence of tobacco and alcohol. She herself smoked from an early age, though she was never what would be called a drinker. Neither does her father appear to have been an alcoholic, except that his feeble constitution resulted in him getting drunk faster than most men. He could also be a nasty drunk, though Garbo always denied rumours that he had been physically violent towards his family.

Greta had always been closer to her father than her mother, but seeing this mighty rock being toppled during a scrap with a lesser mortal made her feel ashamed of him. She did not know at the time *why* he had been beaten by a weaker man – that he was in fact very sick. Therefore she began spending more time away from the apartment, and less time at school, now more than ever determined to become an actress. The major stumbling block towards achieving this goal, however, was that in Sweden not just anyone could step on to a stage and play Shakespeare or Ibsen. Unless one wished to augment one of the more disreputable players groups, one had to graduate via the Royal Dramatic Academy and, like L'Academie Française and other eminent European institutions, they were fussy about who they allowed through their hallowed portals. Besides which, Greta was too young to apply for a place there.

There was, however, another way: the movies. As was happening in Hollywood, each morning hundreds of hopefuls would gather in front of the studio gates in and around Stockholm in the hope of being 'spotted' by a casting director and hired as an extra. In February 1917, Greta and Elizabeth Malcolm set off for the Nordisk Studios, on the city's Lidingö Island – not the easiest of locations to reach in winter, when there was twelve inches of snow on the ground.

Unless the studios specifically requested child actors by advertising in the movie magazines, the legal age requirement for extras in Sweden was eighteen. Therefore, wearing more make-up than might have been prudent, the two girls set off for Lidingö Island. Elizabeth Malcolm later recalled Greta's logical way of thinking: if her (then) favourite movie star Mary Pickford could get away with playing child roles in her mid-twenties, then why could *they* not reverse the procedure? To get to the island, the friends took the trolley-bus to the toll-bridge, but could not go any further because they had no money to pay for the toll. No problem for Greta, who decided that they would *walk* across the frozen water to the island. They were halfway across, Malcolm said, when there was a sudden and violent snowstorm, forcing them to turn back and trudge home because the trolley-buses had stopped running.[14]

Vowing to return to the Nordisk Studios when the weather was more clement, Greta knuckled down to her studies. The war ended in 1918, and the Armistice coincided with Karl Alfred Gustaffson's health taking a turn for the worse. Greta's father had suffered from kidney stones for some time – unable to pay to see a specialist, he had taken a doctor's advice to drink plenty of water and take long walks. Now, there were times when he was too ill to get out of bed. It is possible that he may have been a victim of the influenza pandemic which was wiping out millions worldwide, surviving the malady, but only just. Neither was Karl Alfred's condition helped by the scandal which 'rocked' the Gustaffsons at this time.

Twenty-year-old Sven had fallen for a milkmaid named Elsa Hagerman while working at a local farm, and got her pregnant. One source claimed that, towards the end of her confinement, the family took Elsa in and offered her moral and financial support following the birth of her son, who was named Sven after his father. This seems unlikely: Garbo later claimed that the first time *she* had seen the boy, he had been ten years old.[15]

As there was no Public Assistance in Sweden in those days, it was a case of the rest of the family 'mucking in' to keep their heads above water. Anna was still cleaning the rich folks' homes, while Alva and Sven took ad-hoc work wherever they could. Greta, who does not appear to have yet been told how seriously ill her father was, continued with her dreams of becoming an actress. In June 1919, she arrived home from school and announced that she would not be going back. Neither of her parents attempted to get her to change her mind and a few days later, so that she would not be there when the school inspector came around, she was sent to stay with Anna's relatives in Högsby. Garbo would always regret leaving school early, and spend the rest of her life seeking out and socialising with people she considered more intelligent and intellectual than herself.

When Greta returned to Södermalm in January 1920, she took up where she had left off – helping her mother during the day, then doing the rounds of the theatres until the early hours. Two of her favourite stars were actor-singers Sigurd Wallén and Joseph Fischer, but it was at the Mosebacke, within comfortable walking distance of the South Side, that she met her biggest idol. Kalle Pedersen (1895–1958) was a handsome, 6′ 1″ Danish ex-prizefighter. In 1915 he had been crowned Central European Amateur Middleweight Champion, but he had given up boxing to marry his childhood sweetheart, Cleo Willard, and to go on the stage, where he soon made a name for himself as a musical comedy star. In 1923, having changed his name to Carl Brisson, he triumphed on the London stage as Prince Danilo in *The Merry Widow*, and later carved a successful niche for himself in Hollywood. Whether he reciprocated Greta's advances is not known. She may have lied to him about her age, and if she turned up at the theatre made up as in her later confirmation photo, Pedersen might not have felt it necessary to ask. The actor was appearing in the revue, *The Count Of Soder*, a variation of the one which he had been touring Scandinavia for several years – the theory being that, if the title was changed at every venue to incorporate the name of the city, the locals would be fooled into believing that they were about to see a new piece, written especially for them.

Greta was so infatuated with Pedersen that she collected every cutting and photograph she could find, and pinned these to the wall at Blekingegaten 32. And now she was no longer content just to hang around the stage door – she insisted the doorman let her in, claiming that she was a friend of the star. Flattered by the attention, Pedersen gave her a job as his prompter – each evening she sat in the audience and kick-started the applause when he walked on to the stage, then each time he began a song. According to Greta's version of events, the ruse backfired one evening when a technician turned the spotlight on her and she fled from the theatre, horrified at having been made the centre of attention. Pedersen told a different story: Greta had begun taking him flowers, and one evening sneaked into his dressing room and drew a heart on the wall within which she scrawled, 'Greta loves Kalle'. Subsequently, the next time they met he snarled, 'Go home to your mother, *little* Kata!'

No sooner had Greta recovered from her 'ordeal' than she was given the devastating news that her father had but a few months to live. Her first concern was in getting him the medical care he needed – and that cost money. To raise this, she took a job as a *tvalflicka* (lather-girl) at Einer Wideback's, the barber's shop where she had often accompanied her father to read movie magazines. This was not as unusual an occupation for a woman as it seems. Most of the *tvalflicka* in Stockholm were female, as were many barbers. Neither were Greta's duties restricted to lathering men's faces. She was responsible for cleaning and laying out the razors and scissors, washing the towels, and cleaning the sinks. Besides Wideback's, she worked at Ekengrens, whose owner recalled, 'She was really one of the most beautiful creatures I have ever seen. She was more filled out in those days, almost buxom, and she simply radiated happiness. She was a sunbeam!'

Mrs Ekengren was of course speaking in hindsight, having seen her celebrated former employee on the screen, after enormous changes had been effected on her appearance. Photographs taken of Greta at the time reveal her to have been handsome, certainly, but not specifically beautiful. For Karl Alfred, however, it was too late. By late spring he was completely bedridden, at which point Greta gave up her jobs and hardly left his side. He died on 1 June 1920, of nephritis, aged just forty-eight.

Garbo later told a French friend, Roger Normand, who she met by way of Jean Cocteau, 'It was a slip of a girl who travelled behind the hearse to the [Skogskyrogaarden] cemetery – but a mature woman who walked away from her father's graveside.'[16]

The occasion also proved an exercise in ultimate self control, useful in her later life when, no matter what happened to her, no matter how dramatic or tragic, Garbo would *never* put on the slightest display of emotion while in public. Recalling the time when the bottom had dropped out of her world, she told Lars Saxon:

> There was only sobbing and moaning to be heard in my home. My brother and sister would not even *try* to hide their grief. I frequently had to tell them to shut up. To my mind, a great tragedy should be born with silence. It seemed a *disgrace* to display grief in front of all the neighbours by constantly weeping. My sorrow was as profound as theirs – I cried myself to sleep for over a year. I also fought against the ridiculous urge to rush out in the middle of the night to look at his grave – to make sure that he hadn't been buried alive.[17]

On 13 June, less than two weeks after losing her father, Greta was confirmed. For twelve weeks, she had attended classes given by Pastor Ahlfeld – reluctantly because she had been desperate to spend every precious moment with her dying father. The photographs taken during the ceremony belie her age. In them one sees the Greta who set out for Lidingö Island – fourteen, going on twenty-one, wearing too much make-up, trying to look sensual, her hair over-dressed – as one biographer observes, looking like the picture on a chocolate box. In one picture, wearing her white confirmation dress and holding a bunch of roses, she looks almost gargantuan as she sits on a wooden chair, which has been turned sideways. In the group picture, she towers above the other girls, the ribbons atop her head making her appear even taller.

In the weeks following her father's death, Greta became increasingly paranoid about losing her mother and sister. Sven, she decided, had paved his own pathway to Calvary by getting his girlfriend pregnant, therefore it was up to *her* to look out for him from now on. Her possessiveness became such that, if she saw Anna talking to a neighbour in the street, she would distract her and drag her away. Alva, she declared, needed no friends while her 'big sister' was around. 'I was the youngest, but they always treated me like I was the oldest,' she remembered.[18]

This possessiveness resulted in a massive showdown – by Garbo standards – when she learned that a friend, Eva Blomgren, had been seeing Alva behind her back, as well as other friends of hers. Not only this, Eva had beaten her to meeting another of her idols, a popular actor-singer named Dalqvist. On 27 July, an irate Greta dashed off an imperious letter to the hapless Eva, part of which read:

> One thing you must tell me. How did you meet Dalqvist? The ideas I have are such that I think it will be better for you if you do explain. One other thing I have to say. If you and I are to continue as friends, you must keep away from my girlfriends as I did from yours ... I did not mind your going out with Alva, but I realised that you intended to do the same with *all* my acquaintances. Eva, I am arrogant and impatient by nature, and I don't like girls who do what you have done. If you hadn't written [to me first], I should never have made the first move toward reconciliation. And then you're writing to Alva. Frankly, I think you're making yourself ridiculous. If you hadn't done that, perhaps my letter would have been more friendly ... If this letter offends you, then you don't need to write to me again. If it doesn't, and you promise to behave as a friend, then I shall be glad to hear from you again.[19]

Like Marlene Dietrich (and speaking from experience as her confidante), later in life Garbo would go to inordinate lengths to ensure

that her closest friends never got to know about each other, so paranoid was she that they might meet up or communicate and 'swap
notes'. There is also some evidence that the relationship between
Greta and Eva may have progressed beyond the platonic, that this
is why Greta had such a hold over her. In 2005, to honour Garbo's
centenary, some of her private letters and telegrams were made
public, including those to lovers of both sexes. Though these did
not include missives to Eva Blomgren, references were made by the
author to a 'lovers' tiff', detailed in letters which were believed to
be in the possession of Garbo's surviving family.

There is no record of Eva's reply to Greta's letter, but she must
have apologised for her 'indiscretion' as Greta wrote to her again
on 7 August, though she had by no means finished ticking her off:

> Well, so you promise to mend your ways. Then all can be as before,
> provided I have no cause to complain again. I only do that when
> you behave like a child or make yourself ridiculous, that is,
> when I have reason to, not otherwise. But we can talk about
> that when we meet.[20]

Just days after admonishing Eva, Greta took her first steps towards
venturing out into the real world, so to speak. Alva was now
employed as a stenographer for an insurance company, and had
friends who worked at the Paul Urbanus Bergstrom department
store, more popularly known as PUB – the biggest in Sweden
and the equivalent of today's Harrods or Macy's. This was situated in the Hotorget Placa, in the centre of Stockholm. The store
had several vacancies, and citing Alva as referee, Greta applied
for a job. On 26 July, she began her apprenticeship in the store's
packing department on a more than modest salary of 125 kroner
a month – more money than she had ever seen in her life. She
worked here until the end of November, when she was promoted to
sales assistant in Ladies' Coats & Hats. With the promotion came
an increase in salary: three-quarters of her earnings were handed
over to Anna, while the rest went on Greta's twin passions –
chocolate, and visiting the cinema and theatre.

Today, the PUB store remains a shrine for devotees who visit

the city of her birth and take in one of the 'Garbo's Stockholm'
tours. In the display case in the third-floor millinery department
are photographs of her taken at the time, along with copies of her
employment record, and her signature at the bottom of her leaving
document. Working for PUB did not diminish her aspirations of
becoming an actress, though. 'Can you imagine such a thing – *me*,
a shopgirl?' she wrote in her 7 August letter to Eva Blomgren, 'But
don't worry. I haven't given up on thoughts of the stage because of
this. I'm just as keen as ever!'

Only days after receiving this, Eva was in hot water again. Since
starting at PUB, Greta had insisted that her friend be waiting
outside the store each evening at six, on the dot, to walk her home.
When Eva complained – as much as she dared protest – Greta *told*
her to get a job at the store, mindless of the fact that there were no
vacancies. Next, the poor girl received a ticking off for going on
holiday with her parents, without asking her permission:

> I thought you were going to come back this month and begin at
> Bergstroms, so that we could go to work and come back together,
> to say nothing of the fun we would have there every day ... I think
> you should come home soon, Eva. Why do you want to be in the
> country? Tell your mother you want to go home and work. Write
> when you're coming and I'll ring you up.[21]

Greta's dream of stardom appeared to take a small step towards
fruition when, in January 1921, she was invited to model for PUB's
spring catalogue. This was an important publication – not only was
it handed to customers visiting the store, but 50,000 copies were
dispatched to mail order clients all over Sweden. Greta modelled
five hats, each of which was given a name: Vera, Margit, Vanja,
Edit, and Olga. The prices ranged from 4.75 kroner (for the woman
in the street) to 18 kroner (for the elegant society lady). She by
far resembles the latter in the photographs, and, although still a
teenager, looks every inch a woman in her early twenties.[22]

How much Greta was paid – if anything – for her first professional appearance in front of a camera is not known. The fact
that she proved a natural, preening and posturing like the most

sophisticated of movie stars, ensured her a more prominent position in PUB's summer catalogue. Again she modelled hats, this time from the store's more expensive (10–26 kroner) range, with the then high-class monikers Jane, Ethel, Helny, Solveig, and Clary.

'I was really only interested in selling hats,' she later enthused, when asked why she had never sought promotion, 'I never seemed to have to *think* how to treat the individual whims of each customer. How I envied and admired the actresses among my customers!'[23]

It was almost certainly one of those customers who informed Greta that Mauritz Stiller, one of Sweden's most eminent film directors, was currently on the lookout for fresh new talent. She had seemingly forgotten about making that return trip to the Nordisk Studios, and though at the time she regarded Stiller as no more important than any other, she was intent on meeting him. His custom-built Kissell Kar, painted buttercup yellow, was a familiar sight on the streets of Stockholm, so Greta had no difficulty in recognising it. Stiller was such a madcap driver that, as soon as other drivers saw him speeding towards them in his 'Yellow Peril' they would pull over until he had roared past. He was returning home from the studio one evening and had only just managed to pull up outside the gates to his house when Greta stepped out of the shadows and strode in front of the car. Politely, she requested an audition. Not so politely – still shaking after watching her almost get knocked over – Stiller suggested that she go home, and seek him out again once she was a little older and more experienced. She is said not to have taken the rebuff very well, though it was an 'oversight' on Stiller's part which she was to forgive, for he would soon become the most important figure in her life.

By all accounts, Greta Gustaffson was a competent salesgirl, one who got along well with colleagues and customers alike. The latter, even the rude ones, were treated with the utmost reverence because there was always the chance that they were from the movie or theatre world. Often, Greta was asked to model a particular hat, and if it looked good on her, the client frequently purchased it without even trying it on.

An important client was John Wilhelm Brunius (1884–1937), the actor-director-scriptwriter who ran the Skandia Film Company.

When Greta first saw him, Brunius was casting extras for his new production, *En Lyckoriddare* (*Soldier Of Fortune*), which tells the story of the seventeenth-century Swedish poet and adventurer, Lars Wivallius, portrayed by heart-throb actor Gösta Ekman. When Greta informed him that she could not discuss 'business' at work – it was strictly against the PUB rules to 'moonlight' in any way – Brunius asked her out. Greta, probably assuming that she might be expected to hop on to the casting couch, took along Alva for 'protection', while the director, his intentions never less than honourable, brought his actress wife, Pauline. Both Gustaffson girls were hired for the film: Alva is listed on the roster as 'a servant girl', while Greta appears as 'a virgin'.

No print survives of *En Lyckoriddare*, and its successor, *Karlekens ogon* (*Scarlet Angel*), of which virtually nothing is known, appears to have suffered the same fate. Ironically, in 1934 when Brunius's 'discovery' had become the world's most feted female movie star, he made *False Greta*, featuring Karin Albihn as 'Greta Gustafsson, Typist', and Adolph Jahr as her businessman lover, a part clearly based on Max Gumpel, of whom more later.

News of Greta's movie debut was kept from her employer until now, but when she learned that Paul U Bergstrom had commissioned a seven-minute short to advertise his store, she risked her job to ensure that he was made aware of her acting abilities. The director was Ragnar Lasse Ring (1882–1956), a former cavalry officer and novelist, famed throughout Sweden for his frequently offbeat promotional films.

The whole point of *Herr Och Fru Stockholm* (*How Not To Wear Clothes*) is confusing, particularly as it was devised to *attract* customers to the PUB store and not drive them away! Bergstrom's budget permitted Ring to bring in one professional actress, Olga Andersson – one of Greta's hats had been named in her honour – but Ring still needed someone to play the fashion mannequin, preferably a salesgirl with no acting experience so that she would look like 'just another customer trying on clothes'. While Bergstrom was shortlisting employees, Greta found out where Ring lived and, as had happened with Mauritz Stiller, waylaid him outside his home during her lunch break. This time her cheek paid off and she was offered the part, though the other actor in the film, Ragnar Widestedt, tried to talk Ring out of hiring her. Later she recalled how Widestedt had walked up to the director and said, 'You're not intending to have that fat girl in the film, are you? She won't fit on the screen!' Some years later, when Greta had become Garbo, the two bumped into each other at a reception, and when Widestedt made as if to hug her she walked away, saying, 'No, thank you. The last time we met you called me fat!'

How Not To Wear Clothes is a comic mishmash which makes little sense. In her 100-second PUB changing-room sequence, Greta has great fun sending herself up. She appears wearing high-button-up shoes, an oversized three-quarter-length coat with gingham cuffs and matching cap, and a baggy gingham skirt. Smiling, she poses with her *back* to the mirror, unbuttons the coat, and this material-ises into a riding habit.[24]

The production was screened, between features, in cinemas all over Sweden. Though no critical review survives, Ragnar Lasse Ring was suitably impressed – and amorously interested – to use Greta for at least one more publicity short. *Konsum Stockholm Promo* (*Our Daily Bread*) advertised a local bakery, and offered her another comedy role. In the first scene she and three other well-dressed girls sit at a table in the roof garden of Stockholm's Strand Hotel, gorging on cakes, with Greta stuffing so much food into her mouth that it drops back on to her plate. It was not a cinematic moment upon which she would reflect with pride, though it gave her the opportunity to meet Lars Hanson who within a few years would figure very prominently in her life. He plays the handsome young man who sits at a nearby table, blow-ing smoke down his nostrils, with his back to the scene and there-fore oblivious to the gluttony taking place. The second segment of the film sees the same girls taking a picnic on an island. Greta and two of them frolic at the water's edge, while the fourth girl prepares the food and summons them to eat. Again, she spits and splutters as she tries to cram a large biscuit into her mouth, before washing it down with fruit juice – leaving the spoon in the glass so that it gets stuck up her nose![25]

Another important man entered Greta's life at this time. Max

Gumpel (1890–1965) was a former swimmer and waterpolo player who had won several medals representing Sweden in the 1908, 1912 and 1920 Summer Olympics. They first met on the set of *How Not To Dress* when his seven-year-old nephew, Erick Froander, had played Greta's brother. A big, strapping man and now a wealthy industrialist, Gumpel met Garbo again at the PUB store when he dropped in to pick up a hat for a friend. The two got along, Greta spoke to him of her aspirations, and they began dating. Eventually, he invited her to his plush apartment on Drottning Street, where she experienced the finer aspects of society dining: fingerbowls and artichokes, neither of which she had seen before. If they did enjoy a physical relationship, Gumpel could have been prosecuted for having sex with a minor, though, like Kalle Pedersen, he may not have been aware of her age.[26]

Max Gumpel showed Greta a side of life alien to her until now. At home, 'going to the bathroom' meant descending several flights of steep steps, then a trudge across a dark, smelly courtyard to the row of toilets which stank to high heaven in summer, and whose walls were thick with ice in winter; where bathing meant climbing into the tin tub, usually after everyone else, which had to be filled from the copper in the corner then dragged outside and emptied down the grate. In contrast, Gumpel's apartment had gas mantles, the bathroom had brass fittings and a tub so large that she could get lost in it. 'He filled the tub up and had a kind of liquid soap that made bubbles on top of the water,' Greta told a friend, 'I've never experienced anything so nice!'

Gumpel also bought her her first jewellery, a diamond ring which she described as: 'As beautiful as a diamond in the English royal crown.' Whether she interpreted this as some sort of marriage proposal is not known. Their affair ended as quickly as it had begun – though they would remain friends for life – and he returned to his girlfriend, whom he married the following year. Greta kept the ring.[27]

During her relationship with Gumpel, Greta's other friendships had been cast aside. Now, with no one to fuss over her and succumb to her every whim, she returned to former stooge Eva Blomgrem and on 15 August dashed off another pleading, self-absorbed missive: 'They [at PUB] look at me with astonishment because I'm only fifteen. If you were to come, I'll bet they'll all ask you if it's true. Eva, you and I must go out and have fun together, otherwise I'll die!'[28]

Yet there was really only one thing on Greta's mind, as she concluded, 'Whenever I'm left to myself, I long so dreadfully for the theatre. Everything I want is there!' Eva did not heed the call-to-arms, and two weeks later Greta left Stockholm for what may have been her first proper holiday, a week-long stay in Nykroppa, in Värmland County. The trip was financed by Max Gumpel, by way of a parting gift, along with a second diamond ring, though it is not known if he accompanied her there. This time, the tone of her letter to Eva, the friend she assumed she could pick up and discard at will like an item of clothing, was even more condescending:

> Eva, child. To be honest, I haven't thought of you – for the simple reason that I don't think of anything. I'm quite satisfied to be here, and don't long to be back ... I wanted to get to a place where there weren't so many people, so that I could rest. I have had my wish very well fulfilled in that most of the company I provide myself!

Was the melancholia and neurasthenia most associated with Garbo's later years and her quest for solitude already starting to take over at just fifteen? Or was she merely wishing to grab attention by feigning profound happiness one moment, self-pity the next? Neither was she prepared to allow any of her 'intimates' fulfilment in their own lives until her personal goals had been achieved.

Inasmuch as she had admonished Eva for befriending her sister, so Eva was now instructed to 'save the situation' when she learned that her brother Sven, fresh out of military service, was courting a local girl from the bakery where he worked – not only this, but there were rumours of wedding bells. Sven belonged to *her*, not some floozie who would only lead him astray, as had happened with the mother of his son. In this instance 'saving the situation' meant that Eva would be expected to seduce Sven, and have sex with him – moreover, that his girlfriend would have to *catch* them having sex. Eva may have been sufficiently obsessed with Greta to do anything to please her, but drew the line at this.

Greta had stalked Kalle Pedersen, Mauritz Stiller, and Ragnar Lasse Ring.[29] Now, the tables were turned on her when, in July 1922, a man followed her from Blekingegaten one evening while she was on her way home from work. He made as if to approach her when she paused to look in a bookshop window, and when she entered the store to evade him, followed her inside. Subsequently she fled the building and ran all the way home. She had recently been promoted to junior sales assistant in the dresses department and the next morning the same man walked in, flanked by two young women – actresses Gucken Cederborg and Tyra Ryman – and introduced himself as Erik Arthur Petschler (1881–1945). Petschler was a well-known (although not by Greta) director of slapstick comedies, popularly nicknamed 'The Swedish Mack Sennett', and he offered her a movie contract on the spot. They met the same evening, and Petschler informed her that he was producing a comedy, *Luffar-Petter* (*Peter The Tramp*), and would like her to make a screen-test. Later he claimed that he had also asked her to recite a piece of her choice on the sales floor – highly unlikely, given Paul U Bergstrom's strict ruling against such things.[30] The test took place later in the week, Greta passed, and the day after receiving this news – 22 July – she handed in her notice. Her handwritten reason for leaving, scribbled in PUB's employment ledger, was, 'Left at own request to make movies.'

But Greta could have been cutting off her nose to spite her face. Her salary at PUB had risen to 180 kroner a month, while Petschler paid her just 50 kroner for her five days' work on the film, with no guarantee that her movie career would progress any further, certainly not with him.

Luffar-Petter is a delightful, low-budget piece of whimsy which almost certainly would have disappeared without trace, if not for it being the first film to showcase the budding talents of Sweden's – and later Hollywood's – most famous *femme fatale*. Also appearing in the production were Petschler himself in the title role, and Tyra Ryman and Gucken Cederborg, the actresses who had accompanied him to the PUB store.

Petschler had wanted to shoot the film in Stockholm itself, to cut down on costs and complete the project as quickly as possible. Bathing, however, was not permitted within the city boundaries, so the locations were filmed at Dalaro, an hour's journey from the city by steamer. Here, Petschler said, while the other actors were reluctant to go near the water for fear of catching colds, Greta would not keep out of it. He recalled a sudden rainstorm, where everyone but she and Tyra Ryman dashed for cover: 'As we others crouched unhappily under our chance shelter, Greta and Tyra in their bathing-dresses improvised a wild Indian dance in the pouring rain. It was a stimulating sight for the gods.'[31]

The most historically enduring section of this nonsensical production comes when Greta and her on-screen sisters are enrolled at a gymnastics academy – an opportunity for the trio to strut and stretch in black shorts and vests and, later in the film, skimpy (for the day) swimsuits. The original running time is listed as seventy-five minutes, though surviving prints run to around half this length. It does have its moments, though when watching it today, one wonders what Petschler actually saw in this tall and ungainly, rather plain-looking girl with her thick thighs and waist, unkempt hair and protruding front teeth. She was certainly not *femme fatale* material at this stage, though Petschler must have recognised some potential to suggest that she audition for the prestigious Royal Dramatic Academy:

> She was a very determined girl and very willing and anxious to please. She was a bit shy and uneasy at the beginning, which is natural, but when we started shooting she really came to life. She had had no training ... and her movements were quite awkward, but I think she showed signs of having a knack for acting. At least she had the desire, which is not the least important thing.[32]

The government-funded *Kungliga Dramatiska Teater*, to give it the official title, had been founded by King Gustavus III in 1787. Its future alumni would include Ingrid Bergman, Bibi Andersson, Max von Sydow, Signe Hasso, and acclaimed film director Alf Sjöberg – all of whom, with the exception of Bergman, would be vastly overshadowed by Garbo. Petschler introduced Greta to the Academy's elderly former director, Frans Enwall, retired through ill-health and working as a part-time private coach but still carrying some weight with the Academy. This enabled her name to be added to that year's auditions list, which had just closed, with the auditions scheduled to begin taking place on 22 August. Enwall declared that she needed a major overhaul if she was expecting to make the grade as an actress: her stance was clumsy, her accent guttural and unrefined, she hardly ever brushed her hair, she dressed sloppily – and of course, there were those sticking-out teeth. He took Greta under his wing, and coached her until his failing health forced him to stop working altogether – he died the following year and his protégée was assigned to the tutelage of his drama teacher daughter Signe, who later observed:

> The fact that her knowledge of [this] drama wasn't wide didn't matter. What really counts in an actress is contact with real, everyday life and an ability to feel and understand it. In that sense, Greta was probably extremely well-equipped. She was very mature for her age.[33]

Entrance for a maximum three-year scholarship with the Academy was by way of a gruelling audition comprising three five-minute scenes chosen by the student. Out of 300 applicants listed for 1922, only ten were accepted. The auditorium where these tests took place was vast, cold and draughty, and empty save for the long table accommodating the twenty stone-faced judges. Greta, wearing Max Gumpel's diamond ring for luck, would have backed out at the last minute, had it not been for her brother Sven, who insisted on accompanying her. 'All I could see was that black pit, that black open space,' she recalled, 'I said my piece, then I just ran off. I forgot to say goodbye.'[34]

The students were auditioned in alphabetical order, therefore Greta did not have to wait too long before her name was called. Signe Enwall had prepared selections from Vittorien Sardou's

Madame Sans-Géne, Selma Lagerlöf's *The Fledgling*, and Ibsen's *Lady From The Sea*. She finished the first piece to a glacial silence, and was about to continue when the usher was instructed to call for the next student. Convinced she had failed, such was Greta's hurry to get away that she forgot her obligatory curtsey to the jury – in itself sufficient for them to fail her. Three days later, she received notification informing her otherwise, and that her first class would begin on 18 September – her seventeenth birthday. Her joy was ecstatic: 'Oh God, I was happy! I almost died! Even now, I can hardly breathe when I remember. For now, pretty soon I knew I was to be a *real* actress!'

The rules of the Academy were rigid. First-year students were on probation and were expected to devote themselves wholeheart-edly to their work, which comprised an eight-hour day broken into segments: drama and theatre history, deportment, vocal projection, elocution, make-up, gesture, dance, fencing, personality develop-ment, physical training and posture. Most evenings, they and the next-year students put on in-house productions, which left little time for socialising – which in any case was discouraged, particu-larly any forming of relationships with members of the opposite sex. Suffice to say, discreet liaisons among the students were commonplace and, as each student was paired up with another of the same sex so that they could bounce ideas off each other, homo-sexual relationships were inevitably formed. During their second year, students were officially added to the roster, paid a monthly stipend of around 150 kroner, and allowed to accept bit-parts in productions extant of the Academy. Some were loaned out to the film studios. By the time they had completed their third and final year, the ones who had made it thus far were permitted to call themselves legitimate thespians.

Greta, as a probationary student, received no fee. However, her tuition was free, so there was no strain on the Gustaffson family budget: Sven and Alma were bringing in decent wages, and Anna had money set aside from the excess board and lodgings which Greta had been handing over while working at PUB. During her few months at the Academy she preceded the later American exponents of Stanislavsky (Dean, Brando, Clift) in that she very quickly developed a tendency towards indolence, arrogance and rebelliousness, while never losing sight of her essential craft. Film critic Alexander Walker observed, 'To read some of Stanislavsky's manuals on the art of acting after seeing a Garbo film is to find the nature of the performance already analysed, which is not to suggest Garbo consciously employed The Method. It was hers by instinct: Academy training only sharpened it.'[35]

If anything, Greta's off-the-wall behaviour while working, now as later, reflected the part she was rehearsing or playing, which was of course pure Method. If the part called for her to be miserable, she took it out on everyone else until she had left the platform or studio. When studying a comic role, she was giddy towards the point of distracting the whole class with her pranks and jokes. During her first year (billed as Greta Gustavson) she played a whore in a local repertory group's production of Schnitzler's *Farewell Supper*, a lady's maid in J. M. Barrie's *The Admiral Crichton*, and Hermione in Shakespeare's *A Winter's Tale*. Her favourite roles were the male parts in the Russian classics. 'Though I do not like to see men dressed as women, there is something especially thrilling about seeing a woman dressed as a man,' she said.[36]

Greta made few friends at the Academy – she was said to have been too moody for anyone to wish to spend more time with her than they had to. She rejected the advances of Holger Lowenadler, a student who claimed he had been enchanted not so much by her physical attributes as by her 'pompous mannerisms and beauty of voice'. A young banker named Gösta Kyhlberg, dissatisfied with the way she dressed, eschewed the usual flowers and presented her with a lurid green dress to wear on their next date. Greta obliged, wore it for a publicity photograph, then dyed it black. As for the second date, this never happened. At this time, Greta was more interested in relationships with women: Mona Mårtenson (1902–56) was a pretty, dark-haired student three years her senior; and Vera Schmiterlow (1904–87) had already appeared in her first film, and a few years later became a sizeable star in Germany. She and Greta were hired for a photographic assignment advertising the latest Lancia car, talking turns to pose behind the wheel, though neither could drive yet. Vera recalled how, as neither of them had a bathroom at home, they would make weekly visits to Sturebadet, the public baths in Stockholm's city centre, at the time something of a Mecca for lesbian and gay encounters, much like the later bath-houses in Budapest and Los Angeles.[37]

Greta's most profound liaison at this time was with Mimi Pollak (1903–99), a plain-looking Jewish girl from Hammarom in Värmland. As had happened with Eva Blomgren, Greta was the dominant partner in their relationship. They remained close for sixty years, exchanging a long series of letters, telegrams and cards. Some of these, sent by Greta would be auctioned in 1993, while Mimi's correspondence was made public to commemorate Garbo's centenary in 2005. In most of these, the two women scarcely conceal the fact that they were once an item – while other Garbo letters were allegedly considered so revealing by her surviving relatives, desperate that her bisexuality should remain buried in the annals of time, that they have never been made public. The Academy class photograph, taken in October 1922, says it all: while the other students smile and face the camera, Greta looks only at Mimi, and they are holding hands. In years to come, this segment of the photograph would be clipped and appear in newspaper articles and magazines, with no indication that it had once formed part of a larger shot featuring ten other people.[38]

Greta's nickname for Mimi was 'Mimosa', while Mimi called her 'Gurra', short for Gustav. 'The letter from you has aroused a storming of longing within me,' Greta responded to an early missive, when they had not seen each other for a while. Another *billet-doux* reads: 'I keep thinking of you, Mimosa, and thinking that I will meet you any second out in the corridor!' Later, when her fame had forced them to part, she agonised, 'I dream of seeing you and discovering whether you still care as much about your old bachelor. I love you, little Mimosa!' And when Mimi entered into a 'lavender' marriage, and wrote that this was going well and she was pregnant, the message was even more poignant, proof that they had enjoyed a love affair: 'We cannot help our nature, as God created it. But I have always thought that you and I belonged together.'

Mimi Pollak may well have been the first to coin the phrase 'Garbo-esque', when later describing her lover. Greta, she recalled,

always wore black for dramatic effect. Her favourite item of apparel
was an ankle-length, man's black velvet cloak whose purpose was
two-fold: when visiting other theatrical productions using her gratis
Academy pass, the cloak added to her air of sophistication and
imperiousness – but also covered the threadbare clothes she had on
underneath. And Greta, who during her first weeks at the Academy
never stopped talking about her family and upbringing, very soon
refused to acknowledge that she *had* a family. The reason for this,
Mimi believed, was that she did not want the other students –
many from well-to-do-backgrounds – to know how poor hers had
once been. Indeed, to throw them off the scent, she made a point
of *always* wearing Max Gumpel's diamond ring.[39]

Greta was similarly embarrassed about her lack of education
and the fact that she had left school early, as her voice coach, Karl
Nygren, revealed:

> In the classroom she was very quiet. Sometimes I wished she
> would show more initiative. I remember that now and again
> she seemed very depressed and troubled. She often blushed, espe-
> cially when we were discussing things that she wasn't acquainted
> with. I think that this was probably due to the fact that her formal
> education had been meagre, and she was acutely conscious of that
> ... But when I would meet her by chance in the halls or the theatre
> she was not at all bashful.[40]

Mimi Pollak remembered Greta's fanaticism for walking – not just
to save on cab fares, but because of her intense shyness, terrified
should the driver suddenly attempt to have a conversation with
her. Often, she said, she was so paranoid about being out in the
street that a friend had to be with her, whether they wanted to
be with her or not. Yet she would have no problem stopping to
chat with a beggar, and would always drop a few coins into his hat.
On 22 December, Greta travelled with Mimi to Hammaro, where
they spent the festive season with Mimi's parents – Greta's first
Christmas away from home. The friends participated in a concert
at Mimi's former high school, with Greta led to believe this would
be just another run-of-the-mill end-of-term show. In fact, it was

the cultural event of the Hammaro winter season. Such was her stage fright that she had to be virtually carried on to the platform. What she sang or recited is not on record – only that she was paid 100 kroner for doing so. They returned to Stockholm on Boxing Day, where the premiere of *Luffar-Petter* took place at the Odeon Cinema. The only half-decent review came from *Swing* magazine, which observed by way of a backhanded compliment:

> Though American bathing beauties may be lovelier and more subtle, our Swedish ones have more freshness and charm ... Greta Gustafsson may become a Swedish movie star – but only because of her Anglo-Saxon appearance.[41]

Little did they know...

CHAPTER TWO

GARBO & STILLER: BEAUTY & THE BEAST

'I have to thank Mauritz Stiller for everything in this world.'

He became Garbo's mentor, the man responsible for introducing her to the world. Without him, she may never have left Sweden. He badgered her into shape and taught her all she knew: about acting, how to dress, how to speak and think, who to talk to and who to ignore, about being a woman – though he was never sexually interested in women. At times cruel and abrupt, he spared little thought for her feelings. If he felt that she was doing something wrong, he would tell her so – often publicly, in a rant peppered with obscenities. He rarely allowed her an opinion of her own. She in turns revered and loathed him, yet she would mourn his early death for the rest of her life.

Garbo's Svengali was born Moshe Stiller, of Russian-Polish ancestry, the fourth of six children, in Helsinki, Finland, on 17 July 1883. When he was four his father died, and shortly afterwards his mother committed suicide: subsequently he was raised by family friends, the Katzmans, who ran a haberdashery business and whose name he may have used at times, though it was never legally changed from Stiller. As a child, Stiller attended a traditional Hebrew school, where he excelled at every subject, most especially languages – he spoke fluent Russian, German, Swedish and Polish – and learned to play the violin to virtuoso standard. Upon leaving, however, instead of finding a well-paid job, he joined several struggling drama groups. Then in 1904, shortly after his twenty-first birthday and in the wake of Finland's nationalist uprisings, he received his call-up papers. At this time, the country was an autonomous Grand Duchy of Russia. A Conscientious Objector and vociferous opponent of Tsar Nicholas II, Stiller refused to attend the Army training base, and the Russian Military Police apprehended him at the theatre where he was playing Tybalt in *Romeo and Juliet*. Subsequently dispatched to St Petersburg, he was found guilty of desertion and sentenced to six months hard labour.

Exactly how Stiller had escaped from internment and obtained a fake passport is not known – rumours suggest he may have bribed his guard and government official who obtained the document. However he did it, by the end of the year he was living in Sweden, having been stripped of his Russian nationality. He became a Swedish citizen in 1920. Never a well man and already in the early stages of tuberculosis, Stiller settled in one of the poorer districts of Stockholm, where initially he worked on the stage while posing as an exiled German film director. His sterling knowledge of his subject and his flawless command of the language enabled him to get away with this. Gregarious and outgoing, dressed in spivvish suits, pastel-coloured waistcoats, ankle-length fur coats when it was cold and wearing more jewellery than most women, he created an impression wherever he went, and soon wheedled his way into the then developing Swedish movie colony, acting in shorts and writing scripts. By 1912, Stiller was producing and directing his own films – few yet worthy of note but nevertheless moving in the right direction.

For Stiller, international acclaim came with two films: *Thomas Graal's Best Film* (1917) and its sequel, *Thomas Graal's First Child* (1918), light-hearted comedies where the object of fun is the Swedish film industry itself, and said to have inspired Hollywood's finest, Ernst Lubitsch, who later triumphed with Garbo. Appearing in both films, and in Stiller's first major production, *Tradgardmastaren* (1912) was Victor Sjöström (1879–1960), regarded as 'The Father of Swedish Film' and the man who most inspired Ingmar Bergman. Born in Värmland, Sjöström emigrated to New York with his family when one year old, but later returned to Sweden and began his film career in 1917, enjoying tremendous success behind and in front of the camera. He and Greta became good friends, but though always outwardly civil towards Stiller, his greatest rival, he secretly despised him because of the disdainful way he treated most of those around him. Sadly, many of Stiller's and Sjöström's films (though not the best ones) would be lost in a fire which ravaged the Svensk Filmindustri archives a few years later.

Stiller's mannerisms were effete, and many who worked with him referred to him as 'bitchy'. He had never been in the closet, and his sexuality posed few problems in Sweden, but an event of 1 January 1923 – had this been made public at the time – would almost certainly have scuppered his career. Three years earlier he had begun a volatile relationship with Axel Esbensen, the 42-year-old set designer who worked on many of his films. On New Year's Eve, Esbensen was Stiller's date for the annual Svensk Filmindustri dinner. The pair had a massive row – allegedly because Stiller had told Esbensen that it was over between them – Esbensen had returned home and swallowed a fatal overdose of sleeping pills. Stiller had reputedly shrugged his shoulders and only days later taken up with another team regular, actor Axel Nilsson. His callousness tarnished his reputation so far as his Scandinavian colleagues were concerned. Most of them continued working with him for the prestige this brought, but few of them liked him.

Garbo's friend, secretary and subsequent lover Sven Hugo Borg recalled:

> Stiller was ugly, almost hideous in physical appearance. His body was ungainly, his features heavy, lined, gnome-like. His feet were so enormous as to be almost deformed, and his hands huge, prehensile paws, fitted for the plough. Yet beneath this repellent exterior was hidden a soul both beautiful and artistic.[42]

Stiller's sexuality is evident in some of his films, notably *Vingarne* (*The Wings*, 1916) – lost save for a few stills – a tragedy based on the novel by Herman Bang and remade in 1924 by Carl Dreyer as *Mikael*. One of the first films to deal with an openly gay issue, this tells of a sculptor's love for his muse, the beautiful Mikael, an opportunist who feigns affection for remuneration, then latches on to a wealthy woman while the sculptor, bereft, wanders out into a storm and dies. One reviewer defined it as, 'Stiller's subtextual coming-out ... grand and worthy, albeit tragic, next to the sordid and inept obsessions of a heterosexual audience.'[43]

The star of the film was Lars Hanson (1886–1965), the former Academy actor who had blown smoke down his nostrils in *Our*

Daily Bread. Garbo regarded Hanson as a lucky omen because he shared a birthday (26 July) with her brother, Sven. He had begun his stage career playing Hamlet in Helsinki and it was here, in 1915, that he met Mauritz Stiller, safely visiting the city on vacation now that Finland was no longer under Russian rule. Stiller brought him back to Sweden and offered him his first film role in *Dolken* (1915), and for a time they were lovers – as would happen with Garbo, the beautiful blond, famed for his exquisite profile and porcelain hands, was dominated by the unattractive, frequently ruthless Svengali.

Like many gay or bisexual actors, Larson enjoyed a happy lavender marriage from 1922 until his death, with Karin Molander, the daughter of Gustav, the director of the Academy: they met while appearing in Stiller's satirical comedy, *Erotikon*. Phenomenally successful in silent films, his stumbling block when the talkies arrived, despite having a voice that was just as sexy as the rest of him, was his almost incomprehensible Swedish accent. It was for Larson – along with Axel Nilsson still keeping Stiller's bed warm at night – that the director had optioned Selma Lagerlöf's best-selling novel, *Gösta Berlings Saga*.

The story, controversial for its day, tells of a young priest, defrocked on account of his alcoholism, and the effect this has on the new life he chooses for himself. Lagerlöf (1859–1940), whose *The Fledgling* had formed part of Greta's audition for the Academy, was (in 1909) the first female writer to be awarded the Nobel Prize in Literature. Stiller and Victor Sjöström had filmed several of her short stories, but *Gösta Berlings Saga* was her first novel, which she had completed while working as a teacher in her native Värmland. Some years later, the New York theatre critic Bosley Crowther baptised her 'The Bard Of Sweden'.

Stiller had cast the major characters in the film and Greta was one of several students sent by the Academy to be interviewed for the second female leads and bit-parts, with a view to being short-listed for audition, and *then* sent for screen-tests – provided they came up to his excessively high standards.

When the director met her properly for the first time, he had probably forgotten the occasion when she almost ended up under the front of his car. Garbo recalled arriving at his house at the appointed time, and being made to wait for two hours before he turned up, striding into the room with his huge wolfhound bounding in after him. She is said to have been initially terrified of him. Stiller was well over six feet tall, with gaunt features and a shock of unruly iron-grey hair. What frightened her the most about him, she said, was the way that he stared menacingly right into her eyes – the fact that he only had one eye did not help her feel any more comfortable in his company. During the interview, Stiller questioned her about her background and experience, then asked her to remove her coat and hat so that he could better study her figure and profile. After leaving her contact details, she was courteously dismissed. 'Then I knew that it was all over,' she recalled. 'When they're not interested they always ask your telephone number. So I put on my hat and coat and went out. I just didn't think any more about it.'[44]

Several weeks passed. Stiller drew up a shortlist of interviewees for the bit-parts, and just two major parts remained to be cast: the Countesses Ebba and Elizabeth Dohna, with whom Gösta Berling falls in love during the course of the film. Gustav Molander was contacted once more – this time Stiller asked for his two prettiest actors, only to dismiss them on sight for their lack of charisma. He settled on Mona Mårtenson for the part of Ebba after seeing her in an Academy production of *The Merchant of Venice*. It was either she or Mollander who recommended Greta – though both Carl Brisson and Mimi Pollak later claimed the honour.

This time when Greta arrived at Stiller's house she was welcomed by his lover, Axel Nilsson, who had prepared lunch and who made her feel more at ease than she might otherwise have been. As before, Stiller arrived late with his dog in tow and half-frightened her to death by grabbing hold of her, spinning her around and around and exclaiming, 'My dear Miss Gustafsson, you are a little too fat, I believe! Axel, just look at those eyelashes! My dear lady, you'll have to lose twenty pounds if you're going to play the role I contemplate for you!'[45]

Vera Schmiterlow recalled how Greta had gone about this:

Greta had a beautiful body, but was rather plump and Stiller had told her to slim. There was a shower-bath at the theatre school and after everybody had left, Greta stayed on, stretched out naked on the floor taking a hot shower. Day after day she would be lying on her stomach and the water spouting on her back as part of her slimming. She wanted to become figure-perfect in Stiller's eyes as quickly as possible. As her legs were also too fat she bandaged them tightly each night, especially around the ankles, to make them thin ... She adored Stiller, but as far as I know there was never anything between them. Everyone knew that Stiller had a different kind of interest. He saw Greta as some beautiful raw material for him to shape into form. Greta accepted this wholeheartedly.[46]

While waiting for Stiller to make his final decision, Greta and Mimi Pollak attended a supper party at Stockholm's Grand Hotel, in honour of the distinguished Norwegian actor, Halvdan Christensen, who had just played a season at the Academy. Here, the friends put on an impromptu cabaret during which Greta, her confidence boosted by a surfeit of champagne, climbed onto a table and sang in her best contralto a vulgar version of a song from the musical comedy, *The Girl From Hagalund*. Far from being shocked, the thespian audience gave her a rousing ovation, though with the exception of the few snatches in her films, few would ever hear Garbo sing again.[47]

It was now that Kalle Pedersen re-entered Greta's life, albeit briefly. He was in the audience at the Academy when she was playing a harlot in an unspecified play. After the performance, he met her backstage and asked her out. Though with Mimi Pollak, she was still interested in men. Pedersen, however, was expecting too much. The date turned out to be dinner in his suite at the Strand Hotel, and he was clearly expecting her to be dessert. Greta played along with him, eating only the best food and quaffing expensive liqueurs. Then, while Pedersen was in the bathroom, she quietly slipped out of the room.

In June, Garbo was contacted by Stiller, and introduced to his team. The scriptwriter Ragnar Hyltén-Cavallius (1885–1970) was hugely respected in Sweden, and took an instant dislike to the new protégée, dismissing her as 'a lowly farm girl'. The cameraman, Julius Jaenzon (1885–1961), who had been collaborating with the trio of Stiller, Sjöström and Lagerlöf for years, was of the same opinion. Selma Lagerlöf *was* enthusiastic, but only because she, Greta and Mimi Pollak were members of Stockholm's exclusive lesbian 'sewing circle'. Artistic director Vilhelm Bryde (1888–1974) joked that she would prove an on-set liability because she was so big and clumsy, she would keep walking into the sets and demolishing them!

In Greta's defence, Stiller is quoted as having told these detractors, 'She's shy and she doesn't know what she feels, and she is completely lacking in technique, but the important thing is that she is beautiful! Look at her feet! Look at her heels! Have you ever seen such beautiful heels, such fine lines?'[48] What Stiller may not have known at the time was that Greta *loathed* her feet because they were so big.

In the meantime, having won over his production team, Stiller summoned Greta and Mona Mårtenson for a screen-test at the Rasunda Studios, on the outskirts of Stockholm. As had happened with the auditions, the director kept them waiting for two hours – watching them through a spy-hole in the wall and gleaning sardonic pleasure from seeing Greta in particular trembling with terror at the prospect of what lay ahead. She is on record as having jumped to her feet and curtsied the instant he strode into the room, which must have satisfied his ego no end. Throughout their brief but turbulent working relationship, he would alternate between treating her like a princess – when the press were around – and something he had just scraped off the bottom of his shoe when they were not. Greta never really knew where she was with him. For her test, she was instructed to lie on a chaise-longue and pretend to be ill. When she failed to do this to Stiller's satisfaction, he yelled something along the lines of, 'You don't know how to be sick? And you call yourself an *actress*?' The part of the Countess Elisabeth Dohna was already hers – Stiller was just enjoying making her suffer. Greta heaved and almost choked, and *still* this horrible man dismissed her without giving her an answer there and then.[49]

It was not until 23 July, almost six months since her first interview with Stiller, that Greta and Mona Mårtenson learned they would be in the film. Their salary was to be a non-negotiable 3,000 kroner each, around one tenth what Stiller was paying Lars Hanson. Because Greta was a minor, the contract was countersigned by her mother, believed to have been the only time Anna Gustaffson met Stiller, to whom she took an instant dislike. Greta set most of the money aside for a rainy day, buying only a ring for her mother and having a telephone installed at their apartment.

Exactly how Greta Gustaffson became Greta Garbo is not known, save that the formal application to the Ministry of the Interior was completed and signed, again by Anna, on 9 November. The document, equating to the UK Deed Poll, was filed, and the new name made official on 4 December. Long after Garbo had resigned from the movies, Mimi Pollak claimed to have come up with the name, as did Kalle Pedersen – by that time, Carl Brisson. Stiller also claimed unlikely responsibility for the moniker, declaring GARBO was made up from the first letters he had scribbled on a pad while discussing her qualities with a journalist: *Gor Alla Roller Beromvart Opersonligt* (Plays All Roles In Commendably Impersonal Fashion). The likeliest explanation is that Greta herself probably came up with it just by playing with words, and that she was renamed after no one or nothing in particular.

At Rasunda, Garbo and Mona Mårtenson shared a room – the 'official' reason being that, at twenty-two, Mona was the under-aged Garbo's chaperone. Each day, before breakfast, Garbo strolled with Stiller through the woods which surrounded the studio – he voicing aloud his ideas for the day's shooting, she instructed to listen but not allowed any opinion of her own. Later, she accompanied him while he inspected the sets – forty-eight of them constructed around the Rasunda lot. It was not Garbo's company that interested the director, but keeping her away from the rest of the unit. Stiller remained in the room while she was changing into her costumes; he stood behind the chair, staring back at her through the mirror, while she was in Make-up. He vetted which actors she should speak to, which ones she should ignore. While shooting, if she made the slightest error he bawled her out in front of everyone. He is quoted as having compared her with a half-wild filly, saying, 'She's still inexperienced. But I'm ruthless with her. Wait till I've broken her in!'[50][51]

Several times while making *Gösta Berlings Saga* Garbo almost threw in the towel – it was only because of the press interest in the film, and her, that she did not. Earlier in the week, Stiller had been interviewed by *Filmjournalen*'s Inga Gaate, who had been unkind while comparing his actresses to their American counterparts:

> Acting in front of the camera requires calm and concentration above all. You have to be able to relax ... American actors are enormously skilful. Their training is incredible. Here in Sweden we have a short-age of film talent, particularly amongst the women. The Swedish woman eats too much and takes too little care of herself.[52]

Inga Gaate asked to interview Garbo. Stiller permitted them just five minutes together, instructing his protégée that she must speak only about the film and that if *he* entered the conversation, she should only say nice things about him. Garbo warned her, 'I'm one of those people who speak first, think later. So please don't write down *everything* that I say!' Gaate first asked her if she found film-ing tough – though what she really wanted to know was if it was tough working with Stiller. 'Terribly,' Garbo replied. 'I'm finding it very difficult, but Stiller's the most generous person I know. You don't get angry or upset with him, no matter how many times he tells you off. He creates individuals, then shapes them in line with what he wants.'[53]

Garbo and Stiller always addressed each other by their surnames, as she would almost everyone in the future, even close friends. Then, within the space of a minute, with little pressure from the reporter, she was contradicting herself, saying with a laugh, 'I'm a nice, well-behaved girl who *does* get very upset if people are nasty to me. Of course, you *do* have to be a little cheeky at times – though it's not very ladylike. It may well be that *I* don't have too much of *that* delightful quality!'

When Stiller read this he was furious, and gave orders that no reporters were to be admitted to the Rasunda lot unless personally vetted by him. Garbo was instructed to speak to no one, not even the other actors, unless he was present. This suited her perfectly. Her pre-Method style of acting meant that, when preparing a scene, she would psyche herself up to such an extent that it was impossible to relate to anything extant of that scene.

Selma Lagerlöf had published her novel in 1891, when Swedish Neo-romanticism had been at its zenith. A morose epic of bleak landscapes, upper-class grotesques, mystery, decadence, religion and elements of the supernatural, it was inspired by the Icelandic sagas she had read as a child. Stiller spared no expense on detail: the furniture, bought or hired, dated exactly from the Napoleonic period. Costumes were copied from original patterns, down to the last stitch. What Stiller failed to do was to adhere faithfully to Lagerlöf's story incurring her wrath, but for which he may be excused – her book has so many plots, sub-plots and twists, flash-backs, and flashbacks within flashbacks that at times it becomes extremely confusing.

The film opens with Gösta arriving at Borg Manor, where Countess Märta Dohna (Ellen Cederström), *unaware that he is a defrocked priest and thinking him ideal husband material, employs him as tutor to her stepdaughter, Ebba* (Mona Mårtenson). *The Countess's plan is for Ebba to marry a commoner; for some reason this is the only way she will re-inherit nearby Ekeby Castle, confiscated some years before, and guarantee that her son, Henrik* (Torsten Hamméren), *and not Ebba, will inherit Borg. Ekeby belongs to Margaretha Samzelius* (Gerda Lundeqvist), *who also owns the local tinmine. Ebba falls for the cleric, but everything changes when the priggish Henrik arrives home with his pretty Italian bride, Elizabeth.* (Garbo making her appearance with the words, 'Dio mio, in Italia the grapes are sweeter!') *The couple are feted at Ekeby.* (In a split-second scene, removed for British and American audiences, while hoisted onto the guests' shoulders and being carried around the banqueting hall, a breast pops out of Garbo's low-cut gown.) *Ekeby has a sinister side, however, housing a number of debauched drop-outs from Napoleon's army, and it is to here that Gösta flees when he reveals he has feelings for Elizabeth and Märta learns of his defrock-ing. Ebba dies of a broken heart, while Gösta participates in the debauchery and falls for visiting socialite Marianne Sinclaire* (Jenny Hasselqvist). *Marianne brings shame on her family by sleeping with the priest, subsequently wanders off into the snow and for reasons known only to the scriptwriter contracts smallpox and loses her looks. Margaretha, meanwhile, is exposed as an adultress by her husband and is kicked out of Ekeby, returning to set fire to the place, unaware that Marianne is inside. Gösta rescues Marianne, tells her it is over between them, and is driving his sleigh to who knows where when he sees Elizabeth stumbling through the snowy wilderness. He sweeps her up on to the sleigh, and while they are chased by wolves exclaims, 'Is not Don Juan as swift as the wind?' To which she responds, 'Do you think me frightened of a knight's mad whim? Gösta Berling, I have always believed in you. Return to Ekeby, build it up again, and become a real man at last!' – her way of saying that she is in love with him.* (In the condensed version of the film, one assumes Don Juan is Gösta himself, but in the restored print it is revealed that it is actually his horse! A scene was also cut in which Gösta kisses Elizabeth's hand, and she reacts as if having an orgasm.) *It then emerges that Elizabeth and Henrik were never legally married. All ends well when Gösta rebuilds Ekeby, and Margaretha gives it to him and Elizabeth as a wedding present.*

In the film, Garbo and Lars Hanson look exceedingly good together, and one finds it hard to believe that he is thirty-seven, and she twenty years younger. Much of this has to do with the actors' natural beauty, the fact that even before Hollywood had worked on them, there was no such thing as a bad shot for either – Garbo, windblown and dishevelled, and Hanson, smoke-ravaged and covered in mire, still look astonishing, and with Julius Jaenzon's unique halo-lighting, almost holy. Swathed in furs, the snowflakes swirling about them in the icy wasteland, they create a vision of astonishing loveliness.

In her solo scenes, Garbo is equally mesmerising. When picking flowers in her garden, after learning that her marriage is invalid – such is the pained look on her face that she really does appear to be carrying the weight of the world on her shoulders. Her scenes with Gerda Lundequist are no less fascinating. Lundequist (1871–1959), known as 'The Swedish Sarah Bernhardt', appeared rarely in films. 'She has the most amazing eyes of any person. So much *soul*, and so tired, always,' Garbo said of her.[54]

The only 'downside' to the production is the effect the orthochromatic film has on some of the actors' faces. Until 1925, this type of negative was sensitive only to the brightest natural light and large ultraviolet lamps were used universally. As this registered only blue light, anything red – such as the actors' lips – showed up black on the screen. Similarly, flesh-toned faces appeared darker than usual, which is why so many of the early silents' stars wore heavy white pancake make-up. The negative also played tricks with the actors' eyes, particularly if these were blue: Garbo's eyes appear much lighter than they were while Hanson's, which were very prominently blue, appear to be starting out of their sockets – a bonus when portraying the over-excited Gösta Berling in the pulpit and sleigh scenes.

The production also had its moments of very real danger. Stiller refused to hire stuntmen, believing that actors reacted better to hazardous situations if they were actually experiencing them. Therefore, it is Garbo and Hanson that we see on the speeding sleigh – an arduous scene for the cameraman to capture because his own sleigh, along with the heavy equipment, had to be speeding alongside them. Stiller cheated with the wolves, hiring six Alsatians and weighting down their tails so they would not wag. At one point during the lengthy scene, five of the dogs turned on the smallest of the pack and ripped it to shreds. Stiller left the sequence in.

Additionally, Stiller insisted that the Ekeby set be razed to the ground for real during the fire scene – the costliest ever filmed on Swedish soil. Lars Hanson suffered cuts, bruises, and burns to his hands and knees while shooting it. 'I'm burning!' he screamed at one point, bringing the response from Stiller, who had not finished filming the scene, 'Then you'll just have to burn a little longer!' Inga Gaate observed, 'There he was, roaring like a lion, sweat pouring down his face, having fun like a little boy who jumps on his first fire truck to watch his first fire!'[55,56]

The day after shooting wrapped, the eighteen-year-old Garbo became a recluse, setting a precedent for the future. The affair with Mona Mårtenson had not survived the shooting schedule, though as with most of her lovers they would remain friends. She travelled alone to Värmland, where she rented a small cottage in the middle of nowhere:

I went away to the country. Yes, I was alone. I always went away alone. That is what I like. To go away, far into the country alone. Some people need to be with people. I need to be alone, always. It is so wonderful alone in the summer ... you can spend all night long in the open. The little noises of the country, the wonderful air. Ah, it gets to you![57]

The film in the can, and declaring she never wanted to see Stiller again because of the way he had treated her, Garbo returned to the Academy, where she had been elevated to the status of 'star pupil'. This meant that, even though still a first-year student, she was paid 150 kroner a month, and permitted to more or less choose her own roles. In January 1924, she opened in Richard Kessler's German comedy, *The Tortoiseshell Comb*, playing the part of Frau von Brandt.

Meanwhile, Stiller set about editing *Gösta Berlings Saga*, working around the clock, refusing to compromise when asked by SFI to trim the lengthier scenes. Subsequently he ended up with an unheard of fourteen reels – at almost four hours, more than twice the length of a regular feature at that time. It was therefore decided to release the production in two sections: *Part 1* premiering at Stockholm's Roda Kvam Cinema on 10 March, *Part Two* a week later. The notes in the commemorative programme were attributed to the scriptwriter Cavallius, though they were in fact penned by Stiller himself, who boasted there were two potentially great actresses (Garbo, Mårtenson) in his film, and that he alone had made them so:

What are these young and charming girls but clay in the hands of the master modeller? Does then the clay not have the same value as the hands that form it? Infinitely more! In a few years, Greta Garbo will be known and admired all over the world. For hers is the gift of beauty, a rare personal and characteristic beauty![58]

But the Swedish critics were not impressed. Garbo was criticised for the state of her hair, which does look as if it has not seen a brush in months. Indeed, the only time that her hair does *not* look

a mess is when it is concealed beneath a bonnet – when she and
Lars Hanson are flying across the snow on Gösta's sleigh. Fuelled
by Selma Lagerlöf's frequently bitchy comments about Stiller in
the press, detractors also agreed that he had 'mangled' her book to
make it almost unrecognisable, leaving out important scenes while
emphasising and extending the final sleigh scene and the razing of
Ekeby, minor incidents in the novel. This was unfair. The twenty-
minute fire scene had added excitement precisely at the right time
when the scenario had become a little dull – while the one with
Garbo and Hanson on the sleigh remains one of *the* defining
moments of the European *cinéma muet*.

From Stockholm, the trio of Stiller, Garbo and Gerda Lundequist
travelled to Berlin – the director completely undeterred by the
critical panning because Trianon-Film AG, one of the country's
most prestigious companies, had bought the rights to screen *Gösta
Berlings Saga* for 100,000 marks, a fortune at the time, with an
option that if it did well at the German box-office, Stiller and his
protégée would be offered contracts. David Schlatter, the head of
Trianon, had imposed two conditions: firstly, that Stiller re-edit the
film so that it could be viewed in a single showing and secondly,
that Garbo should attend the premiere. Stiller refused to cut one
foot of Garbo's performance, resulting in her sharing equal screen
time with Lars Hanson.

Garbo decided she liked Berlin because of its smell, and also
because something about it had convinced her that this was her
second time on earth. 'The smell of the city,' she later enthused, 'an
amazing smell that has everything in it. I had not been in a big city
before, but I could feel the smell long before we were really in the
city. It was as though I'd smelled it before!'[59]

Roger Normand, who Garbo saw each time she visited Paris,
remembered how she would size up a city, a street, a building, or
even a room just by its smell:

She would walk into a place, glance about her for a moment, then
hug the drapes, close her eyes and throw her head back and exclaim,
'Oh, this is such a good room. How I can smell the love in it!' Then
she would clomp around, touching everything and purring, 'Hello,

sofa! Hello, chair! Good to make your acquaintance! I shall definitely come here again!' Or she would pass a building, a restaurant perhaps, and she would press her nose against the stone and say, 'No, this isn't a good place at all. Let's go eat someplace else!'[60]

The premiere took place on 21 August. 'Berlin received us charmingly. I like the Germans. They don't try to get too near to one,' Garbo recalled. Wearing a fur-trimmed dress and cloche hat, she refused to speak to reporters before the screening, but as the credits rolled, she received such a rousing ovation that she felt compelled to say a few words. 'Thank you very much for coming. And now, if you'll excuse me, I'm very tired,' she pronounced in hesitant German.[61]

The film was a big hit in Germany – Trianon recovered their outlay in just one week. Indeed, it was successful all over Europe, though not in Sweden, where Selma Lagerlöf was still on the warpath, threatening to sue SFI for 'misappropriation' of her work. Garbo had also changed her opinion about not wanting to work with Stiller again. She had become an overnight sensation in Germany, and was not up to being bullied any more. Now, when he was rude to her, she snarled back, '*Fan ta dig* (fuck you) *Stiller!*' She had money in the bank, and independence. Success had gone to her head. Berlin, however, was not Stockholm, and no sooner had she settled back in at Blekingageten than she was returned to earth with a bump. *Gösta Berlings Saga* had not made a profit at the Swedish box-office; no studio wanted to hire Stiller, or employ her while she was still tied to him. She was left with no option but to return to the Academy. In October–November 1924 she appeared in several productions, including Jules Romain's *The Triumph Of Medicine*.

Stiller, however, had every intention of holding on to his star-in-the-making. During breaks from shooting *Gösta Berlings Saga*, scriptwriter Ragnar Hyltén-Cavallius had been adding the finishing touches to a screen adaptation of Russian exile Vladimir Semitjov's novel, *Odalisken fran Smolna* (*The Odalisque from Smolensk*), which had been recently serialised in a Sunday newspaper. Set in the aftermath of the Russian Revolution, this tells the story of aristocrat

Maria Ivanovna, who escapes from Petrograd's Smolny Convent – formerly Lenin's headquarters – to search for her missing lover. Learning he is in Constantinople (now Istanbul), she stows away on a ship which crosses the Black Sea. Discovered by the captain, she is drugged and sold into the harem of a villainous Turkish prince. When he is murdered, she is the prime suspect, but all ends well and she is reunited with her lover.[62]

Having seen what the Stiller had done to Selma Lagerlöf's novel – and not wishing to turn down the reputed 50,000 kroner for the screen rights, which Stiller is said to have paid out of his own pocket – Vladimir Semitjov spent a great deal of time with Cavallius at Stiller's house on Boson Island, ensuring he adhered to the original story. Playing Maria's lover would be Stiller's latest casting-couch discovery, Einar Hanson, but Garbo initially turned down the part of the heroine – changing her mind when Stiller announced that Conrad Veidt had been signed for the part of the prince. The German actor (1893–1943) had risen to prominence as the somnambulist in *The Cabinet of Dr Caligari* (1920), but in the gay circles within which Garbo moved he was revered for the controversial *Anders als die Andern* (*Different from the Others*, 1919). Made during the Weimar Republic, this story of the violin teacher who falls in love with a male student was the first-ever sympathetic portrayal of homosexuality on film.

Garbo found an invaluable ally in Einar Hanson (1899–1927), like most of Stiller's lovers inordinately handsome, much younger than he was, and treated like the proverbial doormat. Hanson was sharing Stiller's bed for no other reason than the advancement of his career, and knew that he would be dropped the moment another submissive young protégé came along, by which time he hoped to have made the big time. He and Garbo spent a lot of time whispering in corners, poking fun at Stiller behind his back, sending him up. This helped them to cope with his frequently intolerable mood-swings.

As before, Stiller insisted that *Odalisken fran Smolna* should be as authentic as possible, no matter the cost. The locations would be filmed in Constantinople, reducing the necessity for expensive sets: the sunshine would be free, and further savings would be made hiring Turkish extras for almost nothing, as opposed to using Swedish actors with darkened faces. He concluded that it would easily be completed in less than three months – half the time it had taken to shoot the last one.

Trianon's David Schlatter had offered Stiller virtual carte-blanche to work on a production of his choice, but balked at a story about the Russian Revolution. Stiller's reaction was to take to his bed – his doctors claiming the shock of rejection had put him there, but that a few weeks working in sunny Turkey would return him to full health. In fact, he was much more seriously ill than perhaps he himself realised. Schlatter capitulated: a contract was drawn up on 10 September 1924 offering Stiller a staggering 150,000 marks to direct the film, while Garbo and Hanson were offered five-year contracts with the studio, starting out at 500 marks a month, whether they were working or not.

Stiller should have been grateful, but demanded more. His actors, he declared, were only happy working with Swedish technicians – Garbo would only ever permit Julius Jaenzon to photograph her, and only Svensk Filmindustri's make-up lady, Ester Lundh, was ever permitted to touch her face and hair. Similarly, Stiller would work with no artistic director other than Vilhelm Bryde. Schlatter put his foot down. Stiller would be allowed Jaenzon, but everyone else would be supplied by Trianon, otherwise the deal was off. Begrudgingly, Stiller agreed to these terms when he and his team returned to Berlin in mid-November.

It was here that everything changed for Garbo. Metro-Goldwyn-Mayer's Louis B. Mayer was visiting Europe with his family to inspect the Rome locations of Fred Niblo's epic *Ben-Hur: A Tale of the Christ*. The film was running way over budget on account of innumerable production problems, and after giving instructions for the set to be closed down and the unit transferred to California, Mayer and his family headed for Berlin.

Mayer (1885–1957) was both revered and feared as one of the most powerful moguls in Hollywood. In 1924 he held the position of vice-president and general manager of the recently formed MGM – a merger between Marcus Loew's Metro Pictures, Sam Goldwyn, and his own film company. He was a man of few scruples: his stars had to toe the line and adhere to his stringent 'family values' rules, for which they were rewarded with massive salaries, and a lifestyle beyond their wildest dreams. And if these rules were broken, such was Mayer's sway that they could be assured of never working in the movies again.

During the afternoon of Sunday 23 November, Mayer and his family attended a screening of *Gösta Berlings Saga*, and his daughter, Irene, recalled his comments the instant Garbo's face appeared on the screen:

> Look at that girl! There's no physical resemblance, but she reminds me of Norma Talmadge – her eyes. The thing that makes Talmadge a star is the look in her eyes ... Stiller's fine, but the girl, look at the girl! ... I'll take her without him, or I'll take them both [but] number one is the girl![63]

In fact, Mayer had already seen the film in Hollywood – but apparently had not taken much notice of Garbo then – at the behest of Lillian Gish, who had wanted Lars Hanson as her leading man in *The Scarlet Letter* – the saga of another priest who goes off the rails, this time getting a married woman pregnant. The film was to be directed by Victor Seastrom – the former Victor Sjöström, now a respected figure in Hollywood. Seastrom had never stopped singing Stiller's praises, and Mayer promised to look him up while in Europe.

When Mayer snapped his fingers, the lackeys jumped to attention. Within an hour of leaving the cinema, Stiller and Garbo were duly summoned to his suite at the Adlon Hotel that same evening. She, however, did not take kindly to being ordered around, and Stiller needed time to prepare for his big moment. Excuses were made – hardly the kind of behaviour Mayer was used to – and the meeting took place on the Wednesday, over dinner in the plush Maiden Room, where Stiller tipped the head waiter to ensure they would be allotted a table in a quiet corner of the restaurant, out of earshot of the other diners and where they would not be disturbed. Garbo's chair was placed in front of a floral display – with a lamp positioned in exactly the right spot so that the light would fall on her profile, showing this to best advantage, reflected in the mirror on the wall next to her. As if to thwart her mentor, she wore the dowdiest dress she could find, and a cheap black taffeta hat.

Tyrannical much of the time, Mayer could turn on the charm if he wanted to, though he was far from polite towards Garbo, as she recalled:

> Mr Mayer hardly looked at me the first time I saw him. Well, maybe out of the corner of one eye. He put a contract [sic] before me. I asked Stiller if I should sign. I always obeyed Stiller instinctively ... Stiller told me to sign it, and I did. I was to get $100 a week for forty weeks the first year, $600 the second year, and $750 the third.[64]

The deal was for five years, and a similar deal was offered Stiller, starting on $1,000 a week – more than he had expected. He and Garbo were then dismissed, but not until Mayer growled at Stiller, 'Tell Miss Garbo that in America, people don't like fat women!'

The next day, 26 November, Mayer dictated a letter of intent to Stiller: he and Garbo would be expected to leave for America no later than 1 May 1925. Similar letters were dispatched to Lars Hanson and Mona Mårtenson in Sweden – though she turned the offer down. A few days later, Stiller and Garbo left for Stockholm, where she was briefly reunited with her mother before returning to Berlin with Einar Hanson, Julius Jaenzon and scriptwriter Hyltén-Cavallius – on the very day that Hanson should have appeared in court on a charge of dangerous driving. The actor, whose passion for fast cars would ultimately cost him his life, had failed to stop after an accident. Stiller figured the police would not come looking for him if he was not in the country, and promised to 'square things' when they got back home. Pausing long enough in Berlin to organise the German crew, who would follow in trucks, the group boarded the Orient-Express.

Intent on taking Trianon for every penny he could to avenge not having had entirely his own way, Stiller booked everyone suites at the plush Péra Palace Hotel, and for three weeks lived like a visiting royal. He hired a roadster for himself and Hanson, a smaller car for

Garbo and Jaenzon, and two trucks for the German crew, which were placed on standby to pick up the photographic equipment, held at the border by Turkish customs officials. Stiller was told this would be released once the necessary red-tape had been dispensed with – and the hefty customs fees paid.

Constantinople, then as now, was a Mecca for rent-boys, of whom Stiller and Hanson had more than their share between trawling the souks in search of artefacts for the film. Jaenzon, restricted to using a hand-held camera, accompanied them, photographing everything but the sex.

Greta, feeling at home here, as had happened in Berlin – and mindless of the potential danger faced by a Western woman walking the streets alone in these parts – wandered off for hours at a time. This was her first Christmas away from Sweden – the first she did not have to wrap up against the cold. And what astonished her most was all the dirt she encountered:

> The Turks dress like European people. Except the very old Turks, who are dirty. The streets are narrow with dirty little shops – dirty cafés filled with food which is oily. The lazy Turks, they are fascinating. One day I was walking alone on the street and I followed behind one of the old Turks, the dirty one with the old pants ... I do not know how many hours I followed him. He was so dirty, but so fascinating. He did not go anywhere, did not have anywhere to go but wander ... I liked it. I liked to be alone in Constantinople. I went to the bazaars. I was so restless. I was alone, but I was not lonely.[65]

The socialite Mercedes de Acosta claimed to have first seen her in Constantinople, in the lobby of the Péra Palace, and mistaken her for a Russian princess, until informed otherwise by the porter:

> I was terribly troubled by her eyes and I longed to speak to her, but I did not have the courage ... She gave me the impression of great loneliness, which only added to my own already melancholy state of mind. I hated to leave Constantinople without speaking to her, but sometimes destiny is kinder than we think. Strangely enough ...

> I had a strong premonition that I might again see that beautiful and
> haunting face on some other shore.[66]

It all sounds very romantic, and Mercedes de Acosta – who later
featured strongly in Garbo's life and wrote a memoir that owed
more to wishful thinking than fact – may have seen some exotic
creature walking through the streets of the city. But it was not
Garbo! In fact, her visit to Turkey had taken place in August
1922, over two years before the object of her desire had set foot in
the place.[67]

Meanwhile, as with all of Mauritz Stiller's relationships, the pairing with Einar Hanson was not an easy one. Stiller made him grow
a beard for his part in the film, which Hanson said made him look
like a down-and-out. Then, after a heated exchange, Hanson headed
for the city's red-light district, where he was arrested after getting
into a brawl. Stiller paid the fine, they made up, and returned to
their rent boys. And the beard came off. On Christmas Eve, several
boys were invited to a party thrown by Stiller at the Péra Palace.
Garbo's date was Ragnar Hyltén-Cavallius. When she complained
to Stiller that she had nothing to wear, he suggested one of the
costumes Trianon had bought for the film: a brick-red, Chinese
silk dress, embroidered with gold. She is known to have been
photographed wearing this, sitting coquettishly on Stiller's knee,
but the dress and other photographs of the event have since disappeared. Years later, Marlene Dietrich sent me a picture of herself
wearing the dress, but refused to say how it had come into her
possession. Roger Normand, our mutual close friend, claimed she
had bought it at an auction in Berlin: 'For reasons known only to
herself, Marlene needed to have something belonging to her greatest rival!' That evening, Garbo and Hyltén-Cavallius danced the
hambo – a lively, polka-style Swedish dance dating from the turn
of the century – until the early hours, then retired to his room.[68]

While Stiller was burning the candle at both ends in
Constantinople and spending Trianon's money, he was unaware
that the studio was experiencing financial difficulties. Matters
came to a head when the corrupt Turkish customs officials, still
holding photographic equipment, threatened to destroy it unless

Stiller paid their fees – which had increased ten-fold and now amounted to more than the equipment was worth. There was a further problem when Julius Jaenzon photographed Garbo and Einar Hanson rehearsing a love scene in the street. Pausing to kiss, they did not realise that they were doing so in front of a mosque until they were suddenly surrounded by a crowd of angry locals, who leered and began throwing stones. The trio managed to run back to Stiller's roadster and were chased all the way back to the hotel. Stiller, fearing he might have to hire bodyguards from now on, and desperately short of funds, wired David Schlatter in Berlin and demanded a 'top up' of one million marks.

In no uncertain terms, Schlatter informed Stiller that there was no money, and the angry director – borrowing the fare from a wealthy businessman staying at the Péra Palace, caught a plane to Berlin the next morning. When he arrived at the studio, he found the place boarded up. Trianon had been declared bankrupt, David Schlatter had been arrested on a fraud charge, and the official receiver handling the studios debts refused to wire funds to Constantinople, where Garbo, Hanson, Jaenzon and Hyltén-Cavallius, by now completely broke, were unable to pay their hotel bills and buy tickets for the return journey to Berlin.

Stiller had funds in the city and could have helped out, but opted not to. Installing himself at the Esplanade Hotel, he resumed his passion for rent-boys, leaving his stranded colleagues with no alternative but to throw themselves on the mercy of the Swedish Embassy. Their hotel bill was paid in full, but there was no question of them returning to Berlin on the Orient-Express; they now travelled in a succession of cramped, uncomfortable, third-class compartments. During the journey, Garbo wrote to her mother: 'In two days I shall be back in Berlin, and we'll see what happens then. But it will be all right – it's been a good beginning, in spite of everything.'[69] The director was waiting for them at the railway station and hugged Garbo as though nothing untoward had happened, while Hanson moved into his suite at the Esplanade Hotel.

Trianon's collapse was regarded as just another hitch by Stiller. None of his team had been paid for *Die Odaliske von Smolny*, but now that the Turkish ordeal was over, they could get on with their lives. Jaenzon and Hyltén-Cavallius returned to SFI, with whom Stiller now opened negotiations, despite the contract with Louis B. Mayer. He was also meeting with executives from UFA (Universum Film-AF), Germany's biggest studio, for an as yet unspecified film with Garbo and Einar Hanson. She, however, appears to have been intent on going to America, with or without her mentor. On 30 January, she dashed off a letter to Metro:

> Gentlemen, in consideration of your providing me with first-class steamer and railroad passage from Berlin to Culver City, USA, I agree to enter into a written contract with you for my services as a motion picture actor ... It is understood that you are to furnish, gratis, the clothes required for the films I am to play in.[70]

One wonders if Stiller had told her otherwise, hoping she too might back out of the deal with Mayer. Had she actually studied the legally binding letter of intent? Maybe not: after all, it had been written in a language she did not understand. At the bottom of the page, she scribbled that *she* would be leaving for America 'no later than 25 April' – five days earlier than originally agreed. Meanwhile, Stiller was wheeling and dealing and Garbo was discovering the seedier but exciting side of Weimar culture. Both had participated in Stockholm's closeted gay scene; nothing, however, compared with what they were seeing in Berlin.

The end of the Great War coincided with a relaxation of morals in Berlin – this and the rapidly mounting inflation had brought about an unprecedented experimentation with democracy. Censorship had been almost completely abolished, and the previously gagged cabaret performers now seized the opportunity to express how they felt about the changing times. Sex was no longer a taboo subject: all aspects of it were discussed openly, sung about, and in some establishments actually practised on the stage. The formerly closeted gay artistic community came out into the open. Garbo and Hanson wallowed in this new-found freedom, he enjoying the company of men whose services did not have to be paid for, while Garbo enjoyed a 'dalliance' with the *sprechsinger*, Marianne Oswald.

Oswald (Alice Bloch, 1901–85) began her singing career by

accident, in Berlin in 1920 when a botched operation for tonsillitis left her with the rasp in her voice for which she became famous. An early interpreter of Brecht and Weill, she took Paris by storm a few years later: her biggest hits included 'En m'en foutant' (Fucking Myself) and 'La chasse à l'enfant', which tells of children being hunted and shot down after escaping from a reformatory. Marlene Dietrich, who first saw Oswald in a revue at the Berlin Wintergarten, said, 'She looked like something out of a nightmare. She had orange hair, and she couldn't sing – and Garbo slept with her!'

Axel Dotti, one of Oswald's later confidants, confirmed her affair with Garbo, as did her manager, Fernand Lumbruso:

> One of the high points of Marianne's then hectic sex life was her brief affair with Greta Garbo. Yes, Marianne *was* ugly, but not to the extent that she was as scary as [Dietrich] claimed. I even slept with her myself! Marianne told me how much Garbo and Marlene adored those Berlin clubs – and believe me, some of the things they must have seen there were not for the faint-hearted! But, so far as I know – certainly according to Marianne – Garbo and Marlene never met away from the film set. They never had an affair, as was rumoured. Marianne would have said. She was always the first to know about such things.[71]

One of the clubs frequented by Garbo, Marianne Oswald and Einar Hanson was Rudolph Nelsen's Chat Noir, in the Friedrichstrasse district, where they saw the greatest Sapphic entertainer of the day, Claire Waldoff, who performed Kurt Schwabacks 'Das lila Lied' (The Lavender Song), generally regarded as the world's first gay anthem. Another haunt was the Weiss Maus, at Jagerstrasse 18, where the clientele rubbed shoulders with Berlin intellectuals and shady underground figures. Those wishing to remain anonymous were handed black or white masks as one of the most notorious dancers in Europe took to the stage. Anita Berber (1899–1929) was a former prostitute whose 'party piece', after performing her expletive-peppered songs, was to strip completely naked, grab a brandy glass from one of the clients and – after downing this in one gulp – climb on to a table and urinate on anyone brave enough not to move out of the way. 'Far from being shocked, Garbo laughed and continued drinking as if she watched this kind of thing every day of her life,' claimed Axel Dotti.

At the Weiss Mauss, Garbo and Hanson encountered another doyenne of Berlin's Sapphic set: Valeska Gert (1892–1978). New to films, she had recently played Puck in a German adaptation of *A Midsummer Night's Dream*. Gert introduced Garbo to the Danish star Asta Nielsen (1881–1972). Both actresses were currently working with a then little-known director named Georg Wilhelm Pabst: the film was *Die Freudlose Gasse*, based on the controversial novel by Hugo Bettauer.

The story takes place in an unspecified Austrian town, during the aftermath of the war when hyperinflation, squalor, poverty, and deprivation are rife. Melchior Street has just two wealthy people: the butcher – and his wife, Frau Greifer, who runs a fashion store and sweet-talks young women into buying clothes they cannot afford on credit so that she can coerce them into prostitution in the brothel upstairs. Two of these were Marie Lechner and Greta Rumfort, who never share a scene. Valeska Gert was playing the evil and manipulating procuress, Frau Greifer, and Asta Nielsen, Marie. Pabst had yet to cast the parts of Greta and Lieutenant Davy, the dashing young American who saves her from shame. He had been impressed with Garbo's performance in *Gösta Berlings Saga* and, when she turned up for her audition with Einar Hanson, Pabst liked him too.

Born in Bohemia, Georg Wilhelm Pabst (1885–1967) was primarily a woman's director, interested especially in the plight of women in German society. Later he made *Pandora's Box* with Louise Brooks and, more famously, *The Threepenny Opera* with Lotte Lenya. He was a pioneer of Die Neue Sachlichkeit – the 'New Objectivity' (aka Post-Expressionist) movement, a genre which flourished during the 1920s but was halted with the fall of the Weimar Republic in 1933, when the Nazis came to power. The movement promoted and frequently satirised life as it really was, raw, unfettered and uncoloured – the direct opposite of the 'Hollywoodisation' of the next generation, which would see the lives of real people fictionalised so as not to offend religious groups and moralists. With Neue Sachlichkeit, religious themes were kept to a minimum, emphasis was placed on the darker aspects of life, while the scenarios lacked any form of jubilation when in real-life, inter-war Europe there was frequently little to rejoice about.

Stiller was furious. *He* had discovered Garbo. Therefore she was *his* personal property. Pabst could loan her for the film, but there would have to be conditions: as his star would never permit anyone else to photograph her, Pabst would have to take Julius Jaenzon as well – and hire him as the film's technical adviser and Garbo's 'spiritual' guide. Pabst refused: he had his own cameraman, Guido Seeber (1879–1940), a pioneer of special effects and a wizard with lighting, whose most enigmatic work had been in the horror movie, *The Golem* (1920). Stiller capitulated – then demanded that, in view of the current state of the German mark, Garbo and Hanson should be paid in American dollars. Pabst agreed to this and both actors signed contracts for an exceedingly generous salary of $4,000 each – the same amount Pabst was paying Asta Nielsen and Valeska Gert.

Die Freudlose Gasse began shooting on 12 February 1925. Stiller drove Garbo to the lot, where the other actors had gathered, waiting for Pabst. Unable to control himself, he grabbed a copy of the script and was dictating to Garbo how her part should be played when Pabst appeared. Within minutes, Stiller was escorted off the set, while Garbo suffered a rare fit of hysterics. Since working on the PUB commercial she had been accustomed to having someone guide her through her paces. Pabst did not work this way, preferring to encourage his actors to rely on their imagination, inner emotions and gut-feeling, and to play their parts the way *they* felt they should be played – effectively, the way Garbo had been taught at the Academy.

The first day on the set, Garbo refused to face the cameras until her mentor was present. Pabst called her bluff and she walked off the set. The next morning, she turned up for work, bright and cheerful as if nothing had happened. During her first days on the set she also developed a twitch in her cheek – part nerves, and partly on account of the powerful lights which were obligatory for the darkened street scenes. In the days when movie cameras were cranked by hand, Guido Seeber solved the problem by increasing the speed – thus, when projected onto the screen, Garbo's close-ups were actually in slow motion, eliminating the twitch.

In getting himself banned from the set, Stiller did not sit idle and content himself just to watch his discovery from the sidelines. Each evening, mindless of the twelve–sixteen-hour shooting, he took her through her scenes for the next day. Permitted to view the rushes, he criticised the grainy quality of the film and asked the cameraman why he was using regulation Agfa film and not the superior-grade Kodak film, which he had used for *Gösta Berlings Saga*. When told this was not available in Germany and that importing it would cost five times as much as Agfa film, Stiller sent to Stockholm for Kodak film, and insisted that it be used only for the scenes in which Garbo was appearing. Subsequently, she stands out more than she would have done, only because of the vast difference in quality of the film used.

The scenario is grim as the main players trudge across the cobbled streets of the mining community, not a happy soul among them as they queue outside the shop belonging to Butcher Geiringer (Werner Krauss), *an obese thug always accompanied by a huge snarling dog, who revels in their misery, knowing only the rich can afforded his inflated prices. When not calling the police to truncheon the queue into orderly fashion, he is at his cellar window, looking up women's skirts.*

Cut to the title 'ORGY' and Frau Greifer's bordello. Then to the home of the Rumforts, where Greta (Garbo) *cooks cabbage for the umpteenth time because this is all they can afford. Later, she queues outside the butcher's all night to no avail* (resulting in arguably the most famous fainting scene in movie history – Greta Garbo caught in the arms of Marlene Dietrich!). *The Rumforts' fortunes momentarily change when a crooked entrepreneur arrives in town. He spreads rumours of a strike, resulting in a drop in share prices, which enables him to buy them cheaply and sell them on to the unsuspecting townspeople. Counsellor Rumfort* (Jaro Fürth) *buys some shares and, finding himself with cash to spare after his bargain purchase, also treats Greta to a fur coat.* (The script called for this to be an ordinary coat, but Stiller chose a fur one, believing a girl of Greta Rumfort's poor social standing would never be able to afford a fur coat and therefore the other characters would assume she had acquired it by selling herself.[72] Her boss thinks so, and when she refuses his offer to pay her for sex, he molests her. Until now, Garbo has been photographed in middle and long-shot, and has not stood out from the other actresses. However, in close-up and despite her over-made-up eyes and protruding teeth, she is mesmirizing.)

When the shares are revealed to be worthless, the poverty of Melchior Street intensifies. The Rumforts take in a lodger, Lt Davis (Einar Hanson), *with whom Greta falls in love. Desperate for money, she agrees to work at the bordello and we see her sitting at a triptych mirror while her client is shown in – Butcher Geiringer! This leads to a high-camp pursuit around the furniture while she fights, screams, cowers, pleads and sobs, finally tumbling through the screen separating this room from the one next door, where a party is taking place. Lt Davis is here and he rescues her – her virtue remains intact. This leads to the citizens of Melchior Street exacting their revenge, wrecking the bordello, then going after Geiringer. Mayhem erupts before the police arrive to restore order. 'I do have meat, but not for your child,' he tells a starving woman before she hacks him to death with a meat cleaver.*

For many years, critics have disputed the identity of the actress playing the woman who kills the butcher: some claim she is Marlene Dietrich, others that she is Hertha von Walther (1903–87), a character actress of the day.[73] In fact, it is both. In a shoddy editing exercise, or perhaps because the footage was badly restored, the woman hammering on the door with her back to the camera is von Walther, but when she turns around and we see her face it is Marlene, wearing the same clothes from the previous fainting scene. In our conversations, Marlene only ever referred to Garbo as 'that other woman', and hated being reminded of her own silent films. 'Of course it was me,' she laughed, when I asked her. 'I should have known if I was in the film or not. It was pure kitsch. I don't even want to remember it, let alone talk about it!'[74]

There was little rejoicing among the cast and crew of *Die Freudlose Gasse* when the film wrapped on 26 March. On this very day, they learned that its writer, Hugo Bettauer, had died in

Vienna, two weeks after being shot by a dental technician named Otto Rothstock. The Nazi party, branding him a 'corruptor of the nation's youth' on account of his outspoken views, had put out a hit on him.

On 18 May 1925, the film premiered simultaneously at Berlin's Mozartsaal and at the Urselines Cinema in Paris, where it played for two years. The original print ran to 10,000 feet. In the French release, *La Rue Sans Joie*, 2,000 feet were removed, including all the exterior shots of Melchior Street. In Austria, all scenes featuring Nazi sympathiser Werner Krauss were removed. In Russia, Lieutenant Davy became Doctor Davy, and the butcher committed the murder. In England, the film was banned, Fortunately, perhaps, for Garbo, about to embark on her biggest adventure, it would not be released in the United States for another two years: in the throes of the Great Depression, Americans had enough hardship of their own to cope with without having that of a country, thousands of miles away, foisted upon them. *Variety* later observed, 'A pretty dingy lot are these Viennese daughters of joy ... The picture's only commercial value is the presence of Greta Garbo.'[75][76]

Garbo's date for the Berlin premiere was Stiller himself, looking pale and tired – the result of his slowly worsening health. SFI no longer trusted him, UFA wanted nothing more to do with him, and a deal with French Pathé had fallen through. Pabst was interested in making another film with Garbo, but did not want Stiller involved – even in the capacity of her adviser. Whatever decision Stiller might have been about to make regarding their future together in Europe was thwarted by an angry cable from Louis B. Mayer, admonishing Stiller for his tardiness – he and Garbo should have left Sweden no later than 1 May, even earlier if Mayer had heeded Garbo's subsequent dispatch, and now they were almost a month late. Even so, Stiller stalled – just in case any other European offers were forthcoming – until, on 31 June, he and his charge set sail from Gothenburg for New York on the SS *Drottningholm*.

CHAPTER THREE

NEW YORK, HOLLYWOOD ... BORG!

'Borg, I think I shall go home now. It isn't worth it, is it?'

Garbo did not allow her mother, brother and sister to accompany her to the docks at Gothenburg. As with her father's death, there would be no public outpourings of emotion. She recalled, 'Both Mother and I were sad about my going, but we never let on ... Mother's eyes were swollen. "Don't cry," I said, "I'll be back in a year – twelve short months that will hurry by!"'[77]

Stiller too had reservations. Before leaving for New York, he took Garbo to the studio of Olaf Ekstrand, one of Sweden's premier photographers, from whom he had commissioned publicity shots for *Gösta Berlings Saga*. Ekstrand took around twenty pictures. The most famous of these shows Garbo, naked from the waist up, but posed sideways so that one shoulder and an arm cover her modesty and smiling coquettishly.

Garbo and Stiller arrived in New York on 6 July 1925 to find the city in the grip of a ferocious heatwave, with temperatures soaring well into the eighties. This, and the noise after the cool and tranquillity of Stockholm affected Garbo the most. Stiller had anticipated a fanfare welcoming committee. Instead, they were greeted by Hubert Voight, a minor MGM publicist, and the only one in New York who spoke Swedish.

Having only seen Garbo's photograph, and knowing virtually nothing about her, Voight had decided to promote her as 'The Swedish Norma Shearer' – though she and the much-loved actress, engaged to MGM's 'Boy Wonder' production man Irving Thalberg – were as alike as chalk and cheese. His first mistake, though they soon became friends, was in pronouncing, 'Welcome to New York, Miss Gustaffson!' Voight's boss, publicity chief Howard Dietz, had

told him how much he hated the name Garbo, claiming that it was
the next best thing to 'garbage'.[78]

Voight had spent several days contacting the press, hoping to
raise interest in this new star, without success, and out of his own
pocket paid a young freelance photographer, Jimmy Sileo, $25 to
snap Garbo and Stiller before they left the ship. Thinking this was
just another routine job, Sileo turned up with only four plates in
his camera. His first shot was of Garbo and Stiller, leaning against
the ship's rail: he wears an expensive English Savile Row three-piece
suit, she a checked twin-set and white hat. Both smile radiantly,
happy to be in this 'land of opportunity', unaware of the difficulties ahead. The other shots feature Garbo alone, one sitting on a
bench with her legs crossed: later she denounced the photograph,
complaining that Sileo had captured her wrinkled stockings and
made her feet appear too big. At the time, however, she was so
keen to pose – and the photographer anxious not to hurt her feelings by confessing that he had used up all of his plates – that Sileo
'snapped' away for another twenty minutes. Garbo never asked
what had happened to the other shots. From the pier, Voight drove
his charges to their quarters – two small suites connected by an
internal door at the Commodore Hotel, on 42nd Street, not far
from MGM's offices on Broadway. Howard Dietz had chosen this
establishment because it was inexpensive – telling Voight, 'These
Swedes are not worth wasting too much money on.' According to
Stiller in his first American interview, a sweltered Garbo spent the
whole of her first afternoon in New York submerged in a bathtub
of cold water.

Two of Jimmy Sileo's photographs made the dailies. The *Graphic*
published the one of Garbo with Stiller, while the *Herald-Tribune*
used a solo shot with the caption, 'A Comely Visitor: One of
Sweden's Most Beautiful Film Stars'. *Motion Picture*'s Adele Whitely
Fletcher caught up with Garbo in the hotel lobby, and asked what
she was most looking forward to while in New York. Fletcher
claimed she replied, via an interpreter, 'I want to go to the *Follies*.
I want to see if those girls are really beautiful. I want to see if they
are any more beautiful than I am!'[79] But did Garbo really say, and
mean, such a thing?

Garbo described the next two months as the most boring of her life. MGM's vice-president, Major Edward Bowes, contacted Stiller with the offer of a screen-test. His response was that Garbo would make the test, but only if the studio upped her salary. Bowes refused: the test took place, and received a thumbs-down. Garbo was denounced as too dowdy and unglamorous, and urged to try again after she had been to a couturier and hairdresser, and smartened herself up. Her response – setting a precedent which would later infuriate and strike terror into the hearts of everyone at MGM – was that if they did not like her as she was, she would finish her 'holiday' and go home.

Within days of arriving in New York, she and Stiller fell in with a small coterie of ex-pat Swedes, who had made the city their home. First up was 25-year-old Rolf Laven, of whom virtually nothing is known save that Stiller picked him up in a gay bar, moved him into his suite at the Commodore, and persuaded MGM to add him to their roster as his translator. On 9 July, Laven accompanied Stiller to the MGM offices, where in the presence of several junior executives – Howard Dietz declared that he was too busy – Stiller signed an agreement agreeing to report to MGM in Culver City on 12 September. He was given no indication what his first assignment would be, and told that his protégée would be sent for at a later date.

As for Garbo, she was pleasantly surprised to learn that one of her old friends from Blekingegaten had relocated to New York. Kaj Gynt, a few years her senior, had appeared in two films, worked on scripts, written several plays and performed on stage in Harlem. Now, she became Garbo's *frangine*, and vied with Hubert Voight for her affection. He may have succeeded in sleeping with her, but it was Gynt who got to share her bed on a regular basis. 'She was in her bed, in lovely silken pyjamas, and I thought then that she was the most beautiful woman I had ever seen. So beautiful did she seem to me that I began to cry,' she recalled.[80]

During the day, if the heat was not too oppressive or if it was raining, Garbo and Laven went shopping: a nightmare, he said, because she was so shocked by the vast difference in prices between there and Sweden that she bartered endlessly, while getting him to translate everything from dollars into kroner. Shopping for shoes, he said, was her biggest problem because most shops did not stock her size – seven-and-a-half – until she hit on the idea of visiting the men's department. On an evening, while Stiller and Laven amused themselves in the gay clubs of Greenwich Village, Garbo, Kaj Gynt and Hubert Voight went to the cinema, where in the pre-talkies era it was not difficult to work out what was happening on the screen even if one could not understand the titles – or the theatre, which was more of a challenge but more exciting because Voight introduced her to some of the biggest stars of the day: Beatrice Lillie, Libby Holman, Katharine Cornell, and Humphrey Bogart, who was appearing in *Hell's Bells*. In those early days Garbo loved to sit in the gallery with the ordinary fans and chat about the show with whoever was sitting next to her. Later, when the paranoia for privacy kicked in, she would always buy two seats, positioned next to the aisle so that she would have no one sitting next to her, and have access to an easy exit, should she be recognised.[81]

Garbo was so impressed by the musical-comedy *Valencia* that she saw it twenty times and learned the title-song – made famous by legendary French revue artiste Mistinguett – by heart. Voight recalled how she sang it all the time and even insisted on being photographed wearing a Spanish dance costume. This gave Howard Dietz, who hated the name Garbo – the idea that she might fare better in the movies as Greta Valencia. Her angry response to this in fragmented English, along with her habit of referring to herself in the masculine gender, was: 'He no flamenco dancer named Valencia. Garbo remains his name or else he sail back to Stockholm!'[82]

Garbo loved Coney Island, riding the rollercoaster for hours at a time and scoffing huge quantities of hotdogs. Occasionally, she and her friends headed for Harlem and the notorious Clam House, a smoky, anything-goes speakeasy on 133rd Street, almost an American version of Berlin's Weiss Maus, where on some nights live sex-shows, hetero- and homosexual, took place in the backroom. Yet it was as if there were two Garbos – the giddy, outgoing teen-ager (she was still only nineteen) and the girl who became suddenly terrified if someone from the press dropped in at the Commodore, and always ensured that the safety-chain was on the door. Just one reporter actually managed to talk to her properly – *Motion Picture*'s W. Adolphe Roberts – in an interview lasting all of five minutes, Garbo on one side of the door, he on the other, her excuse being that she had a cold. Yes, she said, she was looking forward to working in Hollywood. No, she did not like the heat. Yes, she had loved what she had seen thus far of America and its beautiful skyscrapers. Yes, she did like going to the theatre or cinema every day. And no, she did not wish to answer any more questions!

A chance meeting with another expat Swede, retired actress Martha Hedman – formerly a big name on Broadway – resulted in Garbo being introduced to the Berlin-born photographer Arnold Genthe (1869–1942). Known for his studies of San Francisco's Chinatown, and the 1906 earthquake, Genthe had also photographed dancers Anna Pavlova and Isadora Duncan, women whose beauty, he declared, had come from within as opposed to the artificial, contrived glamour of the typical Hollywood star. When he showed her his portfolio and Garbo jokingly remarked how she would like him to photograph her some time, Genthe suggested, 'So, why not now?'

Garbo pleaded that she was not wearing the right clothes; her hair was frizzy and looked a mess. Genthe waved those excuses aside. He was fascinated, he said, not just by her face but what lay *behind* that face. He wanted to photograph her *soul*! The result was an impromptu series of staggering portraits, yet one Garbo insisted should never be shared with the world. As would happen with the characters chosen for her films, each image revealed a separate, integral facet of her complex personality: within the space of an hour she revealed herself passionate, sensual, timid, angry, mournful, jubilant, playful, domineering, orgasmic – each emotion displayed without prompting from the man behind the camera.

Genthe risked showing one of the photographs to his friend, Frank Crowninshield, publisher of *Vanity Fair* and the respected host of the famous Condé Nast parties. Crowninshield was bowled over not just by Garbo's great beauty, but also by her mystique – the vacant stare from those heavy-lidded eyes, the slightly-parted lips, the virtual lack of make-up in an age when vamps were plastered in the stuff to conceal their imperfections. Garbo, however, had no imperfections to conceal: her skin was absolutely flawless. Crowninshield published the portrait in the November issue of *Vanity Fair*. Captioned, 'A New Star from the North – Greta Garbo', it took up an entire page of the magazine. When Stiller saw this, he obtained copies of all of Genthe's photographs of Garbo and sent them by special courier to Louis B. Mayer. Overwhelmed, Mayer ordered Stiller to get her to Hollywood as soon as possible and even agreed to an increase in salary – of a paltry $50.

On 26 August, Garbo, accompanied by Kaj Gynt, visited MGM's Broadway offices for the first time, where she signed a three-year contract. Howard Dietz and his staff found her strange indeed – gliding around the room, drawing her fingers across the tops of chairs, sniffing the walls, caressing the drapes to get the 'feel' of the place. She took an instant dislike to Dietz, and he to her. When he asked her, patronisingly, if she was pleased with her contract, she snapped, 'No, I am not! It is not enough. And I want, too, a car and chauffeur, like all the movie stars have!' Major Edward Bowes is on record as saying after she left, 'What an awkward girl. A peasant type. She'll never live out that contract. The studio will have her back here in six months and on her way back to Sweden.'[83]

A few days later, Garbo was driven to the West 49th Street studio of Russell Ball, who had been commissioned to take a series of pre-publicity portraits, which would be wired to MGM ahead of her arrival in Hollywood. Ball photographed her 'raw' – in everyday clothes, without make-up, and with her hair looking as if she had been dragged through a hedge. He lost patience with her when she suddenly began improvising – removing her leather coat and her top, and draping herself first with a fur rug, then with the curtains. The studio was similarly unimpressed.

On 5 September, bidding Kaj Gynt an emotional farewell at New York's Grand Central Station, Garbo, Stiller, and Rolf Laven boarded the *Twentieth Century* for Los Angeles. Stiller's former secretary-lover, Carlo Keil-Moller, a 35-year-old actor who had appeared with Garbo in *En Lyckoriddare*, was suing him for unpaid salary. Stiller had received several cables in New York, which he had ignored until Keil-Moller's lawyer contacted him to say that he had taken out a repossession order on Stiller's house in Stockholm to get his client's money back. This had been dropped when Stiller paid the debt, but he was taking no chances with Rolf Laven, to whom he also owed money: the young man was promised 'a life of luxury' once they reached Hollywood. Keil-Moller would go on to better things, becoming director of Stockholm's prestigious Lorensberg Theatre, and the Royal Dramatic Theatre itself.

Garbo later said that the five-day journey to Los Angeles had bored her senseless. At one station, she got off the train to stretch her legs, and was still stretching them when it set off again. Leaning out of the window, Laven saw her – sitting on a box, nonchalantly smoking a cigarette – and pulled the emergency cord. The train backed into the station to pick her up, adding thirty minutes to its schedule. Her head had been so in the clouds, Laven said, she never noticed the train had left without her![84]

On 10 September, at Pasadena's Southern Pacific Station, MGM organised a Scandinavian welcoming committee which included, from the acting fraternity, Karl Dane, Gertrude Olmstead, Karin Molander (Lars Hanson's wife) and Einar Hanson – recently arrived in Hollywood and contracted to Paramount, he had just completed *Into Her Kingdom* with Corinne Griffith and was about to begin shooting *Her Big Night* with Zasu Pitts. Also there were Victor Seastrom and, standing at the back of the crowd, a young Swede named Sven Hugo Borg, who would soon feature very prominently in Garbo's life. As she stepped off the train, two small Swedish girls wearing traditional costume presented Garbo with sprays of roses and gypsophila. Then everyone posed for photographs, the budding star smiling shyly and looking away from the camera, Karl Dane, Stiller and Borg towering above everyone else – the director sweating in the Californian sunshine in his heavy English suit.[85]

The event was organised by MGM publicist Pete Smith, who introduced Garbo to the press. When asked where she would be living in Hollywood, she replied that she was hoping to find a room with a nice private family. There were gasps of shock: in those days only a certain type of starlet was not chaperoned around the clock and some journalists were already sharpening their claws simply because she was a foreigner. One, Dorothy Woodridge, cattily observed, 'Her shoes were run-down at the

heels. Her stockings were silk, but in one was a well-defined run.
As a sartorial masterpiece she was a total loss.'[86]

One shudders to think how the press would have reacted, had
they known the truth about Stiller's relationship with Rolf Laven,
the pair sharing a rented beach house in Santa Monica. Garbo took
up residence at the Norwegian-run Miramar Hotel, on Wilshire
Boulevard, in a tiny apartment comprising bed-sitting room,
kitchen and bathroom. Here, on 18 September, she celebrated her
twentieth birthday – alone.

In a town where curiosities were ten a penny, Garbo and Stiller
were initially derided as figures of fun, quite simply because they
made little effort to fit in. He continued wearing his suits, even
on the beach. She was photographed among the palms in fur-
trimmed coats, carrying a man's umbrella to protect her from the
sun. Remembering how Louis B. Mayer had called her fat, Stiller
instructed her to stand sideways and arch her back – which she
does ridiculously in each shot – so that the camera would not
capture her unusually wide hips. Because she hated being stared
at, she refused invitations to parties and receptions, preferring to
wander alone for hours on end, deep in thought, as she had in
Constantinople. In a letter to a friend in Stockholm, she observed:

> God, how I hate this shapeless country ... I live in a dreary hotel in
> the quietest part [of town] and sometimes feel I'm wrong to do it.
> But one can't live in Hollywood. There are millions of motor-cars
> there – I haven't seen any of the stars yet. I dream of our theatres at
> home that must be opening now. Oh, my enchanting little Sweden,
> how happy I shall be to get home to you again! ... I don't go to
> parties, do nothing during the day and just want to go to bed as
> soon as I can. I am not smoking so much either. It's this eternally
> boring smiling sun that takes all one's pleasure away. The doctor's
> told me that the climate here isn't good for me ... There's no atmos-
> phere at all to the restaurants here and you don't feel you're 'going
> out' when you go to one...[87]

Garbo and Stiller visited Scandinavian friends, such as the
Seastroms and their interior designer friend, Erik Stocklossa, who

remembered her being more interested in spending time with the children than the parents and *never* showing up without some little gift.[88] She also spent a lot of time with Stiller and Rolf Laven at their beach house, only taking off her coat to swim with Laven in the sea – most often as dawn was breaking, when no one was around. Because she disliked eating out, she cooked for them – one journalist hoping for an interview rushed away 'in absolute horror' when they saw her sitting on the beach, peeling potatoes for lunch. No one mocked Garbo and Stiller more than Lars Hanson's wife, Karin Molander. 'They were a melancholy pair,' she observed. 'She was really quite unattractive then. Her hair was kinky and her teeth were not good. Nobody paid any attention to her and she was very unhappy. They used to sit on the terrace staring out at the ocean and looking gloomy. I remember we called them Grandma and Grandpa.'[89] Molander did not know one half of it – that 'Grandpa' had slept with her husband back in Sweden, and that 'Grandma' was doing so there in Hollywood. Hanson was shooting *The Scarlet Letter* with Lillian Gish and dropped in on her at the Miramar most evenings.

Louis B. Mayer, meanwhile, was beginning to regret offering Stiller a contract, which had been his only way of securing Garbo, itself seeming like less of a good idea as she was dismissed by the MGM executives as frumpy and unattractive. Mayer had offered her $400 a week to come to Hollywood – an unusually high salary for a virtual unknown – and Irving Thalberg, his production manager, was now faced with the task of making a silk purse out of the proverbial sow's ear. A man accustomed to compromise, New York-born Irving Thalberg (1899–1936) started out as a secretary to Universal's Carl Laemmle and worked his way through the ranks to producer status, joining forces with Mayer in 1923 and helping him found MGM the following year. Mayer had appointed him studio vice-president and, more than any other executive, relied on his tact and experience, though the two never really got along – despite Thalberg's gift of turning everything he touched into box-office gold.

Thalberg was the archetypal Mama's boy, meaning he was used to getting his own way, and suffered extremely delicate health on account of a heart defect. Though he was yet to meet her, he disliked Garbo because a press article had referred to her as 'The Swedish Norma Shearer'. Shearer was his girlfriend (they married in September 1927) and, because of her privileged position, also took too many liberties, demanding and getting only the best parts.

Shearer's name was included as part of the 'catechism' – or list of dos and don'ts which Stiller had written out for Garbo to learn by heart: 'Don't take any notice of other people. Be yourself. Don't try and be like anyone else. Don't try and be like Norma Shearer.'[90] Thalberg learned of this and effected a regime which he hoped would result in Garbo rushing back to Sweden: she would be put on a meticulously controlled diet, her hair would be defrizzed and her 'buck teeth' straightened, and she would be assigned a ward-robe – which she herself would pay for out of her salary – which would not make her look like a 'farmer's wife'.

Garbo complied without a word of protest, though she was less amenable towards the publicity MGM had in mind. Just as Frenchmen in those days appeared on the screen wearing berets and striped jerseys, and Italians were depicted as smarmy villains, so the studios typecast Scandinavians as athletic types who spent all their time on the sports field or in saunas. Garbo was coerced into a series of publicity shots with members of the USC track team looking decidedly out of place. Pete Smith was not satisfied with just having her pose with these testosterone-charged athletes – in one shot he had her standing under the high-jump bar while one of them flies over the top of it, his rump inches above her head. In another, she is crouching while another leapfrogs over her back. She was told to ride side-saddle on a feisty horse and to strum a banjo. She did not *want* to ride a horse, she said – and what was the point in getting her to pretend to play a banjo? The last straw came when she was ordered to pose with Slats, the six-year-old MGM logo lion. Reassured that the animal was harmless, she sat on a chair in his enclosure while the keeper led him in on a leash – then released him to perch on a log, two feet from her face. She remained still long enough for the shutter to click, and when Slats roared at her barely flinched, though she was petrified. The picture appeared with the caption, 'Brave Daughter Of Vikings Visits Lion

In Its Den!' Garbo was not amused: Smith was informed that there would be no more 'stupidly unnecessary' photographs.

One day on the set of *The Scarlet Letter,* Lillian Gish introduced Garbo to Hendrik Sartov (1885–1970), a master of soft focus who had famously worked with her on *Orphans of the Storm* (1921). Such was her power at the time that she was able to march into Irving Thalberg's office to explain how Garbo was wasting her time hanging around a film set when she should be making pictures of her own. She proposed that Sartov should make a screen test of Garbo, which she vowed would be far better than the one Thalberg had seen and dismissed. And it was: within hours of watching it, Thalberg assigned her to the part of La Brunna, the singer in the screen adaptation of Vicente Blasco Ibáñez' *Entre Naranjos* (*Among The Orange Trees*).

Ibáñez (1867–1928) was the Spanish novelist and political activist most famous for *The Four Horsemen of the Apocalypse* (1921) and *Blood and Sand* (1922), adapted into enormously successful films with Rudolph Valentino. MGM thought the title contrived and changed it to *Torrent.* Heading the credits was Ricardo Cortez (1899–1977), a 'Latin' actor being touted by MGM as their answer to Valentino – far from being authentically Spanish, he was Jewish and his real name was Jacob Krantz. Cortez was involved with another actor, but had entered a lavender relationship with actress Alma Rubens, whom he would marry (making him her third husband) the following year. Addicted to cocaine and, having been in and out of mental institutions, Rubens had recently been declared uninsurable and therefore unemployable, and coping with her tantrums made Cortez rude and disagreeable to everyone who crossed his path. Garbo hated him, but she hated the director and the journalists who never seemed to be away from the set even more. *Photoplay* were in the middle of their so-called 'pro-America' campaign, having declared, 'Foreigners are going through the studios with the speed of mumps going through a day nursery.'[91] [92]

Stiller, on the other hand, got along well with Monta Bell and kept his counsel even when Garbo had left the set to visit the ladies' room, and the director bawled through his megaphone, 'Will someone go and fetch that fat woman back here?' A former assistant to Charlie Chaplin, directing only his second film – Bell did not mind Stiller 'lending a hand' in his capacity of translator: the most Garbo could come up with in English were slang terms such as 'Beat it!', along with any number of expletives. Irving Thalberg, however, *did* mind. If Garbo needed a translator, then he would find her one who would not interfere with what was happening on the set.

Sven Hugo Borg (1896–1981) was a strapping, 6′4″ blond from Vinslöv, Sweden. Well-educated, he had eschewed university for a stage career, achieved no success there, and in September 1925 had ended up in Hollywood, hoping to make it in the movies. In the meantime, he had taken a secretarial job at the Swedish consulate and on checking the noticeboard, observed MGM were looking for an interpreter and English teacher for a 'recently arrived Swedish movie star'. Borg, who spoke English fluently, applied for the position, and on 3 November was informed that the job was his. 'I was delighted,' he recalled, 'but I did not know then what I was letting myself in for!'[93]

On 5 November, Borg headed for the film-set, where Garbo was being laid into by both Stiller and Monta Bell. The director had demanded she make another screen test, while Rolf Laven giggled from the sidelines – this time Bell wanted a shot of her legs, and all was going well until Stiller bawled, in Swedish, 'Give them sex, you dumb bitch! Your legs look like pipe-cleaners!' He then denounced her to cameraman Tony Gaudy, 'She's fucking hopeless! She has all the movements of a carthorse. And you're expecting to make a star out of *that*? Bah!' Borg had told him not to be so rude, and he and Garbo hit it off at once: he had fallen in love with her on the spot and she reciprocated a few days later on learning that, like Lars Hanson and her brother Sven, Borg had been born on her 'lucky' date: 26 July, the date she also started work at the PUB store in Stockholm.

Garbo and Borg only ever addressed each other by their surnames, and even when her English was vastly improved, never spoke to each other in any language but Swedish. Within days, Borg had taken on the duties of translator, bodyguard, confidant, dogsbody and slave. On 14 November, when she arrived at the studio for costume fittings and make-up tests, with Borg carrying her vanity case, one reporter observed, 'Garbo's got a personal maid, and it's a man!' He moved into the California Hotel, opposite the Miramar, so that he could be at her beck and call – but for Garbo, this was not close enough. Before being invited to share her bed, he slept on the floor in her room. He fetched her slippers each morning, ran her bath and helped her dress, and even squeezed the toothpaste onto the brush. When Garbo laughed, Borg laughed: when she cried, he wept with her. Early on in their relationship, when not working, they loved to frolic on the beach – until she realised they were being watched. 'After that, Garbo never danced or sang on the beach again,' Borg recalled.

When shopping, if the item purchased cost a large amount, Borg paid by cheque and she settled with him later – then, as in the future, any cheque signed by Garbo was often worth more than the purchase, even if this was a car, which she now bought to facilitate the twenty-five-mile journey between the Miramar and the Culver City set. Borg taught her to drive but during one of her first outings behind the wheel without him, she was pulled over for speeding. She tried to bluff her way out of a fine, claiming she had mistaken the 60 mph on her dial for kilometres. This, however, was Hollywood, which had its own rules. Borg called Louis B. Mayer's office, who in turn called Richard 'Whitey' Hendry, the studio's Chief of Police. He was responsible for sorting out anything from parking fines to sex scandals and even homicides and his motto was: 'We always cater for the picture people – we want them to be happy with us!' The arresting officer had filed a report, which was duly amended: Garbo had been a passenger in the car, which *Borg* had been driving recklessly. The young man was fined $10, which MGM paid – along with a 'donation' to the station – and the matter was dropped. Not that Garbo learned her lesson: over the next three years there would be six more arrests for speeding, with Borg standing in as the stooge.

Torrent began shooting on 27 November, and wrapped on 23 December. Garbo 'approached the making of this picture as one approaches an electric chair,' Borg recalled. Ricardo Cortez was still picking on her, addressing her as 'Miss Dumb Bitch' or 'Flat Foot'

– until Borg grabbed him by the scruff of the neck and warned him what would happen unless he stopped. After this, Borg said, Garbo would glance at him while he was standing next to the camera-man and mouth obscenities in Swedish, which were picked up by lipreaders when the film was released in her home country.

The story, set in Spain's Júcar Valley, centres around two families: the poor Morenos and their aristocratic landlords, the Brulls. Peasant girl Leonora Moreno (Garbo) *sings while waiting for her sweetheart, Rafael Brull* (Cortez), *at the village shrine. Both have aspirations: she wants to become a famous singer so that her family will be afforded a better life, he longs for a political future with her as his wife. But when Rafael's mother tries to scupper the young couple's plans by kicking the Morenos out of their home, Leonora's mother is forced to skivvy for the Brulls, while the girl and her father head for Paris.*

Several years elapse and Leonora becomes renowned soprano La Brunna, singing Wagner in a blonde wig, sporting some of the most bizarre costumes ever seen on screen, and getting kissed by dishy tenor Salvatti (Arthur Edmund Carewe). *In keeping with the times, he takes her to see* La Revue Nègre, *but the black singer crooning 'Goin' Home' makes her realise she no longer belongs there.*

Leonora returns to her village with a retinue of servants and a pet monkey, and dripping with jewels, leading the locals to assume she has turned to prostitution – only the barber who taught her to sing realises she is La Brunna.

Rafael, now affianced to pig breeder's daughter Remedios (Gertrude Olmstead), *wins the local election and the title announces, 'Then a torrent – as furious and relentless as the passion that surged in the hearts of the lovers.' The river bursts its banks, buildings and bridges are swept away, and Rafael sets out to rescue Leonora, whose house is on an incline beneath the dam. The dam crumbles, but the house remains standing, and when he gets to her, she is reclining on her bed, reading – a vision of breathtaking beauty.*

In the next scene the couple are seen drying off after the storm she supposedly knew nothing about – she draped in a blanket, he wear-ing one of her ostentatious fur-trimmed wraps. When Leonora, who has whored herself to the crowned heads of Europe, accuses Rafael of

*being unfaithful, he rushes off to his engagement party, only to feign a
headache halfway through and instead spends the night with Leonora
under the stars.* (It was unheard of for a woman to be the dominant
partner in Hollywood movies at this time, so when Leonora bears
down on Rafael, despite the director's instructions that the lead
male make the first move, Garbo set a precedent for every one of
her subsequent roles.)

*Leonora's actions bring shame on the community: her mother
disowns her and she leaves to resume her career. Years pass, and she is
performing* Carmen *when Rafael turns up at the theatre. While she
still looks gorgeous, a loveless marriage has aged him, giving him grey
hair and a paunch. He still wants her, but she is wed to her public
and this is how it must stay.*

Shooting the flood scene brought about the biggest altercation
between Garbo, Ricardo Cortez and Monta Bell thus far. Dripping
wet, Garbo and Cortez stumbled off the set, to where Sven Hugo
Borg was waiting with a blanket. Cortez made a grab for this,
remarking, 'Where *she* comes from, she should be used to the
cold!' – adding that *he* was the star of the picture, and not the
'Swedish flatfoot', that if she wanted to get warm she would have
to wait until she reached her dressing room. Garbo laughed, and
pronounced in heavily-accented English, 'Let him haff it, Borg.
You must not let yourself be bothered about a pumpkin like that!'
Minutes later, she was summoned to Louis B. Mayer's office. The
mogul had visited the set earlier in the week (the first time Garbo
had seen him since their Berlin meeting) and posed for photographs with Garbo, Borg, and Rolf Laven. Borg asked her what she
would do if Mayer gave her her marching orders, and she replied
that would not be such a bad thing – she and Stiller would return
to Sweden, taking Borg and Laven with them.[94]

Torrent's photographer should have been Tony Gaudio, but a cut
to his finger a few days before shooting began resulted in his deputy
taking over. William Daniels (1901–70) hailed from Cleveland,
Ohio. In 1919, he had been signed by Universal, and had worked on
six films with the legendary Erich von Stroheim. He will, however,
go down in history as 'Garbo's cameraman' – working on nineteen

of her twenty-four films. He alone knew how to capture her innate luminosity, mystique, and perfectly symmetrical features. She trusted him so implicitly after their first film together that she allowed him to photograph her exactly as he saw fit and never criticised the finished result. Daniels was the only person permitted to photograph a close-up of her feet, yet he was a modest man when discussing his innovative work with her:

> I didn't create a Garbo face. I just did portraits of her I would have done for any star. I didn't, as some say I did, keep one side of her face light and the other dark. But I did always try to make the camera peer into her eyes, to see what was there.[95]

Once the studio executives had seen the rushes for *Torrent* they were amazed. Garbo's contract with MGM – the one she had signed in New York – had been for three years. Then, she had been an unknown quantity and an expensively hired calculated risk. Her next film had already been decided and was scheduled to begin shooting in the spring and Mayer now attempted to butter her up, apologising profusely for keeping her waiting for so long before putting her to work, praising her 'phenomenal' acting talents, and suggesting she might extend her contract by another two years. Garbo responded that she was perfectly happy with the contract she had. Mayer then became patronising, saying, 'Miss Garbo, believe me, when you're sitting there at home eating your herring and potato, you will regret it when you think that you could have stayed here and lived on chicken and ice-cream.' Calmly, Garbo picked up her bag and gloves and said, 'Meester Mayer, I must go home even so!' before walking out of his office.[96]

Torrent premiered at New York's 5,000-seater Capitol Theatre in February 1926, and at Loew's State Theatre, Los Angeles, a few days later. It was a huge success, with Garbo – as would happen at all of her film premieres, conspicuous by her absence – taking the lion's share of the plaudits. *Variety* observed:

> This girl has everything – with looks, acting ability and personality. When one is a Scandinavian and can put over a Latin characterisation

with sufficient power to make it most convincing, need there be any more said about her ability? ... There are other 'names' in the cast and although veterans, they could not overshadow Greta Garbo. Hail this girl, for she'll get over![97]

Pictures hailed Garbo the find of the year: 'She possesses that which has heretofore only been laid at the door of Pola Negri – fire, animation, abandon and all of the other adjectives usually employed to describe a very colourful figure and personality to match.'[98] *Motion Picture*'s Laurence Reid described her as: 'The most important feature in the film, a composite picture of a dozen of our best-known stars.'[99] Garbo herself was less impressed by her performance, writing home to Mimi Pollak: 'The public and critics have been wonderfully kind, but personally I don't think I was good, so I don't get much pleasure out of it all. They don't have a type like me out here, so if I can't learn to act, they'll soon tire of me, I expect.'[100]

How wrong she was!

CHAPTER FOUR

THE TEMPTRESS & THE STRANGE AMERICAN

'He was so terribly good to work with. Every morning at nine o'clock he would slip to work opposite me. He was so nice that I felt better. I felt a little closer to this strange American!'

Thanks to Valentino and now Garbo, Vicente Blasco Ibáñez was the most bankable writer in Hollywood, with three smash hit films to his name. Press mogul William Randolph Hearst had serialised several of his novels in *Cosmopolitan*, and owned the film rights to them, including *La Tierra de Todos*, another controversial story set in a far-flung location, which Irving Thalberg had decided should be Garbo's next vehicle. Co-starring would be Spanish heartthrob Antonio Moreno (1887–1967), who had appeared in the popular Pearl White serials. The title of the film was changed to *The Temptress* and, against his better judgement, Thalberg commissioned Mauritz Stiller to write the script. Though not as popular as Ricardo Cortez, Moreno's position in the Hollywood community had been strengthened by his 1923 lavender marriage to wealthy oil heiress Daisy Canfield Danziger, who may have had shares in MGM. Therefore, when Moreno read the script and declared there was too much of Garbo and not enough of him, Thalberg instructed MGM's script department to extend his part. To make up for Stiller's disappointment, he hired him to direct.

Shooting had more than its share of problems. Garbo complained about the inordinate number of costume changes. 'More than twenty costumes to try on, over and over,' she is quoted as saying, 'Dresses, I wish they were all bags, and all alike, to jump into quick!' There were clashes between Stiller and Antonio Moreno, who Stiller said could not act, and who at thirty-eight was too old to be playing twenty-year-old Garbo's leading man. Thalberg stuck to his guns when Stiller asked for him to be replaced: Moreno was an authentic Latin this time, and got along with everyone, including Garbo. One scene in the film required the hirsute actor to appear shirtless, in an era when the recently set-up Hays Office Motion Picture Production Code forbade body hair, navels, open-mouthed kissing, overt violence and sexual innuendo – all of which are seen in *The Temptress*. Stiller declared the macho chest hair would stay, but objected to Moreno's pencil-line moustache, claiming it made him look like an Italian waiter. He also insisted the actor wear plat-form boots two sizes too large, so that Garbo's feet – bigger than his – would not stand out so much, and so that he would appear taller than her, which he was not. Stiller also refused to have a translator present when shooting began on 17 April 1926 – this, he declared, would rob his direction of continuity. Unfortunately, his bad English caused such pandemonium among the crew – bawling 'Stop!' for 'Go!', and vice-versa, but always getting the expletives right – that the technicians mocked him and cameraman Tony Gaudio threatened to walk off the set.[101]

Five days into shooting, Stiller received a cable from Stockholm. Alva, Garbo's sister, had died, aged just twenty-three. Stiller was rehearsing the complicated opening sequence – the masked ball – and did not wish to infringe on Garbo's jovial mood, so he waited until the next day before breaking the news. With her desire to always keep a stiff upper lip, she insisted on finishing the scene. 'It was the act of a real trouper,' Sven Hugo Borg recalled, adding how he had driven her home, at which point she had gone to pieces.[102]

Garbo had last written to Alva the previous December, thanking her for her gifts of hand-knitted mittens and a tin of home-made gingerbread: 'It almost makes me ill, when I think that I can't come home and spend Christmas with you ... I suppose I'm stupid and ungrateful, when you consider that perhaps there are millions whose dearest wish is to be in my shoes. But, there it is...'[103]

Alva Garbo (she had legally changed her name, intent on follow-ing her sister to America) is listed as having died of tuberculosis on 21 April 1926. Most sources state this as the official cause of death: since early childhood she had suffered from respiratory complaints.[104] Later, during a trip to Sweden, Garbo claimed that she and Alva had appeared in *Tva Konungar* (*Two Kings*), but this was not so: the only time they had worked together had been in *En Lyckoriddare*.[105]

Garbo mourned her sister for the rest of her life, most especially as she had not been with her at the end. Two months later, she wrote to Lars Saxon:

> Don't forget me ... It has made me so unhappy being so far away from my own kin, having to be here without being able to do anything for one's nearest and dearest has been so difficult ... I don't understand and can't learn to understand why God suddenly meant me such harm. It's as though a part of me has been cut away. I've tried to go home, but everyone advises me not to ... But I'll go the first chance I get. It may still be another six months but I'll have to be able to go then. It will be very sad, strange and wonderful to be able to come home, home again.[106]

On 27 April, Garbo was dealt another blow when she arrived at the studio and was summoned to Thalberg's office. Stiller had been fired from the picture and she was introduced to his replacement – Fred Niblo, the man who had been directing *Ben-Hur* in Rome, when she had first met Louis B. Mayer. Without even acknowledging him, she asked Borg to take her back to the Miramar.

There was considerably more to Stiller's dismissal than his awkwardness on the set, and the fact that here, as in Sweden, he never shot anything in sequence – totally unacceptable for Thalberg who, when watching the end-of-day rushes, had no idea which scene would go where, or even if it would stay in the film. To the studio's way of thinking, this was an unnecessary and costly extravagance. Stiller's argument – valid but falling on deaf ears – was that Mayer had brought him to Hollywood *because* he had admired his working methods, and was now refusing to allow him to put those methods into practice. Had this been Thalberg's only concern, some sort of compromise might have been effected. Mayer, however, had recently received a missive from William A. Orr, of MGM's New York office, part of which read:

I think I should tell you that the Department of Labor had heard something antagonistic of Stiller. I was not able to find out what it was, and I can only assume that it was possibly an anonymous letter sent to the Department by someone who wanted him out of the country.[107]

The 'something antagonistic' and the 'anonymous letter' were references to Stiller's private life. William A. Orr had intermediated between Stiller and Carlo Keil-Moller, and almost certainly been made aware of the exact nature of the relationship between the director and secretary. This, and the fact that Rolf Laven was still living with Stiller at the Santa Monica beach house, clearly contravened MGM's 'moral turpitude' stipulation included in every studio contract, from the big stars down to the canteen cleaners. While major stars that were homosexual were shanghaied into marriages to save their careers, directors were not always so lucky but Mayer knew that if he sent Stiller packing, Garbo would go with him. For their part, Garbo and Borg tried to convince Mayer that Stiller was straight – by having her deny she was having an affair with him, the theory being that if any man so much as glanced at the Swedish beauty, he could only be rampantly heterosexual. A few years later, Borg revealed what Garbo is supposed to have told him – and what he, as intermediary, had told Mayer, who of course had been far too shrewd to have the wool pulled over his eyes:

> Borg, people say that I am in love with Mauritz, don't they? That is not true, Borg. I have never been anything to any man, not even Mauritz. I do not love him in that way, nor he me ... You have seen me, Borg, sit on his lap and smoke with him the same cigarette. You have seen him hold me like a child. It is so good when his arms are around me, for sometimes I am afraid. But it is not love, Borg.[108]

With Stiller's six-monthly work permit due for renewal, he was loaned out to Paramount to make *Hotel Imperial*, a World War I drama set in Austria, with vamp Pola Negri. In the meantime, packing only a few essentials, Garbo had Borg drive her to a small hotel in Santa Monica where – setting what would be a precedent

– she checked in under an assumed name. It would appear that while here she suffered some sort of breakdown. Lars Hanson, the only person besides Borg and Stiller who knew where she was, later confirmed this: 'She was still just a little girl from the south side. Young and inexperienced. For her, life was like walking on a marsh.'[109]

Mayer, the bully, mounted his high horse and tore a strip off Garbo, by way of Borg:

> Borg, that girl thinks I am a hard, unreasonable man and that I am paying her a salary far below what she is worth. She forgets that it was I who took all the risk. She has acted like a fool, and ought to be spanked, but unless she behaves herself she will regret it.[110]

Such tactics were hardly likely to tempt Garbo back into the fold, and despite being menaced by Whitey Hendry and the studio police, her trio of confidants refused to divulge her whereabouts. Indeed, for a time Mayer believed that she may have fled the country. Then, she suddenly emerged from her bolthole and informed Mayer, by way of Borg, that she would be suing him for firing Stiller.

No one had ever stood up to Mayer before, and Garbo's indifference – the fact that she did not care if she stayed in Hollywood or not – only made him admire her more. Yet within minutes of returning to the set she was asking Borg to drive her back to the Miramar. During the directorial changeover, Irving Thalberg had ordered all the costumes she had worn in Stiller's discarded scenes to be burned, and the Danish costumier Max Rée (who had dressed her for *Torrent*) had walked off the picture in disgust. Again, Borg was asked to deliver a message to Mayer: 'No Rée, no Garbo!' Mayer refused to budge on this one, so Fred Niblo offered a compromise: to keep Garbo happy and complete the film without further hiccups, he would pay Rée out of his own pocket for whatever time he was needed on the set.

Fred Niblo made changes to *The Temptress* in an attempt to 'de-Stiller' the production. The actor H. B. Warner was replaced by Marc McDermott, and upon Garbo's request, William Daniels was brought in to photograph her, while Tony Gaudio assisted. Dorothy Farnum, who had scripted *Torrent*, was commissioned to re-script this one. All of Stiller's scenes were re-shot, and there is the audacious announcement over the credits, 'Personally Directed By Fred Niblo' before the opening title, 'Spring, and the nights of Paris throb with love and desire'. Every now and then, Niblo throws in footage of all the usual tourist locations, lest American cinema-goers forget where the action takes place. The film also set another precedent, the Garbo 'formula', which would never fail at the box-office: the ageless siren, married to or kept by a much older man, who falls for the handsome younger stud in some exotic location.

The masquerade is in full swing, surveyed by Elena Torre Bianca (Garbo) *and her wealthy 'sponsor' Fontenoy* (Marc McDermott). *He tries to get fresh, but she tells him she has never loved him. While fleeing his advances she finds herself buffeted and pawed by the revellers, until she is rescued by visiting Argentinian engineer Manuel Robledo* (Antonio Moreno), *who falls under her spell when she removes her mask.* (Stiller's opening scene featured Garbo making her entrance on a white horse, in riding habit and high-heeled boots designed by Max Rée, and there had followed a scene in which, dressed in an ostrich feather gown, she dances the tango. Bert Longworth's stills have survived to remind us how magnificent she looked. This first love scene with Moreno is unconvincing, however: Garbo kisses him over-cautiously, as if expecting his fake moustache to detach itself.)

The lovers spend the night under the stars, while barges drift along the Seine and a shooting star signals that 'it' is about to take place. He does not even know her name.

Cut to the home of Torre Bianca (Armand Kaliz), *who holds court at the piano and welcomes a surprise guest: Robledo. The Argentinian compliments Torre Bianca on the opulent surroundings paid for by his wife, Elena, who with his blessing is prostituting herself to Fontenoy. How Robledo and Torre Bianca know each other is not explained, but all three have been invited to Fontenoy's Last Supper* (not the first Biblical allegory in the film, and a scene which would have benefited from a retake, since the shadow from the overhead camera can be seen hovering above the table).

While the guests play 'footsie' under the table in anticipation of after-dinner partner-swapping (the scene for which Stiller had wanted Moreno to wear bigger shoes), *Fontenoy toasts his special guest, Elena: 'At the back of every man's failure, there is a woman! I lift my glass to the lady who has honoured me. To the Temptress, who asks for nothing but takes all a man can give, and more!' He has put poison in the glass and promptly drops dead.*

Bereft of his wife's sponsor, Torre Bianca faces ruin, until Elena gives him the jewels Fontenoy bought her to sell and pay off their debt. Robledo, meanwhile, leaves for Argentina – 'The Land of Men' – to be reunited with his sweetheart and finish building the huge dam that will bring him world acclaim. The thorn in his side is singing bandit Manos Duras (Roy D'Arcy, who with gnashing teeth and slimy aplomb performs a camp emulation of Douglas Fairbanks' Zorro).

No sooner has Robledo knuckled down to work than the Torre Biancas roll into town. The locals react like they have never seen a female before – Elena wears gold lamé and the workmen drool over her exposed armpit. Then Duras and his mariachi mob turn up, and when he grabs and kisses her, Robledo challenges him to an 'Argentine', a traditional duel with twelve-foot stock whips.

For the three-minute sequence, no stand-ins were used – remarkably, considering the way they go at it, neither actor sustained serious injury. Aroused by this masochistic display, Elena clutches her breast and pants for breath. Robledo wins, but is badly hurt and temporarily blinded, enabling Elena to make her move: tending his wounds (badly painted on with beetroot dye!), *she very nearly licks the blood from his chest and, like Mary Magdalene, kneels at his feet.* (What makes the scene more controversial is that he initially thinks she is one of his men – and gives the impression of enjoying the experience. The scene was heavily cut before being granted release in some parts of America, and removed completely for others.) *Duras, however, has the last laugh, shooting Elena's husband dead before riding off.*

Having had enough of her, Robledo arranges for Elena to leave for Europe, but before this can happen, Duras dynamites the dam. While the whole town fights to repair the dam before the floods come, the local priest rants, 'God – if there is a God – this woman shall destroy no one else!' Robledo stumbles home, finds Elena in his bedroom and tries to strangle her, but changes his mind and makes love to her instead.

The scene then moves forward six years. Robledo has rebuilt his dam and is in Paris with his fiancée when he sees Elena again. Downtrodden, she is working her beat and does not recognise him. He buys her cognac and leaves, and in her drunken stupor she mistakes the grubby painter at the next table for Jesus – a halo encircles his head as she gives him her last possession, a ring given to her by Robledo, and begs forgiveness for the wrongs she has done. 'After all, you died for love,' she says.

Sensitive American audiences, however, would never tolerate a prostitute talking to Jesus, and after the September 1926 previews, Irving Thalberg commissioned an alternative ending, which was shot on 13 October:

Robledo has completed his dam and after being commended by the Argentinian President thanks those who supported him, particularly his fiancée Celinda. (It mattered little to Thalberg that she had scarcely featured in the film until now.) *It is Elena's face that he sees in the crowd, however, an illusion which persists until he steps down to kiss her, at which point we see that it is his far less attractive future wife.*

Shooting wrapped on 26 July, Garbo's 'lucky' date, and, despite feeling disgruntled that Stiller had been removed from the picture, she presented Fred Niblo with a signed photograph, the only time she would ever do this: a head-and-shoulders shot by Arnold Genthe, on which she wrote, 'To Fred Niblo. With a piece of my heart, Greta Garbo.' She then offered her apologies for not attending the post-wrap party, and returned to the Miramar to host a rare 'Swedes-only' private birthday party for Lars Hanson and Sven Hugo Borg. Because this was also her brother Sven's birthday, an empty place was set at the table. This would be the last anyone extant of her closest friends would see of her for several weeks.

On 23 August, Hollywood and the world were plunged into the deepest mourning with the death in New York of Rudolph

Valentino, aged just thirty-one, from a burst appendix. Pola Negri, Rudy's lavender date, currently shooting *Hotel Imperial* with Stiller, went into publicity overdrive as the 'grieving widow' – claiming he had asked her to marry him, which was wholly untrue. Stiller left her to her histrionics: to get away from her, until after the Hollywood funeral, he and Rolf Laven spent much of their time with Garbo and Borg at the Miramar. No comment was forthcoming from Garbo then, or ever.

At around this time, Crown Prince Gustav and Princess Louise of Sweden arrived in Hollywood on a state visit. Louis B. Mayer asked Garbo if she would escort them around the MGM lot. No, she declared, she would not. Instead, they were driven to Paramount, where Stiller had been shooting *Hotel Imperial*. Here, Garbo and Borg joined them for lunch – she taking her place at the table next to Gustav, while Louise was forced to sit elsewhere. Writing of this to Mimi Pollak, she ended on a dour note: 'I am so tired. I never go out, just collapse into bed. Oh, God, to be able to go home when the time's up! If I have a bit of money then, it would be fine. But no increase in my salary yet – they are mean!'[111]

The Temptress opened in New York on 10 October 1926, just ten days after Fred Niblo had finished the editing. Garbo hated it. 'Terrible, the story,' she complained to Lars Saxon. 'Everything is so rotten. It is no exaggeration, I was *beneath* criticism!' The real reason she disliked it so much was because it would always remind her of two great tragedies of her formative years: her sister Alva's death, and the enforced professional separation from Stiller.[112]

But the critics disagreed. The *New York Times* hailed the film, 'A distinguished piece of work,' while Harriette Underhill gushed in the *New York Herald Tribune*, 'Such a profile, such grace, such poise – and most of all, such eyelashes! They swish the air at least half an inch beyond her languid orbs!' Dorothy Herzog observed in the *New York Mirror*, 'She *is* the Temptress. Her tall, swaying figure moves Cleopatra-like from delirious Paris to the virile Argentine. Her alluring mouth and volcanic, slumbrous eyes enfire men to such passion that friendships collapse.' Robert E. Sherwood, writing for *Life* magazine, enthused:

I want to go on record as saying that Greta Garbo in *The Temptress* knocked me for a loop ... I am powerless to formulate an opinion on her dramatic technique, but there can be no argument as to the efficacy of her allure. [It] is a lavish, luxurious picture with all forms of audience appeal. It would however be pretty dreadful, were it not for the individual and unassisted efforts of Greta Garbo, who qualifies herewith as the official Dream Princess of the Silent Drama Department of *Life*.[113]

And Garbo, in real life the unlikeliest temptress of them all, was about to meet the man regarded as the greatest love of her life, though apparently not by her.

John Gilbert (John Cecil Pringle, 1895–1936) was born in Logan, Utah. As a teenager, recovering from a tough childhood, he arrived in Hollywood, where for a while he was employed with the Thomas Ince Studio. Working through the ranks by way of writing scripts and directing for Maurice Tourneur, in 1921 he acquired national acclaim opposite Mary Pickford in *Heart o' The Hills*. Following a spell with Fox, where he triumphed in *The Count of Monte Cristo*, he moved to MGM, where his biggest hits were *The Merry Widow* and *The Big Parade* (both 1925). The latter, directed by King Vidor, told the story of World War I through the eyes of an ordinary soldier and had made Gilbert a household name. A first marriage to Olivia Burwell lasted five years – what would be a long time for him – and in 1922 he wed actress Leatrice Joy (1893–1985). The couple had one daughter, also called Leatrice who (as Leatrice Gilbert Fountain) would write an uncompromising biography of her father. Their marriage had thrilled Louis B. Mayer 'beyond compare', whereas their divorce – with Joy citing her husband's 'compulsive philandering' – had earned Gilbert his enmity.

John Gilbert could never be called a matinée idol; he possessed neither the physique nor the looks but a gawky frame, bullfrog eyes, a scraggy neck, sunken cheeks, a thin-lipped expressionless mouth, which when he smiled gave the impression that he was wearing ill-fitting dentures, and a high-camp voice which did not befit his macho image. His greatest strength, the critics of the day declared, was his on-screen charisma, which, it has to be said, does not come across as overtly potent. Some regarded Gilbert as Valentino's natural successor – while others thought him even greater than the Latin lover. Neither claim stood up then and, eight decades on, stands up even less today.

Whatever attributes Garbo, or any other woman, saw in Gilbert – none of them stayed with him for long, even his four wives – is anybody's guess, particularly as it was he who replaced the phenom-enally good-looking Sven Hugo Borg in her affections. Gilbert was arrogant, loud-mouthed, temperamental and, much of the time, a nasty drunk who all too often engaged his fists before putting his brain and common sense into gear. Like Valentino, he fancied himself as a boxer and often challenged his enemies – mostly jour-nalists who refused to pander to his self-importance – to fist fights. Unlike Valentino, who excelled at the sport, Gilbert's challenges invariably ended up with him coming off worst.

Gilbert was currently the highest-paid actor in Hollywood – at the height of the Depression he earned a staggering $10,000 a week. Garbo was on a fraction of this amount, yet Louis B. Mayer expected her to be grateful when offering her top billing with Gilbert in the film he planned – *Flesh and the Devil*, based on Herman Suderman's novel, *The Undying Past*. This tells the story of two boyhood friends, Leo and Ulrich, who grow up to be soldiers in Germany and end up falling for the same woman, an obvious recipe for disaster.

To direct, Thalberg hired Massachusetts-born Clarence Brown (1890–1987), who had first met Gilbert while working as Maurice Tourneur's assistant, and moved to MGM around the same time as him. Brown's biggest hit to date was *The Eagle* (1925) with Valentino. In a lengthy career, he would become Garbo and Joan Crawford's favourite director (six films for each), but Garbo remained his favourite actress: 'For me, Garbo starts where they all leave off,' he said. 'She was a shy person: her lack of English gave her a slight inferiority complex. I never gave her a direction above a whisper. Nobody on the set ever knew what I said to her.'[114]

Garbo was less interested in money and equality than she was in denouncing the title, devised by Thalberg to capitalise on her vamp status, acquired from her first two Hollywood films. 'Always the vamp I am, always the woman of no heart!' she told Borg, dispatching him to Mayer with yet another message – she was too ill to work right now but she hoped that by the time she was better, the studio would have found her a better part than this one. In fact, she was not bluffing: she had recently been diagnosed with anaemia.[115]

There was some consolation in that Gilbert did not want to do the film either, declaring it too much of a 'buddies' movie' and lacking in romance. He and Mayer detested each other because of a spat which had occurred while discussing on-screen vamps. When Mayer had denounced such women as 'just prostitutes', Gilbert shot back, 'What's wrong with that? My own mother was a whore!', and Mayer had almost decked him. Gilbert and Thalberg, on the other hand, were friends, and it was Thalberg who talked him into accepting the part, with Gilbert's ultimatum being that he would only do the film with Garbo. Therefore, on 4 August, Mayer sent her an angry missive, part of which read:

> You are hereby notified and instructed to report at 4.30 p.m. today at the office of Mr Irving G. Thalberg, for the purpose of receiving instructions with reference to the part to be portrayed by you in *The Flesh And The Devil*. Failure on your part to comply with this demand, particularly in view of the attitude heretofore displayed by you, and your general insubordination, will be treated by us as a breach of your contract of employment.[116] [117]

If he was hoping for her to jump to attention, however, Mayer had another think coming. Words such as 'demand' were not a part of the Garbo vocabulary, and she purposely ignored him and did not report for duty until 8 August. Production began the next morning – though Garbo would not film her first scene until mid-September – and wrapped at the end of this month, by which time she would have celebrated her twenty-first birthday and embarked on what is regarded as one of the greatest romances of the twentieth century, and one which had begun with a rebuff, after Gilbert marched up to her on 17 August, stuck out his hand and pronounced, 'Hi, Greta. Pleased to meet you!' Her response was a gruff, 'It is Miss Garbo,' wherein she promptly headed back to her dressing room.

Later, she attributed her sullen mood to nerves – she had been expecting Mayer or Thalberg to turn up on the set and bawl her out for being difficult. During her first scene with Gilbert, she fluffed the first few takes, until he guided her through them and told her not to worry. Clarence Brown recalled:

It was love at first sight, and it lasted a long time. In front of the camera their love-making was so intense that it surpassed anything anyone had seen and made the technical staff feel their mere presence an indiscretion. Sometimes they [Garbo and Gilbert] did not even hear my 'out', but went on to the camera-man's amusement.[118]

Sven Hugo Borg was on the set for the railway station sequence near the beginning of the film when Garbo and Gilbert met for the first time. 'Some instant spark, some flash seemed to pass between them the instant they looked into each other's eyes,' he recalled.[119] 'If there was ever a case of love at first sight, that was it.' What Borg did not add was that exactly the same thing had happened when *he* and Garbo had first met. Also, the relationship with Gilbert did not last long, as Brown observed – less than three years, much of it one-sided, and with both parties having affairs between sulks and separations. Two evenings later, Garbo left the studio and drove with Gilbert to his luxurious Spanish-style home at 1400 Tower Grove Road – where she stayed, keeping on the apartment at the Miramar to save face and hopefully fool Louis B. Mayer and the Hays Office spies.

The secret of John Gilbert's success with most women was money and power. Garbo, however, was not most women. Her attraction towards him had more to do with where he was from than what he earned, owned, or looked like. Her previous male lovers had all been hunky Swedes and two of them – Lars Hanson, and Borg himself – were bisexual. Since arriving in America she had been constantly surrounded by Scandinavians – her comfort zone in a country she initially disliked. Her co-stars had been foreigners, neither of them appealing. Gilbert was the first genuine all-American she had come into contact with, and it seems likely that he was more in love with her than she him, precisely because she was different – in the days before extensive overseas travel, she represented the archetypal ice-maiden from a country most Americans had only heard of from newspapers and magazines. Garbo rarely spoke publicly about him. She told one friend, without even mentioning that they had been lovers:

> I don't know how I should have managed if I had not been cast opposite John Gilbert ... He is quite a wonderful man – vital, eager, enthusiastic. If he had not come into my life at this time, I should probably have come home to Sweden at once, my American career over.[120]

Gilbert was gushing when discussing her, partly to bolster his ego, partly to defend her against their common enemy, Mayer:

> Garbo is marvellous, the most alluring creature you have ever seen. Capricious as the devil, whimsical, temperamental and fascinating. When she doesn't feel like working, she will *not* work. Garbo never acts unless she feels she can do herself justice. But what magnetism once she gets in front of a camera. What appeal! What a woman! One day she is childlike, naive, ingenuous, a girl of ten. The next day she is a mysterious woman a thousand years old, knowing everything, baffling, deep. Garbo has more sides to her personality than anyone I've ever met.[121]

Within days of Garbo taking up residence, the workmen moved into Tower Grove Road. 'Yacky', as she called him, forked out a staggering $15,000 for a 'Scandinavian-style' bathroom with black marble walls and tub, and solid gold fittings: when his beloved 'Flecka' (Swedish for *girl*) complained that the marble sparkled too much, he paid another $1,000 to have everything 'de-glittered'. When she told him that she was missing Sweden, he turned part of his garden into a 'mini-Scandinavia', complete with log cabin and pine trees. When she complained that her new patch was *too* quiet, he installed a waterfall. However, the 'house on the hill' was never exclusively Garbo and Gilbert's love-nest, as has been suggested. Scriptwriter Carey Wilson (1889–1962) was a founder member of the Academy of Motion Picture Arts & Sciences, and had famously scripted MGM's *Ben-Hur*. Since the break-up of his marriage, two years previously, he had occupied Gilbert's spare room and become a kind of 'wing man', accompanying his friend on his nightly jaunts in search of prostitutes and showgirls. Their philandering only stopped when Garbo arrived on the scene, declaring herself 'one of the boys'. When Gilbert and Wilson bought matching hunting jackets and boots for their hikes into the hills, she did the same. When they relaxed next to the pool, puffing away at their pipes, she too smoked a pipe. Sometimes, if she preferred her own company, she wandered off into the hills alone, or sometimes hired a horse, and they would go looking for her:

> If I needed recreation, I liked to be out of doors: to trudge about in a boy's coat and boy's shoes, to ride horseback or shoot craps with the stable-boys, or watch the sun set in a blaze of glory over the Pacific Ocean. You see, I am still a bit of a tomboy. Most hostesses disapprove of this trousered attitude to life, so I do not inflict it upon them. Besides, I am still a little nervous, a little self-conscious about my English. I cannot express myself well at parties. I feel awkward, shy, afraid.[122]

Journalists, always welcome at Gilbert's parties, now found themselves excluded – and knew better than to request an interview with the woman who, in their eyes, was the strangest the movie capital had ever seen. Close friends *were* welcome, though aside from Borg, Stiller, Lars Hanson and Rolf Laven, these were mostly Gilbert's friends, some of whom Garbo disliked, and whose arrival usually sent her rushing for the sanctuary of her bedroom. Two exceptions were director Edmund Lowe and actress Lilyan Tashman, the film community's most prominent lavender couple. Most Sundays, everyone piled into Gilbert's two roadsters and headed for a picnic in the mountains. Alternatively there would be tennis parties, after which the guests donned swimsuits and dived into the pool. Garbo, without the slightest hint that she was doing so for titillation, usually swam naked. One of Gilbert's friends was Adela Rogers St Johns (1894–1988), the journalist-novelist-scriptwriter who had started out as a reporter with William Randolph Hearst, and whose subsequent work varies between quality writing and tittle-tattle. Garbo made Adela welcome, though once she read what she had written about her, she never spoke to her again:

> Garbo was never one of the gang. A certain quiet aloofness marks her in the middle of convivial merrymaking. In a bathing suit that never quite fits, with an old straw hat over her long bobbed hair that hides half her face, she will lie for hours in the sun, relaxed, indifferent, looking more like some peasant girl than like an exotic enchantress.[123]

One of Garbo and Gilbert's rare public outings was to the opening night – the only premiere she ever attended – of his latest picture, *Bardelys The Magnificent*, a historical romp he made with Eleanor Boardman. Looking decidedly ill at ease, and wearing a long fur coat despite the heat, Garbo posed for photographs outside the theatre with Gilbert, Irving Thalberg and Norma Shearer, fidgeted all the way through the screening, and insisted upon returning to Tower Grove Road immediately afterwards. Sven Hugo Borg subsequently kept her amused while the party attended the post-performance dinner at the Cocoanut Grove.

Hollywood's promised 'wedding of the year', between Eleanor Boardman and King Vidor, was set to take place on 8 September 1926 at Ocean House, Marion Davies' Santa Monica sumptuous hacienda – described by actress Colleen Moore as, 'The biggest house on the beach – the beach between San Francisco and Vancouver!' One evening, over dinner with Boardman and Vidor, a half-sozzled John Gilbert suggested spicing up the ceremony by making it a double wedding – the other couple being himself and Garbo, whom he claimed he had proposed to several times, something she always denied. In a letter to Lars Saxon she observed, 'I suppose you have read in the papers about me and a certain actor, but I am not, as they say here, "going to get married". But they are crazy about the news. That is why they have picked on me.'[124]

Was the ceremony planned by MGM as a publicity stunt to promote *Flesh and the Devil*? And how did King Vidor and Eleanor

Boardman really feel about having their big day turned into a Garbo and Gilbert media circus, while they were more or less relegated to the background? To be on the safe side – as if predicting what would happen on the 'happy' day – MGM informed the press that the Vidor-Boardman nuptials were to be a private affair. Nothing was mentioned about it being a double ceremony.

An early problem appears to have centred around the chief guests. Gilbert and King Vidor had been close friends since *The Big Parade*. Both wanted Irving Thalberg and Norma Shearer to be there, whereas Garbo did not. Neither she nor Gilbert wanted to invite Louis B. Mayer, whereas Vidor did because he was one of his dearest friends. Sven Hugo Borg was another sore point with Gilbert, for obvious reasons: whenever Garbo needed to get away from her new environment, or whenever she had a problem, rather than confide in Gilbert she would go straight to the handsome Swede – or to Mauritz Stiller, whom no one but Garbo wanted at the wedding.

On the morning of 8 September, Borg arrived at Gilbert's house: minutes later, he and Garbo were witnessed speeding along Tower Grove Road, the last anyone saw of them. According to Eleanor Boardman, thirty minutes after the ceremony was scheduled to start, Mayer followed a very flustered Gilbert into Marion Davies' bathroom, patted him on the shoulder and said, 'What's the matter with you, Gilbert? What do you want to marry her for? Why don't you just fuck her and forget about it?' At this, Gilbert turned and socked Mayer in the jaw, sending him sprawling across the tiled floor – banging his head and breaking his glasses. Mayer staggered to his feet, and would have hit Gilbert back, had they not been separated by Eddie Mannix. At which Mayer levelled, 'You're finished, Gilbert. I'll destroy you, even if it costs me a million dollars!'[125]

Garbo returned to Tower Grove Road that same evening, and the next morning she and Gilbert reported for work as if nothing had happened. Indeed, the fervour and intensity of their performances only seemed to intensify from this point on, suggesting that they really were *so* passionately in love that it did not matter whether they were married or not – or that they were such great actors that they were able to pull the wool over everyone's eyes with the (then) hottest love-scenes which had ever been seen on the silver screen.

A feast of intrigue, sex and homoeroticism, Flesh and the Devil *opens at the Prussian Army barracks. Leo von Harden* (Gilbert) *has missed roll call, and he and best buddy Ulrich von Eltz* (Lars Hanson) *are assigned to mucking out the stables.* (Here, fans get to see Hanson's muscular torso, his toned physique belying his forty years, while the scraggy Gilbert keeps his shirt on.)

In the next scene they are at the station, on leave, about to meet the woman who will try but fail to come between them. Garbo, whose whole demeanour instinctively tells us she is trouble, is rushing to her carriage when she drops the flowers she is carrying; Leo retrieves them and plucks one for a keepsake. The demonic-looking Pastor Voss (George Fawcett) *looks on and hints at the men's relationship, 'I christened those two boys separately, but since then I've never seen them apart.'* (Throughout the entire scene the men appear to only have eyes for each other, and their interactions are no less erotically charged than Gilbert's with Garbo.)

On the ferry home with Leo's mother and Ulrich's fifteen-year-old sister, Hertha (Barbara Kent), *the two men stop within an inch of kissing against the backdrop of their favourite haunt, Friendship Island. A flashback reveals them as boys, cutting their wrists and swearing fealty as blood brothers in front of a statue of two naked Greek warriors.*

Cut to a society ball, where Leo espies his mystery woman – identified only as 'Von Rhaden's wife' – across the crowded room. (Recalling Valentino's debut, William Daniels' first close-up of Garbo, projected on the thirty-foot screen, made audiences gasp. Like Valentino, Garbo was androgynous and attractive to both sexes: her heavy-lidded eyes, when they stared into the lens, were sensuous and suggestive and she had a unique gait, 'schlepping' from the shoulders as a man might, yet by swaying her thick hips maintaining an intense femininity.) *She and Leo dance around the room, then through the open door and into the garden, where she seduces him.*

When Leo asks her name, she asks, 'What does it matter?', and when he tells her how beautiful she is, she declares, 'You are very young!' (Garbo was actually six years Gilbert's junior.) *She sucks the tip of his cigarette before placing it in his mouth. He strikes a match and the glow* (from a tiny carbon arc lamp concealed by Gilbert in the palm of his hand) *lights up their faces, rendering her expression surreal, her face almost corpse-like. The match is extinguished – the sign for her to make the first move – and she kisses him before retreating to the boudoir. There, cradling his head in her lap, she toys with his hair and* (in defiance of the Hays Office) *almost devours him, open-mouthed.* (Though Garbo looks divine, Gilbert does not deserve the title of 'the handsomest man in Hollywood'. Wearing too much kohl around his eyes, he resembles a moustached woman in drag, and his hands, when she slips a ring on his finger to remember him by, are hairy and unattractive.)

The lovers are rumbled by her husband (Marc MacDermott) *and the matter settled by pistols at dawn – with Leo, the victor, exiled to Africa. She promises to wait for him but we know this will not happen because, much to her satisfaction, Leo has asked the wealthy Ulrich to console her while he is away.*

The story moves forward. Ulrich's influence has earned Leo a reprieve and he returns home. The horses' hooves, the pistons of the ship's engine and the train wheels spell out 'FE-LI-CI-TAS', the first time her name has been mentioned, and her face is superimposed over the scene. The two men meet at the station, and again almost kiss. Then Ulrich introduces Leo to his wife – Felicitas. She has manipulated him into marrying her, knowing Leo is so in love with Ulrich that he will never be able to keep away from him – and will therefore be easier to ensnare.

Hertha is now grown and has a crush on Leo, who has developed an unexplained Oedipus complex, planting profound, lingering kisses on his mother's mouth not dissimilar to the ones Felicitas planted on his.

Pastor Voss, who earlier suggested that Leo and Ulrich's relationship might not be platonic, tells Leo that because he loves his friend's wife, he must also give up the friend who has been pining for him. The trio attend church, where the cleric gulps down whisky and rants from the pulpit, 'David hath done evil in my sight, and his deed stinks before heaven because David hath seduced Uriah's wife!' Felicitas fixes her lipstick, then faints. Once revived, she kneels between the two men and when passed the chalice from which Leo has drunk, she turns it around so that her lips can touch where his have been. (Religious groups were outraged but powerless to complain because, morally, Garbo had done nothing wrong. 'She shows a frail physique and a fragile, ethereal air, and is infinitely more civilised and all the more subtle for not being so deliberate,' one critic defended, while Alexander Walker observed, 'A woman who could sin and suffer simultaneously was a god-send in a censor's world where moral misdeed had to be balanced by statutory repentence or inevitable destruction.'[126] [127])

Felicitas persuades Leo to run away with her, and she is packing when Ulrich comes home unexpectedly. He has bought her diamonds, a reminder of why she married him in the first place. Knowing that she will have to give all of this up, she changes her mind about leaving: instead they can meet secretly when her husband is not around.

Distraught, Leo tries to strangle Felicitas. She tells Ulrich that Leo has molested her, and once again it is pistols at dawn – this time on the friends' special island.

Felicitas suffers a fit of hysterics (an ultra-camp climax and the silliest sequence in any Garbo film), *tearing at her hair, rolling her eyes and windmilling her arms before attempting to go after them across the frozen lake – plunging to her death through a hole in the ice. The friends, unaware of this, lower their weapons and fall into each other's arms. 'Everything is suddenly clear to me, as if a veil has lifted,' Ulrich says, as the bubbles rise to the surface from Felicitas' watery grave. And as the camera pans out to long shot, they really do appear to kiss.*

This being a moral tale, however, and bowing to the dictates of the Hays Office after the first preview screening, MGM commissioned a new ending:

Leo and Ulrich are in the garden with Leo's mother. She knits while Ulrich reads a book and Leo holds the skein of wool. Hertha appears. Today she turns eighteen – she is leaving, and will not return. Leo rushes off after her carriage. Ulrich, wearing an anguished expression, is about to stop him, but the old lady holds him back. The implication is that Leo has loved Hertha all along (despite the fact that throughout the film he has found her a nuisance!).

Today, Clarence Brown's explanation for this alteration might be perceived as homophobic: 'You can see my problem. How to have the two leading men wind up in each other's arms and not make them look like a couple of fairies?'[128]

Flesh and the Devil opened in New York on 9 January 1927 – an ominous date, for exactly nine years later cinemas would be dipping the lights and announcing that Gilbert was dead. *Variety* observed:

> Here is a picture that is the pay-off when it comes to filming love scenes. There are three in this picture that will make anyone fidget in their seat and their hair rise on end – and that ain't all! It's a picture with a great kick, a great cast and great direction. Miss Garbo, properly handled and given the right material, will be as great a money asset as Theda Bara was to Fox in years past. This girl has everything![129]

The *New York Herald Tribune* was even more enthusiastic:

> Never before has John Gilbert been so intense in his portrayal of a man in love. Never before has a woman so alluring, with a seductive grace that is far more potent than mere beauty, appeared on the screen. Greta Garbo is the epitome of pulchritude, the personification of passion. Frankly, never in our screen career have we seen seduction so perfectly done.[130]

A rare detractor was Jim Tully, the self-styled 'most hated man in Hollywood', a former boxer from Ohio whose scathing attack on the film and its stars in *Vanity Fair* was published the following year. He observed:

> In *The Flesh and the Devil* [Gilbert] was merely a romantic prop upon which Miss Greta Garbo hung an American reputation. Mr Gilbert is not a gifted actor. He plays every role the same ... The Swedish actress is phlegmatic, even apathetic. Of the fire that sets the white screen ablaze, only the ash is visible in real life. She is broad-shouldered, flat-chested, awkward in her movements. Her figure is the seamstress' despair. She has no real beauty, but with clever

lighting and photographing she becomes graceful and fascinating on the screen. Garbo is the only woman who has made capital out of her anaemia. Her indolent movements and half-shut eyes give an impression of exotic sensuality. The real reason for them is fatigue.[131]

After reading this, Gilbert went after him and the two squared up to each other in a bar – but while Gilbert danced around his opponent, bunching his fists and showing off in front of friends, Tully floored him with a single punch. 'It looked to me as if he'd fan himself to death, so I put him to sleep for his own protection,' Tully said.

Despite having three hit films in a row, and despite Mayer reminding her that she was contractually obliged to do so, Garbo refused to give interviews – fleeing from sets, locking herself in rooms, feigning illness, anything to avoid the press. One anonymous female reporter managed to waylay her in the lobby at the Miramar. When asked what she did to amuse herself in her spare time, the response was, 'Nothing.' No, she did not socialise. No, she did not play golf. 'So, what *do* you do?' the young woman wanted to know. Garbo shrugged her shoulders: 'I should prefer to be dead than to love, and I would rather be dead *not* to love. Love comes, love goes. Who can help it?'[132] Then she stomped off, leaving her interrogator totally baffled.

CHAPTER FIVE

13 OCTOBER 1926-22 JUNE 1927: THE GREAT GARBO MYSTERY

'Love is not really dramatic. It is what is behind love and romance that gives us the greatest emotion. I don't know what the greatest emotion really is. Perhaps it is sacrifice. That is of course a big part of love.'

Immediately after finishing *Flesh and the Devil*, John Gilbert flew alone to New York. Rumours persisted of a rupture in his relationship with Garbo, yet while he told reporters that they were 'just good pals', she stayed on at Tower Grove Road, with Sven Hugo Borg and Carey Wilson for company. Within days, Gilbert was back home and once more asking Garbo to marry him. 'Jack wanted her to be the semi-official châtelaine of the house on the hill,' Wilson observed, adding how Gilbert had told the press, 'I am engaged to Miss Garbo, but I don't know whether she considers herself engaged to me.' Gilbert forked out $15,000 for a two-masted schooner and almost as much again for refitting the vessel, which he baptised *The Temptress*. After their wedding, he said, he and Garbo would take a year-long honeymoon trip to the South Seas. Unimpressed by the importance Gilbert attached to material possessions – the fact that to his way of thinking, love could only be bought – Garbo never set foot on the schooner and it was sold at a loss, without even making its maiden voyage.[133]

Irving Thalberg, meanwhile, had decided that Garbo's next film should be *Women Love Diamonds*,[134] the title alone of which made her cringe. This tells the story of Mavis Ray, a girl from the wrong side of the tracks, who lives a life of luxury courtesy of a benevolent uncle, who is actually a sugar-daddy. Borg was again given the task of telling Thalberg that she was not interested, resulting in Garbo's 'unacceptable' behaviour being repeated to Louis B. Mayer, whose reaction was more severe than usual: unless she toed the line, he would have her deported! This cut no ice with her: scarcely a day dawned when she and Borg were not plotting to return to Sweden – Lars Hanson, Einar Hanson and Mauritz Stiller had already made plans to leave Hollywood when their contracts expired. Also, Garbo had another weapon with which to fight her 'oppressors': she could marry Gilbert, become an American citizen, and sign to another studio, which would not treat like a chattel, once her own contract expired.

Once this reached the press, Garbo received hundreds of letters from fans who did not consider the philandering Gilbert good enough for her. One fan, Robert Reud from Detroit, offered to marry her to save her from deportation, then divorce her with no financial restraints once she had sorted out her problems with the studio. Reud so touched her heart with his words of encouragement that she met him and they remained close friends for many years. Mayer attempted to call her bluff and on 4 November sent a telegram, informing her that she had now forfeited her part in *Women Love Diamonds* and ordering her to report to the studio, or else. She ignored this, and the next day Mayer dispatched a letter by personal courier:

> You have disobeyed this instruction and we have not heard from you either directly or indirectly ... We desire you to know at this time that it is our intention to engage another artist to play the part assigned to you. Until further notice you are instructed to report daily to our studio at 9 a.m. During the period of any insubordination on your part, your compensation under the said contract will be discontinued.[135]

Puzzling, on the face of it, was Sven Hugo Borg's letter, dispatched at around this time to Garbo's New York lawyer, Joseph Buhler, which concluded: 'The difficulties with Miss Garbo and the studio are, in my opinion, the fault of Miss Garbo. But as Mr. Louis B. Mayer holds Miss Garbo in high regard, I am certain that everything will be brought to a satisfactory conclusion.'[136]

Buhler's immediate response was to read the letter to her over the phone, or so he alleged, insisting that she fire her 'secretary' at once. Some years later, Borg observed, 'Had I been employed by her instead of the studio, she would have done it.'[137] Considering his utterly selfless devotion towards Garbo – even after she had left him for another man – it is extremely unlikely that Borg would have been acting out of spite. It may well be that she had asked him to write the letter, in the hope that if she adopted a Machiavellian stance and humbled herself to Mayer by admitting, through Borg, that she was in the wrong, then she might get more of her own way. Also, there was no way that Garbo would have dismissed Borg – she could scarcely function without him. Indeed, Borg was Garbo's rock at this time, and had quite possibly become her lover again. John Gilbert was away much of the time shooting *The Show* for horror supremo Tod Browning and, as usual, was unable to keep his trousers buttoned. Within days of beginning work on the film, Garbo received news that he was sleeping with his French co-star, Renée Adorée, his old flame from when they had been shooting *The Big Parade*.

One question must now be posed: could one of the reasons for Garbo's tetchiness and seemingly persistent fatigue have been something more than anaemia? Could she actually have been pregnant? There is a curious passage in Norman Zierold's 1970 biography of Garbo, where he observes:

> An author friend states that he worked for years with Garbo on her autobiography, that Stiller was the obsession of her life, that there was a child which died at the age of five. At the time of Stiller's departure for home, he reportedly begged Greta to come with him ... She stayed and Stiller went, leaving her only with sad memories and guilt. In 1964, when this autobiography was finally completed, Garbo withdrew permission to have it published. There were too many frank revelations, she felt, and now was not the time to air them.[138]

Zierold, writing in the more cautious late-1960s, makes no reference to Stiller's homosexuality and the fact that he, unlike Borg and Lars Hanson, never slept with women meaning that if there had been a child, it would almost certainly not have been his.

Therefore, who was the father: Gilbert, or Borg? Though coming to any satisfactory conclusion may be purely speculative, it is possible to find some convincing answers in the events of the next few months. Garbo confided in Borg about her desire to have a family. Therefore who better with whom to produce the perfect fair-haired, blue-eyed Swedish child than this towering, handsome specimen? Gilbert seems determined not to have wanted children with her: 'She hates Hollywood,' he said. 'She wants to buy half of Montana or whatever state it is that has no people in it, and turn it into a wheat farm and raise wheat and children. Frankly, I don't want to marry some dumb Swede and raise wheat and kids miles from civilisation.'[139]

Her desire to have children is also implied by Borg's recollection of Garbo's reaction when an Italian baby crawled towards them one day while they were on the beach:

Garbo's face became transfigured. With arms outstretched she talked baby talk to him, and when his mother had come and taken him away, Garbo said to me, 'Borg, some day I want a little one like that – all of my own.' I have often noticed this inclination of hers towards children. I have seen the mother-hunger too often not to believe what she said. People have placed Garbo on too high a pedestal. They have made it difficult for her to live a normal life, and it is difficult for them to visualise their goddess with normal womanly instincts. Nevertheless they are there.[140]

These events are reflected in a scene in *The Temptress*, which has absolutely no bearing on the storyline. A peasant baby crawls into Elena's room. At first, she ignores it, then looks like she might be about to shoo it away. Then, her expression melts: she gathers it into her arms and sings it to sleep with a lullaby, sending the message to cinema-goers that even a heartless vamp may have maternal feelings. Why did Garbo insist on such a scene not in the original script? Was she saying, back then, that she wanted a family of her own?

It was only now that Garbo acquired her first agent, though the only way of contacting her would still be through Sven Hugo

Borg: Harry Edington was John Gilbert's agent-business manager, who later married his *Flesh and the Devil* love-rival, Barbara Kent. Edington never charged Garbo for his services – she was listed on his books as a 'prestige item' – though by the summer of 1927 MGM would be secretly paying him $20,000 per picture to 'keep her sweet' and prevent her from returning to Sweden. 'He became convinced that I was not as terrible as the papers made me appear,' she told Ake Sundborg, 'He understood that what I wanted was not to make a fuss. I hate fuss. I wanted only the opportunity to make good pictures.'[141]

The 'good picture' looked like being *Anna Karenina*, based on the novel by Tolstoy. Irving Thalberg had made the decision without even reading the book and was now horrified to learn that the story ends with Anna flinging herself under a train. Obviously, this was unsuitable for Hollywood: while a new ending was commissioned, Garbo – by way of Borg – was instructed to report to MGM's costumes department. His response to this was, 'Miss Garbo is tired and does not want to do it.' Louis B. Mayer exploded, 'Send the dishwasher home!' Thalberg called for patience and understanding, at least for the time being. The studio was finding it almost impossible to cope with Garbo's 'quiet tantrums, illnesses and indifference' – but they had also become used to the vast revenues her films were bringing in.

More speculation over whether Garbo may have been pregnant can be drawn from the compromise which was reached. The studios had a no-nonsense approach to unmarried stars who ended up in the family way: they could have an abortion, or be sent away until the child was born and put up for adoption – or they could marry the father, whence the birth would subsequently be reported as premature. Otherwise they were fired. Garbo was no ordinary star who could be pushed around and did not care whether she stayed in the movies or not. Therefore, as if aware that she would be absent for some time, Thalberg hired a bit-part actress, Geraldine Dvorak, who was not just the exact height, weight, and shape as Garbo – broad shoulders, large feet, wide hips – but who acted, walked, talked (in a fake accent) and so looked like her that anyone meeting her for the first time could not tell them apart. Officially, Dvorak's job was to stand in for Garbo at costume fittings, and in long-shots where her face would not be seen; unofficially, to stand in when her swelling figure might be detected if the shot called for her to be standing sideways.

Privileged journalist Rilla Page Palmborg, who was married to a Swede and who had met Garbo at the home of their mutual friend, Victor Sjöström, was permitted to attend Dvorak's costume fittings, and subsequently watch the pair working:

> 'Gott! She looks like me!' exclaimed Greta the first time she saw Geraldine modelling gowns. Never did any girl enjoy her work more than the double of Greta Garbo. All day long she sat close to the star studying her every movement ... and imagined what it would be like to be the great Greta Garbo. Stardom bored Garbo, and when the day's work was done she left its glittering, dazzling garments at the studio. Then Geraldine, with her hair slicked back from her face like Garbo's, wearing the clinging, exotic garments of the Garbo of the screen, would sit at the table in a gay night club, looking more like Garbo than Garbo herself – while Garbo, dressed in a rough tweed coat, with a slouch felt hat pulled down over her eyes, hurried home to quiet and peace.[142]

Texas-born Dvorak (Jeraldine Matilda Dvorak, 1904–85) appeared in several Garbo films, and as one of Bela Lugosi's brides in Tod Browning's *Dracula* (1931). When Jean Harlow died halfway through shooting *Saratoga* (1937), Dvorak was brought in to double for her in a number of unfinished scenes, where she is seen in long-shot or with her face covered. For a while there was speculation over whether Garbo and Dvorak had actually met, but several photographs do exist of them together. It was she, and not Garbo, who met director Dimitri Buchowetzki in the foyer of the Miramar Hotel in late January 1927. Buchowetzki (1885–1932) had been chosen to direct *Anna Karenina* because of his reputation of being able to handle 'tetchy Europeans' such as Pola Negri and Emil Jannings. According to one journalist, 'Garbo' walked up to him, listened to his protestations on behalf of Thalberg, and of how enthusiastic he was about working with her – then rounded on him with, 'But *I* do not wish to work with *you!*'[143]

Meanwhile, while Garbo was in hiding – only Sven Hugo Borg appears to have known where she was – Harry Edington met with Mayer and attempted to explain that maybe his client was only being awkward because her name was now as big as John Gilbert's, while MGM were paying her less than one-tenth of his salary. Mayer argued that he was paying her what *he* believed she was worth: on 18 September, her twenty-first birthday, her salary had risen to $750 a week. Edington pressed for a minimum $5,000, which Mayer refused to even consider. Borg's response to this was that, until he capitulated, Garbo would be 'staying home'.

Over the next few months, journalists reported numerous 'sightings' of Garbo, none of which actually happened. Dorothy Herzog had Garbo and Gilbert jumping into his roadster and heading for Santa Ana – she thinking that they were about to enjoy a weekend break, until he pulled up at a marriage bureau, whence she fled to the washroom, locked the door and climbed out of the window and hurried to the nearest hotel, where the bellboy called a cab to take her back to Los Angeles. Rival gossip columnists Hedda Hopper and Louella Parsons, who for thirty years made many a star's life a misery with their holier-than-thou preachings and caustic reports, vied for the best stories. Hedda claimed the 'escape' had taken place when Gilbert stopped at a service station. Louella claimed to have seen Garbo, clinging to Gilbert's arm at the 3 February premiere of *Flesh and the Devil* but no one else did, and despite the barrage of press present at the event, there are no photographs to substantiate the story. And when Hedda rubbished the story, Louella came up with another scoop: a Valentine's Day wedding. 'GARBO WEDS GILBERT – FRIENDS SAY!' the headline screamed. Again, the story was made up.

On 23 February 1927, John Gilbert was photographed leaving the Glendale Hospital: the press were told that he had been kept in overnight for observation, but refused to specify why, resulting in more specification. Had Garbo's lover attempted suicide because she had ended their relationship? Had her Swedish secretary *really* driven her to and from the hospital, rolled up inside a rug on the floor of his car? And why were her closest friends – Stiller, Rolf Laven, Lars Hanson, and Einar Hanson – steadfastly refusing to speak to the reporters? Then, four days later, the news broke that Mayer did not know where she was either – moreover that MGM had suspended her, without pay.

Garbo and Borg had in fact retreated to La Quinta, the recently founded resort in California's Riverside County, twenty miles east of Palm Springs. Established by entrepreneur Walter Morgan and later famed for its golf tournaments, in its early days it provided a well-protected hideaway for Hollywood stars and socialites wishing to avoid scandal: the movie moguls brought their mistresses here, actresses recuperated here after secret abortions, or waited out the last months of their confinements safe from the prying eyes of the press. Garbo and Borg rented La Casa, a three-room bungalow tucked into a quiet corner of the resort, so discreet that over the next twenty years she returned time and time again.

On 6 March, Garbo dispatched a six-page telegram of complaint to Robert Rubin, head of the legal department at Loew's Inc., MGM's parent company. In this, she defended her actions for not wishing to negotiate another contract once her current one expired, and accused Mayer of victimisation – obviously she was referring to his threat to have her deported. She berated MGM for purposely giving her a bad press, with their persistent references to her temperament, and their criticism of her for rejecting roles which she found unsuitable – and further accused them of compromising her health by expecting her to make a minimum of three films a year, without breaks in between. Mayer's reaction to her going over his head was to offer another ultimatum: she had rejected *Anna Karenina*, which he now claimed she had asked to play in the first place, and unless she pulled herself together and reported for duty, the part would be given to someone else. Garbo ignored him again and, realising his bullying tactics were getting him nowhere – and that he would be a fool to let her go – Mayer capitulated early in May and offered her a contract which, after some deliberation, she would eventually sign on 1 June 1927.

The new deal was for five years, backdated to 1 January to compensate for the revenue Garbo had forfeited while on suspension. She would be starting out on a weekly salary of $3,000, raising to $5,000 over the term of the contract. It was unique in that she was the only Hollywood star to be paid fifty-two weeks of the year as opposed to the usual forty. She pressed for this because, she said, she never took vacations – therefore what would be the point of her hanging around for the other twelve weeks, doing nothing?

In the meantime, the search resumed. On 18 March, Louella Parsons claimed that Garbo had been waylaid by reporters outside the Miramar, and coerced into giving a brief statement, 'I think a lot of Mr Gilbert. I admire him very much indeed – as a friend, not as a possible lover or husband.' Again, this was pure invention: she was not even at the hotel. On 11 April, Gilbert was arrested after a fracas at the Beverly Hills police station: drunk, he barged into the place claiming that Mauritz Stiller had just tried to kill him and when an officer laid a friendly hand on his shoulder and asked him to calm down, Gilbert drew a gun on him. Cuffed and thrown into a cell, the next morning he was brought before a judge, and sentenced to ten days in jail. The judge was quoted in the press as having told him, 'Nobody makes a monkey of the Beverly Hills police and gets away with it!' Louis B. Mayer let him 'stew' for the night before assigning MGM Chief of Police Whitey Hendry to his case. Money exchanged hands and Gilbert was released: Mayer needed him back at work because he was scheduled to begin shooting *Twelve Miles Out*, with Joan Crawford.

Adela Rogers St Johns recalled how Gilbert had confided in her about one of his rows with Garbo, and of how she had reacted with the same indifference towards this as she did everything else: 'When in sheer desperation he threw her off the balcony and down the Beverly hillside, she climbed back over the rocks and through burrs and tumbleweed.' Often, if Gilbert was in one of his moods, Garbo would call a cab, head for the Miramar, and spend the night with Borg. Gilbert also tried to make her jealous by picking up prostitutes and recounting his adventures with them in clinical detail over the breakfast table – though Garbo did not really care what he was getting up to any more. Howard Dietz recalled an incident when Gilbert told her, one evening before going out, not to expect him home because he had arranged to have sex with sultry Chinese-American star Anna May Wong – to which Garbo replied, matter of fact, 'I'll leave the door open,

Jack.' Borg told the story of how Gilbert once wept on his shoulder, convinced Garbo did not love him but Mauritz Stiller. Little did he know that her real comfort zone was the big man in whom he was confiding.[144]

Gilbert is alleged *not* to have wanted to work with Joan Crawford, but that Mayer ordered the pairing as part of his ongoing plan to destroy Gilbert in the wake of the Boardman-Vidor wedding incident: he was hoping that the two would find each other irresistible – that someone would relay the news to Garbo, who would abandon all hope of ever marrying him. He needed to keep Garbo single once she signed the new contract binding her to MGM – this time, if she stepped out of line again, he really would arrange for her to be deported. Gilbert, however, was not interested in Joan, nor she him. 'He was like a caged animal – he resented every moment he was not with Garbo,' she later told his daughter.[145] [146]

On the day Garbo emerged from her self-enforced solitude, Harry Edington, morally supported by Borg, read Mayer the riot act. From now on, his client would be treated with respect – she was a human being, not one of the studio props or a lesser employee they could bully and humiliate. Also, from now on she should be known *only* as Garbo and any future interviews would be sanctioned by him, and only if Garbo *desired* to be interviewed – which effectively would be never. The idea of 'building up' on her mystique, however, appears to have come from Borg, who told her one afternoon as they lay sunbathing on the beach at Santa Monica:

> I know you are not acting, Greta, when you hide from people. But just the same it is something that fits your personality to be mysterious and secretive. By playing up to it, you will kill two birds with one stone and you will get your privacy and also get people talking about you.

To which she responded, 'You think so, Borg? Yes, maybe it is a good idea.'[147]

A few years later, in her one and only exercise in putting pen to paper for a press feature, she observed:

When I first went to Hollywood under the wing of Mauritz Stiller,
I used to go to parties regularly and attend premieres. But my work
began to suffer. Also, making public appearances destroys the illusion that surrounds the shadows of the silver sheet. The creative
artist should be a rare and solitary spirit.[148]

On 21 April, Garbo reported for work on *Anna Karenina*, the first
time anyone other than her intimates had seen her in twenty-
seven weeks. Sven Hugo Borg drove her to the studio: she had
celebrated her 'windfall' by exchanging her car for a much larger
Packard, too big for her to handle – later, the studio provided
her with a chauffeur. It was the first time she had faced a camera
since 13 October, when shooting the alternative ending for *The
Temptress*, and it was also the first anniversary of her sister Alva's
death. Remembering how Lars Hanson and Lillian Gish had
comforted her then, she dropped in on the set of their latest film,
The Wind, before returning to her own set.

Dimitri Buchowetzki's *Anna Karenina* was doomed from the
start: within minutes of the cameras rolling, Garbo was denouncing Buchowetzki as 'The worst director in the world'. Her co-stars
for the production were Lionel Barrymore, who she liked and, with
John Gilbert still shooting *Twelve Miles Out* – Ricardo Cortez, her
co-star from *Torrent* with whom she had vowed never to work
again. She also disliked the cameraman, Merritt Gerstad, and said
that she would only work with William Daniels. Again, Louis
B. Mayer refused to budge, and on 28 April, Garbo fell ill with
what she said was food poisoning: Borg took her home, and there
followed yet another lengthy period where she seemed to disappear
off the face of the earth.

Though no official statement was given to the press, the ubiq-
uitous Louella Parsons had all the answers. Writing in her column
that Garbo was seriously ill, she added that 'a friend of the star' had
confirmed that she nevertheless was expecting to return to work
within the next few weeks. Again, this was pure speculation. Next,
MGM announced that Ricardo Cortez had been assigned to another
film, and that Irving Thalberg would be replacing him with Norman
Kerry. Finally, when one of Thalberg's secretaries was unable to locate

Garbo, and when her friends refused to divulge her whereabouts, he closed down the production – at a loss of over $200,000.

By 18 May, Garbo was reported to be recovered from her malady – an announcement which coincided with MGM's press-release detailing drastic changes to the *Anna Karenina* production. Dimitri Buchowetzki had been fired and replaced with the more amenable London-born director Edmund Goulding, who had already built up a rapport with Garbo during his Sunday visits to Tower Grove Road. She became especially fond of Goulding (1891–1959) because, like Mauritz Stiller, he never directed 'by the book', preferring to allow his actors to use their initiative as much as possible. His first move was to replace Merritt Gerstad with William Daniels. John Gilbert was also free by now, and Thalberg cast him as Anna's lover, Vronsky. This meant that she would be dropped down to second-billing, but this she did not mind. Next, Thalberg changed the title: *Anna Karenina* too much of a mouthful for some Americans, he declared, so he incorporated the new title into the slogan, 'Garbo & Gilbert ... In *Love*!' MGM were, however, still taking a calculated risk, given Garbo's indifference and mercurial temperament: though she had made a 'gentleman's agreement' with Louis B. Mayer, she had yet to sign her new contract.

This was duly signed, and everyone at MGM breathed a huge sigh of relief. Yet just two evenings later, on 3 June, there was another setback. Garbo, Borg, Mauritz Stiller and Rolf Laven had thrown a small dinner party at the Miramar to cheer up Einar Hanson, who was having problems in his private life. Since arriving in America, Garbo's co-star from *Die Freudlose Gasse* had completed two films with Pola Negri, but was finding it increasingly hard coping with the strain of hiding his sexuality – something which would never have happened in the more liberal Sweden – and begun drinking heavily. Driving home the worse for wear after Garbo's party, and ignoring pleas to stay the night at her apartment, Hanson – accompanied by the latest 'love of his life', his pet Airedale – had skidded off the Pacific Coast Highway, near Topanga Canyon. Trapped beneath the wreckage for several hours before being rescued, and with his faithful dog standing guard, he had died soon afterwards in the Santa Monica Hospital.

He had been two weeks shy of his twenty-eighth birthday and his death hit Garbo hard. Once again, she retreated from the world and there was talk of her giving up her career. What was the point of staying in such a prejudiced environment? Who could do this to a young man? Certainly there was no encouragement for her to stay from John Gilbert: he had cheated on her throughout their now deteriorating relationship with any number of women – though the same may be said for Garbo who, when fleeing back to the Miramar to evade his drunken, bad-tempered binges had invariably ended up back in the arms of Borg.

Who got her to change her mind – Borg or Goulding – is not known. She returned to the set, leaning on Borg's arm for support and informed Goulding she no longer wished to be photographed in close-up during her menstrual cycle when she looked pallid and gaunt. Since the previous summer she had suffered from irregular periods, accompanied by excruciating pains – some sources attributing this to a recurrent ovarian infection. This led to further speculation surrounding Garbo's recent disappearances – a total of 251 days 'in some wilderness', aside from the seven days she had worked on the cancelled *Anna Karenina*.[149]

Again, this leads to speculation. The 'recurrent ovarian infection' could have been the result of a difficult labour and birth, or the result of a botched abortion conducted by a studio doctor. There was also worse speculation: a miscarriage, brought about by a beating during one of John Gilbert's psychotic episodes.

The pregnancy theory was touched upon by Garbo biographer Mark Vieira, who cites 'an unpublished 1962 interview with a television producer,' – given by Garbo's intimate screenwriter friend, S. N. Behrman, wherein a stenographer's notes are reported to have read, 'Mr Behrman said he thought she might have had a couple of abortions and that this had given her a terror of sex.'[150] However, given Garbo's proven maternal instincts and desire to have children, one could assume that an abortion would have been totally out of the question, even to save her career, which she was never really bothered about saving in the first place. Indeed, being pregnant would have offered her the perfect excuse to carry out her oft-repeated threat and return to Sweden. And if there *had* been a baby, and if she *had* given it up for adoption – or maybe asked someone to care for the child until she had decided whether to remain in America or not – who better for the job than one of her trusted Swedish friends, or even Anna Gustaffson? Lars Hanson and his wife had already announced they were leaving Hollywood for good, as had a number of Swedish technicians who had worked with Garbo: any of these would have fit the bill, if required.

So, if there was a child, what happened to it? There seems little doubt that there *was* a cover-up, aided by Whitey Hendry and Los Angeles district attorney Buron Fitts, for whom such things were almost a weekly occurrence. A similar situation would arise in November 1935, when Loretta Young gave birth to Clark Gable's daughter, Judy. To avoid the 'shame', the baby was placed in a San Diego orphanage from which, two years later, Loretta 'adopted' her. It would take another twenty years for the truth to emerge. Yet over eighty years after Garbo's confinement, if there was one, we are no closer to solving the mystery – other than knowing that those missing eight months had nothing to do with any 'strike'.

Another important point to consider is Garbo's sexual preference from this point on: once Gilbert had exited her life, so far as can be ascertained, aside from Borg there appear to have been no more physical relationships with men. Nils Asther and Ramon Novarro admitted to sharing a room with her but denied that sex had taken place. From now on, the only men permitted within her intimate circle would be gay or bisexual and *only* as friends, never to provide her with 'lavender' cover. It was as if she was saying – *if* she had fallen pregnant – that she would not be taking the risk of making the same mistake twice.

Love finally began shooting on 22 June 1927, by which time there were days when Garbo and Gilbert were not even speaking, let alone in the mood for love-making in front of the camera. MGM had employed the photographer William Grimes to take 'candid' shots of the couple without their knowledge, to prove to doubting fans that they were just as much in love as they had always been. Unfortunately, Grimes' pictures told another story and the shots of the couple between takes, looking glum and sometimes hostile, were never used.

Tolstoy's novel begins at one railway station and ends at another. The Hollywood version opens on the road to St Petersburg, during a snowstorm, when Anna's horse drops dead and her troika is stranded. Rescued by a passing captain, Count Alexei Vronsky, she is driven to an inn, where they shelter for the night. (Gilbert, looking considerably more macho than he had in *Flesh and the Devil*, but sports a silly cropped hairstyle and a cheesy grin, and hams it up with one of the worst performances of his career. The restored print, with a haunting new score, was screened at the University of California's Royce Hall in 1984 before a live audience and their reaction – mostly laughter at Gilbert's expense – was left in.)

At the inn, the hostess assumes they are spending the night together and puts Vronsky's clothes in Anna's room. (The shot of their slippers, side by side, and Gilbert fondling Garbo's discarded stockings was cut from some prints.) *He kisses her, but for now that is as far as it goes and when he leaves, she wipes her mouth in mock derision.*

The two meet again at the cathedral, during the Easter service; then at the Grand Duke's ball, where they fall in love and brazenly dance in front of her stuffy elderly husband, Karenin (Brandon Hurst)*; and finally, at a wolf hunt, at which she tells him they must cool things off for a while.*

Cut to Anna in her apartment (and the essential 'Garbo takes stock of herself in front of the mirror' sequence, which had featured in all of her films since *Die Freudlose Gasse*)*, where she realises that the real man in her life is her little son, Serezha* (Philippe De Lacy).

Much has been made of the fact that Garbo was only twenty-two, while her on-screen son was ten years old. In the film, the relationship between mother and son is almost incestuous, resulting in three of their scenes being heavily censored. In the first one, Garbo kisses the former child model (who had played the young Leo in *Flesh and the Devil*) several times on the mouth. One biographer praised De Lacy's 'Pre-Raphaelite sensuality that made him the perfect love object for a repressed and doting mother', while Alexander Walker, comparing her with her later rival, observed:

Dietrich and Garbo, outwardly *femmes fatales* in their films, women of the world who sought out the little boy in the men who pursued them, would deploy their femininity in scenes with children in such a way as to summon forth and flatter the latent manhood of their screen offspring. The flirtatious De Lacy, a remarkable child actor who resembles a male Shirley Temple, behaves like a miniature adult: and the love-starved Anna turns him into a substitute love-object.[151] [152]

A scandal erupts when the lovers meet at the racetrack, where Vronksy rides in the steeplechase: Anna's hysterical reaction when he takes a tumble gives the game away. They leave Russia and travel to Italy, where they are miserable, he missing his regiment and she her son. During a riverside picnic she sees a boy who resembles Serezha and demands, 'Give me a kiss!', causing him to shrink back in horror while Vronsky turns his back in disgust.

The pair return to St Petersburg, where Karenin has told Serezha that his mother is dead. She sneaks into his room: it is his birthday and she has bought him a train set. (This is the film's most heart-rending scene, a moment so genuinely sincere that one can only assume Garbo was thinking about the child she had almost certainly lost.) *Karenin catches her. 'Better you were dead than to live, a constant reminder to him of your disgrace,' he says, ordering her never to see her son again.*

Karenin has arranged for Vronsky to be dishonourably discharged from his regiment, and this Anna's conscience will not support. She visits him to say goodbye, and though she pretends that all is well, the title suggests that Vronsky knows what she has in mind: 'Anna, even death could never part us.' She kisses the handle of his sword, then him, and the next time we see her she is standing at the platform edge, about to end it all as the train's headlights flash in the distance.

Preview audiences reacted badly to such a dramatic ending, however, so Thalberg commissioned Frances Marion to sabotage one of the greatest works in the Russian literary canon:

Vronsky returns to his regiment. The story moves forward three years, during which time he has searched in vain for his lost love, and Vronksy discovers that Serezha is now attending military school. He goes to see the boy and learns that Anna has been coming to visit every day since Karenin's death. Then the door opens, she appears, and (to hysterical applause from the audience) *flings herself into Vronsky's arms.*

Though it fared exceptionally well at the box-office, *Love* did not represent Garbo's finest moment thus far in her career. It was her film – she dominates every scene she appears in, easily out-acting John Gilbert, which by this stage of his career was not hard to do. But it has to be said that she shared the honours with Phillipe De Lacy – and cameraman William Daniels, whose close-ups of her were nothing short of stunning.

In *Flesh and the Devil*, audiences had Lars Hanson to light up the screen alongside Garbo's cool Nordic beauty – along with Nils Asther and Robert Taylor, by far her most engaging and believable leading man. In *Love* they had only Garbo. When the film premiered at the Capitol in New York, the manager of the theatre attempted to dispel the rumours that Garbo and Gilbert were no longer an item by projecting a large red heart on the stage curtains while the orchestra was striking up the overture.

Mordaunt Hall observed in the *New York Times*:

> Miss Garbo may lift her head the fraction of an inch, and it means more than John Gilbert's artificial smile ... It is not often that one feels that the mere watching of a screen actress is more interesting than the story, but it is the case in this film ... Anna, at least, is real and therefore it does not matter that the other characters occasionally look as if they have stepped out of a musical comedy...[153]

And from *Motion Picture*:

> Lovers of Tolstoy will be disappointed. Those who like to study the Garbo-Gilbert embraces will be disappointed. In fact, the only people who won't be disappointed are those who have always thought of Greta Garbo merely as the woman in pictures who dresses worse than Alice Terry. Because Greta is surprising, and her beauty and fine acting make a cheap, melodramatic picture into something at least interesting, if not good.[154]

Variety was certainly off the mark with its predictions for the couple's future:

> Peculiar combination, this Gilbert–Garbo hook-up. Both sprang up suddenly and fast, Miss Garbo from nowhere. The latter isn't now as big as she should or will be, always remembering it's the stories that count ... Miss Garbo and Mr Gilbert are in a fair way to become the biggest box-office mixed team this country has yet known.[155]

There was just one problem. The love affair dubbed by the press as 'The Romance of the Century' – having survived by the skin of its teeth throughout the shooting of *Love* – had ended long before the cameras stopped rolling.

CHAPTER SIX

THE DIVINE GARBO!

'The thing I like best about Hollywood is that here is one place in the world where you can live as you like and nobody will say anything about it, no matter what you do!'

While *Love* was being edited, Garbo withdrew further into her shell. Gilbert had introduced her to the American way of life and with him now out of the picture, she held court at the Miramar – the lonely, disillusioned and exiled Scandinavian princess, surrounded only by those courtiers she felt she could trust. Sven Hugo Borg, still fulfilling the role of secretary, confidant, and occasional lover. Lars Hanson and Karin Mollander, who had opted to stay in America just a little longer: much was expected of *The Wind*, completed the week *Love* had begun shooting, and there was talk of Hanson making another film with Lillian Gish. While the Hansons and Rolf Laven dropped in on Garbo most days, Mauritz Stiller, his health failing fast, saw her only occasionally.

When not at the Miramar, Garbo could be found at her other 'safe haven', the Palisade Avenue home of Victor Sjöström and his actress wife, Edith Erastoff. Garbo was unofficial godmother to the couple's two daughters, Guje and Greta. Since signing the new contract with MGM, she had been given co-star, director and script approval, and she now announced that she wanted to make the film version of *Starlight*, based on the stage play by Gladys Unger, which loosely tells the story of the great French actress, Sarah Bernhardt. Doris Keane, a fine thespian but now almost forgotten, had starred in the original production, which opened on Broadway in March 1925 – two years after Bernhardt's death. Irving Thalberg sanctioned the project at once – after the problems of the past year he thought better of opposing Garbo and risking any more traumas – but he disapproved of Gladys Unger's screenplay, declaring it too strong for family audiences.

Sarah Bernhardt (1844–1923) was the illegitimate, convent-raised daughter of a Jewish prostitute. Sponsored by her mother's wealthy lover, the Duc de Morny, she entered the Conservatoire at thirteen, and five years later joined the Comédie-Française. Known as 'The Divine Sarah', she took dozens of lovers of both sexes and developed strange traits such as sleeping in a coffin. In 1915, following a fall, she had a leg amputated – pretty heavy stuff for 1920s Hollywood, which was why none of these incidents were included in MGM's reworking of her story. Garbo's Sarah is renamed Marianne and moulded to fit in with the now regular formula of the woman of indeterminate age, forced to choose between the handsome lover and the older man she is using as a meal-ticket. Marianne is sent to live on a farm in Brittany, while her floozie mother, Zizi, lives it up in Paris with a succession of lovers. When one of them makes a pass at her, she hits him and, believing she has killed him, flees into the night, where she meets handsome soldier Lucien. He is about to leave with his regiment, therefore he entrusts her to the care of a laundress friend. Later, Marianne meets another of her mother's lovers, Legrande, a theatre producer who coerces her into becoming his mistress with promises of stardom. Meanwhile, Lucien returns, spends a little time with her before deserting, and ends up in prison. By now, a desperately unhappy Marianne has decided which of her men she wants: after a botched suicide attempt, she ends her with Legrande, but leaves him when Lucien is released and they marry. She gives up her career, and in true Hollywood fashion the two live happily ever after on a ranch somewhere in South America!

Garbo gave Thalberg two conditions before accepting the part: Lars Hanson would play Lucien, and Victor Sjöström would direct. Thalberg agreed wholeheartedly, then began having palpitations when Garbo informed him that this would be an 'all-Swedish production', with herself, Hanson and Sjöström speaking only this language while shooting was taking place. Thalberg's major concern was that another Stiller-*Temptress* situation might arise, with the technicians downing tools because none of them could

understand what was going on. Garbo assured him that this would
not happen. Sjöström himself hired the supports: Polly Moran,
Lowell Sherman, and future Westerns star Johnny Mack Brown.
Playing Marianne's strumpet mother, Zizi, was Dorothy Cumming
– something of a volte-face as she had recently played Mary in
Cecil B. DeMille's *The King of Kings*. Much would be made of the
fact that Cummings was only six years Garbo's senior.

The Divine Woman began shooting on 28 September 1927, the
day before Thalberg married Norma Shearer. Garbo was asked to
delay the proceedings by just one day so that she could attend as
guest of honour but refused. She and weddings did not mix, and
she much preferred to be branded rude rather than a hypocrite for
publicly congratulating a couple she could barely tolerate. She was
also angry at Thalberg for taking William Daniels off her picture
and assigning him to Shearer's next production, *The Latest from
Paris*, set to begin shooting after their honeymoon.

Sadly, we shall never really know how well Daniels' replacement,
Oliver T. Marsh, fared. *The Divine Woman* is the only Garbo film
of which no complete print survives: just one nine-minute reel,
with cyrillic subtitles, located in a Moscow vault. However, what
little we have does prove, as had happened twice already, that
Lars Hanson was far better suited to partnering Garbo than John
Gilbert ever was.

Marianne (Garbo) *prepares dinner for her soldier sweetheart, Lucien*
(Hanson)*; he, meanwhile, is pictured in his rented property, sad to be
leaving for Algiers, though his landlady says he will find many dark
beauties to make him happy again.*

*There is only one girl for him, however, and next we see him 'singing'
outside Marianne's apartment. The lovers laugh and kiss a lot; he hoists
her on to his shoulders* (a very un-Garbo pose)*, marches with her
around the table and gives her a necklace he has bought. 'They say you
must be cautious when you're this happy,' she warns him, and a glance
at the clock informs him that they have little time left.*

*This is the first she has heard about him leaving and after supper she
tries to persuade him to stay by making him jealous. 'There are plenty
of other soldiers left in Paris,' she says. Suddenly angry, he grabs her by*

the wrists; they argue and he is leaving in a huff when she calls him back and makes him promise never to leave her. Pushing him on to the chair, she straddles his lap and smothers him with kisses, and they topple backwards onto the floor.

A shot of the lighted lamp is an indication of what happens next: the clock now says midnight, and they are reclining on the window seat, the night lights of Paris twinkling behind them. Lucien has deserted, and reassures her, 'Lovely geisha girl, don't be sad about a thing!'

Garbo had given explicit instructions that no one – not even Louis B. Mayer himself – was to approach her while she was working. Screens were now erected around the set, and for one street scene she was hidden from view by sheets slung over washing lines. Rilla Page Palmborg got past the security by masquerading as an extra, and claimed the star had spoken 'quite candidly' about John Gilbert. Asked if she was missing him, Garbo had allegedly confided:

> I will be very frank with you. The only American I have gone out with at all is Mr Gilbert. But it is only a friendship. I will never marry. My work absorbs me. I have time for nothing else. But I think Jack Gilbert is one of the finest men I have ever known. He is a real gentleman. He has temperament. He gets excited ... I am very happy when I am to do a picture with Mr Gilbert. He is a great artist. He lifts me up and carries me along with him. It is not scenes I am doing – I am *living*![156]

Shooting on *The Divine Woman* wrapped on 7 November, with Garbo customarily refusing to sit in on the rushes or attend the previews, shutting herself in her Miramar apartment – sometimes with Borg keeping her company, much of the time alone now that her Swedish 'community' was shrinking. Lars Hanson and Karin Mollander left for Sweden in the middle of the month, followed a few days later by Mauritz Stiller and Rolf Laven. None of these people would return to Hollywood, though Stiller aside, Garbo would see them again.

The film's reviews were mixed. Harriette Underhill wrote in the *New York Times*:

We insist that all those who, in their foolishness, have cried, 'There is no screen acting – the figures are but puppets with the director pulling the strings,' go to the Capitol Theater and take a look at Greta Garbo and Lars Hanson ... Many who admit that there *is* acting on the screen have stated that Miss Garbo did not act, however, that she was only a beautiful woman with a strong appeal ... In the first place, we are not at all sure that Miss Garbo *is* beautiful. It seems to be a soul, rather than prettiness, which makes her face so attractive, and no one could call Lars Hanson handsome. Still, we cannot for the moment think of any two performances as fine as those offered by a Swedish actress and a Swedish actor.[157]

On the other hand, *Screenland*'s Delight Evans did not like the film at all:

This picture is a huge disappointment ... The most potent personality on the screen – the girl who made Hollywood actresses look like stock company ingénues – the Swedish marvel at emotional massage – she was all of that. And now ... here is a new Garbo, who flutters, who mugs. This interestingly reserved lady goes completely Hollywood all at once ... Miss Garbo seems to me to have only one scene in her usual marvellous quiet manner. But for the rest – excuse me! 'I go now!'[158]

After the hugely successful *Hotel Imperial*, Stiller had made *The Woman On Trial* with Pola Negri and Einar Hanson and *The Street of Sin* with Fay Wray and Emil Jannings, both of which bombed at the box-office. Stiller's stint with Paramount had seen even more rows than the one with MGM: both studios blacklisted him and he left Hollywood under a dark cloud, assured that he would never be made welcome there again. Garbo, Borg, and Victor Sjöström (who also returned to Sweden not long afterwards) accompanied Stiller and Laven to the same Pasadena railway station which had fanfared their arrival just a few years earlier. 'I will see you soon, Moje,' Borg remembered Garbo saying to the man who had put her name on the map. In New York, Stiller spent a few days with Hubert Voight, the publicist who had welcomed him there, before boarding the ship for Gothenburg.

Garbo was at her lowest after Stiller's departure. He is purported to have handed her a letter before boarding the train, part of which read:

> I am leaving you your freedom. Perhaps you, when I am gone, will blossom anew. Perhaps your face will get its peace back ... I am gone, obliterated from your life. And you shall not think about me. You don't have to repeat 'Poor Moje' every time we meet. You are free![159]

In fact, she never stopped thinking about him, as if she was aware that she would never see him again. Suffering from depression and fatigue, edgy, suspicious of picking up the phone, Garbo instructed Borg that she neither wanted to see or speak to anyone outside her circle of intimate friends. Therefore, just how she came about giving an 'interview' to *Photoplay*'s Ruth Biery is at first glance baffling – more than this, Biery's ability to persuade her to leave the Miramar and accompany her to 'a discreet tea-room in Santa Monica', when others had failed to get her to step outside her apartment is astonishing. Garbo's reluctance to speak to the press was already legendary, yet here we have her, on the face of it, opening her heart to a virtual stranger.

This was however no ordinary journalist-star interview but a date to an afternoon New Year's Eve get-together. Biery was an aficionado of beautiful women, many of whom she met at the parties of Alla Nazimova and Lilyan Tashman, two of Hollywood's most notorious lesbians. That Garbo may have been amorously interested in her, indeed that they may have had a relationship, *does* make sense. It explains why a woman, paranoid about discussing any aspect of her private life, told Biery so much about herself – obviously trusting her not to repeat a word of what she had said. When the piece was eventually printed, Biery preceded it with what she claimed had been Garbo's opening statement once they reached their destination:

> Let's not talk of me! It is New Year's Eve. In Sweden that means so much, so very much. There, we go to church and eat and drink and see everybody we know. I have been blue all day. At home,

in Stockholm, they are skiing and skating and throwing snowballs at one another. The cheeks are red. Oh, please, let's not talk
about me![160]

In fact, during their five hours together – an inordinately long time
for any movie magazine interview, as most journalists would agree
– Garbo never stopped talking about herself; about her childhood,
her stage and film work in Sweden, Stiller and Carl Brisson, her
adventures in Constantinople and Berlin, Alva's death, Louis B.
Mayer, and John Gilbert – subjects she had not discussed until
now. And when it was time for them to part, reluctantly on Biery's
part, the journalist observed:

> Greta Garbo drew her grey woolly cloak 'such as we wear in Sweden'
> about her. Her eyes sought the windows, as though to penetrate the
> dark secrets beyond them. And as she looked past me, beyond, into
> a world which my eyes could not envision, there was born in me a
> great ambition to acquire this woman as a friend.[161]

There would be absolutely no chance of this happening. During
the first week of January 1928, Biery contacted Garbo – either
directly or by way of Borg – and promised to keep whatever had
been said between them under wraps. She did so, but only until
April, when in the first of a three-part series *Photoplay* published
The Story Of Greta Garbo, As Told By Her To Ruth Biery. The word-
ing of the heading was of vital importance – implying that Garbo
had been forthcoming about her life story so far, with no pressure
from Biery. Garbo called the journalist personally and told her,
'I do not like your story. I do not like to see my soul laid bare on
paper,' and promptly hung up.[162]

It took Biery four years to apologise for her 'act of treason', by
which time the damage had been done. Garbo had never liked talking about herself, and would never do so again – certainly not to
an American journalist. 'Instead of trying to understand her,' Biery
subsequently observed, 'Hollywood has spent every effort to dig an
early professional grave for her. I know how true this is, because,
unintentionally, I have been one of her most active grave-diggers.'[163]

Garbo was probably too wrapped up in her own private anguish to observe the drastic changes taking place in the movie world, which would affect every studio, executive, producer, director and actor not just in Hollywood, but around the world. *The Jazz Singer*, the first talking picture, produced by Warner Brothers and starring Al Jolson, opened in New York on 6 October 1927. The synchronised sound, primarily used for Jolson's musical sequences, sounded crude and rival studios accused Warner Studios of creating a fuss over a gimmick which would never catch on. By the time the film reached Hollywood, many executives revised their opinion: Irving Thalberg did not and boycotted the 28 December premiere.

As the New Year dawned and more talkies went into production, panic rocked the film capital. Eighty per cent of the actors enjoying full-time employment in Hollywood had little or no formal training. Many had never found it necessary to hone their frequently non-existent vocal skills: among the major names who would have a tough time over the next few years would be 'It Girl' Clara Bow, Marie Prevost and Nita Naldi – all possessed of the most horrific 'Bronx honk' which set cinema-goers' teeth on edge. Additionally there were the foreign stars: Pola Negri, Ramon Novarro, Karl Dane, Vilma Banky, Bela Lugosi and, of course, Garbo, were but a few who had rarely spoken English in their films – unimportant in the pre-talkies age unless one happened to be a lip-reader. Some made the transition, but many did not.

By February 1928, Warner Brothers were producing *only* talkies and the other studios were about to follow suit. Louis B. Mayer did not see any point in rushing into the new process – though by the late summer MGM would have released *Shadows in the South Seas*, a curiosity with synchronised sound effects – and worried about the risk of the additional expenditure if, as Thalberg predicted, sound would prove but 'a flash in the pan'. Garbo was similarly against the idea, informing Irving Thalberg that she would not be appearing in talking pictures in the foreseeable future – and even then not without an 'appropriate rider' to her current contract.

MGM had purchased the rights to Ludwig Wolff's novel, *War in the Dark* for a song – a little over $2,000 – with a view to casting John Gilbert as the Austrian intelligence soldier who falls for a

Russian spy, who, naturally, they wanted to be played by Garbo. She agreed to do the film but only without Gilbert. With Fred Niblo at the helm and William Daniels returned to the fold, shooting began. Her first complaint was about the powerful 'Mole' lights, recently brought in to light the set for the new-style panchromatic film. For the first time, Garbo could see the extras standing in front of the screens which she had asked to be erected to keep unwelcome 'gawkers' at bay. Subsequently they were banished from the set until required.

There was another 'quiet tantrum' over one of Gilbert Clark's costumes. Though she does not wear a bra in the film (her nipples are clearly visible through the flimsy fabric of the dress she wears for the party scene) claiming that, as a 'flapper' and liberated woman, Tania would not have done so, Garbo complained that the dress was too revealing and asked Clark to change it. He reacted by walking off the picture. For Garbo, this was a plus. Clark's replacement was Adrian (Adrian Adolph Greenberg, 1903–59), who in a lengthy career with MGM designed the costumes for over 250 films. Adrian, who was openly gay, had first worked for Valentino's wife, Natacha Rambova, then for Cecil B. DeMille. As 'one of the girls', he and Garbo got along famously. 'Her natural aloofness and the manner of her bearing make it possible for her to put meaning into simple clothes,' he once said.[164]

Everyone involved with the production hated the title – even more so the alternative devised by Irving Thalberg: *The Glorious Sinner*. MGM then hit on the idea of an 'in-house' competition, where studio employees were promised a $50 bonus for coming up with the title which would please Garbo the most. It did not take a genius (probably Thalberg himself) to come up with *The Mysterious Lady*, particularly as the mystery 'winner' asked for his name not to be revealed.

Garbo got along well with her leading man, Conrad Nagel (1897–1970), her dullest so far. Much more fascinating is the second lead, German-born Gustav von Seyffertitz (1862–1943), nicknamed by his peers 'The True Hollywood Aristocrat' – and by Garbo, in a rare outburst of public humour, 'Mr Safer Tits'. Von Seyffertitz was a master of disguise – almost completely bald and unwrinkled, once he removed his make-up, most moviegoers would never have recognised him off the screen. Like his character, he was also a bit of a rogue where the ladies were concerned – to date he had had five wives, and dozens of mistresses.

In pre-war Vienna, outside the State Opera House, Captain Karl von Raden (Conrad Nagel) *boasts to his friend Max* (Albert Pollet) *of his latest conquest, whose husband caught them together and joined in. Karl is there to see* Tosca, *but he does not have a ticket – until a suspicious-looking character returns one, and he finds himself sharing a box with Russian beauty Tania* (Garbo with a fluffy new hairdo).

The attraction is mutual. They leave the theatre. It is raining; Tania has no money for a fiacre, so Karl takes her home and is invited in for a nightcap, while the coachman tells his impatient horse, 'Sorry, sweetheart, but you know it's spring!'

In Tania's room, Karl sits at the piano and, with a flashback to the opera, accompanies her while she sings 'Vissi d'arte'. (In the late 1920s, the piano music would have been played by the cinema musician, but in the restored (2002) print, though we can lip-read Garbo performing the aria, what we actually hear is syncopated rhythm, robbing the sequence of its original emotive content.) *For Karl, this is too much and he tries to ravish her, his big hands encircling her breasts. This horrifies Tania, but only because she must be the dominant one – she turns the tables and seduces him, the shot of the lighted chandelier telling us what happens next.*

Cut to the lovers enjoying a day in the country, making the best of their time together because that night Karl must deliver top-secret military plans to Berlin; Tania's next assignment is to steal them. Later, Max, Karl's friend from before, arrives at Tania's apartment to arrest her, but they have sex instead. She meets Karl again on the train, by which time he has been made aware of her identity. Nevertheless, she manages to steal the plans. Karl is court marshalled and branded a traitor, while the real culprit – the man who slept with her before letting her go – looks on.

The scene shifts to the Warsaw home of Tania's elderly lover, General Boris Alexanderoff (von Seyffertitz), *who wants to 'make her happy'. Tonight, though, she is tired and he must wait – something, he reminds her, she has been saying for years. When Tania learns that Karl is in jail because of her, she says she hates the way she serves her country and Alexanderoff responds, 'When one takes the oath to serve the Tsar as a spy, the only release is death.'*

Karl is sprung from jail, determined to track Tania down and prove his innocence. Arriving in Warsaw on a fake passport, he finds work as a pianist in a society café and is invited to a private party, where Tania and Boris are guests. Tania warns Karl that he is in danger, but he is caught and arrangements are made to kill him in front of her. In Alexanderoff's private quarters, Tania begs him to spare Karl's life, and when this fails she shoots him. He slumps in his chair, while upstairs at the party Cossacks dance wildly, their frenzied movements representing what is happening inside her head.

When Boris' henchmen announce that they have brought Karl to him, Tania is sitting on the dead man's lap, one of his hands on his arm, while she feigns the preliminaries of lovemaking to put them off the scent. (This is the so-called 'necrophilia' sequence, controversial at the time, though today one wonders what all the fuss was about. It was not a 'kinky' scene by any means: merely the actions of a desperate woman who does not know what to do next. The scene was shot with the back of the chair facing the camera, so that the viewer and the soldiers see only Garbo and von Seyffertitz's hand.) *Tania announces that Boris wishes to see the prisoner alone, and this offers the lovers the chance to escape. When next we see them, they are crossing the Austrian border as man and wife.*

Shooting wrapped on 15 June, seven weeks ahead of the 4 August premiere. The reviews were mixed, leaning towards the unfavour-able: Garbo and Conrad Nagel just did not gel. The *New York Times'* Mordaunt Hall observed, 'None of the actors are able to do much about [the storyline] save to wander through and hope for something better next time. Miss Garbo is pretty, but she doesn't make too good a Russian spy.' The best the *New York Evening Graphic's* Betty Colfax could offer was a back-handed compliment: 'Miss Garbo takes a close-up like no other star in Hollywood. She overcomes the handicap of an atrocious wardrobe, big feet, and widening hips with a facility of expression which still keep her in a class by herself.'[165]

For a while, Garbo had been asking MGM to let her do the film version of Michael Arlen's novel, *The Green Hat*, with Clarence Brown directing. Hailed 'A tale of a lost generation of post-war Bright Young Things,' this had shocked and titillated thousands of readers around the world since its publication in 1924. Arlen (1895–1956) was born in Romania and for years lived in England – he was a friend of the outrageously outspoken Tallulah Bankhead, whose portrayal of the heroine, Iris March, in the stage play had packed London's Adelphi Theatre to the rafters. Katharine Cornell triumphed with the part on Broadway.

Irving Thalberg, who had paid next to nothing for the screen rights for Garbo's last film, was forced to cough up a whopping $50,000 for this one. Mayer's only worry – oddly, as there would be no sound – was whether Garbo would prove as convincing as a 'rustic Englishwoman' as she had when playing all those exotic Europeans. With this in mind, Adrian was instructed to tone down her wardrobe: aside from one scene where she wears jewels and a party gown, Garbo is dressed very much like a spinster from an Agatha Christie novel – short tweed skirts, sensible shoes, pullovers, and that ubiquitous green felt hat.

Thalberg's chief concern was the Hays Office. The 'Bright Young Things' were radicals who lived life to the full, drank alcohol and smoked, insulted their peers, and shocked society by shedding their inhibitions: the play's topics included adultery, suicide, abortion and venereal disease, and running throughout the storyline was a very potent homosexual subplot. Arlen's own screenplay was rejected, and scriptwriter Bess Meredyth instructed to remove all references to venereal disease. Thalberg then changed the title to *A Woman of Affairs*, changed the names of all the main characters and removed all references to Michael Arlen and *The Green Hat* from the credits and publicity material – not that this would prevent virtually every reviewer from revealing the film's original source.[166]

When asked to choose her main love interest in the film, Garbo surprised Thalberg – and herself – by asking for John Gilbert. He accepted the part at once, though he would not be on screen as much as supports Douglas Fairbanks Jr, currently engaged to Joan Crawford, and former all-American halfback Johnny Mack Brown, who hailed from the Deep South and amused Garbo by persistently addressing her as 'sugah' or 'honey chile'. Neither did Gilbert object to being billed below Garbo for the first time.

Narrated by the family doctor (Lewis Stone, 1879–1953, in the first of seven films with Garbo), *the opening title reassures us, should we wish to judge, that this is, 'The story of a gallant lady – a lady who was perhaps foolish and reckless beyond need, but withal a very gallant lady.'*

We soon get to see evidence of this – Diana ripping through the countryside in her Hispano-Suiza – then the camera cuts to her wastrel brother, Jeffry (Douglas Fairbanks Jr), *drinking heavily while being gently chided by university jock David Furness* (Johnny Mack Brown), *the man he 'hero worships'.* (Brown, 1904–75, and Fairbanks Jr, 1909–2000, are the typical, upper-crust English, not-so-closeted gay couple, the precursor to Sebastian and Charles in Evelyn Waugh's *Brideshead Revisited*: snooty but not overbearing, sophisticated, affectionate, beautiful, idealistic, unequivocally masculine but unafraid of revealing their feminine sides and discreet when exchanging hurried amorous glances.) *'There are few chaps in the world as fine as you. I want to be like you – you've always stood for decency,' Jeffry gushes.*

But while he is in love with this perfect specimen, he loathes the fact that David only has eyes for Diana – who, in turn, is besotted with the weak-willed Neville Holderness, to whom she pledged herself when they were children. The two first kissed underneath their favourite oak tree, a symbol of their love to which the camera will persistently return.

Hoping to force Neville to forget Diana, Neville's father sends him overseas. Knowing that this will mean he is now in danger of losing David to Diana, Jeffry hits the bottle with a vengeance.

Cut to Deauville, two years down the line, and David and Diana are on their honeymoon – a wedding night interrupted by a visit from detectives, which ends with David flinging himself out of the sixth-floor window.

Back in London, his family hold an inquest. Why should a man as happy as David wish to kill himself? When the doctor says it was an accident and a distraught Jeffry goes to pieces, Diana says, 'David

wanted *to die. David died for decency!' Jeffry mocks her, 'Bravo, David.
You died for decency!'* (This is a discreet reference to their feelings
for each other – to the fact that though Jeffry may have *wanted*
David to consummate their relationship, legal constraints may
have prevented this from happening. Bearing in mind no explanation is given for David's arrest until after Jeffry's own death, it could
be assumed that it was for what 1920s Hollywood termed 'sexual
deviancy'. Not only was homosexuality illegal in Britain – where
the story is set – until 1967, Jeffry was only eighteen and therefore
a minor.)

*Accused of having David's blood on her hands – though in fact she is
beyond reproach – Diana leaves for Europe and seven years of dissipation with a succession of lovers: crowned heads, playboys and sportsmen.
She returns to London upon learning that Jeffry is gravely ill, but he
refuses to see her. Neville has moved on and is to marry Constance*
(Dorothy Sebastian)*, though this does not prevent him from sleeping
with Diana. Then Jeffry dies.* (We are not told the cause of Jeffry's
death: alcoholism, madness, a broken heart or a combination of
all three. In a touching scene that was badly in need of a retake,
Douglas Fairbanks Jr is still visibly breathing after the doctor
pronounces him dead. Filmographer Jerry Vermilye later observed,
'It's a pity Jeffry never forgives Diana – sinking deeper into alcoholism and eventually expiring of it, from what little information we
are given, we can only surmise that his feeling for Furness was a
closet case.' Suffice to say, David's photograph is close at hand.[167])

*Several months elapse: Neville and Constance are married and
Diana is seriously ill in Paris.* (As with Jeffry's death, we are not
told the cause: mental breakdown, the after-effects of an abortion,
the loss of a baby. The scene must have caused Garbo no little
anguish in view of her own recent experiences, and the way she
handles such a heartbreaking scene reveals what a truly magnificent
actress she was.) *'Where are my flowers?' she asks, stumbling into the
corridor in search of Neville's bouquet, which the doctor has removed
from her room. She sees them, and in her confusion thinks they are
Neville himself. Clutching them to her breast, she savours and gains
strength from their fragrance, caressing them as she would a lover: 'I
woke up and you weren't there. I don't want much, only you!'* In a

moment's lucidity, Diana sees Neville with Constance, and her treatment is complete: now that he is happy she will soon be well again. She cradles the flowers in her arms, like the baby she may have lost.

And from this point on it is all downhill. The 'truth' emerges about David: he was an embezzler. At a family gathering Neville reveals how Diana secretly paid off David's debts. Taking a card from the pack on the table that will decide her fate, she says, 'You've taken from me the only gracious thing I've ever done.' Minutes later they find her dead, having crashed her car into the oak tree – the Ace of Spades in her hand, her green hat next to her body.

The film opened in New York on 19 January 1929, to exceptional reviews. 'By long odds the best thing she has ever done. Without her eloquent acting, the picture would go to pieces,' *Variety* observed. *Photoplay* told anyone who might not have already known that 'Despite the change of title, despite the Hays ban, despite new names for old characters, it is still Michael Arlen's *The Green Hat*, and it is corking!' Pare Lorenz enthused in *Judge*:

> The most interesting feature of *A Woman of Affairs* is the treatment accorded it by the censors. As is obvious ... as every reader of that Hispano-Suiza advertisement will recollect, the heroine's white feather was borne for the proud fact that her suicide husband suffered from the ailment enjoyed by some of our most popular kings, prelates and prize fighters ... [Garbo] shuffled through the long, melancholy and sometimes beautiful scenes with more grace and sincerity than I have ever before observed, and the fact that she rode down and practically eliminated John Gilbert's goggling is in itself grounds for recommendation.[168]

There were no arguments between Garbo and Gilbert during shooting, which began on 27 July, and wrapped on 11 September, one week before her twenty-third birthday. Both had moved on. He was seeing Canadian actress Beatrice Lillie, among others. Whether Douglas Fairbanks Jr 'fancied his chances' with Garbo is not known, but it seems likely. Certainly his father, swashbuckling star Douglas Sr, and his stepmother Mary Pickford believed that he could do better than marry Joan Crawford, whom they had denounced as 'common'. Overjoyed that he was working with Garbo, Pickford invited her to Pickfair, their Beverly Hills mansion. The importance of the Fairbanks at this time – Hollywood's 'royal' couple – was such that an invitation from them was deemed such a privilege that not even those who loathed them dared refuse. Garbo was the first.

Rarely emerging from the safety of the Miramar, she was currently spending most of her time with Borg and the young, up-and-coming actress he had recently introduced her to: Eva von Berne. Today, Eva would probably be labelled a groupie. Born Eva Plentzer von Schameck, in Sarajevo in 1910, she moved to Vienna as a child, where she would be discovered by Irving Thalberg while he and Norma Shearer were honeymooning in Europe. Thalberg, in what proved for him a rare error of judgement, had boasted that here was a 'new Garbo', and assigned her to a Hollywood contract – changing her name to Eva von Berne, after his friend, MGM executive Paul Bern, adding an 'e', he claimed, to make her sound more aristocratic.

Eva arrived in New York on 28 July, the day after Garbo began shooting *A Woman of Affairs* – like Garbo, she was handled by Hubert Voight before being sent to Hollywood. Scarcely giving her time to adjust, Thalberg cast her into a social whirl of receptions, premieres and interviews and assigned her to her first film: *Masks of the Devil*, starring John Gilbert and the ill-fated Alma Rubens and directed by Victor Sjöström, was scheduled to begin shooting as soon as Gilbert had finished his film with Garbo.

As an actress, Eva would prove a disaster. She spoke very little English, and even with the help of an interpreter was hopeless at taking direction. Like Garbo in her formative years she was over-weight and was ordered to go on a diet. Unfortunately, her way of dealing with this was to eat whatever she liked and swallow an emetic after every meal. She also had a severe problem with her complexion, relying on a surfeit of pancake make-up, which frequently made her features appear bloated and grotesque. And naturally, when Garbo learned there was a 'new Garbo' in town, one who would soon be working with Gilbert, she wanted to meet her. Borg, who had recently taken up acting himself – with a small part in *Rose Marie*, starring Joan Crawford – was asked to arrange this. For Eva, this was the answer to her wildest dreams.

Garbo's opinion of Eva von Berne the actress is not on record – she hardly ever went to the cinema and was not interested in watching her own films, let alone anyone else's. Eva the woman, however, she soon found an embarrassment, not just because of her bulimia and the fact that she spent much of the time they were together in the bathroom, throwing up what she had just eaten – but also due to her indiscretion, discussing their affair with other members of Garbo's circle, including Lilyan Tashman and Beatrice Lillie. Though by no means a spiteful woman, Garbo would take whatever steps she felt were necessary to get Eva 'out of her hair', worried that one day she might blab to the press.

In November 1928, two weeks before *Masks of the Devil* premiered, and 'by mutual agreement' with MGM, so that she could 'go home and learn English' – a lame excuse if ever there was one – Eva von Berne returned to Europe with just $300 in her possession, her severance pay from the studio. Here, she appeared in a clutch of forgettable films before succumbing to the excesses of dieting, aged twenty. Garbo's parting gift was a signed photograph – in itself a rarity – upon which she scrawled, 'To Eva von Berne – from her friend, Greta Garbo.' And with Eva gone, and with her next picture, *Heat*, not scheduled to go into production until 22 October 1928, she used the time to develop her relationship with Lilyan Tashman, enabling a close friendship to blossom into a full-blown affair.

Born in Brooklyn, Lilyan Tashman (1896–1934) was the tenth and youngest child of a Jewish clothing manufacturer. In 1914, having enjoyed success as a fashion model, she began working in vaudeville, married the comedian Al Lee, and began a three-year stint with the *Ziegfeld Follies*. This marriage, like her subsequent one in 1925 to actor Edmund Lowe, was entirely lavender and enabled both parties to engage in same-sex relationships without ever being questioned by the press or their peers. By this time, Tashman was enjoying a reasonably successful movie career, though she would never be regarded as a major star. Tall, not particularly beautiful, she was often typecast in supporting roles as the catty but loveable 'other woman'. She also shared a trait with Eva von Berne – bulimia.

Like the Fairbanks, though on a less lavish scale, Tashman and Lowe threw parties at 'Lilowe', their Beverly Hills home – effectively orgies where, behind locked doors, even the most cautious stars could let their hair down and engage in gay sex without being found out. For the rest of Hollywood, there were afternoon fashion shows. Tashman's wardrobe was valued at over $1 million – most of the items she modelled were purchased by her, but many were donated by fashion houses, well aware that her friends would only want to copy whichever hats, gowns and jewellery she was wearing. Tashman boasted that she had never worn the same outfit twice.

Garbo, meanwhile, was still unaware that the only reporter she really trusted – Rilla Page Palmborg – was gossiping about her behind her back, and that she had interviewed Lilyan Tashman, hoping to find out what was really going on and pick up some juicy titbit to pass on to one of her columnist friends. 'She puts in long days,' Lilyan told her. 'I can't keep up with her myself. She has the strength of ten ordinary women. I don't know anyone who gets less sleep than Greta. When she isn't working, she wakes me up before nine in the morning, asking me over the telephone, "What shall we do today? Where shall we go?"'[169]

Palmborg's boasts to friends that she knew the 'real' Garbo did not go unnoticed by Mayer who, to quell any gossip which might erupt regarding his biggest asset, started up a rumour of his own – that Garbo was back with Gilbert. The two were given parts in James Cruze's latest production, *A Man's Man*. They appear in just one scene – as themselves, attending a film premiere with director Fred Niblo. It was, however, sufficient to hoodwink the press and draw attention away from Tashman. The press were soon speculating that Garbo and Gilbert would be properly reunited in her new film. She, however, had already decided on her next co-star.

Danish actor Nils Asther (1897–1981) was one of the most glamorous men ever to have appeared on the silent screen and was already known in Hollywood circles as 'The Male Garbo', though only on account of his exemplary looks – when it came to his love-life, Asther was anything but discreet and was currently involved with

Johnny Mack Brown. Garbo had known him for a while. Over six feet tall, he had been born in Copenhagen but raised in Sweden, where he attended the Dramatic Academy a few years before Garbo. In 1915, aged eighteen, he was discovered by Mauritz Stiller and cast alongside Lars Hanson in *Vingarme*. He became Stiller's lover while shooting the film, Hanson's afterwards. 'One evening [Stiller] came up to me and I was initiated into the art of loving someone of your own sex,' he recalled. Asther subsequently worked with Victor Sjöström in Sweden, and Michael Curtiz in Germany, arriving in Hollywood in 1927, where initially he lived an openly gay life. Brought into line by Mayer, the 'Swedish fagelah', quelled the rumours about his sexuality and proved to the film capital's naive that he was as heterosexual as the next man – by growing a moustache.[170]

The title of the new picture – Garbo's first where she would be playing an American – was denounced by the Hays Office as 'pornographic' when someone suggested that, along the lines of the earlier billboards pronouncing, 'Garbo & Gilbert...In *Love*!', the slogan for this one might read, 'Garbo & Asther...In *Heat*!' Thalberg changed the title to *Wild Orchids*. For Garbo, partnered with her most dashing leading man since Lars Hanson, this was a return to the exotic: the love triangle of a shy young wife, her middle-aged husband, and a lothario prince. Such was her importance by now that MGM were able to get away with having just three names in the credits: herself, Asther, and Lewis Stone as the impotent husband. The script was by John Colton (1887–1946), who had written the titles for *The Divine Woman*. Directing was Sidney Franklin: his film with Garbo was slotted between two Norma Shearer projects, *The Actress* and *The Last of Mrs Cheyney*.

Synchronised sound effects make for a noisy opening as Lillie and John Sterling (Garbo and Stone) *set sail for his tea plantation in the Far East, a trip she regards as a second honeymoon.*

It is clear that there will be problems the moment Prince Ferdinand appears and Lillie sees him whipping his servant (the camera alternating between Garbo's horrified expression and Asther's wide-eyed stare, enables us to witness the ultimate in male and female Scandinavian beauty). *Next we see the Prince dressed for dinner in high style, his hat slanted over one eye, while he struts alongside John. It is almost as if he is 'on the pull' and he seems taken aback to learn John has a wife: 'Oh, you are married!' He invites the couple to stay at his palace, which is located near to John's plantation.*

Lillie tries to feign indifference, but ends up dancing with him while a singer croons 'Wild Orchids' on the synchronised soundtrack:

PRINCE: Your country has always interested me, with its worship of the great god, business. The East is a country of the senses: warm, mysterious, like the kiss of a lover. You are like the white orchids of your country. You have the same cold enchantment. In Java the orchids grow wild and their perfume fills the air.

LILLIE: And the women of Java – do they grow wild, too?

PRINCE: Not wild, but natural. They do not pretend to be cold. The everlasting heat strips everyone of all pretence. It would be fascinating to learn whether your coldness is only pretence!

Though he desires her, the Prince does not yet know her name (as in so many of Garbo's films). *He kisses her hungrily; she rewards him with an almighty slap.*

Later, in her twin-bedded room after the obligatory self-analysis in front of the mirror, Lillie confesses all to John, who does not hear because he is asleep. She dreams that the Prince is whipping her, screams and gets into her husband's bed. (For American audiences, the 23-year-old Garbo being kissed and comforted by the 49-year-old Lewis Stone was regarded as obscene – unions where the age difference was so vast were invariably condemned by religious groups.)

Once their ship reaches port, the trio board a train. Lillie faints and it is the Prince, not her husband, who revives her, unbuttoning her blouse in order to do so. In the Prince's palace John sees the four-poster and exclaims, 'Good Lord, a double bed!' (Because the Sterlings *were* married, the censor could not cut the scene in which Garbo climbed into Stone's bed, but this line and the look of horror on the actor's face was MGM's way of assuring audiences that although she may have slept with this feisty old man, nothing sexual ever happened.)

Cut to the banquet and the Prince looking even more effete than before, plying John with drink so that he can make his move on Lillie, who is only interested in the female dancer. Later, the Prince sends the dancer's costume to her; she puts it on and tries to seduce John, who responds, 'You look silly, dear. Take off that junk and go to bed!' Instead she heads for the moonlit balcony, knowing the Prince will be waiting.

We do not see him approach (the original title, 'His shadow crawls up her body', was removed by the censor, though this is exactly what happens). *He grabs and kisses her; she flees, guilt-ridden.*

The next day the trio head for the plantation and are caught in a storm, but while John travels on alone, Lillie and the Prince take shelter in a nearby house. He turns his back while she undresses, but drops his hat so that he can peek at her removing her stockings and washing her feet. John returns and sees their entwined silhouettes through the closed blinds.

Cut to the jungle, with Lillie (not Garbo but stand-in Geraldine Dvorak) *looking uncomfortable on the back of an elephant. The group are there to hunt tigers but John removes the bullets from the Prince's gun – only to have an understandable change of heart, shooting the tiger when it mauls him. Next, she is seen wearing hunting trousers with a man's shirt and necktie for an almost homoerotic scene in which the Prince risks making a move on her. John, pretending to be asleep, does not see her push him away.*

The next day, assuming that Lillie is interested in the younger man, John decides to leave. She, however, is waiting in the back of the car to convince him (unconvincingly, one might add) *that he is the only one she has ever loved!*

Some critics disliked the film, believing Garbo had played against type – they did not want to see her portraying the 'good girl' who went back to her boring, sexless husband when the alternative was a dashing, handsome prince! *Variety* observed: 'Sex is the meat and marrow of [the film's] drama, the protagonist of its characters. The dames will probably feel that having their marital fidelity tested and tempted by so natty a sheik [sic] as Asther is a possible source of pleasurable tremors.'[171]

Garbo, meanwhile, was well aware of Mauritz Stiller's fragile health, but had genuinely believed that, once he returned to

Sweden, he would start to improve. His career certainly had. In April 1928, he sold the house on Boson Island and moved to a city centre apartment with a new lover – one of the actors in *Broadway*, a musical comedy he staged at the Oscar Theatre. This proved successful and Stiller begun making grandiose plans for the future. There was talk of film projects in England and Germany and a possible return to America – though not Hollywood – at the end of the year. These plans were postponed indefinitely when his health took a turn for the worse; an emergency operation for a lung infection necessitated the removal of several ribs, and rheumatic fever set in.

The news that Stiller was fighting for his life – relayed to Mayer by Victor Sjöström, currently working in London – was withheld from Garbo while she was shooting *White Orchids*. For the mercenary MGM executives it was imperative that her work schedule should not be interrupted. For his part, Sjöström flew to Stockholm on 6 November, and spent several hours at his friend's bedside in the Red Cross Hospital. Later, he said how Stiller had been excited about a new project he was working on: 'I want to tell you a story for a film. It will be a great film. It is about human beings, and you are the only person who can make it.' At this point in their conversation, the nurse intervened, telling Sjöström that they would have to resume their discussion in the morning. 'There would be no morning,' Sjöström concluded. The next day, Stiller was too weak to speak and the day after this, 8 November, he died, according to one report clutching one of the Arnold Genthe portraits of his most celebrated protégée. He was just forty-five. Two days later, he was buried in the Jewish section of Stockholm's Northern Cemetery, where the mourners included Sjöström, Lars Hanson, a whole coterie of former lovers, and just about everyone – from the technicians and canteen staff to the director and major stars – from the Swedish film industry.[172]

As had happened when Alva died, Garbo received no sympathy from Mayer and Thalberg, who were cabled at once by Sjöström. Thalberg's only concern was that the film should not run over budget. After some deliberation, Mayer dispatched the cable to Garbo – along with a tiny bottle of cognac 'to help her get over the shock'. Nils Asther recalled finding Garbo in her dressing room in a state of near-hysteria, a mixture of mirth and grief, having read the card which accompanied Mayer's 'gift', upon which the mogul had scrawled, 'Dear Greta. My sympathy in your sorrow. But the show must go on.'[173] Asther called Borg, who stayed with her until she had recovered from the initial shock. Ever the professional – she was filming the palace balcony scene – Garbo insisted on completing the sequence before leaving the set. For two days she shut herself away at the Miramar – even the faithful Borg was barred from seeing her. Then she asked Borg to call Mayer and inform him that once the film was finished she would be taking a month's compassionate leave so that she could visit her friends and family back home, whether the studio approved or not:

> After Moje died, I could not sleep nor eat nor work. For me it was a time that was very black. I wanted to drop everything and go back to Sweden, but the studio said no ... 'You must be faithful to us and your work.' I said to them, 'You will have something dead on the screen. It will have no life.' But they wouldn't let me go.[174]

Four years later, still mourning him, she wrote in *Liberty*:

> Stiller's death was a great blow to me. For so long I had been his satellite. All Europe at that time regarded Stiller as the most significant figure in the film world. Directors hurried to the projecting rooms where his prints were shown. They took with them their secretaries and, in the dim silence, they dictated breathless comments on his magnificent techniques. Stiller found me an obscure artist in Sweden, and brought me to America. I worshipped him. Some say it was a love story. It was more. It was the utter devotion which only the very young can know – the adoration of a student for her teacher, of a timid girl for a master mind. Stiller taught me how to do everything. How to eat, how to turn my head, how to express love – and hate. I studied his every whim, wish and demand. I lived my life according to the plans he laid down. He told me what to say and what to do. When Stiller died, I found myself like a ship without a rudder ... By degrees I dropped out of the social whirl.

I retired into my shell. I built a wall of repression around my real self, and I lived (and still live) behind it. In the gayest, maddest colony on the world, I became a hermit. I did not go to parties. I was too tired. I went to bed when my work was done.[175]

Henceforth, Mayer and Thalberg found themselves almost pathologically loathed by their biggest star. Garbo had long been thinking about returning home for the festive season. At the end of October she had written to Mimi Pollak:

I just think how glorious it will be to come home. It will feel like coming out from a lovely bathe. Just imagine being able to walk about in peace, round all my old haunts. As soon as this film is finished, I leave the factory. I long to get away from this factory life.[176]

Three days after learning of Stiller's death, Garbo turned up for work an hour late. When this happened three mornings in a row, Nils Asther and Lewis Stone – unable to complete their scenes without her – began having a lie-in. Subsequently, the first morning she did turn up on time, Garbo was waylaid by Sidney Franklin, who asked, sarcastically, 'Oh, Miss Garbo, do you think you can manage it? Do you feel inspired?' To which she shot back, 'Yes – if you'd only leave the studio!' Franklin was so incensed that he marched into Thalberg's office and asked to be taken off the picture. The response was that, like everyone else when Garbo was being tetchy, Franklin would have to grin and bear it.[177]

Nils Asther was set for travelling to Sweden with her, but changed his mind when Mayer threatened to fire him. During Garbo's absence he spent much of his time with Borg. The fact that she was not taking Borg with her eased Mayer's mind somewhat, and gave him some confidence that she would be coming back. On 3 December, wearing a black wig and dark glasses, Garbo huddled in the back of Borg's car as he drove her to the railway station at Pasadena. She had made the reservation under the name 'Alice Smith', the first of several pseudonyms she would adopt over the years in an effort to lose her public identity. She got as far as the changeover at Chicago, when an unnamed actor recognised her and alerted the studio. Mayer wired her on the train: 'Return, or great loss and damage will be caused us.'[178] Scenes in both *A Woman of Affairs* and *Wild Orchids* required retakes: if she returned for these at once, she would still make it back to New York before her ship set sail on 8 December. Garbo ignored him, and fearing MGM's New York representatives might be waiting for her at the Central Station, she left the train at Croton-Harmon and travelled the remaining forty miles into the city by taxi.

News that Garbo was about to arrive in New York had travelled like wildfire: every major hotel had pressmen stationed in the lobby. She fooled them by meeting up with Hubert Voight, who drove her to the Commodore, the hotel where she had stayed with Stiller, seemingly a lifetime ago. Here, on 5 December, she read in one of the evening papers that Mayer had suspended her, indefinitely, without pay – not a wise move, for had Garbo been looking for a legitimate excuse to stay in Europe, he had given her one. The press caught up with her three days later when she boarded the *Kungsholm* – shielding her face from photographers with a magazine and muttering that she was going home to put flowers on Stiller's grave.

Contrary to what was expected of her, Garbo did not lock herself in her cabin until the ship reached Sweden. The more miles she put between herself and Hollywood, the more relaxed she became – it was as if free from the constraints of the studio system, the shackles had been removed and she was once more becoming Greta Gustaffson. Among the passengers was Ragnar Ring, returning home from a holiday in New York, and Prince Sigvard (1907–2002), the second son of King Gustav VI Adolph of Sweden, with whom she was rumoured to have engaged in a shipboard romance. She was invited to sit at the captain's table as often as she liked, and was introduced to two more members of Swedish society who became lifelong friends: the Count and Countess Wachtmeister (Nils and Ingrid, aka Horke) owned one of the largest estates in the country, and were returning home from a wedding.[179]

Bad weather added twenty hours to the voyage, and there was a further delay when, on 16 December as the ship docked in

Gothenburg, Garbo consented to meet the barrage of reporters who had invaded its portals, and threatened to wreck everything in sight unless she gave them an interview. She afforded them just five minutes in the ship's library, insisting there should be no photographs, and that only Swedish journalists should be allowed in. Sitting in an armchair, with a magazine in her hand just in case someone had sneaked a camera in, she responded to a series of mostly innocuous questions:

Yes, she *was* glad to be home: 'America is the same as anywhere else. One has happy times, one has sad times!'

On *The Garbo Waltz*, a classical piece commissioned especially to welcome her home: 'No, I will not say that it is good. I'm back in Sweden now and I want to be honest. How can I say that I like something when I have never heard it?'

On the subject of her favourite director: 'After Stiller, Clarence Brown. He's not as strong a personality, but he usually gets the job done well.'

On her favourite actor: 'My favourite American actor is John Gilbert. Of the others, Lars Hanson.'

And finally, and impatiently, on the subject of whether she intended to marry Gilbert: 'I am *not* going to marry!'[180]

Shortly afterwards there was a tearful meeting between Garbo and Mimi Pollak – now married to the actor Nils Lundell and the mother of a one-year-old son. The pair were exchanging pleasantries when mass hysteria erupted: an estimated 5,000 screaming fans crowded the docks and extra police were drafted in to escort the two women to their waiting car. A dozen fans clambered onto the roof, while others clung to the running-boards, and two of the windows were smashed before the police dragged them off. When told that the train for Stockholm would not be leaving for another two hours, Garbo asked the driver to take them to the Grand Hotel, where they spent a quiet night before taking a taxi to the station the next morning. They managed to board the train unscathed, but when some of the passengers recognised her, Garbo asked the guard to cable ahead to her mother – the idea being that Anna and Sven Gustaffson, Nils Lundell, and Garbo's journalist friend Ake Sundborg would be waiting at Sodertaje, on the outskirts of the city. As had happened with the journey to New York, she was hoping to avoid the media circus by then driving into Stockholm. The guard tipped off reporters and when the train arrived at its destination, such was the size of the crowd that once the four passengers had boarded, along with fifty pressmen, her police escort advised her to stay put. In the excitement, the curtains to her compartment were torn down and she spent the rest of the journey sitting with her back to the door while photographers jostled to snap the back of her head. Despite the discomfort, she told Sundborg:

> I am unspeakably happy. Of course Hollywood is fascinating. But I also had many unpleasant experiences. And don't believe the silly stories about life in Hollywood. I am sure there are just as many temptations in Stockholm as there are in Hollywood. The American film colony means, above all things, work, and I have worked as hard as anyone. I am exhausted now. It will be lovely to have a real rest![181]

In Stockholm, the crowds were even bigger than at Gothenburg but the police presence was stronger as thousands of fans lined the route between the station and Karlesbergsvagen 52, Lars Hanson's former apartment, which had been assigned to Garbo for the duration of her stay. Hanson was there to greet her, along with Victor Sjöström. The next morning, Garbo made the pilgrimage – alone – to the Northern Cemetery, where as promised she laid a cross on Stiller's grave. A few days later she returned to find it broken in pieces – the Jewish faith did not permit Christian floral tributes. Accompanied by his former lawyer Hugo Lindberg, now executor of his estate, she visited the storeroom where Stiller's effects were being housed until being auctioned off to help settle his debts. Lindberg recalled her walking around the room, touching and smelling the contents as if memorising them – a scene which she would revisit in *Queen Christina*. For keepsakes, she was given a portrait of her mentor, along with the heavy oak chair she had sat in while waiting for her interview during her first visit to his home. She also bought a chest of drawers, which had stood in Stiller's study.

In Stockholm, there were countless requests for interviews: Garbo turned them all down and similarly declined invitations to receptions, parties, premieres, and store openings. Aware of her problems with MGM, the UFA approached her with an offer to work in Germany. She was not interested, but seriously considered a proposal from SF, with one condition: Alva's early death had robbed her of a potentially lucrative film career, so now it was up to the SF to put her brother Sven into the spotlight. Garbo demanded that he be given a screen test, the idea being that he would cut his acting teeth in a few minor Swedish roles before joining her in America. She personally directed the test, which Stiller's cameraman, Julius Jaenzon, filmed – and which was rejected. 'No Sven, no Garbo,' the studio was informed.

After spending Christmas with her mother and brother at their new apartment, still in Stockholm's south side, Garbo spent the New Year with Mimi Pollak and Nils Lundell, and on New Year's Eve attended the Dramatic Academy's annual party at the Strand Hotel, where she bumped into Gösta Ekman, the star of *Soldier of Fortune* and widely acknowledged as Sweden's greatest stage actor. A few evenings later, Ekman escorted her to a performance of Stiller's *Broadway*, still running at the Oscar Theatre. Instead of one of the beautiful outfits she had bought with Lilyan Tashman, Garbo turned up in a brown chiffon dress and the cloche hat she had worn in *A Woman of Affairs*. Ekman placed a lighted candelabra on either side of her head and pronounced, 'Look, Lucrezia Borgia!'[182] adding that Garbo would be perfect playing her on the stage and inviting the comment, 'No, she was a bitch!' The Academy was thrilled beyond belief when Ekman persuaded her to play Katinka, the lady's maid who turns to prostitution, in Tolstoy's *Resurrection*. She learned her part and attended several rehearsals, but on the eve of the premiere, nerves got the better of her and she dropped out of the production.

The party at the Strand Hotel had been gatecrashed by Prince Sigvard and his best friend, Wilhelm Sorensen, the son of a wealthy local industrialist. Garbo took to Sorensen at once, yanking his

handkerchief out of his top pocket, flicking him across the face
with it and posing, 'What kind of sailor are *you*?'[183] There was more
to this quip than met the eye. 'Sailor' was the term Garbo applied
to bisexual men and 'fuck buddies', her theory being that while
sailors were renowned for having a girl in every port, while at sea
they frequently had each other. But while she took to Sorensen,
allowing him to chauffeur her around Stockholm, Sigvard annoyed
her by boasting that he and Garbo were an item and even thinking of marriage. Later she would say of his fawning over her, 'I'm
interested only in *men*, not kids.'

During this first trip back to her homeland, Garbo and Mimi
Pollak were virtually inseparable – there is little doubt that,
despite Pollak's marital status, they resumed their affair. For Garbo,
then as always, men were good to be seen with on very rare public
outings, or to be linked with her in the press but once the doors
were locked and the blinds pulled down, she sought comfort – not
necessarily sex – from her Sapphic friends. Such was her dread of
being alone on home ground – she who had *yearned* for solitude in
Hollywood – that she never ventured out on an evening unless assured
that one of these women friends would escort her back to her apartment and, after a hot bath and endless nightcaps of hot chocolate, sit
with her until she fell asleep. An unnamed friend is cited as saying:

> After this, Greta would throw herself on the couch, weeping and
> bemoaning her tired state. With her head cushioned at last on the
> other woman's lap, she would gradually calm down and finally go to
> sleep. It was a nightly ordeal.[184]

Before bidding them farewell in Gothenburg, Garbo had promised
to 'look up' the Wachtmeisters. It was they who contacted her,
inviting Greta and Mimi Pollak to spend a week at their home,
Tistad Castle, just south of Stockholm. Another guest was Willhelm
Sorensen, with Prince Sigvard, who she was not so happy to bump
into again. Pollak later recalled how Garbo loved to wander through
the long, draughty corridors late at night and how by day they
spent hours sitting on the castle roof, gazing across the landscape,
happy to be temporarily excluded from the rest of the world.

Back in Stockholm – at the Northern Cemetery – Garbo struck up a friendship with Marte Halldén, one of Stiller's regular actresses and a member of Selma Lagerlöf's circle she had never shown interest in until now. Halldén persuaded her to pose for two sketch artists in the foyer of the Palladium Cinema, where they were about to premiere *A Woman of Affairs*. Garbo's only condition was that there should be no photographers. When she arrived, she was greeted by over 200 cheering art students armed with pencils and pads, but posed for them just the same.

While in Sweden Garbo had as little contract with Hollywood as possible. John Gilbert claimed she called him on New Year's Eve, Borg that her only call to America was to tell him she would be leaving Gothenburg on Sunday 10 March 1929. To avoid the mass hysteria and media frenzy of her arrival, she boarded the *Drottingholm* on the Saturday. Willhelm Sorensen and Marte Hallén drove her to the port. By the time the *Drottingholm* reached New York ten days later, the news of her earlier arrival had been leaked, and she was greeted by thousands of noisy fans. Her official reception was handled by Hubert Voight and Nicholas Schenck, standing in for MGM publicity chief Howard Dietz. Garbo would never forgive Dietz for his harsh treatment of her when she had arrived in 1925 and her opinion of Schenck – who she learned had supported Mayer's plan to have her deported – is said to have been unrepeatable. 'Mr Metro', as she scathingly referred to him, hugged her and handed her a huge bouquet of flowers at which she visibly cringed. As Garbo was about to get into Voight's car, a ten-year-old girl stepped out of the crowd and presented her with a scrapbook of photographs and magazine clippings – then promptly fainted! In a touching scene, she knelt at the girl's side, helped bring her round and, grabbing a pen from Voight, promptly wrote her name across the book – so far as is known, the only time she ever signed an autograph in public. She turned to Voight and pronounced, 'I am so popular now, and I don't want to be. Make them go away like a good boy and we'll go out later.'[185]

Voight had set up a press conference at the Hotel Marguery, which Garbo refused to attend. The next morning, she begrudgingly granted a ten-minute interview to the *New York Times*' Mordaunt

Hall, where she talked about nothing in particular, other that one day she would like to play Joan of Arc and make a film with controversial actor-director Erich von Stroheim. The next day, Garbo and Voight dined at the apartment of one of her favourite singers, the New York Metropolitan Opera's Lawrence Tibbett. The renowned baritone gave a private performance just for her and, carried away by the excitement and an excess of champagne, Garbo sang along with him – in Swedish. 'I saw a new sophistication, a polishing off of the rough corners,' Voight recalled. 'But there, underneath, not bothering to remain hidden was the real Garbo, a marvellous friend and child of the sun. She was the most beautiful creature I have ever seen, that night, simply shining with life.'[186]

A few days later, Voight drove Garbo to the railway station and, while awaiting the train, discussed her now inevitable move to talkies. MGM had contracted her two more silent, but if she was going to attempt the transition, she said, it would be with a production of her own choosing. She therefore asked Voight to find her a Swedish translation of Eugene O'Neill's Pulitzer Prize-winning *Anna Christie*, and send this to her in Hollywood.

CHAPTER SEVEN

A CLEAN SWEEP & THE FIRST TALKIE

*'In Hollywood, where every tea table bristles with gossip-writers, what
I might say might be misunderstood. So I am as silent as the grave
about my private affairs. Rumours fly. I am mum. My private affairs
are strictly private.'*

After the hysterics of Gothenburg, Stockholm and New York,
Garbo was intent on having a fuss-free welcome when she
reached Hollywood on 26 March 1929. She cabled ahead to
Mayer, informing him of the expected time of her arrival. He
and Thalberg could not make it to the station but other studio
executives were there, along with dozens of pressmen and several
thousand fans, who cheered as the train pulled in. But Garbo was
not on it – she had alighted at San Bernadino, where John Gilbert
picked her up in his roadster.

Gilbert's career was in decline, not helped by his womanising
and heavy drinking. He needed a publicity boost to get him back
on track and what better than the announcement that Garbo had
finally agreed to become his wife. When he proposed again, the
answer was the same as before, though Adela Rogers St Johns
claimed that Gilbert had confided in her that Garbo had suggested
they might live together again. 'You are a very foolish boy, Yacky.
You quarrel with me for nothing. I must do it my way but we need
not part,' she is supposed to have said, to which Gilbert responded,
'Not this time, Greta. This time it's going to be all or nothing.'[187]

Anticipating such a response, Gilbert had a 'substitute' waiting
on the sidelines. He had begun dating actress and former vaudeville
star Ina Claire (1892–1985) while Garbo had been on her way home.
And Garbo, of course, knew he would never change, and that so
long as they were together he would cheat and attract only the
worst publicity. Now, he turned to Claire – the woman he would

have dropped, had Garbo said yes. According to Gilbert's daughter, Claire may not even have liked him when they first met – she is on record as dismissing his acting as 'a kind of ham.' Balancing the equation, so to speak, and unbeknownst to Gilbert, Claire was unofficially engaged to the scriptwriter Gene Marley – had Garbo accepted Gilbert's marriage proposal, she would have wed Marley, who was now given his marching orders.[188]

On 15 April Garbo headed for Catalina Island to shoot the locations for her penultimate silent, *The Single Standard*, devised during her absence as a vehicle for the combined talents of Joan Crawford, Nils Asther and Johnny Mack Brown, who had recently triumphed in *Our Dancing Daughters*. During shooting, Joan made a play for both actors, who were less interested in her than in each other. Though she would work with Brown again, Crawford did not take kindly to being snubbed, and dropped out of filming. Subsequently, the two actors petitioned Irving Thalberg to offer the role to Garbo, who accepted it without hesitation, despite the imminent shooting schedule and her complaints that she was still feeling 'travel weary'.

The film was heralded as Garbo's first '100 per cent all-American' role – obviously MGM had forgotten that she had played an American in *Wild Orchids*. Directing was John S. Robertson (1878–1964), a Canadian today best remembered for John Barrymore's *Dr Jekyll & Mr Hyde* (1920). Garbo asked for him because he had directed Lars Hanson in his last big Hollywood picture, *Captain Salvation*. With William Daniels assigned to Norma Shearer's new film, the cameraman was Oliver Marsh, who had photographed *The Divine Woman*. The Art Deco interiors were by Cedric Gibbons.

Arden Stuart is a modern San Francisco girl who believes in equality: if guys can fool around, so can she. Tommy Hewlett (Johnny Mack Brown) *wants to marry her, but she finds him dull. More exciting is Anthony, her chauffeur, secretly the ace aviator son of a lord.* (Why he is masquerading as such is not explained. The character is played by Fred Solm, a 6′ 3″ German singer who showed great promise as a matinée idol, but disappeared with the advent of sound. In German and Scandinavian prints of the film his voice was added to the soundtrack to complement this scene, performing 'Den Har Man Med Sej'.

Tonight Arden feels like doing seventy mph, so she takes Anthony for a spin in her convertible. They head for the dunes (where the moonlight catching Garbo's hair makes her look lovelier than ever). *At first they hug, then it is an all-out kiss – maybe the first time he has kissed a woman – a prelude to them making love on the beach.*

Back at the house, Arden's irate brother, Ding (Lane Chandler), *confronts them. He gives Anthony a hard stare and tells him he is fired. That there is history between the two men is obvious: Anthony rewards Ding's guilty glance with a satisfied smirk and then drives the car into a wall, killing himself – not what one would expect after a one-off tumble in the sand.*

Several months elapse and Arden, still mourning Anthony, visits an art museum, where there is an exhibition by sailor-turned-artist and aspiring boxer Packy Cannon (Nils Asther). *The attraction is instant. He invites her to his next* (much speeded-up) *fight, which he wins, then to his apartment, where she drifts around, caressing everything. Tomorrow he is taking his yacht* (the All Alone!) *to the South Seas, and a passionate kiss persuades her to accompany him.* (None of Garbo's co-stars kissed with the same rough, animal passion as Asther.)

The months fly by as we witness a truly beautiful couple in love: clad in white and lounging in each other's arms on the deck, donning skimpy swimsuits (Asther's leaving little to the imagination), *diving off the yardarm and swimming underwater* (both refusing stunt doubles), *and Arden crawling across the deck on her hands and knees to nuzzle his thigh. Then Packy decides to end their romance and return to San Francisco, despite her pleas that they are both happy and single. 'No, Arden, we must go on – alone! Our love has been so perfect, we must keep it so, always in memory,' he tells her, before sailing off to China.*

Three years pass, and Arden is now married to Tommy and has a small son. Packy returns and is horrified to see the child, which he thinks may be his. When he discovers that Arden wants to run off with Packy again, Tommy grabs a gun and confronts his rival on the All Alone. *'Coffee and pistols for two?' Packy jokes. Though by this point Tommy is willing to kill himself so that Arden might be 'honourably free', a mother's love dictates the outcome of the situation* (the intervention of the Hays Office, perhaps, as in *Love*) *and she pronounces, 'One man will always be first in my life, and he is my son!'*

The film was edited in record time, and premiered on 27 July. Despite sterling box-office receipts, the reviews – some journalists still lamented the loss of the Garbo-Gilbert partnership – were not always complimentary. Pare Lorentz, who had gushed over her performance in *A Woman of Affairs*, wrote in *Judge*:

> For the first time since she hit these shores, grim Greta Garbo has done a good piece of work ... she actually walks, smiles, and acts. I have never been able to understand the universal palpitation that has followed her slow but stupid appearance on the great American screen ... Nice legs and much hair might be 'it', but it doesn't make an actress. Nevertheless the lady can, and does, act in her latest movie, and the fact that she is homely and awkward while so engaged only makes me like her more.[189]

Variety, whose critic gives every impression of having skipped the scenes on the yacht, observed:

> What some girls do today, and a lot more would like to, Greta Garbo does in *The Single Standard* ... But the thousands of typing girlies and purple-suited office boys will find this made to their order ... as Arden Stuart, throwing off the cloak of conventionalism for free plunges claimed so common in spots here and on the Continent, the actress is most unfeline in her brazen directness. While censors probably expect to leap on this point, when the picture gets to them, they will find no show, except a veiled peep at Arden's garters. The star keeps well-wrapped throughout.[190]

At the end of April, John Gilbert announced his engagement to Ina Claire. The wedding was set to take place in Las Vegas on 9 May, after which the couple would be sailing for Europe on the *Ile de France*. The scriptwriter Lenore Coffee later said that she had been standing outside Harry Edington's office when a call had been put through from a distressed Garbo, on location at Catalina Island.

According to Coffee, who claimed to have heard every word through the half-open door – which given Garbo's quiet, sultry voice one finds hard to believe – Garbo ordered Edington to stop the wedding, only to be told by him that *she* was the only one capable of doing this. The story was utter nonsense: Garbo had turned down at least a dozen marriage proposals from this man – for Gilbert, if the penny had not dropped by now, it never would. Her initial comment to the journalist who brought her the news was a sarcastic, 'Thank you. I hope Mr Gilbert will be very happy.' Another source quotes her remark to a young Swedish admirer (almost certainly Nils Asther) when their cars passed each other in the street, 'Gott, I wonder what I ever saw in him. Oh well, I guess he *was* pretty!' As with all Gilbert's relationships and marriages, this one would not last. The rot set in immediately when Ina Claire tore a strip off the editor of a newspaper, which ran the headline, 'JOHN GILBERT WEDS ACTRESS'. This, she declared, *should* have read, 'Ina Claire Weds Movie Star'. Days after the wedding, when asked how it felt to be married to a great star, Claire barked, 'I don't know. Why don't you ask Mr Gilbert?'[191 192]

While shooting the film, Garbo and Nils Asther were virtually inseparable, retreating to her dressing room or his between scenes and always locking the door. When not working, there were treks into the mountains, or picnics in the country. Like Garbo, Asther frequently felt like a fish out of water in this strange town both had reluctantly adopted as home. 'I am rather like Greta in that I like to be alone,' he recalled. 'I love peace and quiet. Hollywood is really no place for me; I stagnate there. I only really feel awake when the air is fresh and crisp, as in my native Scandinavia. I believe it is because Garbo is from Sweden that she feels the same.'[193]

Asther too was having problems with MGM. Aware that he was bisexual, and unashamedly so – but probably not aware that he was involved with the married Johnny Mack Brown – the studio pressured him to marry. Garbo herself had given the game away while shooting one of their love scenes on Catalina – when Asther grabbed her a little too roughly before kissing her she remonstrated, albeit in jest, 'Hey, stop that! I'm not one of your sailor friends!'

Asther's first American film in 1927 had been *Topsy & Eva*, starring Vivian Duncan of the Duncan Sisters vaudeville act. Since then he had been using her as a lavender date; her sister, Rosetta, had tagged along with Asther and Brown to make up a foursome. However, the rumours stopped abruptly when the press began reporting on a romance with Garbo, sparked off by the kiss on the set of *The Single Standard* – an affair which, though short-lived and not as highly publicised, proved no less passionate than the one with John Gilbert. Neither was this the first time that Asther had fallen for her. He recalled meeting her in Stockholm, when she had been studying at the Academy and he had proposed back then:

> I didn't notice anything special about her except that she had a wonderful voice, dark, almost plaintive. She lowered her eyes and when she finally raised them I was thunderstruck. I stared, bewitched and bewildered ... Without mercy, she turned me down. She said she definitely would not marry me or anyone else for that matter. She had decided to dedicate herself to art, to film and the theatre.[194]

Had Asther made such a statement in 1929, he might have been accused of proposing to Garbo as a means of covering his tracks, as would happen the following year when he finally married Vivian Duncan – a marriage which lasted just over a year but produced a daughter. Because his remarks came after his Hollywood career was over, when he had nothing to lose, one may only assume that his feelings for Garbo were genuine and he really did want to marry her. During a long weekend break from shooting, he persuaded her to accompany him on a trip to Lake Arrowhead, where he rented a small log cabin. This was certainly no love-nest, and from his point of view there was no pressure for sex: while Garbo slept downstairs on the floor, Asther occupied the loft. By day, they swam naked in the lake, and on an evening relaxed and fantasised about building, 'A Swedish log-cabin [of our own] high up on a hill, where we could withdraw from the rush of the movie colony.' It was here that Asther proposed again. The response was the same as before – she had no intention of marrying, ever. Some years later, another close friend, Sam Green, further explained Garbo's special affinity with gay and bisexual men, even when she was an old lady: 'I didn't want to marry or sleep with her, but she was the ideal romantic companion,' he recalled. 'You just wanted to put your head on her lap, or bury your face between her breasts or have her kiss you. It didn't matter how old she was.'[195]

During the autumn of 1932, Garbo – in what would be the only feature penned by herself, partly in English, partly in Swedish – offered a rare and lengthy philosophical insight into what she believed were the benefits and pitfalls not just of movie marriages, but of marriage in general, and into Hollywood's fascination with delving into the private lives of its stars:

Why are people so interested in the matrimonial status of film stars? After all, the marriage is nobody's business except the two people concerned. It is strictly their private affair. Moreover, it is damaging to have the intimate details of their domestic life broadcast far and wide. It is particularly unfair (if not actually unwise for an actor who plays great lover roles) to stress having a wife and children, no matter how he dotes on them in private ... Personally I should hate to have my husband lose his identity. Instead, I should want to forget I had ever been Greta Garbo. With so many broken romances littered about, Hollywood is not keen to draw attention to the love affairs of its players ... What chance has a marriage in these circumstances? Can you wonder that film stars hesitate to exchange single-blessedness for wedded bliss?

The particular problem that faces the film star, however, is this: Have I the particular kind of genius and temperament that makes of matrimony a holy and lasting bond? Am I a fit person to be anybody's 'lawful wedded wife'? Can I make a success of married life? With a male star, it is different. When he marries, convention expects that his wife shall subordinate her interests to his...

How embarrassing, on the other hand, is the situation of a non film acting husband married to a famous film star! He is bound to lose something of his own identity. Imagine a man being known as 'Mr Garbo' – just that and nothing more! In sections of society still impressed by the false glitter of the limelight, and where the spectacle of a woman who has made her own way in the world is still a matter for surprise and idle chatter, this is what would surely happen...

Only a fool or a hero could abide such an anomalous position. The only good reason for two people getting married is so that they can be together most of the time. That is impossible for me so long as I remain on the screen...

A marriage contract which has to make the best of whatever is left over after the film contract has been fulfilled seems a makeshift affair. A husband needs his wife's spiritual support as well as her physical presence. Unless one marries a fellow film artist, there is little chance of this ideal union of sympathy and interests. A star's career is a whole time job ...[196]

The sweeping changes continued. After four years of living at the Miramar, Garbo was looking to put down roots – though the threat of returning to Sweden would always be there. At the Miramar, she was surrounded by too many memories, albeit good ones – Stiller's visits, the intimate soirées with Swedish friends, of whom only Asther and Borg remained. Though they would remain friends, she had ended her relationship with Lilyan Tashman, having been made aware of her indiscretion when speaking of her to others.

Borg was next. Exactly what he had done is not known – probably nothing. Since returning from Europe, Garbo was at her most paranoid that even her closest friends had talked about her during her absence – even this man, who had been her rock since the first day she had faced an American movie camera. There were no arguments. Borg helped her pack her meagre belongings, and drove her to the Beverly Hills Hotel, where she rented a small apartment. Then he more or less withdrew from her life, returning to work at the Swedish Consulate until his film career as a character actor took off. During World War II, Borg was very much in demand, playing both Nazi officers and Scandinavian resistance fighters. He also appeared in two films with Errol Flynn, who became a friend.

Garbo's move to the Beverly Hills Hotel proved a big mistake. Though she never used any of its facilities, the elevator down to the crowded lobby and the seemingly never ending walk through here to her waiting car proved a daily trip to Calvary, with newspapermen and fans keeping a round-the-clock vigil in the hope of snaring her for the interview or autograph they knew she

would never give. The crunch moment came when a fan – identified only as 'a dentist's daughter from Milwaukee' – having seen
her leave the elevator, rushed outside and hid behind a clump of
bushes, leaping out in front of Garbo's car and screaming, 'I love
you, Greta!' as it sped off to avoid the pursuing pressmen, forcing
the driver to slam on the brakes and almost catapulting her over the
windscreen. Once she had recovered from the shock, Garbo called
Harry Edington and asked him to find her somewhere less intrusive to live – a house, this time, where she would be protected from
such madness.

Edington found her a rented, two-storey Spanish-style property
at 1027 Chevy Chase Drive, off Benedict Canyon Drive. The house
was far too big: eight rooms including three en-suite bedrooms,
a living room, dining room, library, two kitchens, a utility room
and servants' quarters. What attracted Garbo to it were the pool and
the landscaped garden, planted with lemon trees and surrounded
by a ten-foot concrete wall and cypress hedge – essential to protect
her from 'peeping Toms' during those naked early-morning dips.
To fool the neighbours, when inspecting the place she donned
the 'Alice Smith' disguise she had worn on the train to New York,
and was accompanied by her 'family' – MGM hair-stylist Sidney
Guilaroff and his two children. She signed the lease, then brought
in workmen to seal off the rooms she would not be using, having
their doors padlocked, just in case intruders broke in through the
barred windows.

At the Miramar, Garbo had managed with just her 'personal
maid', Borg. Now, she asked Edington to hire a live-in couple.
Naturally, these would have to be Swedish, and she would personally conduct the interviews in this language. She plumped for the
first couple who applied – unusually for one so paranoid about
her privacy and security, she never checked their credentials.
Gustaf Norin (1905–88) hailed from Malmo, the son of Josef, a
former prosthetics laboratory technician with the SF. The whole
family had emigrated to Hollywood during the early twenties, but
whereas Josef found work with one of the studios, his son was not
so lucky. Later, Gustaf became a leading exponent of prosthetic and
cosmetic make-up, working in over 700 films – including, with

his father, *The Wizard of Oz* (1939). But for now, he and his wife, Sigrid, would be responsible for protecting Greta Garbo from the interfering outside world. The Norins' first job was moving in her personal effects – a single journey which involved transporting two trunks, three suitcases, boxes of books brought over from Sweden and not yet opened, and Mauritz Stiller's chair, chest of drawers and portrait. A few weeks later, Garbo hired MGM's costume designer Gilbert Adrian to 'do the place up' – this involved fitting one carpet, rearranging what little furniture she had, and hanging curtains in the two rooms she decided to use.

At home, Garbo ran a tight ship. MGM were now paying her $5,000 a week but she allowed the Norins a household budget of just $25 a week. Initially this panicked them, until they realised that most of the time there would be just the three of them. Garbo *never* threw parties like other Hollywood stars – her only guests during her first month here were Harry Edington, the Jannings, and Nils Asther, who often stayed the night. She had also acquired several pets: two stray cats, whom she named Big Pint and Half Pint, a parrot named Polly, and a chow called Fimsy. Sigrid Norin's job description called for her to cook and clean, and answer the door, *always* to announce that the lady of the house was not home, even if she was. She was also responsible for replenishing Garbo's wardrobe, an uncomplicated task because most of the time she wore men's clothes and, apart from the size of her feet, she was exactly the same height and build as Gustaf. Her specific requirements were cotton shirts and neckties, Oxford twill jackets and trousers, waistcoats and gabardine raincoats. Gustaf himself purchased her favourite brown brogues, essential for those long, solitary treks in the country. 'Just the thing for us bachelors,' he recalled her telling him, adding how she had given him and his wife a little black book, with instructions to list every purchase they made – and to include the receipt – then hand this over for her to check the figures at the end of each week.[197]

Gustaf's first daily duty was a walk to the local drugstore to buy the day's papers and magazines: Garbo flicked through these, and if there was no mention of her in them they were returned for a refund. Foreign publications were sent by friends and contacts in Europe to Harry Edington's office, so that the mailman would not know who resided at 1027 Chevy Chase Drive. Just as she hid whenever the man came to clean the windows or tend the pool, Garbo *never* answered the telephone. Whichever of the Norins took the call would announce: 'The Norin residence. Who's speaking?' The caller would then have to give a special secret code before the receiver was passed to Garbo. Callers blocked from speaking to her at home were Mayer, Thalberg, any actor or actress who was not Swedish, and everyone from the press. Garbo *always* left the studio at 5.30 sharp, whether or not she had turned up late for work that day. Sigrid Norin prepared her bath as soon as she arrived home. Then, after dinner, usually taken in bed, she read or listened to the gramophone. Her favourite singer was Sophie Tucker and often she played the same record twenty times in succession. By ten, unless she had guests, she would be back in bed. The next morning she would rise early, around six, and spend an hour in the pool before breakfast. This was a hearty, Scandinavian affair: fruit juice, a grapefruit, creamed chipped beef, fried potatoes, an egg, coffee and coffee cake, all eaten on china given her by Emil Jannings.[198]

After breakfast, Garbo often went for a walk, or asked Gustaf Norin to drive her to the riding stables. She especially loved these activities if it was pouring with rain – the bad weather, complimented by the obligatory dark glasses and wide-brimmed hat, offered her extra protection from passers-by who otherwise might have recognised her. She so loved the rain that she often stood in her garden, fully-clothed, until she was soaking wet – her only way of keeping cool, she said, in the oppressive California heat. If there was a prolonged dry spell, she turned on the sprinklers and stood under them. Invariably she caught colds, which she dealt with not by seeing a doctor, but by dosing herself with nasal sprays and hot chocolate. If the cold was severe, she made an appointment for treatment at one of the local Turkish baths where, she said, she would have less chance of being pestered if everyone was wearing just towels.

Wearing her Alice Smith disguise, Garbo spent a lot of time at the cinema. She loved Gary Cooper and would always regret not having worked with him. Her favourite director was Ernst Lubitsch, who she would one day work with. She enjoyed witnessing audiences'

reactions to her own films, deriving immense pleasure from the
fact that they had no idea that the woman they were applauding
was sitting among them. Garbo and Nils Asther also frequented
some of the Hollywood clubs. Their favourites were the Russian
Eagle, with its Slav theme nights, and the Apex, an establishment
popular with black musicians. With Asther, she was never afraid of
being accosted by fans or pressmen; as had happened with Borg,
one hard stare from the big Swede was sufficient to keep most
'intruders' at a safe distance.

During the late spring of 1929, Garbo slightly extended her
tight-knit circle of friends. British actor John Loder (1898–1988)
had served at Gallipoli, been captured by the Germans, and spent
time in a war camp. Soon after meeting Garbo he appeared in
Paramount's first talkie, *The Doctor's Secret*. Loder was married
to the Austrian actress Sophie Kabel, the first of five wives. He
said of Garbo at the time, 'There is no doubt that at times she is
a most unhappy person but she has the divine flame that carries
her along and makes her the great actress that she is.'[199] Belgian
director Jacques Feyder (1885–1948) had established a reputation as
one of French cinema's most innovative directors – most famously
for *Thérèse Raquin* (1928), the film which led Mayer to invite him
to Hollywood. Married to the temperamental French actress
Françoise Rosay (1891–1974), he quickly became disillusioned with
the American studio system, publicly declaring his disapproval and
staying for just four years before returning to France – though he
did get to work with Garbo. Another important friend was F. W.
Murnau (1888–1931), the eminent German director who gave the
world its greatest early horror movie, *Nosferatu* (1922).

With these friends, Garbo and Nils Asther held regular soirées
at Chevy Chase Drive, where she was able to let her hair down
and be her true self – not some miserable, anti-social recluse but a
woman who loved music, laughter, and intellectual conversation.
As the only language that everyone could speak with any degree
of fluency was German, this was the language used at Garbo's
gatherings – with her or Loder acting as interpreter if she invited
anyone else to join their circle.

In June 1939, Irving Thalberg added Garbo's name to the cast of

Hollywood Revue of 1929, an all-talking, part-technicolor, plotless mishmash showcasing the cream of the MGM roster. The *Revue* included musical numbers by Joan Crawford and Marie Dressler, comedy sketches from Jack Benny and Laurel & Hardy, John Gilbert and Norma Shearer – twice the age of the star-crossed lovers – hamming it up in the balcony scene from *Romeo and Juliet*, and the whole cast splashing about the set in a *Singin' in the Rain* finale. Garbo refused to appear, and Thalberg attempted to pull rank until Harry Edington pointed out that she was yet to sign a contract with MGM obliging her to make sound films.

Meanwhile, there was Garbo's final silent film to contend with before the studio began negotiating this new contract. Thalberg suggested *The Woman Accused* (subsequently changed to *The Kiss*), which she approved after reading the script. The storyline, a murder mystery, followed more or less the same pattern as her previous films: a young woman, married to an older wealthy man, becomes involved with rival suitors, the twist in the tail being that she ends up in the dock charged with murder. Garbo wanted Nils Asther to co-star, but he had been assigned to another film, so she once again ended up with Conrad Nagel, no less wooden here than he was in *The Mysterious Lady*.

Playing her young admirer was Lew Ayres, a discovery of Jean Harlow's future husband, Paul Bern. Known as 'Little Father Confessor' on account of his puny build and fondness for listening to other people's problems – though not always helping them to resolve them, or indeed facing up to his own – German-born Bern (Paul Levy, 1889–1932) was Irving Thalberg's right-hand man at MGM. Sophisticated, intellectual but unattractive, his all-powerful position with the studio enabled him to date some of the biggest names in Hollywood of both sexes, many of whom owed their stardom to him. A rare failure was 29-year-old Barbara Lamarr, six times married, who in 1926 died of a drug overdose, 'Hollywoodised' for the press as 'death by over-rigorous dieting'. Bern had moulded and promoted Joan Crawford to take over where the luckless Lamarr had left off, and put her into *The Taxi Dancer*, since which time she had not looked back. Now, he was hoping to turn his latest protegé, Minnesota-born Lew Ayres (1908–96), a former banjo player with the Henry Halstead Orchestra, into the new John Gilbert. Garbo was shown his screen test, and liked what she saw. To direct, she asked for Jacques Feyder, whose eccentricity appealed to her offbeat nature: instead of calling 'Cut!' like other directors, Feyder always waved a coloured handkerchief.

Like his character in the film, Lew Ayres developed a crush on Garbo. For the duration of the shooting schedule, which began on 16 July 1929, he became part of the 'gang' at Chevy Chase Drive. Because he was the only member of her entourage who did not speak German, and none of them wished to speak English, she acted as interpreter. Soon after working with her he was offered a starring role in *All Quiet on the Western Front*, the film which made him a household name.

At the Musée des Arts, snooty society matrons gossip as Irene Guarry (Garbo) *and her lawyer lover André Dubail* (Conrad Nagel) *discuss their relationship.* (It's back to the Garbo of glamorous gowns for this contemporary story set in Lyons and the opening title, 'Irene, we can't go on meeting like this,' gave the world a new catchphrase, still used today.) *She wants to end their affair, or run away with him, but he is too honourable. He would rather confess all to her elderly husband, Charles* (Anders Randolf), *who she fusses over as she would a grandfather – frowning, scowling, shoulders hunched, depressed – but Irene will not hear of this.*

Then comes the obligatory mirror scene, this time as seen by the mirror itself: Garbo in extreme close-up, repairing her make-up as if shooting a commercial, mentally conversing with the camera as if saying, 'I'm not really miserable. I'm beautiful and having fun, and all this is just play acting!'

Charles has hired a private detective, who sees her with Pierre Lassalle (Lew Ayres), *the son of Charles' business partner: the boy has fallen for her, though she will not take his attentions seriously until it is too late.*

Cut to a society dinner, where André turns up and announces he is leaving for Paris – he will not be back. No sooner has he gone than Pierre arrives. He and Irene dance, and the next day they play tennis at his father's house. He has just turned eighteen and tells her, 'You women just don't know how love affects a man like me' – only to have her chide,

'You're just a boy, Pierre!' (Garbo and Ayres were able tennis players, but MGM would not permit them to play in the film and used stock footage of professionals. And was it purely by chance or a coy reference to Ayres' alleged endowment that the music played over this scene was 'The Donkey Serenade?') *Tomorrow, Pierre returns to college and he wants a photograph to show his friends. When he calls on her later, after ensuring her husband is not there, she reveals a whole stack of 14 x 11 inch glossies for such requests. Her attitude is maternal until Pierre asks for a kiss. She obliges but he wants more, and she is fighting him off when Charles comes home. Charles gives Pierre a thrashing and knocks Irene about while she clings to his thigh, begging him to stop. The door closes on the camera and a shot is fired, but we will have to wait until the denouement to find out what really happens.*

When we next see Pierre, he is stumbling home bloodied and battered, and we discover that Charles is dead. Irene is arrested for murder. (A huge blooper follows. When she is arrested, Garbo's formerly long hair is now short, but has grown again when she arrives at the court house, then it is back to short for the scene, subsequently cut, that takes place in her jail cell. These scenes were filmed several weeks after shooting wrapped.)

In the dock, wearing her widow's weeds, Irene is resolutely imperious towards the gossips and the judge – who assume that because she married a much older man, she must be a strumpet. (This haughteur is perfectly captured by William Daniels, who filmed Garbo from ground level looking up.) *The circumstances of the shooting make it clear that Irene has committed a crime of passion, but André* (the only available defence lawyer in town, despite the fact that he is supposed to have left Lyons for good) *argues that Charles' death was suicide, as that same day he had revealed to a friend that he was close to bankruptcy.* (During a flashback, we see Irene fire the gun from the far side of the room. In the real world, André's defence would never have been possible but in the film the investigating officers never check the weapon for fingerprints!) *Exonerated, Irene faces the two men in her life, but it is André who walks off with the prize when, having told him the truth, she adds, 'I couldn't let him kill that boy.'*

The film opened in New York on 16 November. *Screenland* observed, 'The Swedish charmer carries this load of a mediocre story on her splendid shoulders and makes *The Kiss* worth seeing ... Next to Greta, the most interesting thing is the film debut of young Lew Ayres, a smouldering boy who is a real find.' The reviewer for *Motion Picture*, who found Ayres' 'display of adolescent passion' almost too embarrassing to watch, was eager to hear what Garbo would sound like, observing, 'The last stand of the silent pictures, the last hope of those who like 'em quiet is Greta Garbo ... In spite of unworthy stories, in spite of her stubborn silence in this talkie day, I would gladly pay for my own ticket to see a Garbo picture – which is the greatest compliment a reviewer can pay!'[200]

While shooting *The Kiss*, Garbo received a parcel from Hubert Voight: unable to find a Swedish adaptation of Eugene O'Neill's *Anna Christie*, he himself had paid to have it translated into a rough draft. Garbo read this quickly and informed Thalberg that this was what she had in mind for her first talkie, despite the fact that it was not the kind of scenario *he* would have chosen: set on a waterfront, with Swedish characters that could almost have come out of a *Joyless Street* scenario.

On 27 August, instead of attending a meeting with Thalberg to discuss the new film, Garbo spent the entire afternoon with Clarence Sinclair Bull (1896–1979), the head of MGM's stills department and believed by many to have been the greatest American portrait photographer of his generation. With his assistant continuously replenishing the gramophone with Sophie Tucker records, Bull took 200 photographs – between now and 1929, there would be 4,000 more. During this first session, not one word passed her lips until she was ready to leave. Bull recalled, 'As she rose and moved to the door, obviously tired yet somehow showing she had enjoyed our efforts, she said, "I was quite nervous, Mr Bull. I'll do better next time." At the door, I reached for her hand. It was as moist as mine. "So will I, Miss Garbo."'[201] One of Bull's most celebrated portraits of Garbo came about as the result of an experiment, in 1931. For 'The Swedish Sphinx' he superimposed one of his close-ups of her over a photograph of the Sphinx at Giza, from which he had airbrushed out the face. Friends advised Bull not to show Garbo this, certain that she would take offence. Amused and delighted, however, she gave permission for its worldwide distribution and the picture sold many thousands of copies.

At a meeting that Garbo failed to attend, Thalberg assigned her a personal press aide. Katherine Albert (1902–70) had worked as a film extra before becoming a staff reporter for *Photoplay*. Garbo refused to have anything to do with her. Thalberg next urged her, by way of Harry Edington, to grant an audience with Hedda Hopper or Louella Parsons. Absolutely no Hollywood star worthy of their salt would have wished to risk career suicide by refusing to be interviewed by one or other of those harpies. Garbo did now, and in so doing earned their enmity, but also the respect of her contemporaries, who only wished they might have the courage to take a leaf out of her book.

On 16 September, Garbo received a cable from Wilhelm Sorenson, the young Swede who had squired her around Stockholm. Perhaps not expecting him to take her up on the offer, she had told him to look her up, should he ever visit Hollywood. Indeed, when in subsequent correspondence he had confided that he was hoping for a career in the movies, she had tried to put him off, declaring even she was apprehensive about the future:

> If you really wish to come you are heartily welcome, but I must warn you that you may never understand me completely – *how* I really am, *what* makes me so. If I am working on a movie when you are here, we would not see much of each other because then I must be alone ... They are making sound movies here now and nobody knows what is to happen to me. Perhaps I will not stay here much longer. Already some of the top stars intend leaving Hollywood, and it is questionable for how long I will remain a film tramp.[202]

Sorenson arrived in San Pedro by freighter and Garbo insisted on driving there alone to meet him. Very much the narcissist, he presented her with a bust he had commissioned of himself: this enjoyed pride of place on her piano next to Stiller's framed photograph, for years the only 'ornaments' she possessed. That night she did not sleep alone, though early next morning Sorenson moved into a nearby hotel, where he stayed until his return to Sweden.

For 'Soren', as she called him, Garbo almost came out of her shell. He visited her house every day, drove her to and from the studio and socialised with her most evenings. After his first week in Hollywood he even fell in with her 'early to bed, early to rise' routine. He and Nils Asther were the only ones permitted to use her pool – all three swam naked, with the children who lived next-door selling tickets to their friends, who would climb on to the roof to watch. During the daytime, when Garbo was at the studio and the Norins out shopping, those same children broke into her garden and collected her cigarette butts, which they sold to fans. Sorenson also accompanied Garbo and Asther on their outings to the Russian Eagle.

On 18 September, in the company of her Swedish beaus, Garbo celebrated her twenty-fourth birthday with lunch at the Ambassador Hotel. That same evening, they escorted her to a dinner party given in her honour by Pola Negri, at the home of the director Ludwig Berger. Who else was present is not on record, save that Garbo went to inordinate lengths to look good for her hostess. Instead of wearing her usual tweed trousers, pullover and brogues, she went to the couturier, and followed this up with trips to the beauty salon and hairdressers – probably Sidney Guilaroff, who gave her the style she sports in the out-of-continuity scenes towards the end of *The Kiss*. According to Sorenson, when someone at the party commented on how good she looked, Garbo responded drily, 'You know, one often makes mistakes in life!'[203]

At some stage during Sorenson's visit, Garbo took a week off and they headed for San Francisco in her car – she heavily disguised as usual – and checked into a hotel as brother and sister. They stayed there for several days, and spent much of their time strolling around the city's Chinese quarter, where Garbo believed there would be less chance of her being recognised. She came unstuck when she tried to cash a cheque at a bank – the teller observed the signature and, believing this to be a hoax, asked for proof of identity. When Garbo showed him her passport, the man caused such a fuss that 'Miss Sorenson' made a hasty exit. As she had no intention of returning to Los Angeles until the end of the week, she and Sorenson headed for La Quinta, where she had stayed with Borg during her 'indisposition'. Here, for three days she did nothing but sunbathe and read.[204]

Upon their return to Hollywood, Garbo and Sorenson attended a Sunday afternoon showing of Ernst Lubitsch's *The Love Parade*, starring Maurice Chevalier. Sorenson recalled how, after leaving the cinema, she sat on the edge of the pavement for several minutes, telling him, 'I must sit and think. I am so happy to know that pictures like that can be made.'[205] Stopping off at a florist's shop, she bought a bunch of red roses, and asked her escort to drive her to the director's home. Here, a dinner party was about to begin. Flinging her arms around Lubitsch's neck she exclaimed, 'Ernst, I love you for this picture!' Garbo, wearing her trademark tweeds, brogues and cloche hat, was hardly suitably attired for one of Lubitsch's 'black tie and evening dress' events but he invited her in just the same and she soon coaxed him away from his other guests so that their conversation would remain private. Henceforth, she would drop in on Lubitsch when he was least expecting her but would *never* accept an official invitation to one of his parties.

It was at one of Ernst Lubitsch's gatherings that Garbo met the scriptwriter Salka Viertel (1889–1978), arguably the best friend and closest confidante she ever had – one who would never stab her in the back, unlike some of the others. Born Salomea Steuerman into a wealthy Jewish family (her father was mayor) in Sambor, Galicia – then a part of Poland belonging to the Austro-Hungarian Empire, and today a part of western Ukraine – Salka was astute and intellectual, fluent in eight languages and had never wanted to be anything but an actress. She had played Mary Stuart and Medea on the stage in Teplitz in Southern Bohemia (now in the Czech Republic), but on the outbreak of World War I gave up her career to volunteer as a nurse with her sister, Rose. Arriving in Vienna as a refugee fleeing from the Germans, she met the then-married writer and director Berthold Viertel (1885–1953), who subsequently divorced his wife to marry her in 1918. The couple would have three sons, of whom Peter (1920–2007) also achieved fame as a scriptwriter, besides becoming the second husband of British actress Deborah Kerr.

In 1922, the Viertels relocated to Berlin where, courtesy of Salka's acclaimed pianist brother Edward, they were hired to work for the legendary Max Reinhardt. Six years later, the equally acclaimed F. W. Murnau summoned Berthold to Hollywood to script *The Four Devils* for Fox Pictures, a venture encouraged by the Feyders, who the Viertels already knew. Berthold subsequently directed Françoise Rosay in Fox's last silent, *The One Woman Idea*. In Hollywood, the Viertels quickly integrated with the emigré intellectual clique – Murnau, the Feyders, Ernst Lubitsch (who they had known in Berlin), the Jannings, Conrad Veidt, Einstein, and eventually Garbo. Their base, where they held regular 'anti-establishment salons' similar to the ones they had hosted in Berlin, was an English-style house at 165 Mabery Road, in Santa Monica.

Garbo and Salka almost got off to a bad start when Salka confessed that she had seen only one of her films: *Gösta Berlings Saga*. Fortunately, she had said the right thing – according to Salka, Garbo responded that it was the only one of her films *worth* watching! The conversation then turned to their common interest – Berlin – though only minutes into this, Garbo suddenly excused herself and slipped away into the night, only to turn up at her house unannounced the next day. 'Gaily, she announced she had come to continue the conversation of the last night, and stayed all afternoon,' said Salka. 'We went for a short walk on the beach and then sat in my room.' The two women would remain close friends for life.[206]

Salka and Sorenson helped cushion the blow when Garbo began suffering panic attacks in the wake of John Gilbert's infamous lampooning by fans and the press, which accompanied his transition to the talkies. His actual sound debut was in *Redemption*, based on Tolstoy's *The Living Corpse*, a sombre tale of drinking, dissipation and suicide, almost a reflection of what the actor's life had become. His marriage to Ina Claire had proved an abject failure. He was sleeping around indiscriminately with anyone from major stars to women he picked up in bars or off the street. Night after night he was drinking himself senseless, and always getting into trouble. Dissatisfied with the finished print of *Redemption*, MGM opted to delay its release until after Gilbert's next film, *His Glorious Night*, a Ruritanian pot-boiler directed by Lionel

Barrymore, released on 28 September. In one scene, Gilbert kisses love interest Catherine Dale Owen and three times in succession pronounces 'I love you!' in a tone that was not just high-pitched, but profoundly effeminate, bringing hoots of derision from audiences across America. In fact, Gilbert's voice was nothing like this: it was widely rumoured that the sound had been sabotaged by a technician acting on Mayer's orders – payback time for the actor hitting him at the aborted Garbo–Gilbert 'wedding'.

This debacle took place nine days before *Anna Christie* went into production and Garbo was terrified that she would soon be heading in the same direction as Clara Bow and Nita Naldi, despite reassurances from friends and studio executives that she had absolutely nothing to worry about. Mordaunt Hall, who had briefly interviewed her, observed, 'If any voice suits a personality, it is that of Miss Garbo. It is deep in tone, and her utterances are always distinct.'[207] Yet even at the eleventh hour, Garbo held Mayer and Thalberg to ransom: unsure how she would sound pronouncing her lines in English, she declared that she would only make the film providing MGM allowed her to shoot an 'export' version in German, to be directed by Jacques Feyder and with Salka Viertel playing second female lead, Marthy Owens. German was still her second language after Swedish and the studio must have been aware of her reasons for wanting this – her first films with Stiller and Pabst had been smash hits in Germany, and if the Americans did not take to her in the English version of *Anna Christie*, she knew that the Germans would.

Thalberg paid Eugene O'Neill a whopping $570,000 for the screen rights to *Anna Christie*, and brought in Frances Marion to write the script. The familiar Garbo formula was amended slightly: replacing the older love rival was Anna's cantankerous father, Kris Kristofferson. Clarence Brown directed, and there was never any question of Garbo not being photographed by William Daniels. The play had opened on Broadway in 1921, with Pauline Lord in the title role, and George F. Marion as Anna's father – a role he had reprised for the 1923 film version. Then, the *New York Times* had enthused of Blanche Sweet's Anna: 'It would be difficult to imagine any actress doing better in this role.' Little did they know!

The part of Garbo's brash Irish love interest, Matt Burke, was given to Charles Bickford (1891–1967), himself a rough-and-ready character. At the age of nine he had been tried (and acquitted) for the attempted murder of a trolley-bus driver who had killed his dog. After years as a drifter, he ended up working in burlesque, then in supporting roles on Broadway. *Anna Christie* made him a star.

Unquestionably, the film's *coup de grâce* was veteran Canadian actress, Marie Dressler (Leila Marie Koerber, 1868–1934), who plays Kristofferson's dilapidated elderly lover, Marthy. Dressler was a tragi-comic genius who had worked in vaudeville then for many years on the legitimate stage, and who arrived in Hollywood way too late – not making her first film until the age of forty-two. With her 'lived-in' features and 'fuller figure', Dressler was unrivalled at playing loveable harridans, as she does here. Garbo adored her, not just as a person but for her supreme professionalism, and the feeling was reciprocated:

> Greta works almost to the point of exhaustion, and her capacity for work is contagious. The fact is, an actor must put forth every last ounce of effort every minute of his working time, or his role will fall short miserably in comparison to Greta's uniformly splendid work. There are several actors who, for this very reason, have risen to great heights when playing opposite Garbo, only to fall back to their natural levels when appearing in other casts.[208]

Within a year of finishing *Anna Christie*, Dressler would be hailed Hollywood's number one box-office draw after Garbo, a position she retained until her death, winning an Oscar for *Min & Bill* (1931), in which she starred with Wallace Beery and scored further hits with him in *Tugboat Annie* and *Dinner at Eight* (both 1933). While working on the latter she was taken ill and Mayer had her examined by his personal physician. Incurable cancer was diagnosed, but the news was kept from her to keep her working. When Dressler finally found out, Mayer offered fake sympathy by imposing a three-hour working day so as not to tire her, and promised her a $100,000 bonus – so long as she promised to 'hang on' and complete the three films he had earmarked for her. She did, only to have Mayer go back on his word and pay her just $10,000 shortly before her death in July 1934. Because of this, Garbo is said to have loathed him more than any man on earth.

On 7 October, Clarence Brown assembled the entire cast of the film for a week's rehearsals. Garbo had never done this before and he had a tough task persuading her to turn up: in the past, she had rehearsed each scene at home – a chair or some other inanimate object standing in for whoever would be in the scene with her – then improvised when it came to doing the scene in front of the camera, *always* getting it right. Then, she need not worry about dialogue – or rather, her co-stars fluffing their lines. Nine days later, Wilhelm Sorenson drove a very apprehensive Garbo – hiding on the floor of her car – to the studio for her voice-test, and to shoot Anna's first scene in the picture, the one with Marie Dressler. Many years later, he recalled the event for a British newspaper:

> Suddenly it occurred to me that she must have stage fright, though she didn't betray herself with a word. I did not say anything either ... Then I heard a voice from underneath the rug in the car. Instead of a rich, deep timbre I heard the moving plaint of a little girl. 'Oh, Soren, I feel like an unborn child just now!' ... Just before noon, Garbo called me up to her dressing-room. 'Well, it wasn't really so bad,' she said, 'Though I became a little scared when I heard my own voice. I almost jumped out of my chair when I heard those lines played back to me ... and you should have seen how the others reacted. Alma [her maid] makes a dramatic gesture towards her forehead and appeals to the Lord. Billy [her make-up man] gets hysterics and runs out. Some of those tough boys on the set start clearing their throats. [Clarence] Brown comes up, gives me a big kiss and says, 'Wonderful, Greta!'[209]

The film opens with Kris and Marthy enjoying a spat. Anna, the twenty-year-old daughter he has not seen since she was a child, is on her way here from Minnesota, where he left her with relatives, and Marthy does not want to get in the way. While deciding what to do they head for the local bar to get plastered.

When Kris has gone home to sober up, Garbo makes her much-anticipated entrance, fifteen minutes into the film. World-weary, she drops her battered suitcase, slouches over the table and drawls the now infamous line, 'Gimme a visky. Ginger ale on the side. And don't be stingy, baby!' Henceforth her speech will be entirely in the vernacular – she utters phrases with which even some American audiences were unfamiliar, all in a thick Swedish accent that offers a delicious touch of tragi-comedy to whatever situation she is in. *The two women strike up a conversation, without Marthy letting on who she is, though not before flinging a few home truths. 'I got your number the minute you come into the room,'* Marthy admonishes, while the streetwise Anna responds, *'I got yours, without no trouble. You're me, forty years from now.'*

Anna has been somewhat economical with the truth when writing to Kris. He thinks she is a nurse because she is *'yust outa hospital for two weeks'.* The reality is that she ran away from the farm after a cousin raped her, and ended up working as a prostitute. The hospital is, in fact, a prison hospital, where she has been since she was picked up by the vice squad: *'The yudge gave all us girls thirty days ... If my old man doesn't help me, it's men again. Men all the time. Oh, how I hate them, every mother's son of them!'*

At this point, *Kris returns and the barman assures him that Marthy is still here, 'and another tramp with her.'* While he wants to get to know his daughter, she sees living on a coal barge as an unwelcome but necessary temporary arrangement: *'I could rest up for while until I felt able to get back on the yob again.'* (This gave British moviegoers a new vernacular phrase for sex.)

The next morning, father and daughter set sail. They run into a storm and are forced to rescue a group of shipwrecked sailors, one of whom is Irish loudmouth Matt Burke (what happens to the others once they are on board is not explained, nor why Kris' skipper, Johnson, appears only in this scene). *Burke tries to molest Anna, she knocks him out, and he concludes that for the first time in his life he is in the presence of a real lady.*

They dock in New York and head for Coney Island. (Garbo having fun on the Big Dipper – an image few fans expected to see on the big screen!) *Back on the barge, Anna kisses Burke, telling him this is her way of saying goodbye: she has never loved a man as much as him, which is why she cannot marry him. Then, when the two men in her life begin fighting, Anna goes into meltdown. Actress and character merge as Garbo delivers one of her personal philosophies: 'You can go to blazes, both of you ... Nobody owns me, see, excepting myself. I'll do what I please. And no man, I don't give a darn who it is, can tell me what to do ... I am my own boss. Now, put that in your pipe and smoke it!' Anna admits that she has been raped and for two years she has worked in the same kind of 'house' that Kris and Burke visit while on shore leave – she only ended up in such a mess because her father abandoned her, she says. She decides to return to her former life, while the two men aim to give her and each other some space by sailing for South Africa, though ironically they end up signing to serve on the same ship. In the end, all turns out reasonably well: Anna swears on Burke's crucifix that she never loved any of the men she slept with – an oath which means nothing because she is Lutheran – and the men begrudgingly make up, leaving us with the impression that the wedding will take place when they come home.*

Shooting wrapped on 18 November on what had been for Garbo her toughest schedule to date: five-day blocks comprising two days of rehearsals, two days shooting, and a day off while Clarence Brown filmed scenes not involving her. Unable to come up with a suitable tag-line for a movie about an ex-prostitute which would not offend moral and religious groups, Irving Thalberg plumped for the obvious: all over America, hoardings proclaimed in large letters, 'GARBO TALKS!'

Thalberg also warned Harry Edington that his client had better turn up for the previews, if not the actual Hollywood premiere, fixed for 22 January 1930. This was an important milestone in MGM's history and absolutely everyone involved with the production would be there – even the sound stage cleaners. Garbo ignored the command – though 'Alice Smith' is known to have sneaked in to watch the film when it went out on general release.

One of Garbo's fiercest and most unrelenting critics who emerged at around this time was Mary Cass Canfield, the influential sister of publishing executive Augustus Canfield, president of Harper

& Row. Her 'Letter To Garbo', later published in *Theatre Arts*, was very definitely *not* appreciated by its subject, and fortunately appeared too late to damage her reputation as a serious actress. While applauding Garbo's grace, glamour and finesse, Canfield did not reckon much to her performance here:

> Emotionally, Miss Garbo, you were walking in your sleep. Your Anna Christie was a wind-blown dryad, quite adequate in make-up and attitude, and never once touched the core of the character. Those of us who remember Miss Pauline Lord in the original theatre production will always celebrate her Anna: the infinite patience of her suffering, her foiled affection indicated with that reticent, glancing beauty ... You gave no such wistful overtones, no sense of being a lost soul at bay. Your acting was in one competent dimension, without vistas or variety. Your performance was picturesque, but there was no wisdom in it and there were no tears.

Many would have argued that Garbo played a 'lost soul at bay' in virtually *all* of her films. The plot of *Anna Christie* could almost have been inconsequential. The costumes, accredited to Adrian, were, aside from the one Garbo wears during Anna's trip to Coney Island, little better than could be purchased at the bargain counter in any department store. The acting, Garbo and Marie Dressler aside, is lamentable. George F. Marion looks and sounds silly much of the time – his pronouncing his daughter's name at the end of almost every line, and his persistent reference to the sea as 'that old devil' soon becomes monotonous. One also finds it hard that even an allegedly hard-bitten prostitute such as Anna Christie would have looked twice at an ever-yelling oik like Matt Burke extant of her patch. It was of course the Garbo *voice* that everyone was interested in and whether this would disappoint, as had happened with the near-defunct Clara Bow, Mary Pickford, Pola Negri, and of course John Gilbert. Richard Watts Jr observed in the *New York Herald Tribune*, 'Her voice is revealed as a deep, husky, throaty contralto that possesses every bit of that poetic glamour that has made this distant Swedish lady the outstanding actress of the motion picture world.'[210] Mordaunt Hall, who had applauded the quality of Garbo's voice long before the public heard it, wrote in the *New York Times*:

> Whether she is dealing with straight English or the vernacular, she compels attention by her deep-toned enunciation and the facility with which she handles Anna's slang ... She is a real Anna, who at once enlists sympathy for her hard life. The words and expressions of this girl make one think of her in character, and cause one almost to forget that she is Miss Garbo ... who proves here that she can handle a forceful role with little or no relief in its dull atmosphere just as well as she can play the part of the fashionably dressed, romantic wife of a moneyed lawyer.[211]

The review which amused Garbo the most came from Norbert Lusk of *Picture Play* because, having witnessed John Gilbert's vocal downfall, Lusk assumed that studio wizardry was again involved, but this time to the star's advantage:

> The voice that shook the world! It's Greta Garbo's, of course, and for the life of me I can't decide whether it's baritone or bass ... and there isn't another like it. Disturbing, incongruous, its individuality is so pronounced that it would belong to no one less strongly individual than Garbo herself. Yet it doesn't wholly belong to her, but seems a trick of the microphone in exaggerating what in real life is merely a low-keyed voice, slightly husky...

Of Garbo's acting skills, however, Lusk was in no doubt:

> The Swedish star attempts one of the most difficult roles in the contemporary theatre. The part is almost a monologue, a test for an actress experienced in speech, a brave feat for one who is not ... a magnificent effort, a gallant fight against great odds. She emerges not quite victorious but crowned with laurels, nevertheless, for her courage.[212]

CHAPTER EIGHT

WELTSCHMERZ

'I will probably remain a bachelor all my life. Wife is such an uggly [sic] word!'

Anna *Christie* was the highest grossing film of 1930. Despite the emergence of soup-kitchens and bread-lines in the wake of the Wall Street Crash, impoverished Americans could still find those crucial few cents to get them into the movies where, for a few hours, they could escape the miseries of the Depression. Yet Wilhelm Sorenson recalls Garbo's disappointment with the American version, remarking, 'Isn't it terrible? Who ever saw Swedes *act* like that?' On the other hand she was so impressed by Marie Dressler's performance that, as had happened with Ernst Lubitsch, she had Sorenson drive her to Dressler's house, where she presented the ageing star with a huge bunch of yellow chrysanthemums.

Garbo's friends, meanwhile, were stunned when she announced that she would be hosting a Christmas Eve party at Chevy Chase Drive, moreover, that as most of her guests would doubtless end up worse for wear, she would be expecting them to stay overnight. So far, the only ones to do this had been Sorenson and Nils Asther. Few of her friends took her seriously: Garbo was notorious for inviting people around, then instructing the Norins to announce that she was not in or suffering from some mysterious malady when they turned up on the doorstep, when all the while she would be hiding upstairs. This time, she carried it through, buying a huge pine tree and decorating the living room with holly, poinsettias and mistletoe. Asther and Sorenson were recruited to help with the Christmas shopping – at the local five-and-ten-cents store. Her purchases befitted her warped sense of humour: toothbrushes, boys' neckties, tins of soup, and boxes of dominoes! William Daniels was the exception, receiving a solid gold cigarette lighter. Besides her two beaus, the guests included the Viertels, the Jannings, the Feyders and the Loders. This being a traditional Swedish Christmas party, everyone was expected to arrive with a hearty appetite: the Norins served a twenty-dish smorgasbord starter, followed by goose with all the trimmings, aquavit, and apple cake. Afterwards, instead of being allowed to sleep off their excesses, Garbo insisted that *everyone* strip off and jump into the pool.

In January 1930, the great Spanish dancer La Argentina (Antonia Mercé y Luque, 1890–1936) visited Los Angeles with her troupe. Garbo had always admired her neo-classical flamenco style, and may have seen her in Berlin – her costume in *Torrent* was modelled on one of La Argentina's stage outfits. Sorenson secured a box at the theatre for Garbo, himself, the Loders and Nils Asther, and the actress stuck out like the proverbial sore thumb wearing a gold lamé pyjama jacket, knee-length black skirt, dark glasses and a cloche hat. She met La Argentina before the show – the dancer acknowledged her after her first tableau, and throughout the rest of the revue all eyes were focused on Garbo and not the stage, forcing her make a hasty exit before La Argentina took her curtain calls.

Since Feyder would not be available to shoot the German *Anna Christie* until the summer, Garbo and Thalberg mutually agreed that her next project would be *Romance*, produced by Paul Bern and directed by Clarence Brown. The story, the subject of a play by Edward Sheldon, was very loosely based on the life of Lina Cavalieri (1874–1944), the controversial Italian soprano whose career began in the café-concerts of Paris. Four times married, Cavalieri became a stalwart with the New York Metropolitan Opera and partnered the greatest names of her day, including Caruso. Garbo had seen the play in Stockholm while studying at the Academy, and asked that the screenplay adhere as closely as possible to the singer's life. By the time scriptwriter Bess Meredyth 'cleaned up' the singer's story to placate the censor, virtually nothing remained of the real Cavalieri, or anyone associated with her.

Garbo's first choice of leading man was Gary Cooper, then contracted to Paramount. 'She knew that he was going to be making *Morocco* with me, and she wanted him first,' said Marlene Dietrich.[213] Marlene was expected in Hollywood at the end of April, having been signed by the studio to compete with Garbo, and Garbo was hoping that *Romance* would be completed by then. Paramount, however, refused to loan out Cooper, and Thalberg suggested Douglas Fairbanks Jr, who Garbo had accused of 'dying badly' in *A Woman of Affairs*. She was happy to consider him – until she learned that his stepmother, Mary Pickford, had persuaded Thalberg to offer him the part because she felt that, since marrying Joan Crawford, Fairbanks had been pushed out of the spotlight and needed the big boost that working with Garbo would provide. Eventually she settled for Gavin Gordon (1901–83) – a strapping, 6′ 2″, Mississippi-born stage actor who had recently made his Hollywood debut, *His First Command*, opposite Dorothy Sebastian. Shooting was set to begin 17 March.

There were rumours of a romance between Garbo and Gordon, which he quickly dispelled, declaring she was way out of her league: 'If I had the dynamic personality of a David, the gifts of Sophocles and the appearance of Helios, I should perhaps dare to endeavour to win Garbo's attention and favours!'[214] Gordon was perhaps selling himself short. He was well-educated, possessed of a sparkling personality and extremely handsome with a perfect profile comparable to that of John Barrymore – but he was also spoken for. Garbo knew that Gordon was in a relationship – and would be for another forty years – with the actor Edward Everett Horton, fifteen years his senior. Horton was famed for his 'Nervous Nellie' roles; the mode of portrayal for the majority of on-screen homosexuals in 1930s and 1940s Hollywood.

Marie Dressler recalled Garbo's plight while they were working on *Anna Christie*: 'Garbo is lonely. She always has been, and she always will be. She lives in the core of a vast aching loneliness.'[215] Sorenson was starting to get on her nerves: often when he turned up at Chevy Chase Drive she made an excuse not to see him. Lilyan Tashman called several times, but the Norins had been instructed to hang up on her. Sven Hugo Borg tried to see her, but Garbo had heard rumours that he was writing a book about their time together, and wanted nothing more to do with him. Nils Asther was still in touch, but their outings were few and far between now that, against Garbo's 'brotherly' advice, he was about to marry Vivian Duncan, having decided to stay on in Hollywood for the time being and take his chances with the talkies, despite his limited English. There were, however, still the soirées with the Viertels, and every now and then Garbo dropped in on Ernst Lubitsch.

But Garbo was not lonely for long, having set her cap at somebody else. She had recently seen *They Had to See Paris*, a Frank Borsage comedy starring Will Rogers and Fox's latest 'import', Fifi d'Orsay – a trite story about an American oil tycoon who takes his family on a trip to Paris, mindless of his pathological hatred of the French. Garbo was knocked sideways by the 'French' star who knew Jacques Feyder and, upon hearing from him that Fifi may have a crush on her, asked him to arrange an intimate supper in a darkened corner of the Russian Eagle.

Though nicknamed 'The French Bombshell', Fifi (Marie-Rose Lussier, 1904–83) hailed from Montreal, Canada, and had never set foot in France. As Yvonne Lussier she relocated to New York in 1924, where she successfully auditioned for the *Greenwich Village Follies*, and introduced the French-language version of 'Yes, We Have No Bananas'. Having lied to the producer that she had been born and raised in Paris, and worked at the Folies Bergère, she was billed 'Mademoiselle Fifi'; the d'Orsay, after her favourite perfume, came later.

Feyder 'chaperoned' Garbo's first date with her at the end of January in case it resulted in another 'unfortunate situation', as had happened with Ruth Biery. This meeting went well, and the two began seeing each other on a regular basis but if Fifi telephoned Garbo a dozen times every day, she was never invited to her home. She was also indiscreet, something which Garbo only became aware of when it was too late. In New York, Fifi had had relationships with several men but the affair which had been the talk of the theatrical world was with torch singer Helen Morgan. In Hollywood, the gossip columnists picked up on this, drawing attention to the title of her latest film, *Women Everywhere*. That Garbo was alarmed when Gustav Norin returned home with the newspapers one morning and she read what had been written in the *Los Angeles Record* may have been putting it mildly:

Greta Garbo and Fifi d'Orsay have become inseparable friends. Everywhere that Greta goes, Fifi is sure to tag along ... Greta stays in her shell and is so reserved that Hollywood has been greatly amused and interested in this dalliance. Fifi is Greta's first pal since Lilyan and Greta parted company. Greta sings the songs Fifi sang in *They Had To See Paris*, and Fifi retaliates by trying to talk Swedish. Just how long it will last, no one knows, but the two 'gals' are certainly a colourful pair ...[216]

Obviously, the writer of the piece was 'in the know' about Garbo's more intimate relationships, probably having been enlightened by Fifi herself, possibly by way of a little pillow talk. It is extremely unlikely that Hedda Hopper, Louella Parsons or any other top-ranking journalist would have penned such a story – most were too straitlaced and (particularly Louella) fanatically religious to report a sex scandal involving two women. One thinks, therefore, of two reporters with Sapphic tendencies, who had been snubbed by Garbo in the past and therefore had axes to grind: Katherine Albert and Ruth Biery, who later observed:

Fifi was young, impulsive, unable to understand upon such a brief acquaintance the reasons for Garbo's reticence. In fact she was incapable because of the differences between the French and Swedish natures of comprehending at all the complex motives for Garbo's silence. She gabbled all she knew.[217]

An outraged Garbo refused to speak to Fifi d'Orsay again but rather than submit to defeat, Fifi complained in person to the newspaper which had broken the story, only to have them lampoon her by publishing her 'confession' exactly as she had pronounced it:

Most of ze interviewairs say theengs I never say, like saying I am from ze Folies Bergère when I nevair have been to Paris. And zat I am ze inseapairable friend of Greta Garbo! All zat ees a big lie. I have seen Greta Garbo maybe four times in my whole life ... I theenk she ees ze greatest of all actresses. You can tell everybody Fifi say zat. But I am not her – inseapairable friend, even eef I would like to be![218]

As had happened with Eva von Berne, getting on the wrong side of Garbo put paid to Fifi d'Orsay's Hollywood career. Unable to cope with the humiliation, she broke her contract with Fox and was blacklisted by all the major studios. Later in her career she worked successfully on television, mostly appearing as herself on variety and game shows, and made her Broadway debut, at sixty-six, in the Tony Award-winning musical, *Follies*. She died in 1983, aged seventy-nine.

Meanwhile, *Romance* hit a snag on the first day of shooting when Gavin Gordon was injured in an accident en route to the studio. Excited about working with Garbo, he later said, and not concentrating on the road, he failed to swerve when another vehicle pulled out of a side street and collided with him. Gordon was flung out of his car and landed on the pavement, dislocating his shoulder and fracturing his collarbone. Though in agony, he managed to reach the studio and was shooting his first scene with Garbo when he passed out. When he came to in the hospital, she was at his bedside, having accompanied him in the ambulance. His next visitor was one of Irving Thalberg's assistants – not to offer get well wishes, but to inform the actor that MGM were replacing him. But Garbo was having none of this: if this happened, Thalberg would have to find himself another leading lady. Gordon was reprieved, and until he was well enough to continue, Clarence Brown worked around him.

Romance is a rarely seen, truly beautiful film – a juxtapostion of worldliness, sensitivity and sexual innocence, complimented by a series of stunning performances from the lead actors. Garbo is the temptress who comes good in the end – imperious, conceited but eventually not without heart. Gavin Gordon is out-and-out camp in his portrayal of the timid virgin cleric, but this works in his favour because his persistent fidgeting and over-the-top mannerisms evoke how any sexually inexperienced young man might feel when under the spell of a man-eating diva such as Rita Cavallini.

Bishop Tom Armstrong (Gavin Gordon) *is visited by his grandson, Harry* (Elliott Nugent), *who is about to bring shame on the family by marrying an actress. To help him make up his mind, Tom recalls his 'great adventure', half a century ago, which ended one New Year's Eve such as this.*

We hear a recording of Rita Cavallini performing 'The Last Rose of Summer' and return to the home of New York millionaire Cornelius von Tuyl (Lewis Stone), *who is throwing a party for his lover, Rita. She will sing here tonight. Alone with him, Rita bemoans the fact that she has never been in love, and delivers the first of many speeches in which her character's philosophy fuses with the actress's own: 'Sometimes I wish that I had died before I ever heard those words, 'I love you!' ... What is love? It's made of kisses in the dark, hot breath on the face, a heart that beats with terrible strong blows. Love is just a beast that you feed all through the night. And when morning comes, love dies!'*

Cornelius leaves her to rest until her performance and Tom, who has not seen her until now and does not recognise her, wanders into the room. He tells her he does not drink, though by the time she has finished flirting with him he is sharing her wine, and she purrs, 'How do you like it when I drink to what I see in your eyes, and you drink to what you see in mine?' When he scolds her for embracing an admirer's flowers as she would a lover, she philosophises once more: 'They were born to die. Our meeting here tonight – what is it but a bunch of flowers that we love and smell, then throw away? Why should we take them home and watch them die?' Moments later she sings and the penny drops for both of them: they fall in love.

The weeks pass, and Cornelius is relegated to a 'father-confessor' figure, who begs Rita to end her relationship with Tom before she breaks his heart, as she has done with all the other men in her life. New Year's Eve arrives. She is to give her farewell performance before returning to Europe, and she tells the young rector, 'A dream. I guess that's all that I am. A dream that's lost her way and rests a minute in your sleepy heart. Tomorrow you will wake up and the dream's all gone!' She wants him to sail with her but he declines with the plum line, 'I've got a meeting at the Board of Charities tomorrow at eleven, and Patrick Crowler's funeral at twelve!' More debate follows, and a plum line of her own: 'Let me tell you something that I hope you will remember. Yesterday's a dream that we have forgot. Tomorrow's the hope for some great happiness that'll never come. Before, behind – just clouds and shadows. Nothing that is real but just this little minute that we call today ... Oh, mon Dieu! Why do you keep the oar over there?' (She is referring to the memento from his college days, when he rowed

Garbo and her Svengali, Mauritz Stiller, arriving in New York at the start of her Hollywood adventure, July 1925.

With her favourite co-star, Lars Hanson, in *The Divine Woman* (1928), the only Garbo film of which no complete print survives.

With Nils Asther in *The Single Standard* (1929). Though openly gay in a prejudiced Hollywood, Asther did have an affair with Garbo. © Getty Images Ltd

As Helga, the poor girl rescued from prostitution by a rough and ready Clark Gable, in *Susan Lenox* (1931).

'I am tired of being a symbol. I long to be a human being!' Garbo's finest role, in *Queen Christina* (1933), one of the greatest films of all time and this author's favourite.

'I shall never yearn for spring again!' On the set of *Marie Walewska* (1937).

'Perhaps it's better if I live in your heart, where the world can't see me.' As the dying courtesan Marguerite Gauthier in *Camille* (1937).

With Robert Taylor in *Camille* (1937). Just seconds after this photograph was taken, Garbo's gown caught fire. Headlines screamed of the co-stars' burning passion; in reality Garbo was almost certainly not Taylor's type! © Getty Images Ltd

'Stalin won't like it. Molotov may recall his envoy from MGM,' observed one critic when faced with Garbo's lampooning of Russia in *Ninotchka* (1939).

Greta Garbo flanked by Sven Hugo Borg (left), who may have fathered her child, and Victor Sjöström (right).

for his team, but religious groups believed Garbo had pronounced the word 'whore' and wanted the line cut, which did not happen.)

Tom gives Rita his mother's pendant, which causes her to recall her miserable past, and they discover they share the same favourite song, 'Annie Laurie', though it is he who sings it, while she accompanies him at the piano. They kiss while a choir sings out in the vestry. Then the spell is broken when Tom tells her he loves her, and when Cornelius arrives, she confesses to Tom that they were once lovers. (In the original scene Rita says, 'Until the night I met you, I was his mistress!' This was deemed 'indecent' by the Hays Office and Thalberg ordered a retake in which Rita says, 'I was his–', enabling Cornelius to cut her off sharply by exclaiming, 'Rita!')

The next day, Tom tries to 'save her soul', though he ends up trying to seduce her, forcing her to push him away: 'Don't treat me like the others have. You're a man that God sent to help the world … Go away, Tom. My heart will go with you always … if only you will let me keep my soul!' (The next scene was the most intensely moving that Garbo had filmed to date. William Daniels photographed her in close-up, before slowly panning out to long-shot: for one whole minute, accompanied by a heavenly choir, she stands in the centre of the room, motionless and proud, becoming almost holy.)

As 'The Last Rose of Summer' is reprised, we return to the older Tom, telling his grandson that he should follow his heart and marry the woman he loves – for tonight he has read in the newspaper that Rita has just died in a Swiss convent. (The real Rita lived on until 1944, when she was killed during a bombing raid on Florence.) *Not one of Garbo's best-known films, but a masterpiece just the same!*

The film wrapped on 25 April, and premiered on 22 August 1930. After criticising producers Thalberg and Bern for casting Garbo in the role of an Italian soprano, when in his opinion she did not look like one, the *New York Times'* Mordaunt Hall saw fit to praise her in the end: 'Her fascinating countenance and her graceful movements are admirably suited to the role in this slender narrative which moves along so easily that there is never an instant one would take one's eyes from the screen.'

Norbert Lusk enthused in *Picture Play*:

Her performance is a thing of pure beauty, an inspiring blend of intellect and emotion, a tender, poignant portrait of a woman who thrusts love from her because she considers herself unworthy of it ... It is the same voice that was heard in *Anna Christie*, but it is better suited to the present role, because the character has many moods and none of the bitterness of Anna ... What matter if Garbo's accent only suggests the Italian's efforts to speak English? The Garbo voice itself is not of Italian quality or inflection but for all one cares Rita Cavallini might as well be Portuguese or Romanian, for it is her emotions that are conveyed by Garbo to the spectator, and her nativity counts for nothing at all.[219]

Garbo was Oscar-nominated for both *Anna Christie* and *Romance* but lost out to Norma Shearer, who won the Best Actress Award for *The Divorcee*. Many accused the Motion Picture Academy of favouring the boss's wife, and they were right.

Around the same time, Garbo also lost her housekeepers. Gustav Norin told Rilla Page Palmborg that he and his wife had handed in their notice because they could no longer put up with her mood-swings and inordinate demands. He added:

She was always ringing the bell all through the night. She would call me to put the cats out and bring them back in. She would want a glass of water or a certain newspaper. There was always something she wanted in the middle of the night ... After a gay time, Garbo often lapsed into a moody spell ... She would stay in her bedroom for days, coming out only to swim or take walks at night. She didn't want to talk to anyone when she was in one of her moods ... Day after day we saw the real Garbo, without pause or pretence. Yet we never felt that we actually knew her. There was something distant and aloof about Garbo that neither of us could penetrate.[220]

In fact, the Norins were fired because Garbo had found out about Gustav's double-dealings with the press. The couple were the latest in an increasing roster of 'traitors': Ruth Biery, Lilyan Tashman, Fifi d'Orsay and Wilhelm Sorenson, the one she had trusted more than most, had all talked about her to reporters. Until Edington could find replacements, Garbo hired a new maid – her name was Ettie but she always answered to the name 'Whistler' – who moved into Chevy Chase Drive to take care of her. There was also a helper named James, who turned up one day to clean the windows. Unusually for her, instead of hiding until he finished his work, Garbo invited him in for tea, took a shine to him, and employed him on the spot as her chauffeur-factotum. She would be even more demanding with Whistler and James than she had been with Borg and the Norins but they remained loyal throughout their time with her and never spoke about her to the press.

Not long afterwards, Garbo moved to a property on Camden Road, formerly occupied by Marie Prevost and close to a streetcar station. Complaining that the noise from this kept her awake at night, she moved out after three weeks into a two-storey, three-bedroom stucco house at 1717 San Vicente Boulevard, near the beach in Santa Monica. Approached by a long drive lined with cypress trees, its only drawback was that there was no pool – a problem which Garbo solved by getting up at the crack of dawn each day, when hardly anyone was around, and going for a swim in the sea. On 9 July, she began shooting the German *Anna Christie* – with Salka Viertel in the Marie Dressler role, and two of Germany's finest actors imported by Thalberg for the other leads: Hans Junkermann (1872–1943) played her father, and Theo Shall (1896–1955) was Matt Burke.

Garbo always favoured this version of *Anna Christie*, which premiered in Cologne in December 1930, to the American one. It is certainly more in keeping with the great German films of the day – *The Threepenny Opera* and *The Blue Angel* – in that it does not 'pussy-foot' around the contentious issue of prostitution. What Clarence Brown's film implies, Feyder's applauds in no uncertain terms. Anna is not just a girl from a 'house' who hates men – she is a 'whore' who loathes 'dirty pigs'. By increasing the fog levels and dinginess of the waterfront scenes, and by getting the make-up department to add a few lines to Garbo's face and dark rings around her eyes, he makes us *believe* she is a dockside doxy, as Pabst does Lotte Lenya in *The Threepenny Opera*. Garbo becomes, vocally and physically, as wretched as one would expect

from a twenty-year-old girl who has been raped and forced to sell
her body to any wreck of a man in order to survive. She smokes
and drinks more and makes more of her first scene. Dressed like
one of the Reeperbahn's finest (though this is still New York) and
uncannily resembling Joan Crawford (who, one year later would
base her portrayal of 'swamp tramp' Sadie Thompson in *Rain* on
Garbo's performance here), she is less slouchy at the table when
demanding of the barman, '*Whisky – aber nicht zu knapp!*' Salka
Viertel's Marthy, though not a patch on Marie Dressler's, is *very*
different – there is no mistaking the intonations as she glances
sideways at Anna, licks her lips and pronounces, 'You look all
done in. You been on a bender?' Theo Shall is also less abrasive
than Charles Bickford: kindly, sensual and handsome – the sort
of man Anna would feel drawn to, and comfortable about spending the rest of her life with after all the creeps she has known, as
opposed to Bickford's caveman bravado and bullying.

Meanwhile, on 31 August, John Gilbert and Ina Claire announced
they were separating after just fifteen months of marriage. Garbo
was surprised, but only that, considering Gilbert's record, they had
lasted so long. The next day, Sorenson, the man who had clung to
her like a limpet for almost a year, stormed out of her life. He had
received word from his wealthy parents that they were tired of his
loafing around, and that they would be cutting off his monthly
allowance unless he found a worthwhile profession and refrained
from hanging around movie stars. When he asked Garbo's advice,
her response was a curt, 'Go home, Soren!'

In the middle of September, MGM announced that Garbo's
next film, *Inspiration*, based on Alphonse Daudet's *risqué* 1884
novel, *Sappho*, would begin shooting on 15 October. This had been
filmed as *The Eternal Sappho* in 1916 with vamp Theda Bara. In
Daudet's book, Fanny Legrand is a courtesan, the kept woman of
a number of wealthy patrons but her true love is Jean, a young
engineer. MGM would not consider the idea of Garbo falling for
a mere engineer, and there was no way that the Hays Office would
have permitted a name like Fanny (in the Bara film, she is Laura
Gubbins). Garbo's *demimondaine* was called Yvonne Valbret and
given a fluffy hairstyle.

Playing her main love interest was former stage actor Robert Montgomery (1904–81). Only marginally less dull than Conrad Nagel, though he would improve and go on to better things, Montgomery had appeared as an extra in *The Single Standard*. 'Working with Garbo is an education in screen art,' he enthused at the time, though he soon changed his tune when, after completing the film, she decided that she would rather not work with him again as he had kept fluffing their love scenes. In 1968, when biographer Norman Zierold approached some of the people who had worked with her for anecdotes and reminiscences, Montgomery was the only one to offer a negative response: 'I'm not interested in discussing Garbo.'[221]

In a Paris club, a quartet of elderly artists toasts their muse, Yvonne Valbret, who they have all sponsored and slept with. Her friend Lulu (Marjorie Rambeau, who gets the best lines here) *explains to a group of horizontalistes who this creature is: 'She's as well known as the Eiffel Tower and twice as beautiful. Half the men in Paris are crazy about her, and the other half are trying to forget her. She makes the rest of you trollops look like scrubweeds!' And Yvonne's favours are not restricted to the rich: when someone asks her chauffeur if she rewarded him for taking her luggage up to her room, he beams, 'I'll say she did. And my breakfast on a tray besides.' One of her many suitors is a gentleman called Delval* (Lewis Stone), *whose latest squeeze is seventeen-year-old chorus girl Liane* (Karen Morley) – *she later flings herself off a balcony when he dumps her. 'All alike, you men,' Yvonne drawls. 'You only want the situation of being through with us first. So far I've had the satisfaction of beating you to it, so I'm heartless.'*

When Yvonne sees handsome student diplomat André Mantell, she pounces on him. 'I lak yoor rice (I like your eyes)!' she says, and within minutes he is carrying her up the stairs to his apartment. The next morning, over breakfast, she gives him flowers and tells him all she wants him to know about her: 'I'm just a nice young woman, not too young, not too nice.' He assures her that this is just a fling and that once he graduates, he will leave Paris. This suits her: he will be gone before he finds out the kind of woman she really is. Lulu warns that she will end up in the gutter, and this amuses her: 'That will not be so bad. I know some very nice people in the gutter.'

When André finds out that Yvonne's opulent home is being paid for by a former lover, he is disgusted and ends their relationship, though he himself is a pretty obnoxious character who balks at introducing Yvonne to his snooty family because he thinks her beneath him. The next time he sees her she is in a café, unable to pay her bill. Moved to pity he rescues her and installs her in his country house. But she soon learns that he has brought her there because he has a fiancée in Paris, so she slips off into the night to meet up with a former lover who has been imprisoned for forging cheques to keep her in her accustomed style – he has promised to turn over a new leaf and asked her to marry him.

Shooting wrapped on 10 December, and the film was premiered in February 1931. Elizabeth Yeaman of *Hollywood Citizen-News* believed that with such material, Garbo had had her day: 'There is something about the appearance of Garbo which suggests a vitriolic past and an empty future. As Walter Pater so aptly said of da Vinci's painting of the *Mona Lisa*, 'She has been a fisher in deep seas and the eyelids are a little weary.' Katherine Albert, writing for *Photoplay*, was less interested in the film than in Garbo's supposed revelation to her that she was hoping to return to the stage, providing the rehearsal techniques were the same as in the studio. 'I'd have the whole cast rehearse and have another woman do my part. Then when it was ready, I'd come in and play the role,' she told Albert.[222] *Variety* declared it the best film Garbo had ever made, which was perhaps going a little too far, adding, 'Replete with heavy stuff, she plays it easily and convincingly, even contributing a sparkling brief bit of light comedy and often helping long passages of awkward dialogue to sound almost real.' But *Picture Play*'s Norbert Lusk, while still adoring his favourite actress, disliked it intensely:

Handicapped by the material provided for her, Greta Garbo still shines with such brightness that it is only when the picture is well under way that one realises the weight and dreariness of her burden. For not even the greatest artist maintains effulgence in the murk of a poor picture. That is why laurels for Garbo should be dewed with tears of regret. She makes her heroine sensitive, intelligent, alluring, with a shimmer of laughter like sunshine after an April shower. So superior indeed is Yvonne to the trite circumstances of her story that you feel the player, aware of the disparity, is spurred on to greater effort.[223]

Several times during shooting, Garbo told Clarence Brown that after this film she was thinking of returning to Sweden for good, and that this time she meant it. At the back of her mind were fears that she might be about to be gazumped by Marlene Dietrich. *The Blue Angel* was yet to be released in America but *Morocco* had opened in November 1930 and proved a box-office sensation. Now, there was talk of Marlene playing Dutch spy Mata Hari, a role MGM had earmarked as the next-but-one for Garbo. Paramount would subsequently change their minds and cast Marlene in *Dishonoured*, directed by her mentor Josef von Sternberg and playing another sultry spy called X-27. Garbo-like, she drawls at the beginning of the film, 'I am not afraid of life, though I'm not afraid of death, either,' and who, at the end of the production suffers high-camp martyrdom by checking her reflection in a soldier's sword when there is a hitch with the firing-squad. Garbo favourite Norbert Lusk sarcastically observed of this scene, 'It is as if the Delphic Oracle has stepped down from her pedestal to give her opinion of the weather.'[224]

In the *Los Angeles Examiner*, Louella Parsons exacted her revenge on Garbo for all those refused interview requests: 'There is a definite likeness to Greta Garbo, although Miss Dietrich is prettier.'[225] Whether Garbo did seriously consider throwing in the towel because of the fuss being afforded to Marlene is not known – she had vowed to return to Sweden so many times that few took the threat seriously any more. MGM grew worried, however, when Harry Edington told *Motion Picture Classic*'s Jack Grant that his client could leave Hollywood any time she wanted because she had invested enough money to afford her to live in luxury for the rest of her life. 'If Garbo retires, it will not be because of a loss of popularity,' Edington concluded, 'But if she does go back to Sweden – I say *if* – my bet is that someday she will return and make the greatest picture of her career.'[226]

Garbo may have forgotten the slightly older German extra who had caught her as she fainted outside the butcher's shop in *Die Freudlose Gasse* – she certainly had not linked the film's murderess with the Lola-Lola of *The Blue Angel* until enlightened by Salka Viertel. Though in her later years Marlene pretended not to like Garbo – usually referring to her as 'that other actress' or 'the Swedish woman', and never by name – she and Garbo did admire each other's work. At her apartment in Paris, Marlene would regularly watch *Queen Christina* after its release, and in 1931 her recordings of *Ich bin von Kopf bis Fuss auf liebe eingestellt* and *Quand l'amour meurt* were hardly ever off Garbo's turntable. In fact, Marlene was not that much of a threat: she left Hollywood after completing *Dishonoured* to embark on a trip to Europe, and did not return to New York until April 1931, to be served with a writ from Josef von Sternberg's wife for 'alienation of a husband's love'. The case amounted to nothing and if anything bought MGM a little time – by the time Marlene began her next film, *Shanghai Express*, Garbo was preparing for *Susan Lenox: Her Fall and Rise*, the story of another prostitute who redeems herself in the last reel.[227]

That spring, Garbo also faced two personal dilemmas. The first was the abject humiliation wrought upon her by 'the actor who never was' – her brother Sven, to whom she had written only occasionally since seeing his failed screen test in Stockholm. In 1929 he made his film debut with the SFI in *Konstgjorda Svensson* and the following year in London he played the lead in *When the Roses Bloom*, an Anglo-Swedish production, and the first Swedish talkie, released in America as *The Hole in the Wall*. Garbo might have been less upset had he been billed under his own name and not as Sven Garbo. What incensed her the most was the review in *Photoplay* attacking his phoney matinée idol presumptions: 'He's a tall, limp, black-haired boy with a minute moustache, and doesn't bear the faintest resemblance to his famous sister. And he's a punk actor, if this is an example.'[228] Suffice to say, Sven made just one more film before calling it a day. For a while, Garbo gave him the cold shoulder for stealing her name but she later forgave him when he married an American woman, Marguerite Baltzer, and embarked on a new career studying art.

The second incident, much more distressing, was the death on

11 March of F. W. Murnau. He had recently completed a South Seas documentary, *Tabu*, and while shooting had hired a fourteen-year-old Filipino houseboy, Garcia Stevenson. It was he who was at the wheel of Murnau's Packard, on the highway between Los Angeles and Monterey, when it swerved to miss a truck and plunged down a steep embankment. The boy died at the scene, and Murnau the next day in the Santa Barbara Hospital. This, however, was no ordinary automobile accident, for the position of the two men when discovered in the wreckage – along with the teethmarks on Garcia's penis – left no doubt that, when the vehicle had left the road, 42-year-old Murnau had been administering a blow-job to his companion, a story which naturally travelled around Hollywood like wildfire.

Murnau would eventually be interred in Berlin's Southwest Cemetery but in the meantime he was given a paltry send-off on account of the controversy surrounding his death. Harry Edington begged Garbo not to attend the event, and Mayer is thought to have *ordered* her to keep away. Her response to this was that if she could not bid her friend farewell here in Hollywood, she would accompany his body back to Berlin and stay there, where she had been offered a position with the Max Reinhardt Theatre Group. Regardless of Murnau's esteem and popularity, only eleven people risked turning up at the ceremony. Silent stars Janet Gaynor and Charles Farrell, whose films Murnau had directed, making them household names – Farrell is alleged to have had an affair with him – offered their excuses, but Garbo was no hypocrite. She led the handful of mourners, read the eulogy – and even let it be known that she had commissioned a death-mask of her friend, which for many years would stand next to Mauritz Stiller's framed photograph, on her piano.

Garbo had wanted Clarence Brown to direct *Susan Lenox* but it now emerged that they had argued over script changes in their last picture together and he did not want to direct her. 'Brown is through as Greta Garbo's director, and King Vidor will direct her next pictures, starting with *Susan Lenox*,' observed the *Los Angeles Record*, a paper Garbo had loathed since the Fifi d'Orsay debacle.[229] And *Photoplay*'s Katherine Albert, whom she hated even more, took it upon herself to act as Brown's official mouthpiece: 'Said Clarence Brown, "I would not direct Miss Garbo again under the same conditions that prevailed during the last picture."'[230] Brown would return to the fold but not for a few more years and Thalberg brought in Robert Z. Leonard (1889–1968), who had recently directed Norma Shearer in *The Divorcée*.

The big news however was her co-star: new-kid-on-the-block Clark Gable, a thirty-year-old former labourer from Cadiz, Ohio, who, in the space of twelve months, had taken Hollywood by storm. In 1931, the year he worked with Garbo, Gable released a dozen films – from the dross of *The Painted Desert*, his movie debut with RKO, to the quality productions he made under contract to MGM. He supported Jean Harlow in *The Secret Six*, Joan Crawford in *Dance, Fools, Dance* and *Laughing Sinners*. In *A Free Soul*, he knocked Norma Shearer around, and almost caused Thalberg to have a coronary with his description of their love scenes: 'She kisses like a whore on heat – she was naked down below and I made her wet as October under her dress!' Thalberg and Gable loathed each other unconditionally, almost as much as Gable hated Mayer, but like Garbo, he was earning the studio a fortune, and got away with much more than he should have.

But if Garbo was looking forward to working with Gable, he did not share her enthusiasm. Though he had nothing against her personally, he was well aware that *any* leading man, no matter how high-ranking, would in comparison with her be regarded as little more than an 'also ran' by fans and critics alike. As a sweetener, Mayer upped Gable's salary from $650 to $1,100 a week, still only a fraction of what he was paying Garbo. The scriptwriter (the first of twenty-two) was then asked to 'customise' Gable's part by adding terms the actor used in everyday life – 'sweetie pie', 'sugar', 'honey' and 'broad'. Such words had peppered Johnny Mack Brown's vocabulary while they had been working together but Garbo did not want them on the screen and they were blue-pencilled.

Next there was the question of Gable's personal life, complicated to say the least, and which Mayer declared needed 'sorting out' sooner rather than later. Already having problems with his second marriage to Houston socialite Ria Langham, Gable was also involved with Joan Crawford *and* Johnny Mack Brown. The studio was also paying hush money to his first wife, Josephine Dillon, who was threatening to expose him to the press. In pre-fame days, while married to her, Gable had slept around indiscriminately as a way of getting himself on the Hollywood ladder. There were discreet affairs with actors Earl Larrimore and Rod La Rocque, an episode in a Beverly Hills Hotel mensroom with William Haines, which would enter Hollywood folklore, and relationships with several 'baritone babes' – movie parlance for lesbian actresses who slept with men to kill off any rumours. Indeed, one of these had been Dillon herself. Mayer was hoping that, by way of his cheque-book, all those murky secrets would stay buried, certainly while Gable was under contract to MGM. Still in his pre-moustache days, he is much better-looking here than in previous films, though he struggles to keep up with the macho, caveman image he was known for. Indeed, *who* could get away with playing tough in an amorous situation with Garbo, notorious for holding the upper hand in all of her on-screen relationships?

When the film opens we see Helga, raised in a hovel by her uncle, Ohlin (Jean Hersholt), *following the death of her unmarried mother. He treats her like a skivvy and expects her to marry his odious friend, Monstrum* (Alan Hale). *When Monstrum tries to rape her, Helga rushes out into a storm and is forced to take shelter in the garage of mining engineer Rodney* (Gable). *He asks her if she is a girl and growls, 'You'd better take your clothes off ... Aw, I didn't mean it that way. I meant change your clothes!' She dons a pair of his pyjamas and still looks gorgeous. She cooks him breakfast; he takes her fishing – and quickly they fall in love.* (This scene was dictated by Gable's MGM publicist friend, Howard Strickling, to tie in with the actor's new 'rugged he-man' image: the theory being that fans would not believe the rumours that Gable was sexually attracted to men if they saw him participating in outdoor sports because homosexuals were too 'lily-livered' for such things. Similarly, according to the dictates of 1930s Hollywood, if Garbo could fix a man breakfast, then there was hope for her one day becoming a domesticated, 'normal' wife.)

*Rodney has to go away for a few days and leaves Helga alone. Ohlin
and Monstrum try to kidnap her but fail – she steals their trap and
heads for the railway station at Lenoxville, where she decides to change
her name to Susan Lenox and boards a carriage occupied by circus
performers. The troupe is run by an elderly pervert, who agrees to
protect her from her pursuers provided she performs on stage as Fatima,
the phoney ex-favourite of a sultan. Secretly, she writes to Rodney,
who catches up with them, chins her mentor, and tells Helga they are
through. When she says she could never survive without him, Rodney
snarls, 'I tell you what'll become of you: you'll go from one man to
another just like every woman in the gutter.' If such a thing happens,
she retorts, she will make it a worthwhile gutter.*

*Helga travels with the circus, finding a new man in every town, and
ends up as the mistress of crooked politician Mike Kelly* (Hale Hamilton).
*Rodney, meanwhile, loses his job after causing a mining accident and hits
the bottle, unable to stop thinking about Helga. When Helga learns of
his plight, she cons a friend into inviting Rodney to a society party she is
hosting, on the pretext of an offer of work. They trade insults across the
dinner table and then he leaves, ending up a bum* (albeit one with sexy
designer stubble) *working for a construction company.*

*Rodney bumps into Helga again in a sleazy dancehall in Puerte Sacate.
She has now hooked up with a sea captain, who wants to marry her,
but she could never love him the way she loves Rodney: 'Since I last saw
you, no man has had a minute of me, not even a second.' Rodney treats her
as he would any whore until he realises that she is sincere. She adds that
she would love nothing more than to cook, clean and slave for him in the
dump they will be forced to live in because they are both broke* (Garbo
effectively offering to fulfil the dream of every female fan) *and when
a genuine whore propositions him in the middle of this conversation, he
promptly tosses her over the balcony! Then comes a loaded piece of dialogue,
exchanged to the strains of 'La Golondrina'* (while going over the heads
of the general public it made closeted gays everywhere whoop with
delight at a time when homosexuality was regarded by many – not
least the movie moguls and the Hays Office – as an affliction)*:*

*HELGA: We're just two cripples, twisted. Only together can we ever
become straight.*

RODNEY: You have a queer way of looking at things.

In Britain, *Susan Lenox* ran foul of the censor. David Graham Phillips (1867–1911), upon whose novel the story was based, was a women's rights activist who had been shot dead by a lunatic accusing him of promoting female depravity. Initially, the film was banned, but following a petition from MGM's London representative, 125 feet was cut from the finished print and the movie given a new title. Irving Thalberg suggested *The Stain*, but when a shocked censor argued that critics might begin speculating what *kind* of stain this was referring to, the studio settled on *The Rise of Helga*.

Shooting wrapped on 19 September 1931 and the first preview (with 'Alice Smith' sitting in the audience) took place on 10 October, six days ahead of the premiere. Like its predecessor, it drew mixed reviews. *Variety*, drawing comparisons with the 'destiny hounded woman' Garbo had played in *Anna Christie*, concluded, 'Once more she achieves an acting effect by means that baffle while they provoke.' The *New York Times'* Mordaunt Hall also disapproved:

> Being an accomplished actress, Greta Garbo makes the most of a bad bargain in the picturisation of David Graham Phillips' novel … It is rather disappointing to find her in a production which is directed along the lines of old silent film techniques, with halting and often crudely-written dialogue and episodes.

British journalist Hannen Swaffer, loathed by just about everyone in the movie industry because he rarely had anything good to say about anyone – to the extent that he even received death threats for his poisonous comments, laid into both stars:

> Why does she always have the same sullen expression and the same face, the same meaningless stare, and the same vacuous look? Genius writes a book and then mediocrity murders it … Greta Garbo has never yet shown that she has the capacity to act such a part as Susan Lenox. Duse might have played it, or Sybil Thorndike, but not Greta Garbo … And whatever started all this fuss about Clark Gable? He is moderately good-looking. He has a moderate voice. But there is nothing to distinguish him from hundreds of similar young actors

... If he died, or lived, or went on not living, you would still refrain from noticing what he could not do.[231]

The anonymous reviewer from *Photoplay* wrote of Garbo's co-star, 'If you like your romance spread thick, your passion strong and your Garbo hot, don't miss this. And take notice, you Garboites! If you were mad about her before, just wait until you see her teamed up with this manifestation of masculine S.A. called Clark Gable!'

MGM's biggest headache was condensing David Graham Phillips' two-volume, 1,000-page novel into a 75-minute scenario without dispensing too many of its key issues, and while maintaining its essential themes of sex, vice, corruption, prejudice against women and eventual redemption – without falling foul of the Hays Office. Rather than attack Garbo personally, the self-appointed guardians of public morals, headed by *Variety*'s Ruth Morris and a colleague who preferred not to be named, blamed cinema-goers for supporting and nurturing this 'current wave of on-screen filth', not America's men folk, but their wives, girlfriends and mothers. 'The smug and contented housewife subconsciously envies the glamour that surrounds cinema mistresses,' Morris opined, 'Luxury, excitement, and dangerously stolen romance are an alluring opposition to her own conventional life.'[232] Her fellow critic was more direct, heading his/her feature 'Dirt Craze Due To Women':

> Women love dirt. Nothing shocks 'em. Women are responsible for the ever-increasing public taste in sensationalism and sexy stuff. Women who make up the bulk of the picture audiences are also the majority readers of the tabloids, scandal sheets, flashy magazines and erotic books.[233]

By the end of June 1931, when the *Variety* feature appeared and the Hays Office began kicking up a fuss, twenty-two writers had worked on the *Susan Lenox* script, sometimes effecting changes while the actors were halfway through shooting a scene. Finally, on 11 July, Irving Thalberg closed down the production until a satisfactory script had been agreed upon. Garbo had also walked off the set six times – once after Clark Gable had called her a 'stuck-up broad'. It was during one of these walk-outs that Garbo formed and cemented arguably her most bizarre friendship.

Mercedes de Acosta (1893–1968) was an American playwright, costume designer, feminist, poet, vegetarian, student of the astral plane and Sapphic socialite, born in New York City of a Cuban father and a Spanish mother reputedly descended from the Dukes of Alba. A strange-looking individual with bird-like features, dark hair and shifty eyes, she invariably wore black-and-white male attire and in some photographs looks like a cross between Charlie Chaplin and a penguin. In 1920 she baffled friends by marrying the painter Abram Poole – they were hardly ever together, and divorced in 1935. Immediately after their marriage Mercedes began a stormy relationship with French actress Eve Le Galliene – prior to this there were affairs with Alla Nazimova, Tallulah Bankhead, and Isadora Duncan. Mercedes boasted over fifty female conquests on both sides of the Atlantic, sleeping with anyone so long as they had a name and, as she is known to have made up as many of those affairs as the ones which genuinely happened, it is impossible to separate truth from hearsay when discussing her sex life. Ones confirmed by personal correspondence include Pola Negri, Natalie Barney, Edith Wharton, Katharine Cornell, and Amy Lowell.

The two affairs that overshadowed the others are those Mercedes claimed to have had with Garbo and Dietrich – which must be taken with liberal pinches of salt. Whatever may have happened between Mercedes and Garbo, and Mercedes and Marlene, appears to have been wholly one-sided. Mercedes may have *claimed* to have had physical relationships with them, as opposed to the well-documented close friendships, as a means of adding to her prestige and 'pulling' power when attempting to seduce lesser mortals. She was always the one doing the chasing, frequently making a nuisance of herself in the process. Marlene confessed to having been her friend, but denied any romantic involvement. 'If that woman spent as much time having sex as she claimed, she would never have found time to eat or sleep,' she said. 'Most of the things she wrote, she made up. And there would have been no point in all of us suing her – by the time her book came out, she had no money.'[234]

Mercedes' autobiography, published in 1960, did not cause much of a splash, though it cost her the friendships of most of the women – Garbo included – who she purported to have known intimately. When she died, in 1968, penniless and in obscurity – many believed this was no less than she deserved. In 1982, author Martin Greif observed of Mercedes de Acosta, in an aptly tongue-in-cheek way:

> What is one to make of this long-forgotten writer. In old age she still affected jet-black hair slicked down with brilliantine, and her autobiography, *Here Lies the Heart*, is just as slippery. An account, in part, of her friendships and amours with famous women, it manages to say everything without saying anything, and its cast of characters is dazzling ... The best scenes, and the most hyper-ventilated, are those with Marlene Dietrich and Greta Garbo. They have to be read to be believed. Since none of the characters uttered a public peep when the book was published, we can only assume that the book was either too silly to refute or, sillier still, even true.[235]

Mercedes arrived in Hollywood in June 1931, summoned by RKO, who were interested in *East River*, a screenplay she had written for old flame Pola Negri. This was subsequently shelved but she was asked to contribute to *Rasputin & The Empress*, starring all three Barrymores, only to have her name struck from the credits – such was Hollywood's impression of her writing talents. Not long afterwards, she wormed her way into Salka Viertel's court, and it was here, and not in Constantinople, that she first met Garbo. For Mercedes, who always wore her heart prominently on her sleeve, particularly when 'collecting' celebrities, it was love at first sight:

> As we shook hands and she smiled at me I felt I had known her all my life; in fact, in many previous incarnations. As I had expected she was remarkably beautiful, far more than she seemed in her films then. She was dressed in a white jumper and dark blue sailor pants. Her beautiful straight hair hung to her shoulders and she wore a white tennis visor pulled well down over her face in an effort to hide her extraordinary eyes, which held in them a look of eternity.[236]

Mercedes adds that she presented Garbo with a slave bracelet (simi-lar to the ones favoured by Rudolph Valentino), which she had bought some time before in Berlin, anticipating this very moment, and that in their next meeting the Viertels dispatched the love-birds to the house next door whose owner, the set-designer Oliver Garrett, was away on vacation. Here, playing records non-stop, they sang and danced for hours and ended the evening doing the tango to 'Just A Gigolo'. A few evenings later, Mercedes says, she was attending a dinner party chez Pola Negri when Garbo called, summoning her at once to San Vicente Boulevard – the first time anyone had ever been invited there. The fact that Mercedes claimed that she found the almost pathologically shy Garbo waiting for her in the driveway *outside* the house, wearing a black silk dressing-gown and men's slippers, is enough in itself to suggest the event never happened.

On 12 July, the day after shooting wrapped on *Susan Lenox*, Garbo headed for Silver Lake, in the Sierra Nevadas, where she had hired Wallace Beery's log cabin, situated on an island half a mile from the shore. According to Mercedes, she set off in 'The Bus' (her name for her black Lincoln Packard) with her chauffeur, James, and after spending just two nights at the idyllic location ordered him to drive her back to Hollywood to pick up Mercedes because she was lonely. The fact that a woman, who much of the time *lived* for solitude, actually hated being alone is a paradox of the Garbo psyche. However, that this involved an 800-mile round-trip suggests in reality there was only one journey to Silver Lake, and that all three actually left together to begin with, Mercedes fabricating the story to make it appear that Garbo could not bear being away from her.

The time scale of events suggests that Garbo spent no more than ten days at Silver Lake, while Mercedes describes their vacation as, 'Six perfect weeks out of a lifetime ... with not one second of dishar-mony.' She recalled how it never rained, how Garbo had rowed them back and forth each day to the mainland to pick up supplies from the lumber-store, how they had swum naked in the lake. There may have been nothing remotely sexual in this: Garbo had done exactly the same during her vacation with Nils Asther and, by his admission, they had slept in separate rooms. The only difference is that Mercedes photographed Garbo topless and, it would appear from studying the expression on her face, with her full approval. 'No one can really know Greta unless they have seen her as I saw her there in Silver Lake,' she wrote. 'She is a creature of the elements. A creature of wind and storms and rocks and trees and water. A spirit such as hers, cooped up in a city, is a tragic sight.'[237]

Back in Hollywood, Mayer and Thalberg were so enthralled by the Garbo-Gable chemistry in *Susan Lenox* that there was talk of pairing them again in *Red Dust*, a Far Eastern drama based on the stage play by Wilson Collison. Garbo was pencilled in for the part of Vantine, the wise-cracking tart with a heart who, on the run from the Saigon police, shows up at the rubber plantation managed by the Gable character. Garbo read the script, and objected to the scene calling for Vantine to bathe in an outdoor vat containing the men's drinking water, avowing any red-blooded man would *want* to drink the water all the more after she had been in it. Producer Hunt Stromberg might have been willing to compromise had not Gable kicked up a storm about the billing – much as he liked Garbo, he would not permit her name to appear above his in the credits a second time. The part went to Jean Harlow, who made it one of her most memorable, and MGM returned to their original plan for Garbo's next vehicle: *Mata Hari*.

This film has the distinction of being the campest Garbo appeared in and bears little resemblance to the real Mata Hari story. Scripted by Benjamin Glazer and Leo Briansk, it was directed by George Fitzmaurice who, in 1926 had directed Rudolph Valentino's final film, *Son of the Sheik*. Adding to the *Carry On*-style drama are the over-the-top antics of the notorious dancer's lovers – an extremely hammy Lionel Barrymore as the half-crazed, eye-rolling General Shubin, and Latin idol Ramon Novarro as the much-younger Lieutenant Alexis Rosanoff. Both are Russians, and neither actor is even remotely capable of affecting a Russian accent.

Through the circles she moved in, Garbo knew Ramon Novarro's story better than the studio which employed him as he was a frequent visitor at the Viertels. Born José-Ramon Samaniegos, in Durango, Mexico, he arrived in Hollywood in 1913 after fleeing the

Huerta Revolution. His first job was washing dishes in a restaurant, and there followed numerous occupations: tango-dancer, summer stock, dancing in Anna Pavlova's chorus and working as an extra in Mary Pickford films before hitting the big time with *Ben-Hur*. Since Valentino's death and John Gilbert's fall from grace, he had become the highest paid actor in Hollywood. Muscular, narcissistic and extremely handsome, José-Ramon had amassed a coterie of male lovers – including Valentino while working as an extra in Rex Ingram's *The Four Horsemen of the Apocalypse*. The French singer-dancer Mistinguett, who knew Novarro well at this time and whose Austrian dancer-lover Frédéric Rey left her for the actor, recalled how Ingram had discovered him posing nude for art students in Los Angeles and, after a session on the casting couch, had commented how his hirsute buttocks reminded him of his favourite haunt, the Novarro Valley: 'That's how he got his name – because his arse looked like a tourist attraction!'[238]

Thalberg's problem in securing Novarro for the film was his salary: currently he was earning upwards of $150,000 per movie. However, he was so eager to work with Garbo that he agreed to a pay cut: $5,000 on signature of the contract, and $5,000 a week for the shooting, scheduled to run from 30 September to 23 November 1931. He also demanded equal billing, which Garbo accepted: the opening credits would read, 'Greta Garbo & Ramon Novarro in *Mata Hari*.'

Mata Hari (Margaretha Geertruida Zelle, 1876–1917) was born in Leeuwarden, Holland. In 1895 she married Dutch Colonial Army officer Rudolph MacLeod, and moved with him to Java, in the Dutch East Indies, where she adopted her exotic name (Malaysian for 'eye of the dawn') and began her dancing career. MacLeod was a violent drunk and no less promiscuous than his wife – the couple's two children both died of syphilis, contracted from them. In 1906, Mata Hari divorced him, by which time she had returned to Europe and settled in Paris, where she achieved notoriety, not just in the music-halls but also as a courtesan. She slept with high-ranking military officials, including the Russian lieutenant, eighteen years her junior, upon whom the Novarro character is based (ironically, Novarro was actually six years older than Garbo). Because Holland remained neutral during World War I, as a Dutch citizen she was able to move more freely for her work as an alleged double-agent. She was arrested by the French in February 1917 and executed the following October. Recent revelations however reveal her to have been used as a scapegoat by the head of French counter-espionage and almost certainly innocent of the charges brought against her.

On the first day of shooting, Novarro sent Garbo a huge bouquet of pink roses. The inscription read, 'I hope that the whole world will be as delighted to see the Mata Hari of the film as I am to be able to act with her.' When he arrived at the set to rehearse their first scene together, shaking on account of his nerves, he was perturbed to learn of her no-rehearsals policy but was later staggered that such was her professionalism, there was rarely a second take. 'Her emotional intensity is genuine,' he recalled. 'The instant she begins a scene, her whole being seems to change. Her role acts as a complete metamorphosis. At once she is Mata Hari and not Greta Garbo. It is an inspiration to work with her. You find yourself living the role, not merely acting it.'[239]

Garbo made an exception when Novarro expressed concern over their more intimate scenes in the film, secretly terrified that he would mess these up if he stumbled into them blindly, since he was not used to making love to women. These, she said, she *was* willing to rehearse but only in private and with *her* telling *him* what to do. 'She needed to be able to concentrate,' he said, 'She had to convince herself before she could convince anyone else ... She would say, "Well, in the last one *you* sat, and in this one *I* sit."' Having had affairs with several inordinately handsome bisexual men, maybe Garbo was amorously interested in Novarro, though as he always claimed to have been exclusively gay, one doubts she would have had much luck in getting this particular stud between the sheets. They socialised while making the film, visiting the Russian Eagle, though these were not 'lavender' dates aimed at keeping the actor's sexuality a secret. Ramon Novarro was almost unique among Hollywood stars at the time in that he was *never* in the closet.[240]

The film opens in 1917 with Dubois (C. Henry Gordon) *presiding over the executions of French traitors, one of whom refuses a pardon*

in exchange for the name of his leader – Dubois believes it is Mata
Hari, but needs proof. Cut to General Shubin, the Russian military
chief, meeting Lt Alexis Rosanoff, who has flown in from Moscow with
secret military papers. Exhausted after his flight, Alexis perks up when
Shubin announces that he is taking him to watch Mata Hari dance.
After all the hype, her act (performed by Garbo with Rae Randall
doubling in the frames where her face is not seen) *is something of a*
con. 'Shiva, I dance for you tonight as the bayadères dance in the sacred
temples of Java,' she drawls, before cavorting around a huge statue of
the god. Wearing breastplates, several layers of silk, a headdress resem-
bling a Christmas tree and with a wealth of Amazonian thigh exposed
(just like the real Mata Hari), *she struts, writhes, sticks out her bottom*
and flails her arms, and in less than two minutes it is all over.

The press reported how, at the premiere, the cheers and applause for
Garbo's first dance in the film went on for several minutes, mingled
with gasps of horror from the prudes. Viewing the film today one
wonders what drove the crowd to such distraction – until we realise
we are watching the 1939 re-release, with four crucial minutes cut from
the original. The 1931 sequence, which replicated Mata Hari's actual
tableau, performed at the Alcazar de Paris in 1916, ends with Garbo
shot through light gauze, kneeling at the foot of the statue and almost
totally nude for several seconds, until one of the other dancers covers
her with a gold lamé cloth. In the next scene, she wears an ensemble
based on one of the designs by Paul Poiret for Diaghilev's first Ballets
Russes, staged in Paris in 1909. Resembling body armour more than
an actual garment – with tight metallic leggings, an embroidered gold
lamé tunic and sweeping train – this weighed an astonishing 52 pounds
and took Garbo thirty minutes to get in and out of. Throughout she
wears replicas of Mata Hari's original headgear: a diamanté skullcap,
a cloche-helmet hung with eight-ounce brass medallions, a jewelled
pillbox hat and a black yarmulke.

Captivated, Alexis says that he must have her, but she is already in a
clandestine relationship with Shubin: in exchange for sexual favours he
gives her secret information about Russian military movements, which
she in turn passes on to her German boss, Andriani (Lewis Stone,

playing the heartless villain, aided by sardonic grins and a make-up department goatee beard). *Alexis follows Mata Hari to her Art Deco apartment. Last spring he saw her in the Bois de Boulogne, he tells her, and he is sure that by next spring the war will be over. Sinking on to a chaise longue, she sighs, 'I never look ahead. By next spring I shall probably be quite alone.' Then sends him packing.*

In the next scene – in which we see her hair for the first time – she is sniffing orchids sent by Shubin when Alexis barges in, flings flowers at her feet and declares his undying love. Again, he is shown the door: she may be attracted to him, but in her line of work it is unwise to fall in love. She changes tactics, however, when Shubin informs her that Alexis now holds the secret information. He orders her to visit Alexis' rooms and seduce him, keeping him occupied while a henchman sneaks in to photograph the messages. Everything goes according to plan, but before they make love Alexis shows her his shrine to the Madonna, given him by his mother, whose votive flame he has sworn on the high altar to keep perpetually burning in her memory. Since the henchman will need to wait until the room is in total darkness before he can break in, Mata Hari has to exercise all her power over the profoundly passive Alexis. There is too much light in the room for love making, she says, and after he has extinguished the lamp she indicates the shrine, her once seductive voice now taking on a cruel tone: 'Put that one out, too!' He must break his oath or she will leave. The next morning, while he is sleeping, she slips away, though not before re-lighting the flame.

A 68-second sequence from the original print was cut by the censor for the 1939 re-release. The scene is played out in total darkness, save for the glow from the couple's cigarettes: Alexis wants to look into Mata Hari's eyes, but when she offers to light the lamp so that he can, he jokes that he would never be able to see them anyway because of her ridiculously long lashes. Another brief scene, also cut (though the stills have survived) features Garbo framed in the archway leading to her bedroom, wearing a diaphanous negligee, under which she is naked.

Alexis has asked Mata Hari to marry him, and though she loves him she knows she must not see him again. 'A spy in love is a tool that has

*outlived its usefulness,' Andriani observes. She visits Shubin, who has
learned of the affair. In a fit of jealous rage Shubin calls Dubois, reveals
that she is the spy he is looking for, then threatens to set up Alexis as her
accomplice. 'I never knew that anyone could be so vile,' she spits out,
before shooting him dead and trying to make it look like suicide.* (It is
at this point in the story that Hollywood fiction takes over. Because
of this scene, on 17 October 1932, the fifteenth anniversary of Mata
Hari's death, her surviving relatives sued MGM for portraying her
as a murderess, a case which failed only because they also accused
the studio of wrongly portraying her as a spy.)

*To save Mata Hari from arrest, Andriani arranges for her to leave
the country, but she refuses and resigns her position upon learning that
Alexis' plane has been shot down. 'The only way to resign from our
profession is to die,' Andriani says. Alexis has been blinded in the crash
and she goes to see him in the military hospital. Touching her own eyes*
(in reference to the cut love scene), *she soothes, 'Here are your eyes,
with those ridiculously long lashes, as you said.' They make plans for a
future they will never have; Dubois arrests her as she leaves.*

*At her trial, her only hope of acquittal is for Alexis to perjure himself
by saying that she was with him when Shubin was killed. This she will
not allow, and she is sentenced to be shot. Shriven and attended by
weeping nuns* (Garbo now resembling Joan of Arc, a role she had
always longed to play), *she is visited by Alexis, who has been told that
she is in a sanatorium and about to have an operation. Only now do
we see them kiss, before she is led to her execution.*

In *Dishonoured*, audiences actually watched Marlene Dietrich
being shot, but for some reason the British censor contacted
MGM while *Mata Hari* was in production and announced that
he would oppose the British release should Garbo be filmed facing
the firing squad. Under normal circumstances, when the ending
of a film proved controversial – like Garbo's *The Temptress*, *Flesh
and the Devil* and *Love* – alternative endings were filmed to placate
moralists and religious groups. In this instance, MGM sided with
the British censor, granting Europe's most notorious female spy a
dignified, saintly death. At the box-office, this was Garbo's most
successful film to date. 'Miss Garbo may not be more like Mata

Hari than the film narrative is like an authentic account of the spy's career,' Mordaunt Hall observed in the *New York Times*. 'There is, however, in the skilfully arranged series of incidents, enough truth to make a most compelling drama.' *Screen Book* declared it the best role of her career: 'The real Mata Hari was a colourful person, but she could in no way touch the personality displayed by the Swedish star.' *Variety* thought her 'sexy and hot' in a less subtle way than in her previous films, but was disappointed by the love scenes: 'Both times they turn out the lights.'[241]

CHAPTER NINE

'I WANT TO BE ALONE!'

'I feel I have lived before. I am never terribly surprised at anything. I feel always, I have been here before, that it is not exactly a new experience.'

Viennese-born Vicki Baum (1888–1960) had published several novels, but it was *Grand Hotel* that made her a household name. Irving Thalberg purchased the stage rights to *Menschen in Hotel* for a 'bargain' $13,500 in 1930, with Garbo in mind for the part of fading ballerina Grusinskaya when it was brought to the screen. He commissioned William A. Drake to write the play to 'test out' on Broadway audiences before giving the go-ahead for the film. Eugenie Leontovich, the great Russian actress, triumphed as Grusinskaya, with Albert Dekker playing the Baron, as a result of which MGM forked out a further $35,000 for the screen rights and confidently assigned a staggering $700,000 budget for the film, though the box-office takings during its first season would more than quadruple this.

Like the later *Gone with the Wind* (1939), dozens of major Hollywood stars were involved in a battle of over-sized egos. By the time casting concluded, Thalberg had assembled the most scintillating roster of names ever seen in a Hollywood film, one which today would prove impossible to finance even if there were comparable talent around. 'A galaxy of stars that have just made the Milky Way sit up and keel over,' *Motion Picture* observed. Unquestionably, Garbo was the star of the show, not that this prevented the other actors from complaining that, as she was spending less time on the screen than most of them – just twenty-seven minutes – their names should appear in the opening credits in letters the same size as hers. This never happened.

Marlene Dietrich and Marie Dressler offered their services for free, just to play character parts – in Marlene's case, Paramount refused to loan her out, while MGM considered Dressler too big a star to be playing Garbo's maid. Douglas Fairbanks Jr petitioned Mayer for the second lead, Baron von Gaigern, as did Clark Gable – going back on his earlier refusal to appear beneath Garbo in the credits. Neither would have been suitable and in any case, the part had already been assigned to John Barrymore (1892–1942) in what many consider the greatest role of his career. The youngest member of Hollywood's *true* acting royal family, Barrymore was a tremendous presence, revered by critics and colleagues alike as 'The Great Profile'. When Buster Keaton dropped out of the production, Barrymore's brother, Lionel, was brought in to play doomed clerk Otto Klingelein. Completing the distinguished line-up were Wallace Beery, a recent Oscar recipient for his portrayal as a has-been boxer in *The Champ*; Garbo stalwart Lewis Stone and Jean Hersholt; Italian character actress Rafaela Ottiano, recreating her stage role as Grusinskaya's fussy, birdlike maid. Playing Flaemmchen, the flighty stenographer, was Joan Crawford, a move which delighted her because it meant she had 'got one over' on Norma Shearer, whom she could not stand and who had been pencilled in for the part since the film's conception. Shearer had been compelled to step down after receiving hundreds of letters from fans declaring that it would not be appropriate for 'the boss's' wife to be playing a prostitute on the screen.

Garbo had been closely following Crawford's career. Culturally, they were worlds apart. Born Lucille LeSueur in Kansas City, in 1904, neglected by her mother and abused by her stepfather, she had clawed her way to the top by way of appearances in tacky revues and, allegedly, even porn films to become the heroine of working-class women across America. MGM paid her $60,000 for the film, just $8,000 less than Garbo, and more than John Barrymore. Garbo was suspicious that she might attempt to steal her thunder, as had recently happened with Clark Gable in *Possessed*. She therefore announced that she would *not* be appearing in any scenes with Joan, upon pain of dropping out of the film. She also avoided bumping into her 'rival' by insisting that Joan should not be allowed on the set until *she* had left for the day, though Joan would not hear of this and later recalled how she had walked past

Garbo's 'cocoon' each evening and called out a greeting, but was always ignored. Then, the first time she did not call out, Garbo emerged from her dressing room and caught up with her:

> I just wanted to say hello to Garbo and curtsy ... I was on the top step, she was two steps below me and I didn't know what to do. I said, 'Excuse me, Miss Garbo!' And she took my face in her hands and she said, 'Oh, I am so *sorry* we have no scenes together.' And I looked at this beautiful face with the sun [coming through the window] in the West, and she was the most beautiful thing I have ever seen in my life.[242] [243]

Grand Hotel was scheduled to begin shooting on 31 December 1931, the day of the *Mata Hari* premiere. This was also the last day of Garbo's MGM contract, which she had shown no interest in re-negotiating. Mayer had expressed concern over a feature in *Movie Mirror*: 'IS GARBO GOING HOME – WILL THE VIKING VENUS RETIRE AT THE TOP?' When Garbo last visited her homeland, the piece went on, she had had a solid reason for returning to Hollywood – John Gilbert. Now, she was unattached. She had no property to dispose of, few personal possessions to crate up, the Swedish friends she had clung to during her early Hollywood years had all left, and even her closest friend, Salka Viertel, was planning an extended trip of Northern Europe and Russia, and might not return to America.[244]

Also, despite losing $100,000 in the Wall Street Crash (news she kept to herself, afraid that MGM might try and reduce her salary if they suspected she was strapped for cash), Garbo was still a wealthy woman. For five years she had lived like a miser, unlike her contemporaries spending next to nothing on clothes and jewellery and never entertaining. She owned just one second-hand car and was reputed to pay her staff stingy wages. The writer of the piece estimated that she had banked or invested over 80 per cent of her earnings, after tax, and that she had $300,000 in her bank account. Rilla Page Palmborg claimed to have 'inside information' that Garbo had arranged to buy an island at Marlen, an hour's drive from Stockholm, where she planned on building her retreat from the world. Additionally she was buying *two* apartments – one in the city for entertaining friends, the other in Berlin, where she would be working much of the time. The editorial concluded:

> One day in April, her contract ends. Perhaps a few days later a Swedish freighter will lie at a pier in Los Angeles harbour. It wouldn't surprise those who know Greta if, a few hours before the ship sailed, a mannish-coated woman with a suitcase or a handbag should walk unobtrusively up the ship's gangplank to a cabin reserved in advance.[245]

Mayer breathed a sigh of relief when Garbo announced that she *was* moving – to a new home where she hoped she would be afforded more privacy now that she had found out about the neighbours' children charging peeping Toms to watch her sunbathing and swimming in the nude. The property was a house on North Rockingham Road, in Brentwood, which she rented on a whim because it had a tennis court. To her distress, she discovered this could be seen from neighbouring properties, a problem she tried to resolve by inviting prospective partners to 'drop by' for a game – at five in the morning. When this did not work, she had the perimeter fence of the court draped with tarpaulins, which everyone found depressing. Giving the place up as a bad job, she moved to North Cliffwood Avenue in a part of town where Joan Crawford and Mercedes de Acosta were near neighbours. When Mayer learned that she was unhappy here too, he contrived to keep her in Hollywood by 'tagging' her previous studio absences to her current contract, adding not just the days when she had stayed at home, claiming to be ill while not providing a sick note, but the long break in the middle of shooting *Susan Lenox*, which had not been her fault. The expiry date was now extended from 1 January to 24 April, time enough, he believed, for her to complete *Grand Hotel*. But he was wasting his time. Had Garbo wanted to leave, she would have done so, mindless of whether she was breaking her contract or not. Mayer was told that she *would* stay long enough to make the film but only because she *wanted* to make it and not as any favour to him. Neither was she or Joan Crawford pleased with Thalberg's decision to hire Edmund Goulding with a sort of homophobic logic shared by his colleagues that, if a man was homosexual, he behaved and thought like a woman, therefore he would be more suited to directing tetchy women than men.

As she would not be required on the set until early in the New Year – and as she had no interest in attending the *Mata Hari* premiere – Garbo and Mercedes de Acosta travelled to New York, where they took separate rooms at the St Moritz Hotel, Garbo checking in as 'Fräulein Gussie Berger'. Their first port of call was to see Judith Anderson in Pirandello's play, *As You Desire Me*, which Garbo never stopped raving about. They also saw Mercedes' former lover Eve Le Gallienne in *Camille* – which would provide Garbo with one of her most definitive roles in the not too distant future – before having an almighty bust-up which saw Mercedes rushing back to Hollywood. This argument – the first of many, although they always made up until Mercedes killed off their friendship completely by publishing her kiss-and-tell book in 1960 – came after a matinée performance of *The Barretts of Wimpole Street*, starring Katharine Cornell.

Katharine Cornell (1893–1974) is generally regarded as the greatest stage actress of her generation. In 1921 she entered into a lavender marriage – a happy one which lasted forty years – with producer Guthrie McClintic, who staged most of her plays. Cornell recalled Garbo's backstage visit, when she approached her – coat collar up, hat pulled down over her face and looking like a spy – and drawled, 'Would Miss Cornell see a stranger?' Thinking her to be an impersonator, Cornell ignored her and Garbo slouched away, muttering, 'Miss Cornell, I see, does not *like* strangers!' Having been made aware that this was the *real* Garbo, Cornell called Mayer's office in Hollywood, who confirmed that Garbo was indeed in New York and staying at the St Moritz under an assumed name. A letter of apology was dispatched to the hotel and Garbo – but not Mercedes, hence their subsequent row – was invited to Beekman Place for supper. 'We all sat and talked, easily and comfortably, until about four o' clock in the morning,' Cornell observed in her memoirs, not revealing who the other guests were. 'Miss Garbo turned out to be as delightful, as charming, as simple and as humorous a person as you could imagine. No attitudes, no pose, no star temperament – and such extraordinary beauty, especially when she smiles.'[246]

While in New York, Garbo met Alla Nazimova, appearing in *Mourning Becomes Elektra*. She also dined with Broadway's most celebrated husband-and-wife acting team, Alfred Lunt and Lynne Fontanne. All too soon her vacation was over and on New Year's Day 1932, she returned to Hollywood, where she was met at the station by Salka Viertel. Garbo did not even look at the reporters, let alone acknowledge any of them. During the stop-off in Chicago, when asked what she thought of New Yorkers she had replied, 'They are always in a hurry, and many of them are *so* impolite!' Then she had turned on Clare Boothe Luce, the associate editor of *Vanity Fair* – a publication she had loathed since the attack by Jim Tully – when she asked the by now tiresome question, 'Miss Garbo, when are you going to marry?' Garbo had glared at her and snarled, 'I will *never* marry. Now go away!' In the February issue of the magazine, Luce did not hold back:

> Garbo will be forgotten as a woman in ten years, and as an actress her memory will be dead when Helen Hayes', Lynne Fontanne's and Katharine Cornell's are beginning to grow greenest ... Selfish, shrewd, ignorant, self-absorbed, whimsical, perverse and innocent. She is the perfect realisation of the child left to itself, unhampered and uncontrolled by mature authority. Every man has the love affairs he deserves ... Our generation's loveliest woman is but a phantom on a silver screen – a shadow with the face of an angel of perdition, as substantial as a mist before the moon, the inarticulate, the bad-tempered, and the 'great' Garbo.[247]

Garbo filmed her first scene – the one in her room with Rafaela Ottiano – on 4 January and that same day was introduced to John Barrymore, whose first words to her were, 'My wife and I think you are the loveliest person in the world.' Garbo's response to this was, 'This is a great day for me. How I have looked forward to working with John Barrymore!' Even so, she made no concessions for his stature: like all her other leading men (with the exception of Ramon Novarro), she refused to rehearse any of her scenes with him beforehand.

Mayer was on the set that day, hiding in the shadows with author Vicki Baum. Garbo sensed their presence and stopped the camera. When reminded by director Edmund Goulding how important Baum was and that she was eager to meet her, Garbo shrugged her shoulders and replied, 'She can stay, then – and *I* will go home!' Over the course of the next few years, even some of the big Hollywood stars went to inordinate lengths to get on to a Garbo set: Tarzan actor Johnny Weissmuller disguised himself as a waiter, Una Merkel pretended to be a script-girl, James Stewart posed as a carpenter – all were 'sussed' out and ejected.[248]

The first Garbo film not to have the older-versus-younger lover formula, and beautifully photographed by William Daniels, *Grand Hotel* comprises a series of cleverly linked vignettes spanning a 48-hour period in the lives of a set of odd-bod characters at an exclusive establishment in Weimar Berlin.

The porter frets about his pregnant wife. The terminally ill Kringelein (Lionel Barrymore) *has worked his fingers to the bone and invested his life savings so that he might die here in unabashed luxury. His odious boss, textiles magnate Preysing* (Wallace Beery, the only character speaking with a German accent, his condition for taking the part), *hopes to clinch a deal here that will save him from the receiver. Flaemmchen* (Joan Crawford) *is the hooker he hires as a stenographer. Baron von Gaigern* (John Barrymore) *is a professional gambler, here to rob wealthy patrons so that he can pay off his debts. Grusinskaya* (Garbo) *is the highly strung Russian ballerina whose performances are suffering because she is homesick and mourning her lover, the Grand Duke Sergei.* (This was an unforgivable error on the scriptwriter's part: Sergei was assassinated in 1905, the year of Garbo's birth, which means Grusinskaya would be over fifty and unlikely to have still been a prima ballerina.) *Finally, there is the surly, facially disfigured doctor* (Lewis Stone), *who drawls, 'Grand Hotel. People coming, people going. Nothing ever happens!'*

As Grusinskaya, Garbo makes an unremarkable entrance, twenty minutes into the film. Her maid awakens her from a drugs-induced slumber and she gets out of bed, does a few exercises and picks up her jewels. 'I think, Suzette, I have never been so tired in my life,' she says. 'Pearls are cold. Everything's cold and finished. So far away. The Russians … Saint Petersburg. Imperial Court. The Grand Duke Sergei, dead … Grusinskaya. It's all gone!' (The scene is pure ham. She looks so unlike a ballerina – clumsy and slouching, clod-footed as she stomps across the room. But who cares when the magic is so potent?) *Tonight's performance is imminent, but she has no intention of dancing again to a half-empty hall, and no applause.*

The Baron, meanwhile, has been flirting with Flaemmchen, who mistakes him for a wealthy catch. He would like to take her dancing, but will be otherwise engaged stealing Grusinskaya's priceless pearls. The next scene (Grand Hotel's *most famous) takes place in Grusinskaya's room, to which the tetchy star has returned, still wearing her tutu, having fled the theatre before the show because her entourage have lied to her about it being a sell-out. Leaning against the door-frame she tells them, 'I want to be alone …I just want to be alone!' Her entourage leaves; she changes out of her costume, pausing to kiss her shoes. She has decided to end it all with an overdose of Veronal: 'They didn't even miss me … I always said I'd lay off when the time came. And who would trouble about a Grusinskaya who dances no more? What would she do – grow orchids, keep white peacocks? Die! That's what it comes to at last. To die…' She is startled when the baron reveals himself – the last man she caught in her room was honour-bound to choose suicide over shame. 'I want to be alone,' she repeats, but miraculously he talks her out of her decision. Right there before our very eyes, without make-up or technical trickery, the lines disappear from her face as her expression is transformed from washed-up hopelessness to profound optimism.*

The two fall in love, this lonely woman and the sympathetic thief who has given her the will to live – the man who makes her want to dance and sing. (And sing Garbo does, the snatch of 'Ich liebe dich' suggestive of a voice similar to that of fellow Swede Zarah Leander, who she would part-emulate in her next film.) *She nicknames him 'Flix' and they spend the night together – talking, we are led to believe.*

The Baron returns her pearls, which she says have only ever brought her bad luck. Tomorrow she leaves for Vienna and he must go with her, then to her villa at Tremezzo. He promises to meet her on the train, then it all goes wrong: Preysing catches him stealing his wallet and bludgeons him to death. Grusinskaya, meanwhile, heads for the theatre, gives a triumphant performance and returns to the hotel laden with flowers, only to sense something is wrong: 'The music has stopped. These flowers make me think of funerals.'

The next morning she leaves for the station, expecting the Baron to be there. Gazing up at the sky she pronounces, 'The sun! It'll be sunny in Tremezzo!' Preysing is carted off to jail, while Kringelein and Flaemmchen – who he has promised to take care of because she is the only person in the world to have ever shown him compassion – leave for Paris, where he may be able to find a cure. Then the porter receives news that his wife has had her baby, and only the miserable doctor remains, mumbling as before, 'Grand Hotel, always the same…'

Grand Hotel wrapped on 19 February 1932. Such was the media interest in the film that, leaving no space for ironing out any problems which might arise during shooting, Thalberg fixed the premiere for 12 April. Continuity man William A. Drake's mania for insisting that William Daniels photograph Garbo and Barrymore from every conceivable angle had resulted in 273,000 feet of film, when Thalberg had asked for no more than 12,000 feet for the finished print.

Garbo was aware of Joan Crawford's boasts that she would 'seize the Garbo crown', should she return to Sweden for good. Therefore, when the editing massacre began, upon her insistence more Crawford footage ended up on the cutting-room floor than might otherwise have done. On 17 March, for the first time with a Garbo film, a media preview took place in Monterey, where 'suggestion cards' were handed out to be filled in by the press and paying audience. The consensus of opinion was that there were too many lingering close-ups of Garbo and Barrymore, and too few of Joan. This resulted in the five leading cast members being recalled to the set on 29 March, where several brief retakes took place along with a 'publicity shot' – for many years believed to have been the only time Garbo posed for a photograph with Joan Crawford. In fact, the whole exercise was a scissors-and-paste job: Garbo refused to join the line-up, and her image – wedged between Crawford and Barrymore and looking *away* from the camera – was subsequently added by a studio technician.

The premiere, at Grauman's Chinese Theatre, was *the* show business event of the year. 25,000 fans lined Hollywood Boulevard to cheer the arrival of the stars and guests of honour, who were asked to 'sign in' at the front desk of the 'Grand Hotel', reconstructed within the theatre foyer: the Gables, Mayer, Thalberg and Norma Shearer, Marlene Dietrich on a rare public outing with her husband Rudolf Sieber, Paul Bern and Jean Harlow, who had just announced their engagement, and executives from rival studios. Only Garbo was conspicuous by her absence. 'She's frightened by large crowds, but you may rest assured she's here in spirit,' Edmund Goulding told the press. Later it was announced that she *had* turned up and a near-riot erupted as hundreds of reporters and photographers rushed to the front of the stage, where 'she' had materialised, looking larger than expected. In a stunt organised by Master of Ceremonies, comic Will Rogers, this was Wallace Beery wearing an oversized gown and blond wig!

The reviews were extraordinary, with some journalists almost coming to blows over their diverse differences of opinion – one either liked this film, or loathed it. John Mosher observed in the *New Yorker*:

> In spite of the brevity of her appearance, against what many stars would call ground odds, Garbo dominates the picture entirely, making the other players merely competent performers. By her walk alone, her gait, Garbo is exciting, and it doesn't need the folderol of grand dukes and pearls that this story gives her, the so-conventionalised role of the beautiful premiere *danseuse*, to lend her that exasperating enchantment vaguely described as 'glamour'.[249]

Vicki Baum, despite having been given the cold shoulder when attempting to meet Garbo, wrote in *Modern Screen*: 'The twittering, laughing, hopping about in the tarlatan of a ballet skirt is certainly not what Greta would have sought out as her role. But she has accomplished it ... Unforgettable! Thank you, Greta Garbo!' Her enthusiasm was not shared by Mary Cass Canfield, crabby as always:

Miss Leontovich, who created your role in the New York stage production, rewrote the script in terms of her own Slavic temperament, and managed to make us feel the heroine as a woman in pain, a disillusioned being. But you, gracefully going through the motions of acting this picture, let reality slide, inspired us with no agony on your behalf. Your reflection of the heroine's tempestuous changes of mood was a surface artifice, overacted and without inner flame. And your gaiety was stillborn, unconvincing.[250]

The Garbo-Barrymore love scene would be parodied the following year by Marion Davies and Jimmy Durante in *Blondie of the Follies*. In this, Davies tells her co-star, 'I vant to be alone,' deliberates over this and adds, 'Vell, maybe for von veek!' Garbo offered no complaint, perhaps because the film was also directed by Edmund Goulding. It was another story when the entire movie was condensed into a nineteen-minute Warner Brothers spoof, *Nothing Ever Happens*, directed by Roy Mack. The names of the characters were barely disguised – Scramchen, Waistline, Prizering – and when there was concern over Geraldine Dvorak parodying Garbo as 'Madam, The Paranoid Dancer', the producer merely changed the spelling of her name to Jeraldine and hoped that MGM would not kick up too much of a fuss.

Dvorak's 'Swedish' accent and her appearance reveal how easy it must have been for her to pass herself off as Garbo – indeed, she is so convincing that, filmed in long shot crossing the hotel lobby, some fans believed they were seeing the real thing. The scenario, told partly in rhyme, is almost the same. Madam complains about her surroundings: 'If I don't get a better room, I tank I go home!' Next up she is in her tutu, throwing a tantrum: 'I vant to be alone! I am so unhappy! I vant to be alone!' The Baron emerges – one of *six* men hiding in her room – and barks, 'I heard you the first time!' He tells her he is nuts about her, and she takes a twirl around the room, the emphasis placed on her oversized men's shoes. 'Madam, you dance like nobody's business,' he enthuses, 'And with those *feet*, and my brain, there's no telling where we'll wind up!' Garbo was furious, demanding her stand-in be dismissed at once: Thalberg replaced her with Rae Randall (1897–1934), who had doubled for the dance sequence in *Mata Hari*. Born Sigrun Solvason, she had started out as a bit-part in Cecil B. DeMille's *King of Kings* (1927), and would cause Garbo an even greater headache in the near future.

Since seeing Judith Anderson in *As You Desire Me*, Garbo had talked of nothing but bringing Elma, Pirandello's amnesiac *chanteuse*, to the screen. While *Grand Hotel* was in production, Thalberg hired Gene Markey to write the script and cast the major parts. Owen Moore (replacing Nils Asther, who was assigned to *Letty Lynton* with Joan Crawford) was an alcoholic actor formerly married to Mary Pickford, while ex-Broadway actor Melvyn Douglas (1901–81) had recently scored a success with *The Wiser Sex*, opposite Claudette Colbert. Rafaela Ottiano, who played Garbo's maid in *Grand Hotel*, was, on her insistence, hired to do so again here. She also cast caution to the wind by agreeing to have Hedda Hopper in the film, hamming it up as her on-screen sister while snooping around the set in search of juicy titbits about the stars' love lives for her column, though in this instance there would be none. George Fitzmaurice was brought in to direct.

Garbo must have derived some sort of sardonic pleasure in demanding Erich von Stroheim (1885–1957) for the part of her psychopathic captor, Karl Salter. Mauritz Stiller had idolised the Austrian-born actor-director, who was almost a precursor of Orson Welles in that, in his quest for perfection, he antagonised and alienated just about everyone who crossed his path, earning himself the nickname 'The Man You Love To Hate'. He arrived in Hollywood in 1914, where after working briefly with D. W. Griffith, he played a number of bit-parts, usually sadistic Germans: in *The Heart of Humanity* (1918), his character deals with a crying baby by tossing it out of a window. From then on, von Stroheim had turned to directing, making extraneous demands on the studios. For Universal's *Foolish Wives*, on a then unheard of $1 million budget, he commissioned a life-size reconstruction of the Casino de Monte Carlo on a back lot, and authentic underwear and hosiery for the extras playing Austrian troops, though these were never seen. His extravagance backfired on him the next year while shooting *Merry-Go-Round*, also for Universal – he was fired by the studio's production assistant, one Irving Thalberg, who vowed never to work with him again. He was halfway through shooting *Greed* (1924) for Samuel Goldwyn Pictures when this was merged into MGM, once more bringing him into contact with Thalberg. Again, extravagance was the order of the day: by the time Thalberg relieved him of control of the picture, he had shot forty-two reels of film, which subsequently had to be edited down to ten. Even so, Mayer was willing to give him another chance and *The Merry Widow* (1925) proved a huge success. More fireworks followed, however, on the set of United Artists' *Queen Kelly* (1929) starring Gloria Swanson. This time, von Stroheim was fired not just for pushing the production over budget, but for introducing bordello sequences where the sex, albeit under the covers and unseen, had allegedly been for real. Swanson finished directing the film itself and though never put on general release in America, it developed a cult following in Europe.

The meeting with von Stroheim was arranged by Salka Viertel and took place at her home on Mabery Road, where the creepy star received the Garbo seal of approval. Thalberg hit the roof, declaring 'The Hun' would never set foot in any studio that *he* was involved with. George Fitzmaurice, aware of von Stroheim's inability to learn his lines and insistence on 'idiot cards', refused to direct him. Garbo, however, was adamant: unless von Stroheim was given the part – and on a salary of $1,000 a day, almost as much as she was earning – *she* would go on strike until 24 April, the day her MGM contract expired. Mayer tried to pull a fast one: going through her work record, he discovered a few more 'unauthorised absentee days' and the end date of her contract was extended to 1 June. It made no difference and Thalberg was forced to capitulate.

As You Desire Me began shooting on 7 March and wrapped on 17 April. The oddest of the Garbo talkies, its scenario and script are the most confusing. 'I never knew at any moment what I was supposed to be doing – it was beyond the understanding of any of us,' Melvyn Douglas recalled of the on-set mayhem. Garbo and Douglas aside, the acting is hammy, the gestures so extraneous we might be watching a badly edited early silent. Douglas was the first to complain to George Fitzmaurice about von Stroheim's lack of courtesy and professionalism: 'He was rude and common and had such a hopeless stutter that his scenes had to be shot over and over again. I was very surprised that a man who had shown such gifts had no subtlety, no *savoir-faire.*'[251] [252]

Garbo, who was used to completing a scene in a single take, found herself having to cope with endless retakes because of an actor who not only persistently fluffed his lines, but pronounced them with a marked speech impediment. Thalberg wanted to fire him and risk the consequences but she persevered, aware that von Stroheim's nerves were shot through as this was the first time he had worked since undergoing a serious operation. The two spent a lot of time between scenes in her dressing room. During their long, meaningful conversations she insisted that he took her chair, while she sat at his feet. Von Stroheim's poor health also brought out her maternal instincts, though he was twenty years her senior. If he felt unwell on the set, she fussed like an anxious wife. If he felt too ill to leave home in the morning, he sent word to Garbo, who in turn called Harry Edington to announce that she too was under the weather and unable to work today.

The story opens in Budapest in 1926, where in a smoky café-concert, Zara (MGM believed that by using the original name, Elma, audiences would mistake this for Elmer, a man's name, and think Garbo was in drag!) is performing to an enraptured audience. Because American critics at the time (and some biographers) believed that Marlene Dietrich was the only big name in Europe ever to have sung on a stage, they assumed that Garbo's characterisation was based on her. It was not. Wearing tight black trousers, a bell-necked top and later, a long black dress, and with her cropped, dyed hair (actually a blonde wig), Zara is an amalgamation of Marianne Oswald, the great French singer, Damia, and Zarah Leander, the legendary Swedish star, who Garbo later met.[253]

Like most of the chanteuses réalistes, Zara likes a tipple. She also has an all-important gay following, clustered in the gallery as she finishes her song and trailing her to her dressing room, where she gets plastered – her only way of coping with her problems, she says. (One of her coterie is Roland Varno, 1908–96, a Dutch actor who had socialised with Garbo and Marianne Oswald in Berlin.)

The party is interrupted by Tony (Owen Moore)*, who addresses Zara as 'Maria'. After slamming the door in his face, she heads home with her fans, where the revelry is once again halted by the appearance of Salter* (Eric von Stroheim)*. Creepy and menacing, he pins her to the desk and bears down on her with an upside-down kiss. 'Don't be so vile,' she reprimands, pushing him away, to which he sneers, 'Since when did* you *mind anything vile?'*

Tony shows up again, claiming to be an artist who painted her ten years ago. He is here to return her to her husband, Count Bruno Varelli (Melvyn Douglas)*, who reported her missing when their house was bombed during the war. Zara appears to recognise the name and perhaps finds the story convincing: 'Maria? I wonder. Maybe I am, maybe I'm not. It's all so mixed up. Noises, blinding lights, pictures that fade before I can catch them. Soldiers, soldiers. Walking the streets, hungry and cold. Men, men, until I don't know who I am, or where I am from.' When Salter tries to intervene, she snarls, 'I loathe you, and I loathe everything I've been!' Then as she is about to leave with Tony, Salter draws a gun and shoots her.* (From this point, the story becomes increasingly far-fetched. Pirandello was obsessed with double-identity, and his plots frequently waffle on without saying much at all.)

When we see Zara again she is on the train with Tony, heading back to her supposed former life. Her transformation into Countess Maria Varelli is almost complete: in less than a month, while recovering from a gunshot wound, her hair has grown six inches and she now looks, acts and sounds nothing like Zara. No explanation is given for this radical change, leaving one to assume that Tony has groomed her to be the duplicate of the woman in his painting, which has been kept covered this past decade.

Cut to the Varelli villa, where Maria's sister Inez (Hedda Hopper) *has spent the summer* (and it is at this point that the story becomes virtually incomprehensible!). *The estate belonged to Maria, who left it to Inez in her will, but only if she died unmarried – otherwise, her sole beneficiary would be her husband.* (The screenwriter, however, does not choose to make this clear, opting instead for parody and

high camp – the scene where Maria is reunited with the household, including her maid Lena (Rafaela Ottiano, who had played
Grusinskaya's maid in *Grand Hotel*), is a high-camp hysteria fest
to end them all.) *A condition of her return is that no one but Bruno
should see her. 'She wants to be alone,' Tony says, a line which brought
roars of laughter from preview audiences.*

*Inez has left on the same train that brought Maria-Zara home,
catching enough of a glimpse of her to be convinced she is not her sister,
but Bruno is unsure. 'It's as if we've met for the first time,' he says,
while Maria-Zara stares at the portrait and plunges into a protracted,
world-weary speech: 'Is that who I'm supposed to be? ... I couldn't have
ever been that woman ... Look for yourself. There's nothing of that girl
in me ... I didn't know there was love like this, that there were men like
you. I couldn't be just the woman who has come back. Would you help
me to create her again? ... You can only do it by believing in me. Then
perhaps I can be as you desire me.'*

*Maria-Zara and Bruno rekindle their relationship. He takes her
sailing and attempts to seduce her. Initially she hesitates, but in the
next scene comes to his room wearing a translucent negligee.* (Their
lovemaking is unconvincing: Melvyn Douglas was a capable actor,
but unsuitable for this kind of scene with Garbo. The only eroti-
cism occurs when she places a cigarette between her lips and lights
it by rubbing the tip against the cigarette in his mouth – a sequence
which barely made it past the censor.)

*From here on in she gives every impression that she is a phoney,
dressing like the woman in the portrait, changing her hairstyle again.
Her memory appears to return and she recalls the good times they had
before she disappeared, but it turns out she has acquired this information from Maria's diary.*

*Then Salter turns up and reminds everyone how convenient it is that
Zara has been brought her here, just one week before Maria would have
been declared legally dead and her estate passed on to her husband.*
(Again, the scriptwriter has erred, for earlier it was established that
the estate would go to Inez, who now reappears for no reason!)
*Zara has been unaware of this until now and finally understands why
Bruno has been so willing to forgive her for her past. To prove his point,
Salter has brought along the real Maria. Black-clad and veiled, and*

recently released from a sanatorium, she recognises Lena and Inez. By now, however, all the characters in the drama – and the audience – are beyond caring who is who, and the mystery woman (played by Nella Wallace, a haggard-looking actress twenty years Garbo's senior) *turns out to be the gardener's long-lost daughter. Or is she? 'What does it matter?' Bruno asks, bringing what has been a pointless story to a welcome conclusion. 'I'll simply call you my beloved!'*

On 29 May, two days before her MGM contract was due to expire, Garbo announced that she was leaving for Sweden. No departure date was given, only that she had booked a one-way passage. Adding to the mystery, and Mayer's concern, was Harry Edington's statement to the press that she had taken Max Reinhardt up on his offer – made at the time of Murnau's death – to join his theatre group in Berlin. Edington had made this up in the hope of getting Mayer to offer Garbo a contract with a salary, which befitted the vast revenues she was bringing into the studio. She was Hollywood's biggest star but by no means its highest-paid. While Mayer was deliberating over this, on 3 July Paul Bern and Jean Harlow were married in what was regarded as the film capital's biggest shocker since the Fatty Arbuckle rape scandal of 1921. The two had met while Harlow was shooting *The Secret Six* with Clark Gable and though the producer was twice her age they had got along like the proverbial house on fire. As a matter of course Garbo was invited to the ceremony and, as a matter of course, declined.

Five days later, Edington learned that his ruse had worked: Garbo signed an exclusive contract with MGM for which everyone involved was compelled to swear an oath of secrecy, and for good reason. Mayer had set up her own company, Canyon Productions, within the MGM organisation, placing her on a far higher financial level than any contemporary, and he was fearful that if this got out, every major star in town would rebel. The deal was for two pictures only, the first to begin shooting no later than 6 July 1933, the second to go into production no later than ten months after the first had wrapped. Unusually, no time limit was set for the completion of each picture. The first film would be made in America, the other in Britain or Europe, however Garbo wished. She would be paid $250,000 per film: $100,000 upon signature of the contract, $30,000 on the first day of shooting, $15,000 per week for the next four weeks, nothing for any subsequent weeks, but $60,000 plus interest upon completion of the project. Additionally, she would be given the choice of director from two names put forward by the studio and a choice of leading man from a list of four. She would not, however, be given any say on the choice of scriptwriters.

On 21 July, Garbo left for New York, accompanied by Mercedes de Acosta. Asked if she would be back, Harry Edington told reporters, 'Miss Garbo has not made any definite plans regarding her future in motion pictures. She has not signed any deal with any Hollywood company.' The *Los Angeles Herald* lamented,

> Why speak of a fine performance from Melvyn Douglas, or say that von Stroheim was excellent as always? Why mention that it is a Pirandello story, when afterwards all you remember is a woman going aboard a boat with swelling sails, and sailing away into a moonlit night, leaving one with a sense of ineffable beauty?[254] [255]

Again, every major New York hotel was targeted with reporters, including the Commodore, where she had twice stayed before. Garbo outwitted them by staying out of town – at the Gramaton, in Bronxville. Two days later, there was another bust-up with Mercedes, who returned to Hollywood in a huff. On 29 July, Garbo boarded the *Gripsholm*. To ensure her privacy, the captain had left her name off the passenger list and, in a lame attempt to throw the press off the scent, had posted a notice by the pier: 'Greta Garbo is not travelling on this boat.' This had a reverse effect: the ship was invaded by press. Most of these unwanted guests were ejected before she set sail. A few, like the *New York Daily News'* Grace Robinson, had booked tickets to sail all the way to Sweden. 'From aboard the steamship *Gripsholm*, she will radio stories of Miss Garbo's voyage to her homeland,' the paper promised its readers, 'Nobody knows Miss Garbo now, but *you* can if you read Miss Robinson's daily stories in the news.' There would *be* no stories: during the journey Garbo emerged from her stateroom just twice – to dine at the captain's table, watched over by security men.[256]

Grace Robinson had not acquired the scoop she had anticipated and therefore decided that a 'lesson in humility' might be in order:

President Hoover has the heaviest burden of work in the world, but he does not shrink from shaking hands with ordinary mortals. King George of England, who rules an empire, does not consider himself too good to appear in public. That hero of the Atlantic, Charles Lindberg, who loathes publicity, did not consider that he could deny his admirers' wish to pay him homage. Greta Garbo has left the country that has made her world-famous without saying goodbye, without even suggesting that she was sorry to go. Who is she that she can permit herself such behaviour? The world's greatest actress? Well, what if she is? Sarah Bernhardt was and so was Eleanora Duse, but neither turned her back on the press and the public. Isn't it time that America revised its ideas about Garbo? Crowned heads, millionaires and famous writers visiting Hollywood have expressed desires to meet Garbo. She has refused. Who is she, we ask, to presume to behave like that? ... Well, now she has gone. Among her baggage is a fine leather handbag – a present [sic] from Irving Thalberg which contains the [sic] paltry two-million dollars she has saved up in dreadful Hollywood. The new contract she was [sic] offered was for $15,000 a week, but she refused to sign it. Goodbye, Garbo![257]

The *Gripsholm* reached Gothenburg on 8 August, where Garbo was greeted with the usual mass hysteria. This time, she was better prepared. Some sixty journalists were waiting as she emerged from the Customs Hall, including the ones who had travelled on the ship, where they had taken it in turns to mount a watch outside the door of her stateroom. One asked her why she disliked Hollywood so much and she replied, 'I don't dislike Hollywood at all, but if I did it would be because of people like you.' Another was told, abruptly, that though her work as an actress may have been newsworthy, her personal life was nobody's business but her own: 'Surely the world cannot care what soap I use to wash my face? I'm tired of picking up English, French, German and other newspapers and reading my views on love, cosmetics and health. I have never written a word in my life!' When asked what plans she had made for this trip to Sweden, the response was a snarled, 'None. Don't *you* ever take a holiday?' Then she saw Grace Robinson, who had made a nuisance of herself throughout the journey, and pointed accusingly: 'It was *you* who disturbed my sleep last night by banging on my door. Why don't you just go away?'[258]

Reunited with her mother, and brother Sven – forgiven for his earlier Hollywood faux pas – Garbo waved to the crowds before climbing into a car, which whisked them all off to a hotel in Ganna. Next day, they travelled to Skargarden, a small island off the coast of Stockholm, where Sven had rented a cottage. Garbo was introduced to his wife, Marguerite, with whom there was an instant rapport. Mimi Pollak was here too. Days into the stay, she received word that John Gilbert had married for the fourth time but no comment was forthcoming. For four weeks she did little more than swim, sunbathe and study the script for her next film, *Queen Christina*. Salka Viertel had written it in German and, to her friend's specification, in a treatment which owed more to the 'unconventional' life of Greta Garbo than that of the Swedish queen who had abdicated the throne on account of her sexual and religious leanings, rather than because she had loved the wrong man, as depicted in the film. Garbo had discussed the project with Thalberg the previous December, since which time he had suffered a near-fatal heart-attack. Mayer had replaced him with Eddie Mannix (1891–1963), an unsavoury character with underground gang connections. When told that she would have to work with Mannix, Garbo came close to abandoning *Queen Christina*. The film's saving grace was that Paul Bern would be producing. Then, early in September, she received the news that, just two months after marrying Jean Harlow, Bern's naked body had been found face-down on his bathroom floor, a gunshot wound to the head and a .38 pistol still in his hand.

Over the coming weeks, as the facts emerged, Bern's death was revealed to have been more than a simple matter of suicide. Unable to have sex on account of a genital abnormality, he had hoped the sexually torrid Harlow might have been able to cure him (though he was physically attracted only to men). When this was unsuccessful, he took his frustration out on his bride and severely beat her with a cane on their wedding night. The whole episode might have become lost in Hollywood folklore had it not been for Bern's attempts to please his wife on the evening of 4 September, when he marched into her bedroom wearing a huge strap-on dildo. Whether he attempted to use this is not known, only that she shrieked with laughter. Leaving a note apologising for humiliating her, Bern had shot himself. At least, this was the official verdict at the inquest. There have been numerous theories about the true cause of his death, not least that he may have been murdered.

A few days after learning of Bern's death, Garbo moved to Stockholm, where she again rented Lars Hanson's former apartment. Hanson was one of the first visitors and Mimi Pollak stayed over occasionally, until the unexpected arrival of Mercedes de Acosta who, once she had made up with Garbo, tried to organise her social calendar. This amounted to little more than a few dinner dates and a visit to the Comedy Theatre, which saw her lampooned by the press over the effort she made not to be recognised:

> Isn't there some neat hair-do that could tidy her hair a bit? And is she so hard-up that she has to keep her hat on and her old overcoat on her knees? If so, she may be happy to know that I have deposited five crowns with my editor so that she can observe our civilised conventions when she goes out and not cheat anyone of the cloakroom charge. Smarten yourself up a bit and I assure you that *no one* will recognise you![259]

Garbo was rescued from Mercedes' clutches by old flame Max Gumpel, now divorced from his wife. She called him, invited herself to dinner at his home and was told, 'Dress just as you would for any Hollywood dinner party.' So she turned up wearing tweed trousers, a polo-neck sweater and the diamond ring he had given her. Over the next two weeks, the pair were seen so often in public, always arm in arm, that the press speculated they might marry. They were invited to the Stockholm premiere of *Susan Lenox*, which was supposed to be a family affair. However, while Gumpel, Anna Gustaffson, Sven and his wife turned up for the event, Garbo stayed at home with Mimi Pollak. She and Gumpel also dined with Noël Coward, who was visiting Sweden for the first time. A disgruntled Mercedes made arrangements to leave for New York.

At the end of September, Garbo travelled to Tistad, where she stayed with Countess Horke Wachtmeister. Here she was reunited with William Sorensen and Prince Sigvard, though the real purpose of her sojourn, besides wanting to spend quality time with her friend, was to rehearse the part of Queen Christina in an authentic sixteenth-century castle. She also visited the monarch's castle at Uppsala, where she made sketches which, along with the research notes she had compiled during clandestine visits to library archives in Stockholm, she packed into the attaché case which would be handed over to MGM's sets department when she returned to Hollywood.

On 15 November, Garbo and Horke travelled to London, where she checked in at the Washington Hotel, on Curzon Street, as 'Miss Swanson', not one of her more sensible aliases. By now the disguises were so contrived that even if she was not recognised immediately, anyone seeing her knew that she was no ordinary tourist – the cheap black wig and dark glasses, the turned-up collar, the hat pulled down over her face, the way she stared at the ground when speaking to anyone. Believing she was *Gloria* Swanson, the receptionist alerted the press, causing Garbo to make a hasty escape through the kitchen, from where a waiting taxi sped her to Noël Coward's house, where she laid low for three days before rejoining Horke.

Early the next morning, the friends boarded the boat-train for Paris. Garbo arrived at the Gare du Nord disguised as an English schoolteacher and again fooled no one. By the time they reached their hotel the place was swarming with reporters, several of whom clambered on to the roof and running-board of her taxi. Garbo ordered the driver to put his foot down: one by one the pressmen fell off and almost ended up under the wheels of the fleet of vehicles which had pursued them from the station, enabling her car to finally lose them. They ended at the Castiglione, Horke's favourite hotel in the rue Faubourg-St-Honoré, where Garbo signed in as 'Madame Gustaffson'.

The remainder of the trip was relatively low key. Garbo and

Horke were squired around town by Mitty Goldin, the Hungarian impresario who ran the ABC music-hall. Goldin introduced them to Jean Cocteau, and it was he who escorted Garbo and Horke to Le Boeuf-sur-le-Toit, one of the city's premier café-concerts. Appearing on the bill was Damia, the great *chanteuse* whom Garbo had part-emulated in *As You Desire Me*. 'She came, she saw and she conquered,' Damia recalled, 'A very shy, very humble and unassuming woman. She asked me to sing "La Veuve" because she said she found it an amusing concept, this being the familiar name for the guillotine. Then, after the show, we all headed for my place.'[260]

'My place' was the Concert-Damia, the singer's own café-concert in Montmartre, where she performed most evenings with a single spotlight trained on her face, the first popular singer ever to do this. The idea was that the audience then saw only her face and hands and so concentrated on the song and not the surroundings. One contemporary American source described it as 'one of the most lurid nightclubs in Montmartre, frequented by hard-boiled women of the Paris *demimonde* who go there attired in mannish costumes to give tourists the shock they are looking for by asking them to dance.' In fact, the Concert-Damia was nothing like this and the only dancing that took place was an occasional *apache*, the rough-and-ready routine which Damia herself had introduced to Parisian audiences some years before.[261]

On 19 November, Garbo and Horke caught the overnight express to Stockholm and a four-month period of which virtually nothing is recorded followed. Later there would be speculation of an abortion or a miscarriage as a result of her relationship with Max Gumpel and this is not entirely out of the question. She rarely ventured out in public during this period and for some reason took extreme measures for secrecy, even for her, when returning to America on 26 March 1933. Terrified that the press would pick up on her pasty complexion and the fact that she had lost weight, instead of embarking on the regular Gothenburg-New York route, she boarded the 500-ton freighter, *Annie Johnson*, bound for San Diego via the Panama Canal – a journey which would take thirty-four days rather than the usual seven.

To say that conditions aboard the *Annie Johnson* were Spartan may be an understatement. Garbo was one of just four passengers and when not hiding below deck to avoid the others, emerging to sit on the deck only at night when they were in bed, she occupied one of the lifeboats, where the captain, the only one who knew who she really was, personally served her her meals. Neither had she informed Harry Edington of her unusual travel arrangements, though she did get the captain to cable Mayer from the ship – breaking her rule never to deal with him directly. On 29 March, Mayer cabled her back: two directors were suggested for *Queen Christina* – Robert Z. Leonard and Edmund Goulding. Garbo chose Goulding, but changed her mind the next day when Mayer cabled again to inform her that Ernst Lubitsch was also available, as a loan-out from Paramount. Garbo cabled back: 'Prefer Lubitsch. Also happy for Goulding.' On 17 April, while the *Annie Johnson* docked to pick up supplies before entering the Panama Canal, Garbo called Salka Viertel. Speaking in German, in case someone was listening in, she informed her friend when she would be arriving in San Diego for her to pick her up and gave explicit instructions that no one else should be informed.

The *Annie Johnson* docked on 29 April and Salka drove Garbo to Mabery Road: she had elected to move house again and would stay there until Harry Edington found her another property. Because he had been kept out of the loop during her absence, the press speculated that she had fired him and that Salka would now be looking after her interests. This was untrue – and in any case, as no document had been signed, Edington had never *officially* been her agent: all their dealings had been by way of a 'gentleman's agreement', while his wages were paid by MGM. The press also reported that, henceforth, Garbo's threats to return to Sweden for good might not be taken quite so seriously – she had recently acquired a permanent resident's visa. Mayer breathed a huge sigh of relief: that same morning, Garbo had pocketed the $100,000 down payment for the new film, and he had been terrified of her suddenly changing her mind – something she was entirely capable of – and leaving him in the lurch.

CHAPTER TEN

QUEEN CHRISTINA

'Just imagine – Christina abdicating for the sake of a little Spaniard!'

The idea of Garbo playing Queen Christina was not a new one. Mauritz Stiller had toyed with the project in 1927, but it had been shelved because most Americans – familiar with royals such as Henry VIII and Marie Antoinette – had never heard of this 'obscure' Swedish monarch. Garbo had discussed her with Marie Dressler while shooting *Anna Christie* but it was only after signing the new contract with MGM that she began taking a keen interest in the subject.[262]

Christina (1626–89), remains one of history's oddities. She inherited the throne at the age of six, on the death of her father Gustav II Augustus at Lutzen, during the Thirty Years War. Raised as a boy, at eighteen she took the coronation oath, demanding the word 'King' be substituted for 'Queen'. Intelligent and well-educated, she spoke several languages and was well-versed in art, theology, philosophy and history. Like Garbo, she bore all the complexities of a lonely woman who had reached maturity without the support of a father figure. Like her, sexually and socially she preferred the company of women, which caused her problems as she was expected to marry and provide Sweden with an heir. Unlike Garbo, she was void of beauty, small of stature, equine featured and slightly disabled, having been dropped as a baby by a clumsy nurse, resulting in one shoulder being higher than the other.

Modern sex psychologists have suggested that Christina suffered from a kind of 'adrenogenital syndrome' in that, while possessed of fully functioning female reproductive organs, outwardly and mentally she believed herself to have been a man – dressing, speaking, and behaving like one. Nonsense, of course. Raised to rule a nation, she had been conditioned to *think* like a man, but sexually she was no different to any other woman with healthy Sapphic tendencies, which were only considered 'abnormal' because of her royalty and the expectations arising from it. In European history there are many homosexual kings who married and had sex with their queens purely to continue the royal line, while enjoying the attentions of favourites – Edward II and James I being but two examples. Christina, like Garbo, had a mind of her own and was too headstrong to submit to peer pressure: she did not have sex with men because she did not *want* to. 'I am unable to marry, and that is how it is,' she wrote in her memoirs, 'I have earnestly prayed to God to let me change my attitude, but I have not been able to do so.'²⁶³

The great love of Christina's life was a young noblewoman named Ebba Sparre (1629–62). Christina was open about their relationship, and her courtiers tolerated it so long as it did not interfere with Christina eventually finding a husband. Considerably more serious, had it emerged during her reign, was her secret practising of Catholicism in a fervently Protestant country. Therefore, because she had no intention of marrying and having sex with a man to produce an heir, and because of her Catholic beliefs (she eventually converted to the religion), her only option was to abdicate at twenty-seven, the same age that Garbo was when she portrayed her on the screen. Christina's exile was spent in Rome, though she did return to Sweden upon the death of her nominated successor, Charles Gustavus. Her Catholicism prevented her from re-taking the throne and he was succeeded by his five-year old son. Christina died of pneumonia in 1689 and was buried in St Peter's Basilica.

On 30 April 1933, Garbo announced that she was ready for work, which by the terms of her contract meant that shooting on the film would commence no later than 15 May. If this was not enough to put Mayer in a flap – the director, producer and co-stars were yet to be decided upon – Garbo added that she would be taking a rest period of just one month before shooting the second of her two-film deal, W. Somerset Maugham's *The Painted Veil*. Mayer interpreted her eagerness to complete her obligation to MGM as a sign that she might already have been holding secret negotiations with rival studios.

There was light relief at this time when Garbo met and befriended one of her biggest fans – the outrageous, outspoken, out-everything Tallulah Bankhead. In her younger days, Tallulah (1903–68) boasted that she had slept with dozens of women and during a bust-up with Mayer, threatened to give their names to the press. Her biggest regret, she always said, was failing to seduce Garbo, the woman she regarded as superior to every other being on earth. During Garbo's absence, Tallulah had met Salka Viertel at a party, where she learned that her idol was just as interested in meeting her – though not for the same reasons. A meeting was arranged to take place at Mabery Road, in a scenario which might have been part of a Marx Brothers film, and was typical of the Alabama-born beauty's offbeat humour. Tallulah marched up to Garbo and tugged her eyelashes to see if both they and their owner were real. She then 'swooned' on cue and had to be revived with half a bottle of brandy. Garbo was amused and accepted an invitation to dine at Tallulah's place a few evenings later, where the humour was resumed. Dinner was prepared and the champagne put on ice but Garbo failed to turn up at the appointed time. When Tallulah had almost given up hope, there was a knock on the door and her maid ushered in 'a Chinese woman complete with slanting eyes, a black wig and an Oriental gown.' The woman announced in pidgin English, 'Miss Garbo unable to come – sent me instead!' Tallulah played along with Garbo's game all evening. When she was leaving, Garbo shook Tallulah's hand and said in her own voice, 'Pleased to have met you, Miss. After Miss Bankhead, you're the finest actress on the screen!'[264]

Writing in her autobiography, Tallulah observed, 'Forget all the bilge about Garbo. She's excessively shy. When at ease with people who do not look upon her as something begat by the Sphinx and Frigg, a Norse goddess of the sky, she can be as much fun as the next gal!' The two remained friends for many years, and such was Tallulah's reverence for Garbo that she placed the dining chair she had sat upon in her bathroom, which Garbo had also used: for months, the room became a shrine and if a visitor needed to use the toilet, they were sent next door.

The same week, there was a reunion between Garbo and Borg. Since parting company, the two had not been in contact: Borg had called several times but Garbo had refused to come to the phone. Therefore it came as a surprise when she called him early in May and announced that she wanted to see him. Because she had no place of her own and did not wish to involve Salka Viertel or visit Borg's beachside home she met him at a restaurant near Santa Monica Canyon. 'I thought of Garbo and a little incident which had occurred between us one morning on the beach, years ago,' Borg recalled, almost certainly referring to one of their pre-dawn, *al fresco* trysts.[265]

Garbo had not intended this to be a romantic assignation: she was here to give Borg a piece of her mind because she had heard he was writing a book about her. However, because they shared a past, she wanted to sort things out 'man to man'. He had in fact been commissioned to write a series of features for *Film Pictorial*, but like Ruth Biery overstepped the mark, disclosing too many of her confidences – particularly her thoughts about having children. Instead of bawling him out, she eyed him up and down like the prize specimen he was, and after listening to his mumbled excuses – which ended with him asking, 'How do you like being back and once more reigning as the Queen of Mystery in Hollywood?' – responded drily that she was 'not open to interviews', and promptly returned with him to his house, where she stayed for a week.

For the benefit of his readers, Borg amended the circumstances of this very public meeting, witnessed by several journalists, writing that they had bumped into each other while she had been striding up a mountain trail and he was on his way down. The giveaway was in the way he described how she was dressed for 'hiking', having eschewed her hacking jacket, tweed trousers and brogues for a pretty blue blouse, short white skirt, *women's* low-heeled shoes, and a red beret:

In place of the uncouth Swedish girl of my first recollection was a lady – a polished, sophisticated woman of the world with poise, presence and charm. Since we conversed in both Swedish and English, I was able to note the difference in her handling of both languages. In the old days she had little English, and that little was guttural and incorrect. Today her English was far better, and she spoke it with a freedom she had not known before. Remembering the sloppy, ill-fitting garments of days gone by, the badly-applied make-up in private life, my mind went back to the perfectly-groomed, immaculate woman I had just left on the trail. *Her* hair was soft, lustrous and well-cared for. *Her* make-up was skilfully applied. There was a poise, a presence, a surety about her which had been lacking in her first Hollywood days.[266]

Borg drove Garbo to the studio to inspect her new dressing room. For years, Marion Davies and Norma Shearer had had the most luxurious dressing rooms on the lot and Mayer had hoped to butter up Garbo by having hers renovated and redecorated during her absence. Borg recalled how she exploded upon seeing her new closet, the hooks of which were set barely three feet from the floor: 'Frantic officials hurried to ascertain the cause. It developed that a group of midgets, working at the studio, had been assigned the dressing room during Garbo's absence and the hooks had been set for them.'

The offending dressing room put to rights, on 17 May, Garbo was still awaiting her studio call: the film did not have a producer, whose job it was, traditionally, to hire the director. Mayer stepped in and hired her a helmsman he hoped she would approve of: with Edmund Goulding and Ernst Lubitsch tied up with other projects and Garbo unwilling to wait until they were free, and with Clarence Brown still refusing to work with her, Mayer had brought in Rouben Mamoulian, who had recently directed Marlene Dietrich in *Song of Songs*.

Mamoulian (1898–1987) was educated in Moscow and London, where he produced stage plays in the West End. His debut Broadway production, the very first *Porgy & Bess*, opened to rave reviews in 1927, two years before he began his cinematic career with an early talkie, *Applause*. Since then he had directed the classic gangster movie, *City Streets*, and *Dr Jekyll & Mr Hyde*, for which Fredric March had won an Oscar. Mamouilian now took it upon himself to appoint a producer, despite Mayer's opposition but Garbo was calling the shots, and as Mamoulian had her on side, Mayer backed off and Walter Wanger entered the equation.

Wanger (1894–1968) had just produced *The Bitter Tea of General Yen* with Barbara Stanwyck and Nils Asther and tried his utmost to get Asther for this one. Indeed, once she learned that he was unavailable, casting her leading man proved a nightmare for all concerned, a problem which remained unresolved when shooting began on 7 August. The supports, on the other hand, were a doddle. She asked for Lewis Stone, for what would be their last film together, and approved Elizabeth Young for the part of Ebba Sparre. Veteran English actor C. Aubrey Smith was cast as Christina's manservant, Aage, and eventually she settled for Ian Keith to play her jealous former suitor, Magnus. This left one major role outstanding – that of Don Antonio de la Prada, her Spanish envoy lover in Hollywood's version of Christina's story.

British actor Leslie Howard, who Garbo liked, responded that the feeling was not mutual, that he would never work with any actress who would completely monopolise the production they were in. He had recently refused to appear opposite Marlene Dietrich in *The Scarlet Empress* for the same reason. 'From a critical standpoint, neither Dietrich nor Garbo is a great actress,' he arrogantly declared, 'Garbo might reach true greatness if she corrected some bad mannerisms. It is her own fault that she has been so handicapped by inadequate direction, for she has scared everyone so badly that they don't dare to supervise her, to advise her when she is mistaken.' To which Marlene replied, 'This may have been so, but who was *he* to make such a criticism? He became a great actor later on, but in those days he was virtually unknown, almost a nobody.' Franchot Tone was a strong contender for the part, and would have carried himself well, but he was dropped when Garbo expressed her admiration of a young British actor she had recently seen opposite Ann Harding in *Westward Passage*. This was Laurence Olivier (1907–89), who she said reminded her of John Gilbert in his younger days. But if Olivier would one day be regarded as one of the finest actors of his generation, for American audiences during the early Thirties he was no great shakes – thus far, all his Hollywood films had bombed.[267] [268]

Olivier made the mistake of boasting that he had actually been given the part of Antonio, and that the test he was asked to do with

Garbo to determine how well they 'blended' was merely a formality. He recalled how it all went wrong: 'I was too nervous and scared of my leading lady. I knew I was lightweight for her and nowhere near her stature, and began to feel more and more certain that I was for the chop.' Another problem, he added, was Garbo's coldness towards him – hardly surprising as he gave her every impression that *she* should feel privileged to be working with *him*. He remembered an incident when he had approached her on the set. He was in costume, having just shot a scene which did not involve her, and she was resting – wearing pyjamas, smoking, and sitting on a chest. Obviously she wanted to be alone, and he annoyed her by sitting next to her, uninvited, and chatting about nothing in particular: 'After a breathless pause, she slid herself off the chest sideways saying, "Oh, vell, life's a pain anyway!" I knew then that the end was not far off.' Not to be outdone, Rouben Mamoulian persuaded Garbo to shoot the love scene at the inn with Olivier, which they attempted twice. As he wrote in his memoirs:

> Garbo was unmoved. She, the great actress whom everyone expected to go into this tender scene with convincing abandon, was as frigid to my embrace as if she were a woman of stone ... We walked a little, smoked together, tried to talk small talk. Then we came back and went into the scene again. Garbo froze up as before.[269]

There are three published accounts, all questionable, of how John Gilbert came to once more act opposite Garbo. His eldest daughter, Leatrice, recalled a anecdote by her mother – whose memory was selective at the best of times, depending on her mood and how much she had had to drink – that Walter Wanger overheard Garbo snapping at Laurence Olivier and invited Gilbert to the set to cheer her up. This is unlikely: the subject of Gilbert was so sensitive, no one dared bring his name up in conversation, let alone arrange for her to be surprised by him in her dressing room. Equally ridiculous is the story that Gilbert was persuaded to don Olivier's discarded costume for what he was led to believe was a pre-test dress-rehearsal, but which was actually filmed, that Wanger called him the next day to announce the part was his, *and* with Mayer's blessing. Gilbert's contract with MGM had ended several weeks earlier, with Mayer declaring how relieved he was to be shot of him. The third and only slightly more credible account, again recounted by Leatrice, is that Garbo took pity on a down-on-his-luck Gilbert, marched into Mayer's office and demanded that he would be her co-star or no one else.[270] Additionally, it was claimed, MGM had been inundated with letters from fans asking for Garbo and Gilbert to once more be paired. Garbo of course did not swan into offices and make extraneous demands – she much preferred to retreat and remain invisible until they had been met. The most *likely* explanation is that, with shooting already under way and no other compatible actor available at such short notice, Mayer was forced to swallow his pride and welcome Gilbert back into the fold, while Garbo, eager to finish this and her next film before deciding whether or not to quit, accepted a reluctant re-pairing with Gilbert, rather than waste time waiting for someone better to come along.

First of all, though, Gilbert had to be tested for the part and, as Laurence Olivier was still in the running, Garbo insisted on scrutinising both tests, with both actors sitting in the projection room. Gilbert's daughter recalled her reaction, and Olivier's arrogant response: 'Garbo's face softened. Into her eyes came a strange, beautiful light ... Here I am, supposed to be one of the greatest actors in the world, and this fading Jack Gilbert's test was infinitely better than mine.'[271]

Olivier took Garbo's snub to heart. He was due to test for Irving Thalberg's *Marie Antoinette*, with Norma Shearer in the title role but he left Hollywood in a huff and, despite numerous requests, for several years refused to return. Eventually he made his 'comeback' in 1939, playing Heathcliff opposite Merle Oberon in *Wuthering Heights*. Accompanied by Vivien Leigh, whom he married the following year, and who had just been signed to play Scarlett O'Hara in *Gone with rhe Wind*, Olivier bumped into Garbo at director George Cukor's house and spent part of the afternoon strolling around the garden with her. According to the scriptwriter Garson Kanin, also at the party, this led to a furious row between Olivier and the already insecure Leigh, who suspected him of 'sucking up to' Garbo, or worse, during their promenade, even more so when

Olivier confessed that all they had done was talk about the differences between fruit and vegetable growing in Sweden and America.

As for Gilbert, he certainly swallowed a huge chunk of humble pie in working with her again: MGM paid him just $20,000 a week, a fraction of what he had earned for *Flesh and the Devil*. His humility and gratitude extended to the comments he made to the press on the day he shot his first scene with Garbo, their first meeting in three years: 'Three years ago, I could have sworn that she would never look at me again, and now she has fought to get me this part – when I am down and most in need of encouragement. Incredible!'[272]

Gilbert was in a pretty bad shape. After just one year, and despite, or perhaps because of, a new baby, his fourth marriage was on the rocks. In the early stages of chronic alcoholism, much of the time he suffered from the shakes and some mornings was so ill – vomiting blood on account of bleeding ulcers – that he found it impossible to get to the studio, telling them he had the flu. As had happened with Erich von Stroheim, Gilbert received Garbo's 'sympathy vote': whenever he was too ill to work, she was informed and also called in sick. Mayer was furious, all the more so because he knew that there was absolutely nothing he could do to bring her into line.

To cash in on the publicity while the film was in production, Margaret L. Goldsmith published *Christina of Sweden: A Psychological Biography*, which raised concern among the moralists. Writing in the *New York Herald Tribune*, Lewis Gannet posed, 'The one persistent love of Christina's life was for the Countess Ebba Sparre, a beautiful Swedish noblewoman who lost most of her interest in Christina when Christina ceased to rule Sweden. The evidence is overwhelming. But will Garbo play such a Christina?' The answer was yes, she would.[273]

The trailer for the film, subtitled 'Talk of the World', saw the news of Garbo's comeback broadcast in several languages, with headlines such as 'GARBO DISAPPEARS IN SWEDEN', followed by the announcement, in large letters flashed across the screen, 'GARBO RETURNS: A Queen Whose Love Affairs Were As Modern As Tomorrow's Tabloids! A 17th Century Maiden Who Lived With 20th Century Madness!' And because the trailer was made *before*

John Gilbert was hired, the credits below her name read, 'Ian Keith, Lewis Stone, Elizabeth Young & A Thousand Others'. Also, for the first time, fans could purchase memorabilia, the likes of which Hollywood had not seen since 1921, when Valentino fans had been able to buy *Sheik* perfume, soap, Vaseline, bubble-gum, costumes and even condoms. Now, there were *Queen Christina* papier-mâché heads, paintings, dolls, cups, cut-outs and corsets.

As was to be expected, Hollywood's take on the life of Queen Christina has little to do with historical fact, though in retrospect this is unimportant – it is by far Garbo's finest work and also her personal favourite, though initially she had her doubts over how it might be received. 'It's really bad in every respect, but the worst thing is they'll think *I* don't know any better,' she wrote to Horke Wachtmeister. She revised her opinion upon reading the Swedish reviews, all of which declared that *her* Christina had been far more beautiful and charismatic than the real one. Yet it starts off woefully bad.[274]

A soldier stumbling across the battlefield asks a dying man his name and he replies, 'I was King of Sweden.'

Cut to the court where six-year-old Christina is being crowned 'king'. (Her actual coronation took place when she was twenty-three. Also, why MGM chose Cora Sue Collins to play the young Christina is baffling: she has the most dreadful 'Bronx honk', far removed from the sultry tones of the actress who plays her as an adult.) *The story then moves forward fifteen years.*

Dressed as a man, Christina returns to the castle with her hunting dogs. At first we only see her from behind. Then, as she removes her wide-brimmed hat, we barely have time to take in her staggering beauty before she is accosted by her ministers. Prince Charles (Reginald Owen) *has arrived home after another victory, but she is not interested in him or this endless conflict: 'There are other things to live for than wars ... Spoils, glory, flags and trumpets ... Death and destruction. Triumphals of crippled men. Sweden victorious in a ravaged Europe. An island in a dead sea. I tell you, I want no more of it!' She signs a peace treaty and then when Aage, her manservant, brings up the fact that her ministers are desperate for her to marry, she quotes from Molière: 'All I can say is that I think marriage an altogether shocking thing. How is it possible to endure the idea of sleeping with a man in the room?'*

Earlier Christina flirted with greasy ex-suitor Magnus (Ian Keith), who she can no longer stand, but now the real object of her affection appears: Ebba, her lady-in-waiting. Ebba kisses Christina on the lips and berates her for cancelling their proposed sleigh-ride to attend to matters of state: 'At the end of the day you're never free to go anywhere. You're surrounded by musty old papers and musty old men, and I can't get near you.' Christina says they will go away soon; in the meantime she awaits the arrival of the Spanish envoy with a marriage proposal. She gazes across the wintry landscape that serves as an allegory for her regulated constitutional life: 'Snow again, eternal snow ... Snow is a wild sea. One could go out and be lost in it, and forget the world and oneself!' (For years MGM were adamant that Garbo and Walter Wanger had insisted all *Queen Christina's* outdoor scenes be shot on location in Sweden. It never occurred to the naive critics and reporters to question how the studio had managed this, nor why none of the actors left footprints in the snow. This was because the locations were in sunny California – the 'snow' several tons of oatmeal.)

Christina's Chancellor (Lewis Stone) is next to broach the subject of her marriage, chiding her for being stubborn: 'But your Majesty, you cannot die an old maid...' Christina responds with a flourish: 'I have no intention, Chancellor. I shall die a bachelor!' However, her good mood changes when she overhears Ebba telling a male lover how selfish she finds the Queen and she rages: 'You pretended to be interested in me and my problems. Your sympathy, your concern – all pretence, underneath which you resent me.'

Hurt, she tells Aage that she is going hunting and out in the wilds comes across Don Antonio's coach, stuck in a snowdrift. The Spanish envoy mistakes her for a boy when she helps him out of his predicament and tips her with a coin bearing her likeness. With him none the wiser and she not knowing who he is, Christina rides to the next inn and secures the last room, eating with the locals, who also do not recognise her. Then Antonio arrives. They hit it off and talk of love, an emotion in which Christina does not believe: 'A great love, a perfect love, is an illusion. It is the golden fable of which we all dream, but in ordinary life it does not happen.' Antonio wants a room and the innkeeper suggests they might share, declaring (for the benefit of the censor), *'The bed, as you know, is large. You might both lie on it and never know that you are not alone.' Antonio is game, but Christina has doubts. There is competition for her attention from Elsa, the chambermaid, who kneels before this 'young lord' on the pretence that he might need assistance with his boots, hoping he might hire her services for the night.* (Elsa was played by Barbara Barondess (1907–2000), but apparently only after Katharine Hepburn's pleas to appear in a Garbo film, even as a cameo, had fallen on deaf ears. Currently playing a boy in *Christopher Strong*, Hepburn was later alleged to have wanted the part so that she could study Garbo's acting technique close at hand, though some believe she merely wanted to get close to Garbo.) *Touching the royal thigh, Elsa says she is only good when she dislikes a man, leading Christina to quip, 'That's a true virtue!' Elsa leaves and Antonio reveals who he is. But Christina likes playing this game too much and introduces herself as Count Dohna* (the name she used while in exile). *They get ready for bed, and Antonio is stunned to discover that 'he' is a she. 'Life is so gloriously improbable,' he exclaims* (though one gets the impression that the outcome would have been the same had he really been required to share his bed with this chirpy youth!).

It is only when one reaches this stage of the picture that it is clear what a wreck John Gilbert had become. His nose is bulbous, his eyes glazed through alcohol abuse, his stance gawky. He wears the most ridiculous, ill-fitting wig, as if the props department intended to make him look silly, and all this must have added to Louis B. Mayer's belief that he should have called it quits years ago. Additionally, Gilbert's voice is high-pitched, almost becoming falsetto at times, and it does make one wonder – having visualised Olivier, Asther or Franchot Tone in the role – whether MGM were taking audiences for a ride by expecting them to believe that a queen would have abdicated her throne for such a man.

The next morning, Antonio's manservant announces they may be snowed in for days. The curtains surrounding the bed are closed and from behind them, Antonio says they have no intention of getting up. Then comes the film's second most celebrated scene, one which Garbo practised time and time again off-screen. Much of the sequence is filmed with Garbo in intense close-up. Lying on her back, she munches the grapes Antonio has brought with him, savours their aroma, then gets up and walks around the room while he stares, mesmerised. Her expression changes with each frame as she caresses the mantelpiece, the paintings and walls, smiles back at him through the mirror, hugs the phallic-shaped spool on the spinning wheel (begging the question: why would a bedroom at a country inn contain such an article?) *and savours the scent of the bedcovers. Finally, having watched her clutch the bedpost in an orgasmic embrace, he asks her what she is doing and she responds, 'I've been memorising this room. In the future, in my memory, I shall live a great deal in this room.'*

The rhythm of the scene, to which would be added Herbert Stuttgart's 'plinky-plonky' score, was effected using a metronome. Rouben Mamoulian had employed this technique for the opening scene of Maurice Chevalier and Jeanette MacDonald's *Love Me Tonight*. The kissing, though, is not as passionate as fans would have liked, allegedly on account of Gilbert's halitosis, brought about by his copious vomiting of blood, on and off the set. Garbo's 'official' excuse for curbing the passion was that Gilbert was now a married man, with a baby daughter.

Christina has still not revealed who she really is, all she will say is that 'at home' she lives a constrained life. Antonio promises to show her the world. Dreamily she responds, 'I have imagined happiness, but happiness you cannot imagine! ... This is how the Lord must have felt when he first beheld the finished world, with all His creatures breathing, living.' They bid each other farewell, shaking hands now that she is a 'man' once more, and she promises they will meet again in Stockholm.

At court, she makes up with Ebba and gives her permission to marry her sweetheart (effectively the Hays Office delivering a message that, despite the earlier kiss and talk of dying a bachelor, Ebba's impending nuptials and what had taken place in the bedchamber with Antonio has resulted in a return to 'normality', where these two women are concerned). *Antonio, meanwhile, gets quite a shock when he arrives at court and finds out who she is. He is offhand with her, feeling that she has made a fool of him, until she explains, 'It had been so enchanting to be a woman. Not a queen, just a woman in a man's arms. Forgive me for being a queen.'*

Magnus, jealous of Antonio and concerned that if Christina marries him, Sweden will embrace Catholicism – a situation even more damaging than war – incites the people to revolt. Christina faces the mob alone, quells them and then signs a passport guaranteeing Antonio safe conduct to the border, where she plans to join him; 'I am tired of being a symbol. I long to be a human being.' Next, we see her in full regalia addressing the populace, who are expecting her to announce her betrothal to Charles. Instead, she names him as her successor and abdicates. It is one of the most moving scenes Garbo ever played. Ebba accompanies her on the first leg of her journey into exile – this time when they kiss it is behind the brim of her hat. In the meantime, Antonio has fought a duel with Magnus (in Salka Viertel's original treatment Magnus kidnaps and murders him) *and Christina arrives at the ship to find him mortally wounded. He dies in her arms* (not terribly convincingly) *but she decides to leave Sweden just the same: 'The wind is with us,' she sighs.* (The more observant critics pointed out that it was blowing in the wrong direction.) *She walks to the prow of the vessel and we witness Garbo's greatest on-screen moment. The wind whips back her hair as William Daniels slowly and majestically brings her face closer towards us. Completely immobile for a whole minute – allowing the audience to decide what she may be thinking – this single frame closes one of the cinematic masterpieces of the twentieth century.*

The *New Yorker* hailed *Queen Christina* 'the Garbo film of the season, with the lady doing handsomely', but thought the story of old Sweden sagged a bit. *Photoplay* praised her 'glorious reappearance on the screen' and her 'unfathomable mystery', then spoilt it all by offering undeserved praise to child star Cora Sue Collins, the production's only low point. *Motion Picture*'s Walter Ramsey deemed it a triumph for Garbo, 'One of the great pictures of the past few years, a historical epic making a sustained drive for artistry.' Mordaunt Hall called it, 'A skilful blend of history and fiction in which the Nordic star, looking as alluring as ever, gives a performance which merits nothing but the highest praise. She appears every inch a queen.'[275] Such sterling reviews meant nothing to *Hollywood Citizen-News'* stuffy Elizabeth Yeaman, who had denounced Garbo in *Inspiration*, and complained directly to the Hays Office after walking out of the New York premiere, on 26 December 1933, disgusted by the film's 'homosexual' sequence. In her column, Yeaman seethed:

> There are two scenes which I found distinctly offensive: that in which Garbo is helped into her trousers by a slovenly valet, and that in which orders for a morning chocolate are issued from behind the drawn curtain of a bed in the inn. However, last night's audience roared gustily over both episodes, which I resented and felt might have been handled with subtlety. It remains to be seen what the censorship board thinks.[276]

In the wake of Yeaman's piece, the homophobes jumped on to the bandwagon regarding the scene at the inn. The Breen Office, founded on 1 January 1934 by self-appointed moralist Joseph Breen – a cohort of Will Hays, equally repulsive, no less loathed – declared the new Garbo picture would not pass his 'Purity Code' unless the 'offending homosexual scene' was completely removed – or at least the frames where she 'lasciviously' hugged the cotton spool and the bedpost and appeared to sniff the bedcovers. Breen was supported by Martin Quigley of the *Motion Picture Herald*, who dismissed the scene as 'pornographic', and the Catholic League of Decency, who denounced Garbo as 'perverted' and demanded her name be added to the Hays Office 'Doom Book'. Personally compiled by Hays and Breen, this contained the names of some 200 stars – topping the list were Joan Crawford, Mae West and Tallulah Bankhead – considered guilty of 'moral turpitude'. Garbo's personal life, however, was beyond reproach and despite such protestations, the scene remained intact after Walter Wanger had it vetted by an independent jury of producers who (with the help of a few cash handouts) approved it wholeheartedly, declaring any 'filth' was entirely in the mind of the detractor.

Queen Christina became the third most profitable of Garbo's films thus far, just behind *Grand Hotel* and *Mata Hari*, though if John Gilbert was hoping that working with Garbo again had completely resurrected his career, he would be disappointed. According to his daughter, when shooting wrapped, Gilbert called Mayer to thank him for giving him the part of Antonio. 'I'd hardly opened my mouth before he opened up on me: foul abuse, threats, damnation, and all hell broke loose,' he recalled. But Mayer's spite did not end here. In order to hire Gilbert for the film, he had assigned him to a standard seven-year contract, fully intent on offering him no further work. When this emerged during a heated argument two weeks before the film's premiere, Gilbert took the matter to court and this time there was no support from Garbo. He lost the case, and in March 1934 took out a full-page ad in the *Hollywood Reporter*, announcing that MGM would neither offer him work nor release him from his contract. He was rescued by Columbia Pictures, who put him into *The Captain Hates the Sea* playing an alcoholic. It would be his last part.[277]

Between August and November 1933, Garbo saw a lot of the boxer, Max Baer. Though not overly enamoured of sport, an event which took place as the political climate was darkening in Europe impressed her no end. This was the bout, in June, between Baer (1909–59) and Max Schmeling (1905–2005), Hitler's favourite fighter and the symbol of the Aryan race. Baer, the son of a Jewish hog butcher, accredited his formidable strength and physique (6′2″, 210 pounds) to his 'training' when he had sledgehammered cattle to death with a single blow. In the ring he riled his German opponent by wearing shorts emblazoned with the Star of David (though after the war it emerged that Schmeling, while still serving his country, had saved the lives of Jewish children), and pummelled him through ten rounds until the referee stopped the fight. Henceforth he would be feted as 'The Jews' Boxer' and Garbo was so pleased with his 'mini-victory' over fascism that, when she learned he was in Los Angeles, she invited him to the set of *Queen Christina*. Initially, she and the boxer lunched in her dressing room but the pair found each other so fascinating that they dated for several weeks, until Baer had to return to New York to train for his next fight, and she began preparing for *The Painted Veil*. The following year, he knocked out 275-pound Primo Carnera to be crowned World Heavyweight Champion.

There was also widespread speculation of an affair between Garbo and Rouben Mamoulian while *Queen Christina* was in production, though this appears to have been no more than a working relationship, where they discussed aspects of the shooting schedule in more relaxed and intimate surroundings than was usual for her. The pair dined regularly, in full public glare, and Mamoulian took her dancing to some of the clubs on Sunset Strip. There were also weekend vacations, almost certainly platonic, which continued after shooting wrapped. On 13 January 1934, a 'close friend' of Garbo – Mercedes – tipped off the press that she and the director, driven by her chauffeur James, had set off on a trip to the Grand Canyon, perhaps with marriage in mind. Within the hour, several carloads of reporters caught up with them and as they approached the state border with Arizona, Garbo ordered James to put his foot down and drive past the control-point without stopping. Not surprisingly they were chased and flagged down by a patrol car, compelled to spend the night at a nearby hotel until a senior police officer decided what action to take. No charges were laid, but by now hundreds of tourists augmented the convoy trailing Garbo and Mamoulian to the next stop of their itinerary – the El Tovar Hotel, where they had booked separate rooms under the names 'Mary Jones' and 'Robert Borji'. They spent an uninterrupted night there and continued their journey to the Grand Canyon, where they stayed until 17 January, when Garbo decided that she had had enough of being a 'tourist attraction' and asked James to drive them back to Hollywood, where reporters were waiting to ask if they were about to name the happy day. 'Can you think of anything lower than the people who are in charge of this beast I am a part of?' she wrote to Horke Wachtmeister. 'Out of nowhere come long pieces about how I've gotten married, how I've disappeared, shot myself, gone to the moon, etc. And I never defend myself. However, I'm still not engaged, still unmarried, houseless, homeless, and love walking on pineapples.'[278]

Queen Christina should have set the stall for Garbo's future career, of which little more than seven years remained. After the *demimondaines*, vamps and adulteresses, she had elevated herself to become the undisputed Queen of Hollywood, tugged in opposite directions by rival courtiers Salka and Mercedes, vying to secure her favours and each in her own way turn her into some sort of cinematic Duse or Bernhardt. Caught in the middle, terrified of what stunt she might pull next, were Thalberg and Mayer. Initially, Mercedes had the upper hand – days after her 'adventure' with Rouben Mamoulian, she whisked 'Harriet Brown' off on a vacation to the Yosemite National Park, where she hoped she might persuade her to change her mind about *The Painted Veil* and play Joan of Arc instead. Not satisfied with attacking the gay community when writing about the bedroom scene in *Queen Christina*, the *Hollywood Citizen-News'* waspish Elizabeth Yeaman now turned her venom on the French: 'For the life of me, I can't figure out why *anyone* would want to visualise Garbo as Joan of Arc. Garbo is Swedish, guttural and deliberate. She does not look French, and certainly has not the volatile tongue of a French girl.' Yeaman received dozens of complaints from French people living in Hollywood and was of course wrong: one only has to study the closing sequences in *The Kiss* and *Mata Hari* to see that she would have made an excellent if not definitive Saint Joan, though not with the script Mercedes had written.[279]

In her memoirs, Mercedes writes an account of this trip. The two of them, she says, went ice-skating, but when Garbo realised people were staring at her because she looked so ridiculous – wearing a number of sweaters and a lumberman's cap – she got in a huff and insisted on going for a walk in the forest, where they became lost and ended up at a house occupied by an old man, who took them in for the night and allowed them to sleep on the floor in front of his fire. The next morning, none the worse for their ordeal, they thanked him and returned to their hotel and a few days later, drove back to Hollywood.

In fact, Mercedes made the whole thing up. She was *supposed* to have accompanied Garbo on the trip, and had even paid for her hiking boots. However, on account of Mercedes' persistent stalking, at the last minute Garbo took Mamoulian instead, leaving the house one hour before the dreaded *frangine* was scheduled to arrive. She was also still seeing Borg who, since their reunion, had had a small part in Columbia Pictures' *Let's Fall In Love*, starring Edmund Lowe, one of his closest friends. It was through Borg, at the end of February, that Garbo learned that Lowe's wife and her own former lover, Lilyan Tashman, was dangerously ill in a New York hospital. Two years earlier, Tashman had been rushed into a clinic and the press reported an emergency appendectomy. Where Hollywood stars were concerned, this was all too frequently an excuse used to cover up an abortion – in Tashman's case it had been a concealment for stomach cancer, too advanced to effect a cure.

Courageously, Tashman had kept on working: she had recently played Nelly Bly in Republic's *Frankie & Johnny* opposite Helen Morgan and Chester Morris – some years later, this was remade with Elvis Presley. The film would take another two years to reach the screens, by which time – having observed Tashman's wasted state – the studio cruelly assigned most of her scenes to the cutting-room floor. By the time Garbo and Borg arrived in New York during the first week of March, she had been admitted to The Doctors' Hospital, where she had been given just weeks to live. She rallied sufficiently to chair a benefit for the Israel Orphans Home on 10 March, but a few days later lapsed into a coma. Garbo was one of the last to visit her, hours before her death on 21 March, aged just thirty-seven. Over 10,000 fans and many celebrities attended her funeral the next day at the Temple Emanu-El Synagogue, by which time Garbo and Borg were on their way back to Hollywood.

Three weeks after Lilyan Tashman's death – on the day she learned that Virginia Bruce had divorced John Gilbert – Garbo received the first draft for *The Painted Veil*, a somewhat lame story by W. Somerset Maugham, already considered old hat in literary circles. Not dissimilar to *Wild Orchids*, it is a routine love-triangle involving the stuffy, pompous older man who takes his much younger, attractive wife on a perilous expedition to the Far East, only to have her fall for a handsome reprobate. Garbo chose it because Thalberg supported her suggestion that Salka Viertel should write the script. This caused problems, with Mercedes pestering Thalberg on an almost daily basis to commission her to write for Garbo – she now wanted her muse to play the writer George Sand and claimed that Garbo had also asked her to write a treatment of Oscar Wilde's *The Picture of Dorian Grey*, which, had this reached fruition, would certainly have raised a few eyebrows.

Another woman obsessed with Garbo was her current stand-in, Sigrun Solavason (aka Rae Randall), who it appears had harboured feelings for her for some time and had been upset not to be hired to double for her in *Queen Christina*. The reason for this had been that stand-in Audrey Scott was an experienced horsewoman for the outdoor riding shots. Matters came to a head on 10 May 1934, when police officers, alerted by the neighbours who had not seen her for days, broke down the door of Solavason's apartment and found her dead – spreadeagled across her bed, surrounded by hundreds of photographs and press cuttings of Garbo and herself, though never together. Attached to the mirror was the suicide note: feeling that her career was going nowhere, when she had always believed herself to be as talented as the real Garbo, who had never even taken the time to meet her, she had decided to end it all. A post-mortem revealed that she had swallowed a lethal dose of strychnine and been dead for over a week. Garbo was distressed that anyone could have taken an unreciprocated crush so far and in June, concerned that things might have been moving in the same direction with Salka Viertel – persistently competing for her affection with Mercedes – she moved out of Mabery Road to a house on North Carmelita Drive. Mercedes moved to a property nearby.

Garbo's co-stars for *The Painted Veil* were British-born Herbert Marshall and George Brent – both so incredibly dull, one wonders what MGM must have been thinking of. Marshall (1890–1966) had lost a leg while serving with the London Scottish Regiment during World War I, enabling one critic to observe, 'His acting is as wooden as his leg.' After working for many years on the West End stage, he had arrived in Hollywood in 1929 and appeared in several missable films until partnering Marlene Dietrich in *Blonde Venus* (1932). George Brent (George Brendan Nolan, 1899–1979) was the kind of matinée idol that women went crazy for without ever finding out what he was really like away from the screen. Like Garbo, very much the loner and Bette Davis' favourite leading man and on-off lover for many years, Irish-born Brent had formerly been a member of the IRA and a leading follower of revolutionary leader Michael Collins, murdered in an ambush in 1922. He subsequently fled to Canada with a price on his head and moved to Hollywood in 1930, where he was contracted to Warner Brothers, who were told nothing about his criminal past.

Garbo socialised with Brent – more as a means of getting into their on-screen parts than engaging in the romance the press hinted at, though not, it would appear, through lack of effort on his part. The actor had a mansion at Taluca Lake, allegedly part-financed by his nefarious political activities in Ireland, and when Garbo accepted an invitation to spend the weekend there, aware that she liked to swim and sunbathe in the nude and doubtless fancying his chances, Brent brought in a team who worked round the clock to construct a wall round the place to deter onlookers. Two years earlier, he had married actress Ruth Chatterton, but they had spent most of this time apart on account of his womanising. When he met Garbo, he was half-heartedly trying to effect a reconciliation, but Chatterton was once more cast aside while he nurtured plans to become 'Mr Garbo'. There were long walks in the country, intimate dinners served in the enclosed garden and even the odd sparring match in Brent's gymnasium. Brent bought her meaningful little gifts, while she presented him with a seascape painting, which occupied pride of place above his fireplace for years.

Directing *The Painted Veil* was Richard Boleslawski (1899–1937). A former Polish Lancer, he was career-educated in Moscow and also ran a school, which taught the precursor to Method acting – indeed, one of his students was Lee Strasberg, founder of the movement. Boleslawski had recently directed all three Barrymores in *Rasputin & The Empress* and been responsible for removing Mercedes de Acosta's name from the credits. His and producer Hunt Stromberg's first stumbling block was getting Salka Viertel's script past the censor. Because the Breen Office had lost their case over *Queen Christina*, Joseph Breen vetted this one personally. Breen complained about the 'too-strong sex scenes', of which there were none, and was overruled. He retaliated by joining forces with the Catholic League of Decency and having *all* of Garbo's early sound films, still doing the rounds, temporarily banned from being screened, declaring them, and her, sinful. She simply shrugged her shoulders and delivered a decree of her own via Harry Edington: if these prejudiced people had begun *banning* her pictures using *her* as an excuse, when all she had done was adhere to the script and follow the director's orders, then there was *definitely* no reason why she should stay in Hollywood once this one was in the can.

Garbo was certainly heading towards flight once more, writing to Horke Wachmeister,

> Oh, it's such a pity that I'm not home. I think about it and long for it every moment. But prostitutes are never very happy. I've already been back here for more than two and a half years now, and have only made two films. It's that awful contract I signed. I can do nothing about it.

The letter is puzzling – by calling herself a 'prostitute' she was obviously referring to the fact that she felt she had sold herself to the studio but she had not been back in Hollywood for this amount of time and certainly was not worried about her contract – Canyon Productions would end soon enough, allowing her to choose whichever path she felt best. Even so, not wishing to risk her leaving now, MGM submitted to Breen's demands: one of the love scenes with George Brent was rewritten and the script then given the nod of approval by this odious man.[280]

The name 'GARBO' fills the entire screen and remains thus throughout the opening titles, which are superimposed over it – which must have been disconcerting for the other actors. Neither does the story adhere to Maugham's novel. Indeed, it is halfway through the film before we get to where the book begins.

Set in Austria, the film opens with Katrin Koerber attending the rain-soaked wedding of her sister and sharing an umbrella with her father's stuffy bacteriologist friend Walter Fane (Herbert Marshall). The conversation turns to men: Mrs Koerber feels that Katrin may end up on the shelf because, although there have been many suitors, none were considered husband material.

To get away from her nagging mother, and acting on a whim, Katrin accepts a shock marriage proposal from Walter, who is about to return to China. He says he has secretly loved her since she was twelve, when they attended school together (the scriptwriter forgetting the fifteen-year age gap between Garbo and Marshall). We then see them in China as man and wife, with him introducing her to his snooty friends and pompous married diplomat Jack Townsend (Brent). Wearing a succession of silly hats, she tries to fit in with these people and succumbs to Townsend's advances while shunning those of her husband: 'Vanquished,' Walter says, heading for the spare room.

Walter has seen a picture of the lovers in the newspaper, and so when a cholera epidemic erupts in a remote village, he volunteers to help out, offering Katrin an ultimatum: she must accompany him or stay put, get a divorce and persuade Townsend to marry her. At this she lets rip (from which point the film rises from near mediocrity to the usual Garbo standard of excellence): 'All right then, I fell in love – blindly, madly, I reached for the happiness I could get. Like a fool, I stole it and tried not to hurt anyone … There is nothing cheap about it, and I have no apology. I don't love you. I never did. If you want to make a mess of it because your pride is hurt, then do it.'

Townsend reacts like the cad he is – a divorce would jeopardise his career. Therefore Katrin dutifully accompanies Walter to the village, where people are dropping in the streets like flies. Never in any Garbo film has she looked so glum as she does now, while Walter seethes, 'I despise myself for ever caring anything about you.'

The epidemic is at its most virulent in the next village and Walter gives orders for it to be burned to prevent the disease from spreading. Sensing imminent danger, he arranges for Katrin to return to the city. Instead she follows him and volunteers as a nurse at the local convent (which results in Garbo looking even more saintly than she did at the end of Mata Hari). Walter's plan is opposed by the villagers – a riot ensues and he is stabbed, just as Townsend turns up and announces he has changed his mind about his and Katrin's future. She, however, has seen the error of her ways: he is sent packing while she fights her way through the rabble to get to the husband she realises she has loved all along, hoping she might be able to nurse him back to health.

Garbo attended one of the previews of the film, accompanied by
Salka Viertel and Borg. Much was made of her headwear – the
pillbox hat she wears while playing bridge, with what looks like
a square of metal stuck in the middle of the crown, attracted loud
guffaws, as did the 'trowel' hat she wears when sniffing the bunch
of perfumeless poppies Townsend has given her. Garbo asked for
these scenes to be shot again, Thalberg refused and she subsequently
upset costumier Adrian, suggesting that MGM should think twice
about hiring him for her next film, *if* there was going to be one.
The scenes with Katrin and her mother were shot again after Beulah
Bondi was deemed too hard-faced and severe. Thalberg brought in
Danish actress Bodil Rosing, who had played the innkeeper's wife
in *Queen Christina*, and who Garbo said physically resembled her
own mother. These retakes took place between 8 and 13 November,
by which time Richard Boleslawski had moved to another project.
The man assigned to the retakes was W. S. Van Dyke, the infamous
'One-Take Woody', whose planning of scenes was so meticulous
that this was usually all it took to get them in the can. This suited
the no-rehearsals, words and gestures perfect Garbo, though she
disliked his habit of addressing her as 'honey' and 'kiddo'.

The revised film premiered in New York on 6 December 1934.
Norbert Lusk of *Picture Play* was not so enthusiastic as usual, declaring, 'It is the same story and the same set of characters which might
have served Norma Shearer or Joan Crawford in their respective
moods.' The *New York Times'* André Seenwald disagreed:

> She is the most miraculous blend of personality and sheer dramatic
> talent that the screen has ever known ... Watch her stalking about with
> long and nervous steps, her shoulders bent and her body awkward
> with grief, while she waits to be told if her husband will die from the
> coolie's dagger thrust. It is as if all this had never been done before.
> Watch the veiled terror of her face as she sits at dinner with her husband,
> not knowing if he is aware of her infidelity, or her superb gallantry
> when she informs him of what it was that drove her into the arms of his
> friend, or her restlessness on the bamboo porch in Mei-Tain-Fu with
> the tinny phonograph, the heat and her conscience. She shrouds all this
> with dignity, making it precious and memorable.[281]

CHAPTER ELEVEN

I HAVE DIED TWICE

'If you're going to die on the screen, you've got to be strong and in good health.'

On 23 October 1934, Garbo signed a one-picture deal for MGM, her fee an unheard of $275,000. She had asked for David O. Selznick, married to Mayer's daughter, Irene, to produce *Anna Karenina*, a remake of *Love* but adhering more faithfully to the Tolstoy novel. In anticipation, Salka Viertel was assigned to the script. Selznick was keen to work with Garbo but wanted nothing to do with this one, declaring costume dramas not just old hat, but unprofitable, too. He suggested that a better part might be that of Judith Traherne in *Dark Victory* – the stage play had opened in November 1934 with Tallulah Bankhead and Earl Larimore. Described by one critic as 'Camille without all the coughing', it was a far from happy tale – that of a flapper compelled to amend her scandalous lifestyle upon learning that she has cancer of the brain. Selznick commissioned playwright Philip Barry, not just to script *Dark Victory* but also a biopic of the controversial dancer Isadora Duncan, who had died tragically in 1927, when her trailing scarf got caught up in the wheel of her speeding car, strangling her. Garbo was interested only in *Anna Karenina*.

While shooting *The Painted Veil*, Garbo and Clarence Brown had settled their differences, but because the script was by Salka, who had scripted 'dirty' pictures like *Queen Christina*, he was compelled to have this one minutely scrutinised by the Breen Office, who gave it the thumbs down without even progressing beyond the title page. Joseph Breen's first demand was that Anna should not be depicted as an adulteress, and when Brown argued that *this* was what the whole story was about, Breen capitulated – his condition being that this time Anna *would* be permitted to commit suicide as a way of atoning for her sins. Salka's script was then passed to Clemence Dane to be 'cleansed'. Dane (1888–1965) was a fuddy-duddy English crime novelist who was the first to admit that she was scarcely qualified for the subject she had been asked to write about – she had never been married or even had a love affair. As with *Queen Christina*, S. N. Behrman was hired to write the dialogue.

While everyone was squabbling over the script, Garbo spent a week with George Brent at La Quinta. Even at this late stage, David Selznick was hoping to get her to change her mind and ditch *Anna Karenina* in favour of *Dark Victory*. He drafted a long letter to Garbo and dispatched Salka to La Quinta to personally deliver it. Garbo, displeased that her sojourn with Brent had been so rudely interrupted, sent her friend away with a flea in her ear. The part of Judith Traherne eventually went to Bette Davis, with George Brent playing her love interest.

Garbo had decided that Fredric March (1897–1975) would be perfect for the role of Vronsky. She had known the Wisconsin-born actor for a while. A friend of John Gilbert, he and his domineering actress wife, Florence Eldridge, had often attended the weekend parties at Tower Grove Road. Initially, March turned the part down, not because he disliked her but because, like her other co-stars he was well aware that where fans and critics were concerned, in any Garbo film, it was *only* Garbo that anyone was interested in. A hefty fee persuaded him otherwise. And if March had feigned shock at seeing Garbo dive stark naked into Gilbert's pool, he was not so fussy once shooting got under way. 'We would bounce a medicine ball back and forth during breaks,' he recalled. 'One day she stripped to the waist to take the sun. Then she caught herself and asked if it embarrassed me. It did not.' March enjoyed Garbo's topless displays and developed a crush on her. When her gentle rebuffs fell on deaf ears, she took a more drastic measure, hoping that he would take the hint. 'Before each love scene,' Clarence Brown said, 'Garbo put a small piece of garlic in her mouth. It worked.'[282] [283]

For the part of the sadistic, heartless Karenin, David Selznick chose Basil Rathbone (1892–1967), the South African-born British actor who, since arriving in Hollywood, had achieved some degree of notoriety and adverse criticism brought about by actor-character confusion following his role as the abusive stepfather, Murdstone in *David Copperfield* (1935). Later, he would be feted as the definitive Sherlock Holmes. Though Garbo was courteous towards him on the odd occasion when they met away from the set, Rathbone was always of the opinion that she disliked him. Pre-Method aficionados might argue that she had a valid reason for this: Rathbone's Karenin is so utterly *loathsome*, maybe Garbo felt that being too sociable towards him off-screen might affect her on-screen hatred of the husband who ultimately destroys her.[284]

Freddie Bartholomew, who plays her son, Sergei, was as far-removed from the earlier Philippe De Lacy as can be imagined. Born in Ireland, Bartholomew (1924–92) had been abandoned by his parents and raised by an aunt who brought him to Los Angeles, where David Selznick discovered him and, 'on a whim', cast him as the lead in *David Copperfield*, dropping American child star David Holt, whose accent would only have ruined the production. Bartholomew later triumphed in *Little Lord Fauntleroy*, earning so much money that his parents tried to reclaim him, only to lose most of it in the subsequent court battle. He always praised Garbo but she loathed him on account of his assuming, despite being advised against this, that his position of 'Garbo's son' afforded him the right to enter her dressing room whenever he liked. Currently, the only people permitted through its hallowed portals were Borg and the eccentric English actress Constance Collier, to whom Garbo had taken a liking. Bartholomew went too far by asking Garbo for her autograph and, on the rare occasions when his name cropped up in conversation, she referred to him as 'that little monster'.

The costumes for the film were provided by Adrian and if the tetchy couturier had been upset by Garbo's comments about his hats for *The Painted Veil*, there were no hard feelings when the time came to fit her for her gowns. With Sigrun Solvasun dead and Geraldine Dvorak out of the picture for mocking her in *Nothing Ever Happens*, there was no stand-in for this one and Garbo 'shocked' Adrian by turning up at his workshop and taking him to dinner after the fittings. Shooting began on 25 March and despite the stuffy performance from Fredric March – so lacklustre, one wonders what Anna would have ever seen in him, let alone committed suicide because of him – *Anna Karenina* is far superior to *Love*. Indeed, the 'love' scenes with Bartholomew are highly poignant and convincing, all the more remarkable considering Garbo's dislike of the boy.

The film opens at a rowdy military banquet in Moscow, where Vronsky drinks all the other officers – literally – under the table. After sobering up in the steam room, he and his friend Stiva (Reginald Owen) *meet the train from St Petersburg. Among the passengers are his mother* (May Robson) *and Stiva's sister, Anna Karenina* (Garbo making a muted but spectacular entrance, wide-eyed and lost-looking, as she descends the steps and materialises through a great swirl of steam). *The fleeting glances between Anna and Vronsky are a prelude of the drama to come.*

Vronsky may be in love with Anna's sister, Kitty (Maureen O'Sullivan), *but it is Anna who partners him in the mazurka at a society ball, during which they fall in love.* (The fact that Garbo danced this inordinately well, bearing in mind there was absolutely no rehearsal beforehand, is testimony to her exemplary acting skills.)

From this point on the story is the same as in Love, *save that this Karenin is considerably more repugnant than his predecessor and Anna's spoilt son* (Freddie Bartholomew) *anything but likeable. And this time the ending is true to Tolstoy's story – Anna, ejected from her home, trudges down the staircase, each footstep more leaden than the last, towards the door, beyond which lies her fate. 'I face the truth … that one day I shall find myself alone,' are her words to Vronsky; he is now more preoccupied with enlisting to fight than being with her. 'I'm sick and tired of love,' he snarls. Even so, she feels she must see him before his regiment leaves, and when her message to him is returned unopened she heads for the railway station. A joyous crowd is seeing off the soldiers, leading her to hold back and let him go. And so she waits for the next train, standing on the edge of the platform, her face barely moving as she hesitates only briefly before flinging herself under its wheels – leaving us as beautifully and as mysteriously as she arrived.*

Anna Karenina won that year's Best Foreign Film at the Venice Film
Festival, while Garbo was cited for Best Actress Performance at the
New York Critics Awards. Many tipped her for an Oscar but this
never happened – indeed, surely she had no need of such 'gongs'
to prove herself to the movie world. Surprisingly few critics drew
comparisons between this *Anna Karenina* and the first. William
Boehnel observed in the *New York World-Telegram*: 'Though *Anna
Karenina* can hardly be called one of the best films she has ever
made, it is as exciting as any because of the marvellously restrained
performance she gives in the title role.' *Photoplay* called it 'a weak
and dull picture', but added that Garbo's genius raised it into the
class of art. Richard Watts Jr enthused in the *New York Herald
Tribune*: 'It would be unfair to you if I did not confess that my
verdict on this picture is based in great part on prejudice', in other
words, whether the production was good or bad was immaterial to
a man in whose eyes Garbo could do no wrong. A glowing appraisal
also came from Eileen Creelman, of the *New York Sun*:

> Greta Garbo, after several years of miscasting, is back at last in her
> own particular province of glamour and heartbreak ... Clarence
> Brown may be responsible for the Swedish star's return to enchant-
> ment ... After four years professionally torn apart, years in which
> Miss Garbo wandered through such films as the clammy *Queen
> Christina*, the director-star team is reunited.[285]

On 30 May 1935, Garbo signed a new contract with MGM, for
two films at $250,000 each. The big difference between this and
the contract for *Queen Christina* focused on time which might be
'wasted' on costume fittings and retakes: her 'work period' would
commence with her first consultation with Adrian (she had decided
against having another stand in) and if this extended beyond
twelve weeks because of retakes, the studio would be obliged to
pay her an additional weekly fee of $10,000. Then there was the
question of her films. The next one, Garbo stipulated, would be
Marie Walewska, the story of the love affair between Napoleon
Bonaparte and his Polish mistress. This would be followed either by
Camille, based on Alexandra Dumas' novel of 1848, *La Dame aux*

Camellias, or *A Woman From Spain*, believed to have been a variation on the *Carmen* theme. Both, she insisted, would be scripted by Salka Viertel.

The next evening, 'Karin Lund' left for New York, accompanied by 'Carter Gibson', described as George Brent's stand-in, though almost certainly Brent himself, who later escorted her from the Central Station to the SS *Kungsholm*, which set sail at noon on 4 June. Nine days later, Garbo arrived in Stockholm, where she took up residence in a rented apartment at Klippsgatan 6. This led to rumours that she might not be returning to Hollywood, especially when she announced that she had her eye on a rural property, where she said she would 'settle down and grow potatoes', while planning a new career as head of her own production company, which would see her making only the films *she* wanted to make.

As with her previous visit to Sweden, no one really knows what she was doing most of the time, or whom she was with. She does not appear to have spent much time with her family, and there were no reported reunions with Mimi Pollak and Max Gumpel, though she did visit an ailing Selma Lagerlöf. There were problems with an MGM 'spy' named Prinzmetal, of whom little is known save that the studio hired him to keep an eye on her. Unable to shake him off, Garbo sent him on a wild goose-chase by pretending to be having an affair with Noël Coward, who had recently arrived in town. With Coward and his current boyfriend, introduced as his secretary, Garbo attended an all-night party at the home of actor Gösta Ekman, where they were heard addressing each other in English as 'my little bride' and 'my little bridegroom', for the benefit of reporters who gatecrashed the event. But when Coward suggested throwing a similar bash for her thirtieth birthday on 18 September, Garbo was not interested and stayed home alone.

No sooner had Noël Coward left Stockholm than the proverbial bad penny, Mercedes de Acosta, turned up. Earlier in the year, Abram Poole had divorced her. The news was a surprise even to some of her friends, who had no idea that she was married in the first place. According to Mercedes, Garbo felt so guilty about leaving Hollywood without saying goodbye that she had written her a letter inviting her to dinner at the Grand Hotel and giving her eight days' notice to get to Sweden. Mercedes had subsequently boarded the *SS Europa*, arrived in Bremen with just twenty-four hours to spare, caught a flight to Malmo, then travelled to Stockholm via train and taxi, arriving at the hotel only minutes ahead of her 'date' for the evening. It was of course just another of her wild stories. What had *actually* happened was that Mercedes had followed Garbo across the Atlantic, then waited until the coast was clear – on Coward's departure – before making her move. That same evening, they attended a performance of *White Horse Inn* and the next day left for Horke Wachtmeister's castle at Tistad. Horke, who could not stand Mercedes – in their letters, she and Garbo scathingly refer to her as 'Swartzweise' (Black-White) on account of her eccentric dress sense – put up with her for a week before asking Garbo to take her back to Stockholm, where there was yet another parting of the ways.

At the end of October, Garbo was reported to be seriously ill, suffering from exhaustion and flu-like symptoms. This news was relayed to Mayer by way of MGM's Paris representative, Laudy Lawrence, with whom Garbo had been corresponding in the hope of getting him to persuade Mayer to offer her brother Sven a Hollywood contract, in spite of him having been earlier denounced as a 'punk actor' by *Photoplay*, a publication which carried some sway in the movie industry. Now Lawrence flew to Stockholm, under the pretence that Mayer had asked him to test Sven, the actual reason to find out if Garbo was genuinely ill or just 'swinging the lead'. On 3 December, he reported back to the studio:

> Sven is a nice boy, but that is all ... his health is very bad. Incidentally, the entire family is in bad health, including Garbo ... I believe her younger sister died from TB long ago, and Sven is in bed a whole lot more than out of it. Garbo is rather seriously ill.[286]

Garbo confirmed her malady in a letter to Salka Viertel, who had already begun working on the first draft of *Marie Walewska*:

> I have been in bed for years, I feel. So, you have had troubles. I have no lovers, but I have troubles just the same. Mercedes has been here

... I took her to Tistad as I didn't know what else to do. She is more
quiet than before but otherwise the same. I was a wreck after she
went and I told her she must not write me. We had a sad farewell.[287]

On 8 December, she opened up a little more in a letter to Mayer:
she told him that she had been bedridden much of the time since
September – not entirely true – and there was a possibility she
might need an operation. She further thanked Mayer for considering her brother for a Hollywood contract and informed him that,
though she still wanted to make *Marie Walewska*, she wanted her
next project to be *Camille*. The press on both sides of the Atlantic
did not know what to make of the situation. If Garbo was suffering
from the flu, or even something as serious as tuberculosis, why
should this necessitate an operation? Again, there were rumours
of an abortion. Later it emerged that she had undergone minor
surgery to correct a gynaecological problem, almost certainly to
alleviate painful periods.

Early in the New Year, Garbo cabled Mayer and asked for an
extra month's vacation to recuperate. The request was granted in a
cable of 10 January, which failed to mention the shock event of the
previous day. John Gilbert had died of a heart attack, aged thirty-
six. In fact, she already knew. Besides a call from Borg, she had
received the news that same evening while attending a performance
of Schiller's play, *Maria Stuart*. One report claimed her to have
responded, 'What's that to me?', which one very much doubts.
Another suggests that she managed to stay until the end of the
programme, after which she went to pieces and took to her bed
for several days, which given her fondness for the man would be
more likely.

Of late, Gilbert had been seeing a lot of Marlene Dietrich, who
wanted him in her new picture, *Desire*. Directed by Frank Borsage,
this saw her cast as upper-crust jewel thief Madeleine de Beaupré, a
role which had at some point been earmarked for Garbo. Borzage
had protested, declaring Gilbert unemployable but Marlene had
taken him under her wing and promised to have him in good shape
by the time shooting began in February. An expert with lighting,
she had given precise instructions to cameraman Charles Lang about

how to 'iron out' the lines on his face. She had even advised him to change his will. Though he bequeathed ex-wife Virginia Bruce two $50,000 annuities, the bulk of his estate was left to his eleven-year-old daughter, Leatrice, from his marriage to Leatrice Joy. Marlene was with him the day he suffered his first heart attack while swimming in his pool. She had given him emergency treatment while waiting for the ambulance and had doubtless saved his life. Ernst Lubitsch, who was producing *Desire*, did not want Gilbert dying on him halfway through the film and on 8 January replaced him with Gary Cooper. 'In my opinion, that's what finished him off. Within a few hours, he was dead,' Marlene later said.[288]

Gilbert's funeral took place on 11 January, two days after his death. Marlene and Cooper were among the mourners, and Garbo sent a wreath by way of Salka Viertel, her only public acknowledgment of how much she had cared about him. Marlene had witnessed Gilbert signing his will and later claimed this had substituted a previous one which saw Virginia Bruce acquiring the house on Tower Grove Road, and the bulk of the estate, while his daughter ended up with just $10,000. Soon afterwards, the property was ransacked by fans, most of the items not stolen were auctioned and the proceeds divided equally among his relatives.

Meanwhile, despite having told Mercedes that she never wanted to see her again, this grossly overbearing woman claimed in her memoirs that Garbo wrote to her two weeks before leaving Sweden, asking her to follow George Brent's example and arrange for a ten-foot, impenetrable fence to be built around her home so that *they* would be afforded the ultimate in privacy. In fact, Mercedes had the fence erected around her *own* home, in the hope that Garbo would move in. 'Poor Mercedes,' she wrote to Horke Wachtmeister, 'She has got an extraordinary ability to make people nervous. Even people who are not quite as unkind as me.'[289]

The *Gripsholm* docked in New York on 3 May 1936, and saw Garbo break her own rule by granting a ten-minute interview in the ship's smoking-room. Not that she said much, or that any of the questions thrown at her were less than juvenile. 'I don't know why I should talk to people I don't know, but I am beginning to learn that it is necessary,' she said. She scoffed, when asked if the rumour was true that she had bought an ancient castle and that this was to be dismantled and shipped to Hollywood, stone by stone, 'Can you imagine what a lot of little parcels, all neatly tied up, a castle could make?' And that was it – Greta Garbo's 'major' interview! She was met off the ship by Berthold Viertel, now separated from his wife, the troubles referred to by Garbo in her letter to Salka. With him, she spent the next month doing the usual round of theatre visits and together they boarded the *Santa Fe Chief* for San Bernadino. Here, having heard of the New York press conference, dozens of reporters scrambled on to the train, causing havoc with those passengers trying to get off. 'Why do they insist she belongs to the public, like a park?' Viertel yelled at no one in particular, before Garbo scowled at the little crowd and made it clear that she was interested in speaking to no one. Her escort then drove her, not to her own house, where she feared Mercedes may have been waiting, but to George Brent's mansion at Taluca Lake.[290]

The reason for Garbo's bad mood was a journalist named Kay Proctor, from *Screen Guide*. Proctor was dispatched to Barstow, in the Mojave Desert, where she boarded the train and waited until Garbo was alone before audaciously entering her carriage in the hope of acquiring an exclusive ahead of her Hollywood colleagues. Rather than summon the guard, Garbo granted Proctor just two minutes, which was spent mostly explaining why she hated being disturbed like this:

> It has been a difficult trip. No peace, no rest. I am not well. I am coming back here to get well in the lovely sunshine ... It's not that I don't like people. I do, believe me. But it does frighten me when hordes of strangers rush at me, stare at me. I do not want to be ungracious but they make it impossible for me to do anything but shut myself away where they cannot tear at me ... I am a peculiar woman. I cannot do too much at once, think of too many different things. My health now. Next, the picture. Then maybe a house...[291]

Changes had been made to Garbo's projects during her absence: Salka would continue with the script for *Marie Walewska* but would not be involved with *Camille*. Irving Thalberg brought in Zoe

Akins, Frances Marion and James Hilton. George Cukor would at last get to direct Garbo, William Daniels would photograph her as usual, and Adrian would dress her. Robert Taylor would play her love interest. Nebraska-born Taylor (Spangler Arlington Brugh) was a former cellist who made his film debut in 1934 in Will Rogers' *Handy Andy*. His big break came a year later opposite Irene Dunne in *Magnificent Obsession*. He and Garbo got along very well and she was enthusiastic about him at the time. Some years later, when Taylor was long dead, she revised her opinion, telling her friend David Diamond, 'So beautiful – and so dumb.' George Cukor did not want him in the film and blamed his on-screen 'shortcomings' on his youth, arguing that Armand should have been played by a middle-aged actor, which would of course have been contrary to the Garbo 'formula'.[292]

Not for the first time, there were rumours that Garbo was having an affair with her co-star, particularly when Taylor told one journalist, 'She has a great pair of eyes. In the scenes before the cameras, she seems to use her eyes so little. Yet, when those same eyes appear on the screen, they reveal that they are constantly performing miracles of expression.' Such comments led to rumours that the woman in Taylor's life, Barbara Stanwyck, was none too pleased. In fact, theirs was yet another 'lavender' relationship encouraged by the studios, who were well aware that both Taylor and Stanwyck were bisexual. Later, for a substantial remuneration, they took the charade a step further and married. Otherwise, pending extreme discretion, they were permitted to lead more or less separate lives. As one biographer put it, 'When Stanwyck became involved with Bob, she had to abide by the same rules as he did, or walk away. She managed this by keeping her mouth shut.'[293] [294]

Taylor also had another way of 'affirming' his heterosexuality besides pretending to date beautiful actresses; he would unbutton his shirt and expose his hirsute torso, which gay men were declared incapable of possessing. When this led to 'curious' reporters cornering him in the hope of a cheap thrill, the stock response would be a snarled, 'Ask me anything except about Barbara Stanwyck or if I have hair on my chest!'[295]

In one respect, George Cukor was right about Taylor: in *Camille* his relative inexperience and occasional fumbling is vastly overshadowed by the magnificent Henry Daniell, the British actor playing the villainous Baron de Varville. Daniell (1894–1963) had worked for many years on the stage in London and in New York before making his film debut in 1929, opposite the ex-Mrs Gilbert, Ina Claire, in *The Awful Truth*. Here, as in almost every role he played, he presents the perfect blend of smarmy charm and simpering evil. Lionel Barrymore is miscast as Armand's father, while Laura Hope Crews and Lenore Uric are perfect as Marguerite Gautier's *demi-mondaine* sparring partners.

The Breen Office kicked up a fuss about the script, though such was the reverence for Alexandre Dumas in Europe, where much of the film's revenue would come from, that the studio were compelled to adhere to the novel or shelve the project entirely. Dumas is said to have based Marguerite on the *horizontaliste* Alphonsine Plessis (1824–47), with whom he had enjoyed a year-long romance. When this ended, she latched on to a Count Perregaux, who rescued her from the society she scandalised my marrying her, though they never lived together. He deserted her when she refused to amend her ways, leaving her to die in near-poverty, aged just twenty-three. Thalberg believed that he was rescuing Garbo when he 'defended' Marguerite, issuing a patronising – and positively insulting – statement: 'Men marry whores in our present society – women who have been promiscuous – and they very often make marvellous wives. In this town you find them all over the place.'[296]

As had happened with *The Painted Veil*, Garbo mentally prepared herself for her role by ensconcing herself at the home of someone involved with the film, at George Cukor's hillside Italianate villa. Set in six acres of very private, landscaped gardens, this provided a 'pink retreat' for the director, who invited all of his closeted gay friends here including actor William Haines, with whom he cruised for rough-trade sex, mostly sailors on leave, around downtown Los Angeles' Pershing Square. While she was staying with him Cukor was caught in the act and arrested by the vice-squad, though any charges were quickly dropped when MGM's police department stepped in with some substantial hush-money. Another regular visitor to Cukor's home was Katharine Hepburn, who had had a crush on Garbo for some time. Maybe Hepburn believed that all her birthdays had arrived at once when Cukor drove Garbo to her house in Benedict Canyon, particularly when Garbo asked to be shown around upstairs. Feeling the lump in Hepburn's bed formed by the hot-water bottle under the covers, she quipped, 'Yes, I have one too. Vat is wrong wid us?'[297]

Production was well under way on 29 July when Garbo reported to the studio to shoot her first scene. The atmosphere on the set was reported to have been more relaxed than usual. When she detected that Zoe Akins and associate producer David Lewis were watching from a darkened corner of the set, she grabbed the director's megaphone and demanded that they show themselves – then invited them to take tea in her dressing room. Akins was complimented on her 'beautiful script', and Lewis was greeted with a dry, 'I expected someone a little older and a little uglier.' These visitors were entertained with her latest musical obsession: Paul Robeson, whose records of negro spirituals were played constantly on the gramophone in her dressing room. She even insisted on lunching with the extras and technicians while shooting the locations in the Hollywood mountains, something she had *never* done before. She refused, however, to meet Robert Taylor until moments before their first scene together – she wanted to experience the same emotions, she said, as Marguerite Gautier might have experienced on seeing Armand for the first time, which would not happen if they were compelled to engage in idle chit-chat beforehand. The earth certainly 'moved' when they first faced the camera: the fuse box controlling the lights for the soundstage blew, showering everyone with sparks and compelling Taylor to grab her roughly by the arm and drag her to safety.[298]

If Taylor's act of chivalry caused him to believe that he could get away with pulling a fast one where his leading lady was concerned, he would be mistaken. Several days into shooting, having been told that Garbo *never* signed autographs, he bought forty fountain pens and handed these out among the cast and crew, offering a prize to whichever of them returned first with that invaluable signature. The ruse backfired when Garbo summoned him to her dressing room: she had confiscated one of the pens and now grabbed a sheet of paper, which she 'signed' with a flourish, folded in half and handed to him. Taylor thanked her, and left. When he opened the paper, he observed that it was still blank – Garbo had removed the ink from the pen!

Neither was it all plain sailing with George Cukor away from the 'pink ambience' of his home. Cukor's habit was to sit under the camera, the script on his lap, and mouth the lines to the actors while they were pronouncing them, waving his arms around if the scene was a lively one. Garbo was having none of this, and Cukor was relegated to working from behind a crack in the screen or curtains surrounding the set. Even so, she admired him more than she had most of her other directors because he was able to make her laugh, telling Horke Wachtmeister, 'If I hadn't been so out of sorts, *Camille* would have been one of my most entertaining memories, thanks to the director. He really is extraordinarily nice. He looks so funny with his huge hips and woman's breasts. I'll soon be finished the whole thing, and blessed be the memory.' And she ended the letter, 'That proves that I'm not *always* ungrateful!'[299]

Garbo's portrayal of Dumas' consumptive heroine was not the first, though it is generally regarded as the definitive one. Forty-two-year-old Alla Nazimova's 1921 posturing opposite Rudolph Valentino's moving Armand had been little more than a joke, those of Theda Bara and Norma Talmadge little better. On the stage, the most distinguished Ladies of the Camellias had been Eleanora Duse and Sara Bernhardt, while Maria Callas' would offer the greatest operatic interpretation (as Violetta) in Verdi's *La Traviata*. Garbo's pre-Method style of injecting realism into her roles to the extent that she *became* the character she was portraying would be inherited by Callas. During the death scene, Callas deliberately cracked her notes and hit back at critics who lambasted her for this, 'I was supposed to be dying, for God's sake!' During shooting, Garbo's health took a downward spiral – a combination of exhaustion and her still debilitating period pains – resulting in several brief hospitalisations. By the time she got around to filming the death scene, she could scarcely stay on her feet. She asked for the sequence to be filmed *twice* so that she and George Cukor could decide which one to use – the one where she had several lines, or the one where she said almost nothing. Plumping for the latter, she told Horke Wachtmeister, 'It really didn't feel very natural talking that much when you've just about given up the ghost.'[300]

The action takes place in 1847 (the year of Alphonsine Plessis' death), with Marguerite's carriage stopping at a florist's shop, where an assistant presents her with her favourite flowers: 'For the Lady of the Camellias,' she says. Inside the carriage, Marguerite's best friend, Prudence (Laura Hope Crews), *chides her for her extravagant spending. They head for the theatre, where Prudence, the matchmaker, hopes to fix her up with the Baron de Varville, who neither has seen. This leads to a case of mistaken identity: peering through her opera glasses, Marguerite's gaze falls on the drop-dead gorgeous Armand Duval* (Robert Taylor). *'I didn't know that rich men ever looked like that,' she says.*

Next we see Marguerite's friend of sorts, Olympe (Lenore Uric), *so unscrupulous that she would 'pick a dead man's pocket'.* (Mercedes de Acosta is thought to have been foremost in Salka Viertel's mind when she scripted this scene, for while Prudence and Marguerite never have a good to thing to say about Olympe behind her back, to her face they are always gushing.) *Olympe has seen the real Baron and wants him for herself, cattily warning Marguerite that unless she changes her ways, she will end up back on the farm where she came from. This draws a dry response from Marguerite: 'Cows and chickens make better friends than I've ever met in Paris.'*

Armand makes his way to her box. (Robert Taylor's very first meeting with Garbo, bringing gasps of surprise from both.) *He has worshipped her from afar for some time; she, however, soon loses interest on learning he is not wealthy.*

The story moves forward six months and Marguerite is now the real Baron's mistress – though he was not at her side while she was seriously ill, whereas Armand brought her camellias every day. The pair meet again in a book shop, where he presents her with a copy of Manon Lescaut, *which she says will be auctioned after her death. She invites him to her birthday party, at which he is shocked by the vulgarity of her freeloading, fake friends. The festivities end abruptly when she suffers a fit of coughing while dancing the polka. 'Aw, she's always ill when anybody's having fun,' Prudence scoffs as everyone leaves, taking the food with them.*

Armand wants to take her to the country to recuperate – on a monthly salary of 7,000 francs, he says, he can afford to. 'I spend more in a month and I've never been too particular where it comes from,' she replies. *When he tells her how long his parents have been together, she says, 'You will never love me for thirty years. No one ever will.' She urges him not to get involved with a woman like her but, when she sees his sincerity is genuine, she agrees to go away with him.*

After arranging to have supper together, she gives him a key so that he may let himself into her apartment. This does not happen: the Baron returns unexpectedly and Armand finds the door bolted. The ensuing scene is electric. Marguerite is at the piano when the Baron enters and messes up her favourite piece on account of the state he gets her into. The Baron knows her lover is waiting outside. He joins her at the piano, striking the keys like a maniac, his expression increasingly sardonic, the music reaching a crescendo as they argue and laugh by turns while the doorbell rings. When she stretches the beads she is wearing this becomes a metaphor for her stretching the truth. She asks him for money; he knows she is lying when she says this is to pay off her debts, but offers her one final handout – his condition being that after today, he never wants to see her again.

Armand takes Marguerite to the country, where she is happier than she has been all her life and appears to rally. (The scene where they arrive at the cottage had to be filmed twice – while carrying her from the carriage, Taylor tickled her, Garbo wriggled and he dropped her. In these scenes, Robert Taylor looks only marginally less effete than Nils Asther in *Wild Orchids*. Even so, they make an astonishingly lovely couple.) *Their joy is short-lived, however – they learn that the local castle belongs to the Baron. Armand becomes suspicious when he sees Marguerite slipping notes to her maid, Nanine* (Jessie Ralph), *though she is actually selling her jewellery to pay for a friend's wedding. Yet when he proposes, she turns him down: 'Let me love you, let me live for you. Don't ask any more from heaven. God might get angry.'*

Marguerite receives a visit from Armand's father. (Not one of Lionel Barrymore's finest moments. In a lengthy scene, the final part of which would have benefited from a retake, he addresses her as 'Margaret'.) *Monsieur Duval considers her to be a gold-digger and beneath his son, 'He has a career waiting for him and in his case he can't serve his best interests by being tied to a woman he can't present to his family or his friends.' Until now, Marguerite has come across as a strong-willed woman; therefore it seems strange that she should now be willing to give up the man she loves without a struggle.* (Ultimately, though the script adheres as closely as possible to Dumas' work, this had less to do with turn-of-the-century Paris than a bigoted Hollywood under the watchful eye of the Breen Office and so Marguerite must choose between the lesser of the two evils: ruining the life of a decent young man, or consorting with her own 'kind'.) *If she tells Armand she no longer loves him, he will not believe her; if she leaves him, he will follow. Therefore the only way to set him free is for her to crawl back to the Baron. Armand begs her to stay – last night, she was ready to give up everything for him, but now her attitude is cold. 'Well, that was last night ... People say things they don't mean sometimes at night. Life is something besides kisses and promises in the moonlight. Even you should know that. Wasn't one summer all you wanted?'*

Armand sees her at a gambling club with the Baron, looking miserable. When he wins his game, Armand flings the money at her – all, he says, she has ever been interested in. He and the Baron square up to each other, and the next morning they fight a duel. The Baron is wounded and Armand forced to flee Paris. When he returns six months later, Marguerite is dying; the Baron has deserted her, she has sold the rest of her jewels to survive but is still in debt and the bailiffs have moved into her home, ready to pounce the moment she expires. Her voice is reduced to a whisper as she asks Nanine to send for the priest. Armand arrives, and for a fleeting moment she convinces him that their love will make her well again and begs him to take her back to the country. Then, knowing this will never happen and remembering what his father has said, she tells him, 'Perhaps it's better if I live in your heart, where the world can't see me. If I'm dead, there'll be no stain on my love.' And so she dies in his arms, beautifully, like no screen heroine before or since.

Shooting wrapped at the end of October, with Garbo declaring there would be no retakes. Marguerite Gauthier had exhausted her but was now dead; she wanted to bury her and look towards the future. She changed her mind after the Santa Barbara preview, when critics declared some scenes too lengthy and boring. One retake, in November, resulted in the headline: 'GRETA GARBO CATCHES FIRE IN LOVE SCENE WITH TAYLOR!' This was the scene where Marguerite is recovering from the coughing fit she suffers while dancing the polka. When Garbo stood too close to the fire, the hem of her dress caught alight and two technicians doused her with buckets of water to put it out. It was also meant as a double-entendre: the rumours concerning Robert Taylor's sexuality could not have been true, if his presence could 'set fire' one of the world's most beautiful women!

The film opened in New York on 22 January 1937 to exceptional reviews. Harrison Carrol, sitting in the audience, observed, 'When illness and tragedy overtake the heroine, she involves pathos so deep that many in the audience were openly weeping.' Louella Parsons, also present, was similarly moved:

> Perhaps it is the unexpected humour injected into her charac-
> terisation that gives her a warmth and a human touch noticeably
> missing from many of her previous performances. Even the hectically
> dramatic death scene has been treated with pathetic appeal, and if
> you can watch it without a tear in your eye, you have more fortitude
> than the crowds that poured into Grauman's Chinese yesterday.

Frank S. Nugent wrote in the *New York Times*, 'She is as incompa-
rable in the role as legend tells us that Bernhardt was. Through the perfect artistry of her portrayal, a hackneyed theme is made new again, poignantly sad, hauntingly lovely.' And from an anonymous British critic:

> When she was dying, she had the appearance not merely of being
> ill, but of having lain in bed for months. In her weakness she could
> not smile, but retained the pride of a Bernini statue. There has been
> no diminution of Miss Garbo's flaming genius during her recent
> absence from motion picture acting. Her command of the subtleties
> of an impersonation is even greater than it was in the past, and her

voice has taken on a new range of inflection. The Marguerite she brings to the screen is not only the errant and self-sacrificial nymph conceived by the younger Dumas nearly a hundred years ago, but one of the timeless figures of all great art ... It is likely that Miss Garbo still has her greatest role to play, but she has made the Lady of the Camellias, for this reviewer, hers for all time.[301]

Camille won Garbo her second New York Film Critics Best Actress Award, and an Oscar nomination. This year the competition was particularly strong: Janet Gaynor in *A Star Is Born*, Irene Dunne in a remake of *The Awful Truth*, Barbara Stanwyck in *Stella Dallas*, and Luise Rainer in *The Good Earth*. Rainer won, not that Garbo cared about such things. Much more important to her was the *Littris et Artibus* medal, one of Sweden's most prestigious honours. Previous recipients included soprano Jenny Lind and Sarah Bernhard and it was awarded by King Gustavus V at the end of the year. This should have been presented on his behalf by Borg's former boss, the Swedish Consul-General, but when Garbo learned that the ceremony would take place in front of an audience in San Francisco, she sent her excuses and the medal was posted to her via registered mail.

Later, she would learn that *Camille* was one of Hitler's favourite films and that he owned a private copy. Roger Normand recalled her reaction when this came up in conversation: 'How I would have loved to have put on one of Marguerite Gauthier's dresses and walked into the Reichstag and shot that animal!'[302]

The production was marred by Hollywood's third major tragedy in four years. On 14 September 1936, four days before Garbo's thirty-first birthday, MGM's Boy Wonder, Irving Thalberg, suddenly, but not unexpectedly, died, aged thirty-seven, plunging the movie capital into a state of profound shock. Many of those who had worked with him genuinely grieved – though many more did not. A few weeks earlier, a simple cold had developed into lobar pneumonia. Clark Gable (ordered to do so, against his wishes) and Douglas Fairbanks were ushers at his funeral at the B'na B'rith Temple on Wilshire Boulevard and anyone who was anyone was there to pay their respects – or disrespects, depending on how they had got along with the precocious mogul. Only the crowd-hating Garbo was absent, sending her excuses by way of a huge wreath. Later she said, 'I liked him. But he died much too early. The best die young.'[303]

Thalberg had died at the height of his powers, but with more of his stars hating than liking him, primarily because of his association with Mayer. This might have been about to change. There were rumours that he was planning to leave MGM and set up his own production company and that some of the studio's biggest stars would have followed him: Norma Shearer without any doubt, Joan Crawford most likely, and Garbo almost certainly; though she had initially disliked him, during the last two years she had begun trusting him and they had developed a bond. As with Ernst Lubitsch and very few others, she had often dropped in at his house unannounced and her grief was genuine, some believed more profound than for John Gilbert. His death also set the sombre mood for the closing scenes of *Camille*. Later, Thalberg served as a model for F. Scott Fitzgerald's *The Last Tycoon*, and from 1937 onwards the Motion Picture Academy would present an annual Best Producer Award in his memory.

Not long after Thalberg's death, William Daniels' father died suddenly, causing Garbo's favourite cameraman to go on a three-day bender. When Mayer learned that he was in Chicago being comforted by friends, there was little sympathy; instead of being granted compassionate leave, Daniels was put on suspension and Jean Harlow's ex-husband Hal Rosson brought in to replace him. Rosson had barely completed the wedding scene in *Camille* when Mayer replaced him with Karl Freund, of whom more later.

Thalberg's replacement at MGM was Bernie Hyman, whose approach to making pictures was decidedly different: cash injections, glamour and expensive sets were, he believed, the only key to success. Hyman was faced with an enormous problem when he learned that his star player had taken his predecessor's death so badly that she was consulting a psychiatrist, a daunting task for anyone attempting to unravel arguably one of the most complex minds in Hollywood history. 'A little hunchbacked man who I am dragging down into the abyss of pessimism,' was how she described him in a letter to Horge Wachtmeister.[304]

❧

Marie Walewska (1786–1817) was the Polish mistress of Napoleon Bonaparte, who bore him a son he could never publicly acknowledge. Born into a wealthy family she grew up at Kiernozia, the family seat, where one of her tutors was Chopin's father, Nicholas. In 1805, the year she met Napoleon, she married Count Walewska, almost four times her age. Reluctant to become Napoleon's mistress, she was coerced into doing so by members of the Polish aristocracy, including her elderly husband, in the hope of getting the Emperor to help Poland regain independence from Prussia and the Russian Empire. After this happened, she recalled: 'The sacrifice was complete. It was all about harvesting fruit now, which could excuse my *wystepa* position. This was the thought that possessed me. Ruling over my will, it did not allow me to fall under the weight of my bad consciousness and sadness.' After her affair with Napoleon ended, she married Philippe, Count d'Ornano. The highly fictionalised account of this period of her life, based on Waclaw Gasiorowski's *Pari Walewska* and coming in the wake of the phenomenally successful *Anna Karenina* and *Camille*, is generally regarded as one of Garbo's poorer films, as was reflected in the box-office receipts.[305]

The first stumbling block concerned the title: neither the critics nor the public, Mayer declared, would be able to pronounce it. Garbo was insistent that it should not be changed, but later settled on a compromise: the title would be retained for British and European audiences, while in North America it would be released as *Conquest*. Irving Thalberg commissioned Salka Viertel for the script and S. N. Behrman for the dialogue. Between Thalberg's death and the first day of shooting, 3 March 1937, fourteen other writers were roped into the project but the studio still was not satisfied. Another problem lay with casting Garbo's leading man. Napoleon's nickname had been 'Little Corporal' and he had been considerably shorter than his mistress. All of the old 'chestnuts' were considered, including John Barrymore and Claude Rains, until Garbo decided that her Napoleon would have to be authentically French – enter Charles Boyer.[306]

Boyer (1899–1978) worked on the French stage before being discovered by MGM's Paris agent in 1929, though during his first few years in Hollywood he achieved little. His big break occurred in 1934 alongside Loretta Young in *Caravan*: more recently he had starred opposite Marlene Dietrich in her first Technicolor film, *The Garden of Allah*. Though not the most charismatic of leading men, MGM considered him perfect for the part of Napoleon *solely* because he was one of two available French actors in Hollywood at the time, the other being Maurice Chevalier. Initially, he wanted nothing to do with the film. 'I would have been less hesitant if someone had asked me to play Jesus,' he recalled. 'Which would have been the harder role to play? For a Frenchman, I believe it would be Napoleon. I was fearful that to the French people, no performance of Napoleon Bonaparte, not even a *perfect* one, would be satisfactory.'[307]

As had happened with Fredric March, MGM's offer of a hefty salary – allegedly almost equal to Garbo's – enabled Boyer to change his mind. She was also 'peeved' to hear that Paramount would be paying Marlene Dietrich $450,000 for her next film, *Knight Without Armour*, almost twice what MGM were paying *her* unless she profited from the clause in her contract which guaranteed her an extra $10,000 per week for retakes and delays. In fact, there would be *so* many hitches during this one – nineteen days alone wasted because of her 'indispositions' – that by the time production wrapped after an astonishing 127-day shooting schedule, she would have earned $475,000, just beating Marlene whose new film, like *Marie Walewska*, would flop, resulting in Paramount terminating her contract.

Garbo asked for Clarence Brown to direct – this would be their seventh and last film together – but she did not get William Daniels, who was working with Jean Harlow. Instead, Bernie Hyman brought in Karl Freund, the photographer who had completed *Camille*. Bohemia-born and Berlin-raised, Freund (1890–1969) worked on many German Expressionist films including *The Golem* (1920) and Fritz Lang's *Metropolis* (1927). His first big hit in Hollywood was Tod Browning's *Dracula* (1931) and he had also tried his hand at acting, playing an art dealer in Carl Dreyer's *Mikael* (1924).

Fireworks were expected between Garbo and Freund, who had won an Oscar for *The Good Earth*, an award she believed would have gone to William Daniels, had he not gone AWOL. The two got along fine, however, as did Garbo and veteran Russian stage actress Maria Ouspenskaya (1876–1949), who plays her dotty aunt in the film. Trained by Stanislavski, she had arrived in New York in 1922 and worked on the stage for over a decade before making her Hollywood debut. In her later years, she opened her own drama school.

Garbo did not like the actor playing her son in the film. Hailing from Oakland, California, Scotty Beckett (1929–68) had been a regular in the *Our Gang* comedy shorts from 1934 to 1935: children all over America had emulated his character with the lopsided baseball cap and oversized black pullover. In 1936 he played the young Anthony in *Anthony Adverse* and had since played an Indian boy in *The Charge of the Light Brigade*.

Ouspenskaya, Beckett and Boyer all met tragic ends. The elderly actress died in 1949 following a stroke brought on by severe burns she received in a house fire after smoking in bed. Beckett made a successful transition from child to adult star. In 1947 he appeared in Marilyn Monroe's first film, *Dangerous Years*, though by then he was already going off the rails. His later career would be blighted by drink-driving charges, failed marriages, violent episodes and drug addiction. On 8 May 1968 he checked into a Hollywood clinic after being beaten up and two days later, overdosed on a mixture of alcohol and barbiturates. In 1934, after a whirlwind romance, Charles Boyer married British actress Pat Paterson, a marriage which lasted until her death from cancer in August 1978. Two days later, unable to continue without her, he took an overdose of Seconal. Their son, Michael, had died in 1964, during a drunken game of Russian roulette at his twenty-first birthday party.

Garbo had her own theory as to how Marie should be portrayed on the screen and pleaded with Salka Viertel, 'I have a great longing for trousers, and if I ask you in time maybe you can put in a little sequence with trousers, maybe her dressed as a soldier, going to Napoleon's tent at night, or something.' Thalberg, who had sanctioned the Sapphic scenes in *Queen Christina*, might have approved the request, but Bernie Hyman made it clear that one of the most beautiful Frenchwomen of her day would not be presented to the public as a 'baritone babe'. The Breen Office also had their say, declaring the film's adulterous content should be 'removed unreservedly'. MGM protested that, as a political pawn, Marie had been *ordered* to have an affair with Napoleon in the hope of saving Poland from oppression. Joseph Breen capitulated when Hyman assured him that the script made it quite clear that Marie had only succumbed to Napoleon under extreme pressure, and very much against her will.[308]

Shooting began on 3 March 1937, six weeks later than scheduled, partly due to Garbo's unspecified health issues and problems with the script, which was still being polished when the cameras started rolling. Garbo's mood-swings were not helped by the unwelcome attentions of Mayer and a drunken John Barrymore. Mayer is known to have made a pass at her and received short shrift when summoning her to his office on the pretext of discussing the script. She found Barrymore sozzled at nine in the morning, chatting to Clarence Brown outside her dressing room. The fading actor rushed up to her, threw his arms about her and proffered a kiss. Garbo smiled, shrugged herself free, and without saying a word walked into her dressing room and locked the door. Another unwelcome visitor was John Gilbert's teenage daughter, Leatrice. When Garbo learned that she was there to discuss her father's will, she refused to see her. There were no such problems when Clark Gable and Borg dropped in for a chat: they were invited into her dressing room and, in Borg's case, the door locked for a different reason.

There is no love-triangle in this film, which may be why many fans disliked it. They also disliked Charles Boyer who, though possessed of a powerful on-screen presence as the cold and calculating Napoleon, has no charisma. Indeed, the only males here with any degree of warmth are George Houston, playing Duroc, and Australian actor Alan Marshal as Marie's future husband, Captain d'Ornano, both of whom died tragically young.

The story opens in 1807, with Russian soldiers attacking the home of Count Walewski (Henry Stephenson). Having wrecked the place and ravaged the servants, they encounter the elderly pacifist owner and his wife Marie (Garbo making another muted appearance, descending the staircase and addressing the invaders in little more than a raised whisper). *The rabble leave upon learning that the Polish Lancers are on their tails, captained by Marie's brother, Paul* (Leif Erickson), *who she has not seen since childhood.*

When Paul appears he informs her that their saviour, Napoleon Bonaparte, has arrived in Poland. Marie travels to see the Emperor for no other reason than hero worship and they happen to meet later at a ball. The Emperor is shocked to see a voluptuous young woman married to a statesman fifty years her senior, with a grown-up family: 'I congratulate you, madame. For a grandmother you are extraordinarily well-preserved. I regret I did not know you when you were younger.'

Also at the ball is Captain d'Ornano (Alan Marshal), *who is enamoured of Marie, but she is coerced by the nobles into dancing with Napoleon instead. They have plans for her: if she becomes Napoleon's mistress, they will have a better chance of getting him on side to rid them of Russian tyranny. The little man flirts with her but she is faithful to her husband, of whom she says: 'He has his dignity, he has his honoured name, and so do I.' No one has snubbed Napoleon before and he is offended, therefore the nobles apply pressure. 'Are you suggesting that I can succeed where the Polish legions have failed?' Marie naively asks. 'Perhaps you have been made beautiful, that Poland may be made free. You are a woman. Napoleon is after all only a man,' is their answer.*

Marie obeys the command. Napoleon says she is the only woman whose favours he has ever had to beg for and for a moment behaves like a rational human being. Even so, she does not wish to sleep with him and says that she is only here to beg for her people. But her pleas only excite him and when she tries to leave, he drags her back into the room and, we assume, has his way with her.

Such is her husband's disgust when Marie returns home that he announces he is having their marriage annulled, but that she may keep the house. (In real life, it was Marie who divorced Walewski – in 1812, *after* her affair with Napoleon, and having accepted responsibility for raising their love-child as his own. This essential historical fact was changed upon Joseph Breen's orders to make Marie 'atone for her sins'; in the eyes of her countrymen, her exploits with the Emperor turned her into a national heroine.) *Napoleon turns up, tries to woo her by telling her how lonely he feels and she suddenly finds her mettle: 'Am I to understand that the Master of Europe who can command a million men to die for him cannot command one of them to be his friend? ... You say you are lonely. Where would you receive a friend? In your heart? It's too full of yourself. In your mind? It's too full of the world. And your desires are unworthy of friendship. You will always be lonely, but you'll bear it. You're pitiless, even to yourself!' However, after he speaks of his dream for universal peace and spins her a yarn about his miserable childhood, Marie yields to his phoney charms. 'I shall never yearn for spring again,' she drawls, for she knows they will be together only during the winter, after which he will leave on his next campaign.*

But everything changes when Marie falls pregnant. She visits him to impart the good news. 'I shall never be unhappy again,' she starts – but she never gets to tell him about the child because he drops a bombshell: though nothing need change between them, he must secure his dynasty by marrying into one of the powers he has conquered. His offspring, he says, must be of royal blood, and so he will take Princess Marie-Louise of Austria as his wife. 'Think, the son of Napoleon, born of Habsburg blood,' he beams. She responds with a weariness born of disappoint-ment, 'Ancient blood. Thin, cold, watery. A dead house, and you are going to live in it. A tomb, with a bride who hates you and a family that despises you. Do you think they'd forget that you'd beaten them? How they will hate you for forcing yourself on them ... The liberator of Europe has become a son-in-law!'

Their affair over, Marie leaves, and the narrative zips through several crucial years of European history as if of no importance: Napoleon's wedding, the birth of Marie's son and that of the Emperor's legitimate heir, his army's retreat across a snowy Polish wasteland and, finally, Napoleon's exile to Elba, where he is mollycoddled by his mother while he waits for the ship that will reunite him with his Empress and son. Instead, he receives a visit from his bastard, Alexandre, accompanied by Marie, who feels that they might have some kind of life together now that his campaigning days are over. He manipulates her into helping him to escape and goes on to fight the British at Waterloo (the famous battle taking up just six seconds of screen time), *then, having lost, he is captured and sentenced to exile in St Helena, where he can do no more harm. Again, Marie offers to help him to escape; he refuses to run away like a coward and as he is escorted to the ship by his captors, she tearfully waves him off through the window.*

The film opened in New York on 4 November 1937 to some of the worst reviews Garbo had ever received. Announcing that it was the costliest film MGM had ever made, the *Motion Picture Herald* concluded, 'It *is* super colossal magnifico – but a dog at the box-office.' Louella Parsons observed, 'Garbo is completely overshadowed by Charles Boyer – who takes the picture, wraps it, and walks away with it.' Of Garbo's appearance she added, unfairly and erroneously, 'She has lost so much weight that there are scenes where she is almost emaciated-looking.' John Mosher, writing for *The New Yorker*, was in agreement: 'Madame Garbo's anaemia, I fear, can pull a little. Her performance seems static, though the story covers a period of years ... I think that for the first time Madame Garbo has a leading man who contributes more to the interest and vitality of the film than she does.'[309]

Marie Walewska remains the only Garbo film to have shown an actual loss. Indeed, it was MGM's biggest money-loser to date: though it took $2 million at the box-office, its hugely inflated $3 million budget resulted in a reported loss of $1,397,000. Her next film, however, would see her in a sparkling and much more profitable return to form...

CHAPTER TWELVE

GARBO LAUGHS

'Don't you think it is high time they let me end a picture happily with a kiss? I do. I seem to have lost so many attractive men in the final scenes.'

Garbo had socialised with none of her *Marie Walewska* co-stars: no invitations to her dressing room, no shared meals, very little laughter, and the only person she saw away from the set was cameraman Karl Freund, who it emerged had met her in Berlin when she was with Mauritz Stiller. Freund recalled a conversation he claimed he had had with Garbo, where she had been more forthcoming than usual:

FREUND: G.G., what do you do when you go home?
GARBO: I rest a bit, the maid brings me dinner, then I study the next day's script and go to bed. I've been in my new house for three months and, would you believe it, I've never seen the living room. I eat, study and sleep.
FREUND: And what else do you do?
GARBO: I sometimes play checkers with myself.
FREUND: And what do you do about sex?
GARBO: Once in a while I go out, when I meet a man I like, who enjoys me. When he arrives I peek out at him to see what he's wearing and then I dress accordingly. Many of the men who ask me out go crazy about my Swedish maid, who is very pretty. They pat her on the cheek and flirt with her, but for me, at the end of the evening they say, 'Thank you Miss Garbo,' and they tell me how wonderful it was but no one ever says, 'Let's go to bed.'[310]

But there was a new man in Garbo's life. She first met the British-born conductor Leopold Stokowski on the set of Deanna Durbin's *One Hundred Men & A Girl* during a break from shooting

Camille – though why she should wish to visit another star's set, when no other star was permitted near hers, remains a mystery. Stokowski (1882–1977) had studied with London's Royal College of Music and first took up the baton in Paris in 1909, though he subsequently dispensed with this to conduct 'free-hand', most notably during his tenure at the Philadelphia Symphony Orchestra (1912–36). His Hollywood movie debut, playing himself, was in *The Big Broadcast of 1937*, completed shortly before the Durbin film. A womaniser and a serial cheat, Stokowski's first wife had been the concert pianist Olga Samarroff, but when he met Garbo he was married to the Johnson & Johnson heiress, Evangeline Johnson.

On meeting Garbo, Stokowski reacted like a starstruck teenager, fawning and lusting over a beautiful woman not much more than half his age. There has never been any real explanation as to what she saw in him, other than his promise to 'show her the world', which she was perfectly capable of seeing on her own. According to the writer Anita Loos, who arranged for Garbo and Stokowski to meet at her home – with other guests present so that she would not know she was being set up, if Loos' matchmaking failed – seduction was the *only* thing on the conductor's mind. Inasmuch as Marie Walewska had entered Napoleon's realm without knowing what she was letting herself in for, so Garbo fell for the philosophies of this phoney charmer: he told her that, to get the best out of life one must enjoy it to the full and not sit alone and mope. And though by no means qualified to make such a diagnosis, he also accredited Garbo's poor health and menstrual problems to her diet and the fact that she was eating far too much red meat. Within a week of meeting him, she turned vegetarian, which only made matters worse.

One of Loos' party guests remembered,

> Stoky didn't waste much time with the overture. He told Garbo they were destined to have a history-making romance, like Wagner's with Cosima. It was written in the stars ... It was the direct attack mixed with a little mystical stuff. Any kind of mystical stuff made quite a hit with Greta in those days.[311]

Their next 'date' constituted a visit to Salka Viertel's house, where Garbo's friend was also attempting to recapture her youth – since splitting from Berthold, she had taken up with Gottfried Reinhardt, the producer son of Max, who at twenty-six was twenty-two years her junior. In his memoirs, Gottfried recalled Garbo kneeling at Stokowski's feet, as she had with Erich von Stroheim, while the conductor regaled her with tales of his overseas adventures.

Being seen with Garbo at his side helped Stokowski through what appears to have been his mid-life crisis. Theirs was almost certainly a platonic relationship, not far removed from Garbo's on-off liaison with Mercedes de Acosta. Like Mercedes, Stokowski was decidedly eccentric – he wore bizarre clothes, and looked odd with his sharp features and shock of prematurely white hair; like her, he was prone to boasting that there was more going on between he and Garbo than there really was. Garbo, he claimed, made him feel young again, while he made her feel intellectual and helped rid her of the guilt she felt at not having had a legitimate education. Problems occurred when one journalist claimed that Garbo had described Stokowski as her 'boyfriend', a fabrication, for she would never have been so forthcoming to the press. Stokowski's wife, Evangeline, no less of a reprobate than he was and embroiled in a public affair with an exiled Russian prince, Alexis Zalsten-Zalessky, moved to Reno and on 1 December filed for a quickie divorce, audaciously citing her husband's adultery. Garbo was not named as co-respondent, but seeing her name linked to his in articles made her feel relieved that she was about to leave for an extended visit to Sweden. Hopefully, she told friends, when she returned to Hollywood – *if* she returned – the scandal would have died down. In the meantime, to evade the press she moved into George Cukor's house. One morning, as she was getting out of her car there, she was accosted by Jim Simmons of *Photoplay*, who wanted to know if the rumours were true that she and 'Stoky' planned to marry as soon as his divorce came through. Garbo tried to ignore him, but when Simmons took on an aggressive tone, she turned on him: 'These rumours are absurd. I won't deny that Mr Stokowski and I are very good friends. But as for marriage to him – no, that is out of the question!'[312]

A few days later, Stokowski accompanied Garbo to New York. For the first time, she was leaving Hollywood without having signed a contract, but MGM were not in the same financial quandary as before. Her last film had shown a substantial loss – mostly the studio's own fault – but even Mayer was beginning to think that maybe she had passed her peak and might be better off staying in Europe. As usual, she gave no indication that she would be coming back. On 8 December, Stokowski settled her into her suite on the Gripsholm, reserved under the name 'Jonas Emersen', and ten days later she arrived in Gothenburg.

This time, there was no rented apartment, or hotel suite with a security guard posted outside the door. Garbo had realised her dream of becoming a 'gentleman farmer'. Situated at Lake Gillen, Gnesta, in Sodermanland County and a 45-minute drive south-west of Stockholm, Harby was set in 1,000 acres of mostly forest, with around 150 acres of workable farmland. Sven Gustaffson and Horke Wachtmeister had found the place for her and she had wired the 276,000-kronor asking price without quibbling. Included in this had been a substantial stock of chickens, pigs and cattle. The house, on two levels, comprised fifteen rooms, all with bare red-brick floors, which one imagines would have been dreadfully cold during a Swedish winter.

Sven collected her from the ship and drove her straight to Harby, where her mother had effected a Christmas card welcome – with six inches of snow already on the ground and the roof, Anna had lined the drive with multicoloured lanterns and hung more of the same in each window. Garbo was incensed, though, that Emilie Danielson, a Swedish freelance photographer, had visited the property earlier in the day. Danielson subsequently sold her pictures to the highest bidder, *Movie Mirror*, whose editorial asked: 'Can you imagine Mata Hari in such surroundings? Yet wouldn't you expect the Viking Venus to choose a home as distinctive as this?'[313]

Though Garbo's name was on the deeds, she had bought the property for her mother. For years, Anna Gustaffson had refused to move from Stockholm's South Side, and only did so now because Sven and his family – his wife Marguerite and their daughter, Gray, born in 1937 – moved in with her. Garbo had a contract of

employment drawn up employing Sven as Harby's official care-
taker, a job he apparently did not do very well. 'I live in my
brother's place, which is a mess,' she wrote to Salva Viertel. 'I
tried to find something that would have helped him in life, but
it is not right. He can't take care of it and now I don't know any
more what to do.'[314]

A few days before Christmas, Garbo received a visit from
Screenland's Hettie Grimstead, who had travelled on the same ship
from New York and had taken this long to track her down. When
Garbo refused to see her, Grimstead bribed one of the maids to
inform her readers what 'the world's most mysterious woman' was
getting up to and reported back that Garbo had spent a lot of time
with a woman painter friend (this was actually Mimi Pollak) and that
the two liked to go ice-yachting and attend hockey matches. They
had also visited the ski slopes at Fiskartorpet, north of Stockholm,
and the Garboscope Cinema on the city's South Side, named in her
honour. She also mentioned that Garbo had frequently spent the
night at this friend's apartment. When Garbo learned that one of
her staff had been speaking to the press, she was fired.[315]

Hettie Grimstead sneaked into an impromptu press conference
forced upon Garbo in the lobby of Stockholm's Grand Hotel at the
end of January, when she expressed her admiration for the British
actress, Flora Robson, whom she had recently seen as Queen
Elizabeth in *Fire Over England*. She had been so impressed, she said,
that from now on she would be content to leave the great dramatic
and historical roles to others. Her mood changed when one of
the reporters, who had obviously been contacted by Mercedes de
Acosta, asked her why she had changed her mind when he had it
on 'good authority' that her next role should have been Joan of
Arc. 'No,' she snapped, 'I am *not* going to play Joan of Arc. Has
that silly story got to Europe, too? It is so idiotic. I am tired of
period pictures and I want to do something modern now. My next
film is to be a comedy!' And with this, she had stormed across to
the elevator.[316]

Upon hearing this, MGM went into meltdown. In their opinion,
the *last* thing Garbo was capable of was making audiences laugh. A
far better option, they declared, would be Marie Curie. Universal

had bought the story for Irene Dunne but when it emerged that Garbo was interested in the role – or rather, that Salka Viertel was interested on her behalf – they sold it to MGM for a staggering $250,000. British writer Aldous Huxley was commissioned to pen the screenplay, on a salary of $2,000 a week. George Cukor was pencilled in to direct. Garbo considered him 'lucky' because his birthday was 26 July – the same as her brother Sven, Lars Hanson, and Borg. Luck, however, was not on his side here. According to MGM's scripts department, Huxley submitted a 140-page treatment to Bernie Hyman's office, but this got no further than a preliminary reading by Hyman's secretary, who concluded on his behalf, 'It stinks!' The film would eventually be made in 1943, using part of Huxley's script, with Greer Garson receiving an Oscar nomination for her portrayal of the Polish-French physicist.

Meanwhile, on 5 February, shortly before his ex-wife married her prince, Stokowski boarded the *Conte di Savoia* for Naples. From here, two weeks later, he called Garbo at Harby and asked her to join him. She actually met up with him in Rome on 24 February. The next morning, with Garbo at the wheel of their hired car, they drove the twenty-five miles to Ravello, the picturesque resort on the Amalfi Coast. Stokowski was independently wealthy, which suited Garbo when it came to 'gallivanting' as he would pay his own way and not sponge off her as some 'escorts' had in the past. Indeed, he had rented the opulent and extremely expensive Villa Cimbrone for a month. Within days the press were on to them. Stokowski claimed he had been accosted in the village by a reporter, who asked if the 'Margaret Gustaffson' staying at the villa was actually Greta Garbo and if the rumours were true that they had come here to marry. 'Greta Garbo?' Stokowski posed, 'Oh, you mean the film star? I've no idea *where* she is right now. She most definitely isn't here with me!' Later, he would be suspected of actually approaching the press, such was his hunger for publicity and his desire to feed his ego by advertising the fact that the world's most enigmatic star might have eyes for him alone.[317]

As had happened at Harby, two of the staff – the gardener and a chambermaid – were paid handsomely by the *New Yorker*'s E. W. Selsey and Martha Kerr of *Modern Screen* to keep tabs on the current mistress of the house, though by the time their stories hit the newsstands, the 'affair' was all but history. 'Garbo has found love at last,' Kerr reported, adding that her acceptance of Stokowski's offer to see the beautiful things in the world was 'proof enough of her greatest love for the man whose association she has secretly enjoyed these many months. And as we go to press, word comes to us that Garbo and Stokowski have silently stolen away from their retreat in Ravello and moved to Taormina, a seaside village in Sicily. Rumour is rife that here, under the shadow of the ever-smoking volcano, Mount Etna, they will be married.'[318]

Selsey went one step further. Her informant rifled through Garbo's luggage, but was interested in what it did *not* contain: no dresses, blouses, coats and other outdoor apparel – just a pair of men's pyjamas, and espadrilles. Clearly, she intended wearing as little as possible during this sojourn. And if Garbo was going to be walking around the place half-dressed or naked, the columnists concluded, it figured she and her middle-aged beau would be spending a lot of time having sex. Further 'proof' of this came from the elderly gardener, who could not understand why this mismatched couple, who also did their early-morning exercises in the buff, should insist on addressing each other as 'Miss Garbo' and 'Mr Stokowski'. He did however find it amusing to hear her drilling him during their routine: 'One, Two, Three, Bend! One, Two – Mr Stokowski, you are out of time! One, Two, Three, Bend!' Much was made too of dozens of jars of a 'strange preserve' which Garbo had packed into one of her trunks – each morning she would tip the contents of one of these over her cornflakes, then fill the bowl to the top with black coffee, and eat the whole disgusting mess with relish. The preserve was made from lingonberries – a wild fruit she herself had picked in the Swedish countryside – not unlike loganberries and very rich in Vitamin C.

The real problems for Garbo and Stokowski came when a Rome newspaper (again almost certainly fed the story by Stokowski himself) reported they *were* about to get married, and that Wallace Beery was flying out to be his best man. The village was besieged by hundreds of reporters. When they began climbing trees and lying in wait on neighbouring rooftops, Garbo hired armed police officers with dogs to mount a round-the-clock vigil outside the property. Next, a fan tossed a brassière over the gates, to which was pinned a request for her to wear it and throw it back. By 16 March, the day the ceremony was supposed to be taking place, she made up her mind to leave.

Stokowski persuaded her to change her mind, his theory – part of his ego-boosting plan – being that if she granted a brief press conference, these people would leave them in peace. The gist of this, with emphasis placed on Garbo's infamous 'catchphrase', was reported in numerous columns around Europe:

> I never had any impulse to go to the altar. I haven't many friends. I haven't seen much of the world, either. My friend, Mr Stokowski, offered to take me around to see some beautiful things. I optimistically accepted. I was naive enough to think that I could travel without being discovered and without being hunted. Why can't we avoid being followed and examined? It is cruel to bother people who want to be left in peace. This kills beauty for me. I live in a corner. I am typically alone ... I wish to be otherwise, but I cannot. I don't like this. I only want to be left *alone*.[319]

The press promised to keep their distance and kept to their word – for two days. Also, there was another threat. Mercedes de Acosta had followed Garbo to Europe, travelling extensively throughout France, Germany and Poland while waiting for someone to call or wire her with news of her whereabouts. Now, thanks to the circus which had taken place at Ravello, she knew exactly where to find her. On 18 March, before dawn, Garbo and Stokowski drove to Naples, and caught the ferry to Capri. Here, they were taken in by British singer Gracie Fields, herself no stranger to controversy, having discovered the island some years earlier while touring Europe with her painter lover, John Flanagan, after splitting from her first husband, impresario Archie Pitt. For two days, Garbo languished next to Gracie's pool at her Canzone del Mare complex and at night slept in one of the tiny chalets reserved for the staff rather than at one of the plush hotels where she knew she would be pestered by the press. She, Gracie and Stokowski also lunched with another of the island's famous residents, the blind Swedish psychiatrist Axel Munthe, at the Villa San Michele, his home in Ana Capri.

On 22 March, Garbo and Stokowski returned to Naples, stayed the night at a guesthouse before driving to Rome, then spent four days here before sailing to Tunis, where they managed to evade the media for two weeks. A 'friend of Miss Garbo', in reality Garbo herself, threw reporters off their trail by revealing that the couple were about to leave for Vienna. The press should have had more important issues to deal with, as war-clouds darkened over Europe. Germany had mobilised its troops. France was calling in its reserves. The Führer had recently visited Mussolini in Rome. Neville Chamberlain had met with Hitler and had failed in his attempts to avoid the conflict. Yet for weeks the front pages had only been interested in speculating over whether Greta Garbo was sleeping with Leopold Stokowski.

The European press also missed out on the big news story, which detractors in Hollywood predicted might bring her career to a premature halt. At the beginning of May, the *Hollywood Reporter* published its now-legendary 'Box-Office Poison' feature, a full-page report from the Independent Theater Owners of America, attacking studios and producers for 'promoting stars whose public appeal is negligible, but who receive tremendous salaries necessitated by contractual obligation.' Besides Garbo, the other names on the list included Marlene Dietrich, Katharine Hepburn, Joan Crawford, Edward Arnold, Mae West, Kay Francis and later, Fred Astaire. Paramount had already dropped Marlene, and RKO had dropped Hepburn. No one knew then who was behind the list but the culprit was subsequently named as Harry Brandt, the owner of a cinema chain. Anita Loos maintained that, had Thalberg been alive, Garbo's name would not have been on it. Though they did not know it at the time, there would be no lasting harm as Brandt's victims all found work with other studios and lost none of their popularity with the public.[320]

By 6 May the couple were back at Harby, after which their movements are sketchy until 24 July, when Garbo drove Stokowski to the railway station for the first leg of his journey home. Though they would sometimes speak on the phone, they never met again. Garbo

herself arrived back in New York on 7 October 1938, granting what
would be her final press conference, before leaving the ship. The
war in Europe was foremost on the passengers' minds: many were
heading for America, terrified that Hitler might invade Sweden.
As usual, Garbo had intended keeping to her suite throughout the
entire voyage, but she had emerged from her self-enforced solitude
on the second day to help deliver a baby. Henceforth, she spent
several hours each day with the unnamed mother and child, and
this and the recurring topic of marriage formed the basis of her
ten-minute grilling by journalists:

QUESTION: Miss Garbo, are you actually married to Mr
Stokowski?
GARBO: I wish you wouldn't ask me that question. If I were
married, *you* would know all about it, since nothing escapes you.
QUESTION: Do you *ever* intend to marry?
GARBO: If I could find the right person to share my life with,
perhaps I would marry...
QUESTION: And the mother and baby you helped out with, here?
GARBO: I spent some time with them, of course. I am always very
interested in babies. The birth of a baby is always a miracle.
QUESTION: And would you like to have babies of your own?
GARBO: No! The world is too difficult. I mean, partly because of
the danger of war in the world. I would not want to raise a son or
any children to go to war. But, I don't want any more about that.
I don't know anything about politics...
QUESTION: Miss Garbo, do you hate *all* newspapermen?
GARBO: Oh, I might *like* all of you, removed from your jobs and
your newspapers!
QUESTION: Miss Garbo – have you enjoyed your vacation?
GARBO: No! You cannot have a vacation without peace – and you
cannot have peace unless you are left alone. And now, if you will
excuse me...[321]

With this, shaking a few hands en-route, Garbo walked out of the
ship's library, then immediately set tongues wagging by being met
at the bottom of the gangplank by Reginald Allen, Stokowski's

personal assistant, who drove her to the West 54th Street apartment of a composer friend, Richard Hammond, where she would stay before returning to Hollywood.

In New York she also met up with Robert Reud – the fan, now a close friend, who years earlier had offered to marry her to save her from deportation. He escorted her around the city, and a much-feted photograph of them appeared at the time, snapped while they were sitting in a corner of a restaurant. While Garbo instinctively grabbed her hat to cover her face, she forgot about the mirror next to her, through which the photographer captured her peeved expression. It did not take long for journalists to track her down and when this happened Hammond whisked her off on a week-long boating trip to Gloucester County. Again, the press caught up with her but not until the day she was scheduled to leave, with the New York *Daily News* running the headline, 'GARBO GOES CRUISIN' AND FINDS IT AIN'T AMUSIN'!'[322]

On 18 October, MGM received an official complaint from the Coiffure Guild, holding a convention in the city. Women all over America, they avowed, were emulating Garbo. By allowing their hair to grow straight, and by washing it themselves as she did, they were depriving the hairdressing trade of a living. 'It is wholly unsuitable for wear by her or by the women of this country,' their manifesto proclaimed of her unkempt locks. 'And should such a style ever be popularised, this would have the effect of working vast injury to the hair-stylists of the United States.' There had been a similar hubbub back in the Twenties when Rudolph Valentino – preparing for his role in *The Hooded Falcon*, subsequently aborted – had returned from a European trip sporting a beard. The Barbers Association had kicked up such a fuss that he had been made to shave it off. Garbo, however, was no pushover. What she did with her hair was *her* business and the Coiffure Guild were unceremoniously told to mind theirs.[323]

A few days later, Garbo left for Hollywood. Wishing to avoid a repeat performance of her brush with reporters the last time she changed trains in Chicago, she boarded the *Broadway Limited*, still bound for Chicago, but allowing her to alight at Gary, Indiana, then travel on to Joliet, Illinois, to board the *Santa Fe Chief*. Salka

Viertel met her in Los Angeles and drove her to George Cukor's house, where she stayed until moving home yet again, this time to a property on North Amalfi Drive. During her absence, MGM had assigned Salka to scripting her next film, *Ninotchka*, based on the novel by Melchior Lengyel, who was hired as co-writer. This tells the story of a humourless Russian female diplomat who finds romance in Paris and was a return to the old Garbo formula, save that instead of being rescued from the clutches of an older man by a younger lover, this one would see her rescued from the clutches of Communism.

Directing, at last, was her friend, Ernst Lubitsch. Lubitsch (1892–1947) was the German-born son of a Jewish tailor. He joined Max Reinhardt's theatre group in 1911 and acted on the stage until bitten by the directing bug. His first important production, *Die Augen der Mumie Ma* (*The Eyes of the Mummy*, 1918) starred Pola Negri. Four years later, he arrived in Hollywood, first directing for Mary Pickford, then rapidly establishing a reputation for classy comedies of manners such as *The Love Parade* (1929). Lubitsch was doubly suited to *Ninotchka*, having visited Russia and experienced life in a Communist country, as opposed to having read about it in textbooks, travel guides and spy novels. Garbo did find him a little overpowering at times and his persistent bellowing of instructions, even when standing right next to her, unnerved her until she gently reprimanded him, in German so that no one else would understand: 'Please, when you speak to me, please speak more softly!' Lubitsch's first move was to remove Lengyel and Behrman from the picture; while not wishing to change Lengyel's story, he found his scriptwriting inadequate and Behrman's dialogue not sharp enough to match Garbo's innate sense of dry, offbeat and frequently caustic humour, which he had discovered during her visits to his home. The pair were replaced by Walter Reisch, who had recently scripted *The Great Waltz,* and who, along with Mayer remained to be convinced that Garbo would be capable of making people laugh. Mayer added that in view of the 'box-office poison' tag, there would be a drop in salary: she would be paid $250,000 for the one-off deal, though all the terms of her previous contracts would still be there: script and co-star approval, and the $10,000-a-week fee for retakes and delays. Garbo agreed to this when Mayer explained that, with war seeming inevitable now that Germany had invaded Austria, in these two countries at least, where much of MGM's European revenue had come from, her films would no longer be permitted to be distributed.

From MGM's point of view there was the added bonus in that Garbo's biggest rival, Marlene Dietrich, was out of their hair. Marlene had shrugged her shoulders at the box-office poison slur – if Hollywood no longer wanted her, she would find someone who would. In the spring of 1938 she returned to Europe, vowing never to make another American film. She had the more important issue of getting her mother and sister out of Nazi Germany to deal with, though sadly this would never happen. On the negative side, Mercedes had wormed herself back into Garbo's affections, taking advantage of Salka Viertel's sudden departure. Also anxious about her relatives and friends, most of whom were Jewish, Salka had returned to Poland. This suited Lubitsch, who considered Salka almost as bad an influence as Mercedes.

Salka was replaced by Charles Brackett, then president of the Screenwriters Guild, and Billy Wilder. Born in Sucha Beskidza, Austro-Hungary (now Poland), and a year younger than Garbo, Wilder relocated to Vienna when young and, after dropping out of university, moved to Berlin, where he worked as a journalist and taxi-dancer – charging well-heeled widows for his services, and not just on the dance floor – before trying his hand at screenwriting. After Hitler's rise to power, he fled to Paris where, in 1933, he made his directorial debut with *Mauvaise Graine*, starring Danielle Darrieux. That same year he moved to Hollywood, where *Ninotchka* would become his first noteworthy success, followed by such classics as *Sunset Boulevard* (1950) with Gloria Swanson and *Witness for the Prosecution* (1957) with Marlene Dietrich. Some years later, he enthused about Garbo, while taking a slight dig at her acknowledged *hausfrau* rival, Marlene Dietrich:

> It may be the goddamnest put-on of all time, yet Garbo is the quin-
> tessence of what a star should be. Today's actresses tell us how they
> bring up their children and give us their recipe for scrambled eggs

but Garbo stumbled on a much more compelling idea. She said and did nothing and let the world write her story. She was as incongruous in Hollywood as Sibelius would have been if he had come to write incidental music for Warner Brothers films.[324]

Garbo's original choice of leading man for *Ninotchka* was Cary Grant, whom she admired tremendously. Despite eventually having seven wives between them, Grant and his actor 'room-mate' Randolph Scott remained lovers for many years and, as was her wont, while MGM were casting the other parts for the film, Garbo dropped in at their Malibu home, 'Bachelor Hall', unannounced to announce the good news. Grant was working at the studio, though she did have a pleasant surprise when Noël Coward answered the door – he and his latest male 'secretary' were spending a short holiday there. Coward tried to contact Grant on the set, but by the time he arrived home Garbo had grown tired of waiting: after a cursory nod and handshake, she got into her car and drove away.[325]

The supporting cast – Ina Claire, Sig Ruman, Felix Bressart, Alexander Granach and horror king Bela Lugosi – are mostly excellent. Garbo and Claire, contrary to some reports, did not get along. They were civil towards each other, but only until the ex-Mrs Gilbert took liberties by spying on her from behind the screened-off set, not once, but twice. The first time was when Ninotchka is about to receive flowers from her lover. Ernst Lubitsch asked her if she was ready for the take and Garbo gruffed, 'As soon as Miss Claire gets out from behind that curtain.' Claire was moved on by a technician, only to watch the scene where Ninotchka cries after receiving the censored letter from her lover, this time undetected, from another darkened corner. Catching up with Garbo later, she complimented her on her acting (condescending, perhaps, considering Claire's own performance is lamentable), and added, 'And damn you, I saw you cry!'[326] This brought the surly response, 'Very unmanly of me, wasn't it?' before Garbo turned her back on her and strode off. Throughout the remainder of the shoot, Claire found herself ignored. She also suspected Garbo of attempting to sabotage her career when Ernst Lubitsch cut two of her scenes after reading Hedda Hopper's comment from the first preview on

24 August, in the *Los Angeles Times*, 'Unless the film is slashed and parts redone, Ina steals it.'

Ninotchka was purposely scripted, with her wholehearted approval, to debunk the Garbo myth and poke fun at Russia and its Communist regime – the names of most of the main characters (Yakushova, Swana, Iranoff, Kopalsky, Bulianoff) are not even Russian. More important from a publicity angle was the simple caption flashed across trailers and billboards. For *Anna Christie*, MGM had proclaimed 'GARBO TALKS!', for this one they employed 'GARBO LAUGHS!' She had of course laughed many times before on the screen, but had never delivered a belly laugh as she does here, in a sophisticated comedy such as Lubitsch was acclaimed for. With Europe on the verge of war – actually at war when the film was released – its mockery of another dictatorial regime provided audiences with a welcome light relief against some of the horror stories, which began appearing in the press. The declaration of war also resulted in a few post-production changes, beginning with the opening credits: 'This picture takes place in Paris in those wonderful days when a siren was a brunette and not an alarm ... and if a Frenchman turned out the light it was not on account of an air-raid!' Minutes into the scenario, a passenger alighting from a train pronounces, 'Heil Hitler!' while giving the Nazi salute.

A trio of inept envoys (Rumann, Bressart, Granach) *arrive at a plush hotel to sell the Grand Duchess Swana's jewels, confiscated by their government, so that the proceeds may buy farm machinery for the starving masses back home. Swana* (Ina Claire) *is here too with her playboy lover, Count Leon d'Algout* (Melvin Douglas)*, who obtains an injunction to block the sale and bribes the three into cooperation by introducing them to a lifestyle unknown in Communist Russia.*

The trio's superior is forced to send special envoy Nina Ivanovna Yakushova, aka Ninotchka, to sort out the mess (Garbo, making her entrance twenty minutes into the film – straitlaced, humourless, wearing dowdy clothes and no make-up). *The kind of woman she is is made clear when a porter explains that it is his business to carry her luggage and she retorts, 'That is no business. That is social injustice.'*

Having expected a man, the three feel they should have brought flowers. 'Don't make an issue of my womanhood,' Ninotchka admonishes. And when asked how things are in Moscow she replies, 'Very good. The last mass trials were a great success. There are going to be fewer but better Russians.' She disapproves of the fashions of the country in which she finds herself – seeing a modern hat in a hotel display cabinet, she opines, 'How can such a civilisation survive which permits women to put things like that on their heads? It won't be long now, comrades!' And she is horrified by the cost of her room – the only one with a safe to store the jewels – declaring, 'If I stay here a week I will have cost the Russian people seven cows. Who am I to cost the Russian people seven cows? I'm ashamed to put a picture of Lenin in a room like this.' (The scriptwriter even permits Garbo a moment of self-parody, having one of the envoys ask, 'Do you want to be alone, comrade?') *When Ninotchka asks for cigarettes, these are delivered by a trio of giggling girls who had entertained the envoys last night, causing her to utter her driest line yet: 'You must have been smoking a lot.'*

Ninotchka meets Leon in the street and asks for directions to the Eiffel Tower. He flirts with her, but she tells him, 'Suppress it. Your type will soon be extinct.' Later, however, she accompanies him to his house – he will make an interesting case study. She asks the elderly butler if Leon whips him, then there is more self-parody: 'Go to bed, little father. We want to be alone.' Of Leon she says, approvingly, 'Your general appearance is not distasteful. The whites of your eyes are clear. Your cornea is excellent.' And when Leon says he is falling in love with her, she confesses that she feels the same way, declaring, 'Love is a romantic designation for a most ordinary or should we say chemical process ... I acknowledge the existence of a natural impulse, common to all ... Chemically, we are already quite sympathetic.' Next comes a line that was almost cut. After recalling how, as a sergeant with the Third Cavalry, she was attacked by a Polish Lancer, who she bayoneted but kissed before he died, she asks, 'Would you like to see my wound?'

Their romance seems destined to be short-lived when each discovers the other's identity. However, determined not to give up on her, Leon follows her to a backstreet bistro, where he tries to get her to smile by cracking corny jokes. She remains stony-faced until he falls off his chair, causing her to laugh hysterically. (Cynics questioned at the time, and still do, the authenticity of the sound accompanying this scene. In previous films, whenever Garbo laughed, it was always silently, as she did in real life. Melvyn Douglas recalled, 'She was unable to articulate so much as a titter during the shooting of the restaurant scene. I never learned whether the laughter, which must have been added in the dubbing room, was Garbo or not.'[327])

Ninotchka is a changed woman. She buys the hat she hated, puts on a fashionable dress and wears lipstick for the first time. Leon takes her dancing and they run into Swana, who has brought along her snooty friends to mock 'the Bolshevik', expecting Ninotchka to look like a frump, rather than the belle of the ball (in one of the most sumptuous gowns Adrian ever created).

Ninotchka gets tipsy: 'The closest I ever came to champagne was in a newsreel – the wife of some president was throwing it at a battleship.' Back at the hotel she slurs that she does not deserve to be happy, that by kissing him she has betrayed a Russian ideal and should be shot. Leon stands her up against the wall, blindfolds and 'executes' her, popping the champagne cork in place of firing a gun. (This brief scene, in which she slides to the floor in slow motion, put Garbo on a par with the greatest screen comediennes. According to a report from MGM, during the first screening an audience member wrote on his preview card, 'I laughed so hard, I peed in my girlfriend's hand!') *Mistaking the safe for the radio, she 'switches' this on, turning the dial and thus unlocking it, and sees the jewels. 'The tears of old Russia,' she says.*

The next morning Ninotchka receives a visit from Swana. The jewels are gone and the only way she will get them back, Swana says, is if she boards the next plane to Moscow. Putting her love of her country first, Ninotchka leaves. (Though the Breen Office had given explicit instructions that there should be no exterior scenes depicting Moscow, even ones fabricated on a set, Ernst Lubitsch ignored this and we are now introduced to MGM's perception of life in Russia.) *We see her once more in dowdy clothes, marching in the May Day parade and entertaining the envoys at her flat. For dinner she is making an omelette; a room mate asks, only half in jest, 'An omelette? Aren't you living above your ration?' She switches on the radio but there is no music here, just propaganda speeches, so the friends make their own entertainment – we even get to hear Garbo singing a snatch of Mistinguett's 'Ça C'est Paris!'.*

The story then moves forward and Ninotchka is dispatched to Constantinople by her boss (Bela Lugosi) *because the envoys have messed up again – only this time they have hatched a plan with Leon, who is waiting for her there having been refused entry into Russia. The envoys have opened a restaurant and will not be returning home and, now that she has been reunited with her lover, neither will Ninotchka. 'Once you saved your country by going back. Now you can only save it by staying here,' says Leon. To which she replies, 'Well, if it's a choice between my personal interest and the good of my country, how can I waver? No one shall say Ninotchka was a bad Russian!'*

Shooting wrapped on 28 July, by which time MGM were 'rocked' by the news that Marlene Dietrich was making a surprise return to Hollywood. Universal had signed her to play opposite James Stewart in a remake of the 1932 Western, *Destry Rides Again*, which critics predicted would see her snatching plaudits from Garbo. In fact, *both* films proved smash hits, enabling both stars to shake off the box-office poison slur once and for all. *Ninotchka* opened at Grauman's Chinese Theatre on 29 October 1939 and, as usual, Garbo was unimpressed by her performance, believing that she could have done better. 'My film is finished and I'm afraid it doesn't amount to much,' she wrote to Horke Wachtmeister.[328] The critics disagreed. Howard Barnes of the *New York Herald Tribune* declared it the most captivating screen comedy of the year and rued her not having done this sort of thing before:

> For in this gay burlesque of Bolshevics abroad, the great actress reveals a command of comic timing which fully matches the emotional depth or tragic power of her earlier triumphs ... Whether it is deadpan clowning or the difficult feat of filling a tipsy scene with laughter; whether she is trading insults with a Grand Duchess or secretly trying on one of those current hats, she is a past mistress of comedy ... There is an added verve and colour to her personality in a role such as this which makes her even more magically lovely than in the past.

Frank Nugent observed in the *New York Times*:

> Stalin won't like it; Molotov may recall his envoy from MGM. We
> will say Garbo's *Ninotchka* is one of the sprightliest comedies of the
> year, a gay and impertinent and malicious show which never pulls
> the punchlines (no matter how far below the belt they may land)
> and finds the screen's austere first lady of drama playing deadpan
> comedy with the assurance of a Buster Keaton.[329]

Ninotchka was nominated for four Academy Awards: Best Actress,
Picture, Original Story, and Screenplay. This year, however,
Gone with the Wind swept the board, delighting Vivien Leigh,
who considered *her* Oscar a real slap in the face for Hollywood's
Number One Box-Office Star, while Garbo could not have cared
less. Yet despite the adulation and the sterling reviews, she was far
from content with her lot, writing to Horke Wachtmeister, 'I still
don't know what I'm going to do about filming. I find working
more difficult than ever. I don't know why that's so, but I get so
embarrassed when I'm in the studio.'

Word of her anxiety reached MGM's front office, where Mayer
who, having expected it to flop without those all-important
European returns to boost the coffers, until being made aware of
the reviews and early returns for the latest film, had been resigned
to letting her go back to Sweden for good if this was what she
wanted. Now, eager to put her into another comedy, he went out of
his way to help her as only he could, by coercing her into consulting a psychologist. Dr Eric Drimmer, married to the actress Eva
Gabor, was considered one of the best in Los Angeles and Garbo
went along with the idea because Drimmer was Swedish. Their
sessions amounted to nothing, with Drimmer concluding – for a
hefty fee – that Garbo's psychological problems were linked to her
intense shyness, her inability to communicate with strangers and
her obsessive fear of crowds – something she was already aware of
and not remotely interested in rectifying.

Meanwhile on 1 September, while Garbo was deliberating over
what to do next, Germany invaded Poland. Her first concern was for
Salka, who was still there, or so she believed. In fact, her friend was

in Paris – she cabled Garbo to assure her that all was well, and that she had booked her passage on what would be one of the last sailings from Cherbourg to New York. Two days later, Britain declared war on Germany and suffered its first major tragedy of the conflict when the SS *Athenia*, en route to Montreal in Canada, was hit by a German U-boat sixty miles south of Rockall, Ireland. Of the 1,418 passengers and crew, 117 lost their lives or died soon afterwards of their injuries. Among the survivors were actresses Judith Evelyn and Carmen Silvera (who later appeared in the British television series *'Allo, 'Allo!*), and Ernst Lubitsch's ten-month-old daughter, Nicola, travelling with her nanny. All the studios urged their stars not to cross the Atlantic until it was safe to do so, not knowing when this would be. Garbo had been planning a trip to Sweden but now wired money to her family, urging them to put Harby on the market and board the next available ship. The Stockholm-New York route had been closed and on 24 October, Anna Gustaffson, Sven, his wife Marguerite and their seven-year-old daughter, Gray, set sail from Oslo on the Norwegian steamer, *Stavangerfjord*. This docked on 3 November and MGM laid on a plane to fly them to Los Angeles, something they had never done for Garbo, who put them up at her house for several weeks before finding them a place of their own. Initially, only Marguerite, an American by birth, spoke English.

The Gustaffsons were Garbo's blood relatives, whom she felt it was her duty to support. Having them under her roof, however, when she had lived most of her adult life totally alone, severely affected her and she found herself spending more time with her 'real' family, the gay and Sapphic intimates she felt most comfortable with. There was also a new 'beau': the wealthy nutritionist Gayelord Hauser. Exactly how and where they met is not known. Hauser (Helmut Eugen Benjamin Fellert Hauser, 1895–1984) was a health food guru who had recently published his fifth book, *Eat & Grow Beautiful* – his reputation, and his bank balance, suitably enhanced by his having acquired several already beautiful sponsors including Carole Lombard, Marlene Dietrich, Clara Bow, Eva and Juan Péron, and Adele Astaire, sister of Fred.

Born in Germany, he had emigrated to Chicago in 1911, and soon afterwards almost died of tuberculosis of the hip. When conventional medicine failed to cure his condition, he put himself into the hands of naturopath Dr Benjamin Lust, whose methods completely cured him, and so began his passion for natural remedies. After studying at several European universities, he returned to Chicago to set up a clinic promoting his five 'wonder foods': wheatgerm, yoghourt, skimmed milk, brewer's yeast, and blackstrap molasses, to which Garbo – with her passion for weird concoctions such as lingonberry jam mixed with black coffee – soon became addicted when Hauser served it to her mixed with broiled grapefruit. And if this sounds unpalatable, a few years later he devised a twice-daily 'health drink' for the Duchess of Windsor comprising a half-pint of herbs and warm garlic juice!

Gayelord Hauser lived with his ex-lover, former actor Frey Brown, at his Sunrise Estate in Coldwater Canyon, though so far as the public were aware, Brown was his manager. Tall, handsome, muscular and imposing, Hauser hid his homosexuality for many years by 'dating' a host of beautiful, high-profile women. When in danger of being 'outed', he simply told journalists that he and his current flame were about to marry, the 'relationship' would fizzle out and he would move on to the next wealthy sponsor. He and Brown, who remained partners for life and who are said never to have cheated on each other, owned a second home in Palm Springs, its grounds well-hidden from the public gaze, where they and their friends could indulge in their favourite passions – partying and nude sunbathing – without being disturbed.

Cynics persistently mocked Hauser – he had added 'Dr' to his name though he had no qualifications and, while he enjoyed an extremely opulent lifestyle, the ones he boasted of helping the most were working-class Americans struggling during the Depression to afford the costly foodstuffs he prescribed in his books. His method of 'curing' Garbo involved not just teaching her what to eat, but how to face her problems and insecurities head-on. If she developed a headache or experienced period pains, instead of taking painkillers prescribed by her doctor, he got her to swallow one of his wheatgerm and celery concoctions. If she was suffering from fatigue, instead of going for a lie down, he encouraged her to go for a walk. That Hauser took advantage of her occasional naivety and brainwashed her, much as Mercedes and Salka had done, goes without saying. As one biographer cynically observed, 'Famous names with declining reputations and self-confidence had been cured by his yoghourt and spinach. Having brought happiness to the millionaires of Florida and acquired a considerable fortune and international reputation, he intensified his attacks on Garbo.'[330]

Garbo had always been a health freak, obsessed with vitamins, potions, and terrified of dying young like her sister and Mauritz Stiller – although to today's reader, her refusal to give up her two-pack-a-day smoking habit seems directly at odds with this. Hauser convinced her that her neurasthenia was linked to her vegetarian diet, recalling in his self-applauding memoirs:

> She was at that time following a diet consisting mainly of boiled vegetables and thou-shalt-nots. In spite of her radiant beauty, this diet had had a marked effect on her vitality; she was suffering from overtiredness and insomnia, and was in danger of serious illness ... I made it my task to wean her away from strict vegetarianism and coax her back to intelligent eating – no easy chore with a woman who has a will of steel.

Garbo would adhere to his strict regime for the rest of her life.[331]

Hollywood's oddest quartet – 6′ 3″ Gayelord Hauser and Garbo, and the equally strapping Frey Brown and the skinny, mouse-like Mercedes – lived life to the full during the winter of 1939–40: skinny-dipping on the sheltered beaches, hitting the clubs around Sunset Boulevard by night, driving out to Reno to shoot craps in the casinos, and on one occasion hiring a roadster and taking everyone to a rodeo. On 15 November, the press reported that Hauser had presented Garbo with a diamond ring, with Hedda Hopper claiming to have seen a photograph of her wearing it on 'the right finger' (though no such picture has ever emerged) and to have been given the exclusive that the couple were soon to be married. Hauser *had* given her a ring, but it was not an engagement ring, and the first Garbo heard of the impending 'nuptials' was when she read it in a newspaper.

The mere fact that Hauser had spoken about her behind her back – and to a reporter – would normally have given Garbo grounds for ousting him from her life for good, as had happened with so many who had betrayed her trust. She, however, had a solid enough reason for wanting to hang on to him for the time being.

CHAPTER THIRTEEN

GARBO'S WAR

'It seems crazy that millions are being killed instead of a few thoughtful people getting together to try and sort out what's wrong. But then there would have to be give and take, and no one wants to give.'

In December 1939, Garbo anonymously donated $5,000 to the Finnish Relief Fund. Finland had always been close to her heart, if only for the fact that it had given the world Mauritz Stiller. Throughout the conflict, she would find herself criticised in some circles for not doing more to help with the war effort. Marlene Dietrich entertained the troops in Europe, performing on the front lines where the fighting was most fierce. Garbo was not, however, one of the so-called 'lazy sunbathers', one of the many thousands of US residents who went about their business believing the war was someone else's problem and nothing to do with them. Quietly and without boasting, she became one of the unsung heroines of World War II. Unable to travel to Sweden, she announced that she would be spending her usual between-movies vacation in New York. Absolutely no one other than those who had arranged her mission knew what she was really up to, that she was about to take on the role of a real-life Mata Hari and put herself in considerable danger, not even Gayelord Hauser and Frey Brown, who accompanied her.

Earlier in the month, Garbo had been approached, perhaps not for the first time, by the Hungarian-born British producer Alexander Korda (1893–1956), famed for *The Private Life of Henry VIII* (1933) and *Rembrandt* (1936), both with Charles Laughton. Korda's London Films had begun shooting *The Thief of Baghdad* in England and had moved the unit to Hollywood because of the war, or so everyone believed. He was in fact also working as an agent for British Intelligence (MI6) and throughout the war used his position

as an excuse to visit 'sensitive' areas under the pretext of searching for locations for his films. The Hollywood establishment was
already being closely monitored: Korda and the Liberal politician
Sir John Pratt (Boris Karloff's brother) had engaged director Victor
Saville, among others, to flush out Nazi sympathisers believed to be
operating in the major studios.

For Garbo, Korda organised a very special mission: gathering
information on one of the world's richest men, Swedish millionaire
industrialist Axel Wenner-Gren, who had been for some time on a
United States 'economist blacklist'. Garbo had met him, courtesy
of Willhelm Sorenson, during her last trip to Stockholm. Indeed,
she may even have been working for Korda then.

Wenner-Gren (1881–1961) had amassed his fortune largely from
the patenting of Electrolux vacuum cleaners. Rumoured to be a
friend of Hermann Goering, since being blacklisted and having
his assets frozen, he had retreated to an estate on Hog Island (now
Paradise Island), off the coast of Nassau in the Bahamas. He was
also a friend of the Duke of Windsor, formerly King Edward VIII,
who had abdicated the British throne in December 1936 to marry
twice-divorced Wallis Simpson: in October 1937, the Windsors
toured Nazi Germany and met Hitler at his country retreat, causing immense controversy by giving the Nazi salute. In August 1940,
the Duke would be appointed Governor-General of the Bahamas,
a position he held for five years, and rumours of his alleged Nazi
leanings persisted throughout the war, and beyond.

Considering the fact that there had never been anyone in the
entire history of Hollywood as secretive as Garbo and therefore
as capable of absolute discretion, once she had agreed to help
him, Korda put a call through to Sir William Stephenson, the
London film executive and another agent with British Intelligence.
Stephenson ('Codename Intrepid', 1897–1989) was a Canadian
soldier, inventor and spymaster, British Intelligence's senior representative for the entire Western world during World War II and
thought to have been used by Ian Fleming as a model for James
Bond. He had been providing Churchill with secret information
regarding Hitler's plans since the spring of 1936. In 1976, his biographer detailed at some length MI6's decision to hire Garbo for

a series of missions which, had she been caught, would almost certainly have cost her her life:

'In some mysterious way, Hitler was expected by French and British leaders to wear himself out on the plains of Poland. Neville Chamberlain did everything not to antagonise the enemy,' remembered Stephenson. 'President Roosevelt was afraid Chamberlain might negotiate peace. There was not much the President could do to support those resisting both Chamberlain and Hitler. American public opinion was the target of Nazi propaganda guns, no less than Warsaw had been the target of Nazi bombs. And American opinion was against us.' So Roosevelt wrote an astonishing letter to Churchill ... A correspondence began on 11 September 1939, unique between the chief of state of a neutral power and an unrecognised foreign leader. The President acknowledged that although Churchill might be without power in Parliament, as First Lord of the Admiralty he was directing the secret warriors. The replies, during the next 150 days, called 'the Phoney War', were signed 'Naval Person' and went to POTUS, the President of the United States ... If the President wanted to join this secret warrior, it would help if he gave him ammunition to fight Nazi and isolationist influences in the US ... if the British needed inside information to convince his doubting service chiefs of Germany's ambitions and Britain's worthiness as an ally. Churchill therefore wanted to put Stephenson at the President's side right away as director of British Secret Intelligence and as a practitioner of covert diplomacy. Stephenson could then prepare a base in the United States for an all-over direction of secret warfare if Britain fell, as seemed likely if the appeasers stayed in control. But Stephenson had his own order or priorities ... A beautiful and secretive woman who prized her privacy gave him a clue. Greta Garbo was one of the many actors and actresses who, working in his studios, became his close friends. The Swedish actress had reported high-level Nazi sympathisers in Stockholm. The neutral port was ideal for German intelligence operations...[332]

Some believed that Wenner-Gren had tried to fox the Allies into believing that he was on their side by sending his yacht, the

360-foot *Southern Cross* – at that time the world's largest, formerly owned by tycoon Howard Hughes – to pick up 300 survivors from the *Athenia*. It seemed too much of a coincidence, certainly so far as Stephenson, Alexander Korda and Garbo were concerned, that he happened to be in the vicinity, claiming to be en route from Scotland to Bermuda, when the ship had been torpedoed. It seemed more likely that his real reason for being there was that he had been behind the whole operation. While awaiting further instructions Garbo allowed Hauser and Brown to escort her around New York, showing her off to their society friends during a round of excursions to the Metropolitan Opera, the ballet, and the jazz-clubs around 52nd Street. One afternoon they dragged her along to take tea with the Vanderbilts at their Fifth Avenue mansion, with Garbo hating every minute of it, but persevering with the arch-snobbery so as not to arouse suspicion as to why she was really there.

Two genuine friends who entered her life at this time and lasted the course were Jessica Dragonette and her sister, Rosalinda 'Nadea' Loftus. Like Salka Viertel, Jessica and Nadea ran an artiste's salon at their 57th Street apartment: here, Garbo met the pianist Oscar Levant, who she liked – and Bishop Fulton Sheen, whose persistent preaching and requests for her to guest on his Sunday evening radio programme, *The Catholic Hour*, annoyed her. Dragonette (c.1900–1980) was America's most popular radio star, an exponent of the light-operatic style popularised in the movies by the likes of Jeanette MacDonald. Bisexual, she married late in life – at almost fifty – though there is no evidence that she and Garbo were ever more than friends. Garbo spent Christmas and New Year with her, then early in February 1940 she, Hauser and Brown headed for Palm Beach, where they rented two suites at the Whitehall Hotel, and Garbo finalised her plans, putting a call through to Axel Wenner-Gren, who had a house in the Bahamas and explaining how bored she was with New York, and missing the California sunshine. The ploy worked: Gren invited the trio to Hog Island.

The next day, 17 February, Garbo chartered a plane to Nassau, where they boarded the *Southern Cross* with Wenner-Gren, his wife and several unnamed passengers suspected of being arms and munitions dealers. For ten days, the company cruised the West

Indies, with Garbo making mental notes of conversations and reporting back to Sir William Stephenson each time the yacht docked. On 28 February the yacht reached Miami, at which point Garbo's current 'adventure' ended. After spending three days in Miami, she and her companions flew back to Los Angeles, the first time she had made the journey by plane. As for her 'romance' with Hauser, the press were told that they had decided to cool things but remain friends. It is not known if Wenner-Gren let slip names of possible Nazi contacts in the United States or Europe, but Garbo's mission must have been successful – Stephenson and MI6 would soon call on her services again. And clearly, her espionage work had shown her that there was considerably more to life outside a movie set. On 15 March she wrote to Horke Wachtmeister, 'If peace comes, what I most want is to go home and not to make another film. I don't even want to think about it.'³³³

On 9 April, Germany invaded Denmark and began bombing Norway, which put up a brave fight but eventually capitulated. Sweden, though mobilising its troops, opted to remain neutral. Garbo was distressed to learn that despite this and the banning of arms and munitions transportation to occupied Denmark and Norway, her country was still permitting Nazi soldiers to travel there via the Swedish rail network. She was also faced with another potential dilemma. MGM's lawyers, who knew nothing of her work with MI6 and even less about European politics, were anxious over what would happen if Sweden – who they believed to be merely 'sitting on the fence' – formed an alliance with Germany. Almost certainly, they concluded, she would find herself arrested and detained as an enemy alien and the studio would lose a valuable source of income. She could of course have objected: protected by MI6, there was no way that any such arrest could have taken place, but to protest would have resulted in too many questions being asked, and her cover being blown. She therefore signed a Preliminary Declaration of Intent form, the first step towards becoming an American citizen, though it would take over a decade for her to be 'called to the flag', as she put it. On 4 September, she would be compelled to submit an Alien Immigration Law Registration application. Oddly, she gave her address as 165 Mabery

Road – Salka Viertel's home – and, despite the close proximity of her family, cited Salka as her next of kin.

Meanwhile, on 10 June 1940, the day Italy joined the war on Hitler's side, Garbo was with MGM's Walter Reisch and Victor Saville, her 'next in command', listening to the radio in Gottfried Reinhardt's office, when President Roosevelt delivered his famous speech from the University of Virginia, accusing Italy of stabbing its neighbour in the back, and ending with the call for 'effort, courage, sacrifice and devotion from Americans everywhere.' Reisch recalled how, in an extremely rare show of public emotion, 'FDR's voice so moved Garbo she dissolved into tears. We were all looking at her to see her reaction, but she didn't seem to care. "Does anyone have a Kleenex?" she asked.' On 15 July, Alexander Korda contacted Garbo. Wenner-Gren, accompanied by his wife and sister-in-law, were en route to Los Angeles, aboard the *Southern Cross*. The next day, according to one source:

> Garbo met them at the docks and took them with her in her Buick Sedan, Wenner-Gren sitting in front with the driver, FBI agent Frank Angell following them, to Paramount Studios. Garbo's only contact here was Walter Wanger, who was working in the Korda-Saville network ... She was keeping an eye on Wenner-Gren, as she had on the previous yacht voyage, looking for indications of admiration for Hitler. These loyalties became obvious very quickly. Garbo would soon wind up her contract and head for New York and neutral Sweden.[334] [335]

In mid-December, Garbo received word from Alexander Korda that Axel Wenner-Gren was in New York and, it would appear, up to no good. Dashing off a letter to Horke Wachtmeister, after complaining that she had been suffering from a cold for five months, she added:

> Just now I'm lying on a bench in the desert all on my own. I'm the only guest where I'm staying ... I was invited to our friends in Nassau, Axel W, but I can't travel. I'm off to New York soon for some sort of treatment. If it works, you must come and have it too

... God, if only we could sit in some little corner at Tistad and tell tales from the never-ending story.[336]

Photographs of the Duke and Duchess of Windsor shaking hands with Hitler had recently appeared in the American press and, with the Duke now appointed Governor-General of the Bahamas and with one report declaring that Wenner-Gren may have been allowing the Germans to conceal U-boats on Hog Island, it may be that Garbo and/or Korda no longer felt it safe for her to be travelling there. What she meant by 'some sort of treatment' is not known, but may have been some sort of secret message – for if there was one person in the world whom Garbo trusted absolutely to confide in about her war work, as much as the constrained circumstances permitted, it was Horke. What is odd, too, is that this was the *only* one of Garbo's letters home, so far as is known, to have been opened and certified 'passed' by the wartime censors.

A few days after writing to Horke, Garbo left for New York with Gayelord Hauser and Frey Brown and met up with Wenner-Gren several times. According to the industrialist's biographer, Leif Leifland, who later unconvincingly attempted to exonerate him of suspicious wartime activities, they took tea at the Ritz, dined with the fashion designer Valentina and her husband George Schlee and never saw each other again. Leifland concluded, 'My guess, but it's only a guess, is that she was given a warning by the FBI or MI6 not to go to Nassau again and that she was told Wenner-Gren was suspected of being a German spy.' Garbo, of course, had known this already.[337]

The box-office receipts for Garbo and Dietrich films were affected more during the first year of the war than those of their Hollywood contemporaries. Sixty per cent of their revenue had previously come from Europe and now that it had become impossible to distribute them there the studios were faced with a dilemma. It was no longer feasible to let Garbo and Dietrich go, as had been earlier anticipated: the success of *Ninotchka* and *Destry Rides Again* had changed all this. Universal had assigned Marlene to two adventure films: *Seven Sinners* with John Wayne and *The Flame of New Orleans* with Bruce Cabot. MGM's initial instinct where Garbo was concerned was to return to the tried and tested formula and put her into the drama, *A Woman's Face*. Based on Francis Croisset's play, *Il Etait Une Fois*, this had been filmed in Swedish (*En Kvinnas Ansikte*, 1938) with Ingrid Bergman as facially disfigured murderess Anna Holm, who falls under the spell of a psychopath (Conrad Veidt), and at one point in the story plots to kill a four-year-old boy by pushing him out of a cable car. Directed by George Cukor, Melvyn Douglas was to play her love interest, the surgeon who restores Anna's self-confidence by reconstructing her face – and this would have also enabled Garbo to achieve her long-standing ambition to work with Veidt.

Garbo was horrified – she was starting to become paranoid about losing her looks and there was no way that she was going to play a character who wanted to harm a child, even if Anna does come good in the end. The part went to Joan Crawford, and Mayer made a decision which, perhaps not inadvertently, would bring Garbo's screen career to an end. With no one knowing how long the war would last – and with some Americans no longer wishing to hear European accents on the screen while the conflict was raging – Garbo would have to appeal exclusively to American audiences. The only way to make this happen would be to cast her, at thirty-four, as an 'all-American oomph girl'. The film was *Two-Faced Woman*, a remake of Constance Talmadge and Ronald Colman's 1925 silent, *Her Sister From Paris*, itself based on a German play, *The Twin Sister*, by Ludwig Fulda, who during the spring of 1939 had committed suicide, aged 76, after being refused entry into the United States. The story told of a stuffy ski instructress who invents a sexy twin sister as a means of wooing her husband away from his mistress, getting him to fall in love with her, then revealing who she really is. The producer assigned to the project was Gottfried Reinhardt, in a privileged position, Bernie Hyman believed, as Salka Viertel's lover, to sell the idea to her in the hope that Salka would be able to persuade Garbo to accept the part.[338]

Hyman took no chances with the budget, assigning just $320,000 to the production, of which Garbo would receive $150,000 along with the usual privileges, and Adrian and Cedric Gibbons were instructed to 'go easy' on the costumes and sets. George

Oppenheimer was brought in to assist Salka with the script, and
S. N. Behrman commissioned to write the dialogue. In retrospect,
the project was never going to work: a story set in Renaissance
Italy, written in German, transported to a modern day American
setting and with the 'all-American' lead character pronouncing her
lines with a marked Swedish accent. Garbo again chose Melvyn
Douglas as her leading man: their first comedy pairing had worked
so well, she did not wish to work with anyone else. The supports
included Constance Bennett and Ruth Gordon, George Cukor was
to direct, but Garbo did not get William Daniels to photograph
her. Instead she was given Joseph Ruttenberg, who had recently
worked with Cukor on *The Women*. In an attempt to transform
her into some kind of Swedish Lana Turner, MGM gave Garbo a
shorter fluffy hairstyle, a 'contemporary' wardrobe, and announced
that she would be seen for the first time, extant of *Peter The Tramp*,
in a swimsuit. Obviously the publicity department had forgotten
the diving scene in *Wild Orchids*. Also, there would be no stunt
double: she would actually be *seen* skiing, and performing an exotic
dance – the *chica-choca* – which had been especially devised for her.

Shooting began on 18 June 1941 and proved a nightmare. Garbo
had had fun making *Ninotchka*: Ernst Lubitsch had ruled the
production with a gentle rod of iron and she had trusted him
implicitly. Now there were constant spats between Gottfried
Reinhardt and Salka, who were having relationship problems and
taking it out on everyone else – and between Reinhardt and Cukor,
on account of the former's homophobia. 'He was the type of man
that I didn't go for,' Reinhardt recalled, 'Even though I have had
many friends who were homosexuals, his homosexuality bothered
me. Perhaps above all because he was so ugly, and that made it
ludicrous.'[339] Garbo soon realised what a big mistake she had made.
She disliked the cameramen and though she got along with her
initially, came to loathe Constance Bennett for the trick she played
on her.

Constance Bennett (1904–65) resented the fact that, formerly
one of Hollywood's highest-paid stars, she was now 'reduced' to
supporting a woman she had always looked down on as coarse
and uneducated. She feigned friendship with Garbo by taking

her under her wing and giving her 'tips' on how to dress in the film, claiming that although Adrian was the best couturier in Hollywood, he simply was not cut out for dressing this type of character. Garbo trusted her enough to listen, ignoring Adrian's advice to the contrary. As a result, Garbo received some of the worst notices of her career and Bennett may even be accused of driving one of the final nails into the coffin of that career. She was also nasty towards Robert Sterling, whom Garbo took under her wing. A sensitive young man, he recalled one particular full-cast rehearsal: '"I'm serving tea in my dressing room," Bennett said during a break. She thereupon invited each one, conspicuously omitting me. Garbo refused her invitation, and invited me to tea in *her* dressing room.'[340] Bennett's nastiness, as her career petered out, became legendary. A few years later, during one of her frequent visits to Capri, Garbo learned that the snooty actress had similarly attempted to sabotage Gracie Fields' Hollywood career.[341]

The debacle would bring about the end of Adrian's long association with MGM. The great couturier, who had dressed Garbo beautifully for thirteen years, recalled, 'In her last picture they wanted to make her a sweater girl, a real American type. I said, "When the glamour ends for Garbo, it also ends for me. She had created a type. If you destroy that illusion, you destroy her."' Garbo is alleged to have told Adrian at the time, which one finds very hard to believe, 'I'm very sorry that you're leaving. But, you know, I never really liked most of the clothes you made me wear.'[342] [343]

Magazine editor Larry Blake (Melvyn Douglas) *is taking a break at a ski resort but is not interested in the sport – until he sees instructress Karin Borg, with whom he jokes and flirts, despite the fact that she remains standoffish. She tries to teach him to ski; however, he is hopeless and gets lost in a snowdrift. She disappears too, and for reasons known only to the scriptwriter, when next we see them they are married, living in a rented chalet with Larry's business partner* (Roland Young) *and secretary* (Ruth Gordon). *Larry tells Karin, 'The moment I saw you, I knew I wanted special instructions.' To which she responds, 'The moment I saw you, I knew I wanted to give them to you.'*

At once, their marriage starts falling apart. Larry receives a call from an old flame, Broadway producer Griselda Vaughan (Constance Bennett). *Sophisticated, dressed head to toe in haute couture and dripping with jewels, she is a complete contrast with the homely, sedately dressed Karin. Larry tells Griselda that he is married, and when she lets out a piercing scream and kicks a chair, we know there will soon be trouble.*

Larry must return to the office in New York, but Karin wants to stay put, sensing that she might be more able to hold onto him while they are on 'neutral' territory. He orders her to accompany him; she refuses and goes swimming (Garbo wears a Valentina swimsuit and old-fashioned rubber cap, which, despite the adverse criticism, does not look that bad). *When she returns, Karin accuses him of being two people: the poetic young man she loved and married, and the 'Napoleon' he has become.*

Larry leaves for the Big Apple and, suspecting him of cheating, Karin follows. Wearing glamorous clothes, jewels and with a new hairstyle, she hopes to woo him back, but after tracking him down to the theatre where Griselda is rehearsing a new show and spying on them from the shadows, she realises that stronger measures are required. With the help of Larry's secretary, she becomes Kathryn, her extroverted, worldly-wise twin sister. She is so convincing that Larry's business partner asks to take her out.

Kathryn accompanies her date to the appropriately named Salka's nightspot. Larry and Griselda are here too with their young friend, Dickie (Robert Sterling). *Initially, Larry is taken in* (the penny only drops when Kathryn loses her glove under the table and he picks it up for her, glancing at her painted toenails – a scene which unbelievably brought gasps of horror from Catholic critics). *Aware that Larry is interested, Kathryn arouses his jealousy by flirting with the handsome but virginal Dickie. And when the snooty Griselda asks how she came by her beautiful clothes, pointing out that Karin, who Griselda has never seen, is only working-class, Kathryn declares, 'I order what I like, I wear them and one day I find them paid for ... Outside of love, everything is a waste of time. I like men, preferably* rich *men!'*

Later, in the powder room, Griselda warns Kathryn to lay off Larry; otherwise she will call Karin and tell her what is going on. He, though, (in a supplementary scene which ruins the rest of the plot) *has worked out who Kathryn really is, having called his housekeeper and learned that his wife is in New York. 'Two can play at that game,' he says.*

Larry asks Kathryn to dance, knowing that Karin could not, and she responds by saying that she only dances with professionals. This leads to the film's best sequence. Partnered by the in-house dancer (Robert Alton), *Kathryn's steps are clumsy, as Larry has expected, until she catches her heel in the hem of her dress. The band leader misinterprets her stamping as a signal to up the tempo, resulting in her on-the-spot invention of the 'chica choca'* (which contrary to some reports at the time Garbo performs in its entirety, keeping perfect tempo throughout, without a stand-in). *Larry flirts with her, hoping that if she goes too far she will be forced to reveal her true identity, while she flings herself at him, hoping that he will feel guilty and go rushing back to Karin* (there is even a reprisal of the controversial cigarette-lighting scene from *As You Desire Me*). *And, of course, a happy ending is somehow finally reached!*

Shooting wrapped in the middle of September, and coincided with the first visit to Hollywood of the German novelist, Erich Maria Remarque (1898–1970), famed for *All Quiet on the Western Front* and currently the *amour* of her great rival, Marlene Dietrich. Garbo had met him during her last trip to New York and he had squired her around town, bringing the snipe from Hedda Hopper, 'Fur will fly if Garbo has taken Marlene's beau away from her.'

A handsome, muscular Aryan who had served in World War I, before taking up writing, Remarque had enjoyed such diverse employment as making gravestones, flying an auto-gyro, and test-driving racing cars. He and Marlene had met in Venice in 1935 and built a relationship based on their loathing of what their country had become. Four years later she brought him to America. A manic depressive and heavy drinker, Remarque is said to have held so much information on the Nazi Party that, after giving orders for his books to be publicly burned, Hitler had personally added his name to their hit list. According to him, he and Garbo embarked on a brief but passionate affair. Writing in his journal after one 'romantic' episode, perhaps a little too prosaically for this to have been much more than wishful thinking, he observed, 'She entered the bedroom, the light of the dressing room behind her, softly flowing over her shoulders, enchanting her outline ... the absence of any form of sentimentality or melodrama – and yet full of warmth.'[344]

Two-Faced Woman was released in November 1941, and was at once condemned by the Catholic Legion of Decency, who released a statement: 'This picture is offensive because of its immoral and un-Christian attitude towards marriage and its obligations with its impudently suggestive scenes, dialogue, situations and suggestive costumes.' Founded in 1933, the movement's goal was 'the purification of the cinema', though many of its early members were Jewish or Protestant and many more failed to practise what they preached. The Legion offered three main categories of rating: 'A' referred to 'morally objectionable', 'B' was 'morally objectionable in part', and 'C' – the category awarded the Garbo film – was 'condemned'.

Why the Legion singled out this film, when others released at the same time were more racy, had much to do with Garbo's insider knowledge of New York and Hollywood's closeted gay community and in particular Francis Spellman (1889–1967), the Roman Catholic Archbishop (later Cardinal) of New York. His fear of her exposing him may have caused him to target her specifically. A close confidant of President Roosevelt, he was also a hypocrite and a phoney moralist – referred to as 'Franny' by intimates – who enjoyed liaisons with dozens of young men, mostly altar boys. The journalist Michelangelo Signorile denounced him as, 'One of the most notorious, powerful and sexually voracious homosexuals in the American Catholic Church's history.'[345] His biographer, John Cooney, gleaned much evidence of his secret life from the priests Spellman worked with – one revealing his long-term relationship with a chorus boy from the Broadway review, *One Touch of Venus.*[346]

Spellman denounced the film from the pulpit, while the Manhattan Catholic Interest Committee branded it 'a danger to public morals'. After watching the film in Rhode Island, a group of 'outraged ex-Garbo fans' marched into the local police station, creating such a fuss that officers visited the establishment the following evening and closed it down. The film was banned in Missouri, Massachusetts and New York State: it was shown briefly in Australia and New Zealand, but withdrawn after complaints from religious groups there, one of which publicly denounced Garbo as 'that Swedish trollop'. Finally, on 6 December MGM withdrew the film from circulation. Garbo was devastated. She had done absolutely nothing wrong, sticking to the script and following George Cukor's instructions to the letter, yet here she was, victimised and made to appear dirty. MGM were accused of collaborating with the censor in an attempt to sabotage her career, the Breen Office having passed the script for public consumption, though she had no idea why they should want to do this. 'They've dug my grave,' she told friends.[347]

The next day, a Sunday, was one of the blackest days of the war. The Japanese bombed Pearl Harbor, with a loss of 2,350 lives. Archbishop Spellman was less concerned with this than with attacking Garbo and this 'ninety minutes of filth'. Despite his fear of flying, he flew to New York and demanded a meeting with the MGM executives and scriptwriters. The first thing Spellman saw when he marched into Mayer's office was a huge portrait of himself hanging on the wall, Mayer's way of proving to the outside world that he was on the side of the righteous. Later, he bequeathed Spellman $10 million in his will. For now, the cleric received a hefty pay-off to desist from making any more of a fuss and Mayer organised for Salka Viertel to rewrite the 'offending' scenes. He also commissioned a new scene in which Larry takes a phone call, where he learns that Karin and Kathryn are one and the same. To photograph this at a cost of $14,000 as Joseph Ruttenberg was working on another project, Mayer used Andrew Marton and Charles Dorian, who had been assistant director on *Flesh and the Devil*. A seething Gottfried Reinhardt recalled: 'This prince of the Catholic Church ... even more incensed than his minions, took time off from shepherding X-million souls to wage a one-man crusade – in a world torn by strife, with his own country on the brink of it – against my sinful *Two-Faced Woman*.'[348]

Meanwhile, Garbo had another 'demon' to deal with: Axel Wenner-Gren's name had recently been added to the US government's 'List of Blocked Nationals'. This effectively prohibited him from doing business on both sides of the Atlantic by freezing his assets in Nassau's Royal Bank of Canada. He did, however, have considerable holdings south of the border, and when Alexander Korda informed Garbo that Gren was in Mexico City, she called the industrialist and explained that she was ready for a holiday, but that because of the war she was unable to travel to Europe. An unsuspecting Gren swallowed the bait and invited her to spend time at the house he was renting there while Garbo applied for the requisite permit and arranged her flight. William Orr of MGM's legal department, who had no business interfering now that she was no longer with the studio, learned of her plans – though not *why* she was going to Mexico – and advised her to reconsider. The country was believed to be a hotbed for Nazi sympathisers and dissidents, and Orr's comments were recorded in the INS Travel Control Division's ledger: 'Learned it would be impossible for her to leave until the end of this month ... explained the uncertainties that might arise in the meantime, and now it seems very unlikely that she will change her plans and follow the suggestion.' Garbo, as usual, pleased only herself. Korda provided her with her permit, though who accompanied her on the flight, which took place around 12 December, or what she did in Mexico or reported back to Korda, is not known. So far as Orr and the press were told, she had gone to New York for 'medical treatment' – the term she frequently used when engaged in an espionage mission.[349]

The revised *Two-Faced Woman* premiered on New Year's Eve 1941. MGM put out a publicity sheet, promoting sports equipment, ski equipment, and the benefits of having one's own private instructor, and containing such 'suggestive' tag-lines as 'Garbo Swims Like A Mermaid' and 'Garbo Skis & Finds Romance In A Wilderness Cabin'. It was, however, the slogan they used for the playbills which she loathed and tried, without success, to have changed: 'Who Is The Screen's Rhumba Queen Who No Longer Wants To Be Alone? A Gayer, Grander, GREATER Greta! Every Inch A Lady, With Every Other Man!'

For once, Mercedes de Acosta was spot on when she observed, 'The studio made her feel that she should do a film for the American market, which meant appealing to a very low standard as far as Greta was concerned.' The reviewer for *PM*, who had attended the original screening, hated the way the story had been hacked to bits. Applauding Garbo's 'loveliness, sensitivity, incandescence, timing and technical proficiency', he rightly blamed the studio for saddling her with this mess:

> And this is the woman, so unique in the movies that she's no longer a person but become now a symbol, a legend whom *Two-Faced Woman* does everything it can to destroy. In its story's frenzy to cover up its own emptiness, its sterility, its lack of any fine feelings, it makes Garbo a clown, a buffoon, a monkey on a stick. The fact that it's a comedy doesn't excuse its confused motivation, its repetition, its distasteful heartlessness.[350]

Time called the film, 'An absurd vehicle for Greta Garbo,' adding, 'Its embarrassing effect is not unlike seeing Sarah Bernhardt swatted with a bladder. It is almost as shocking as seeing your mother drunk.' The *New York Herald Tribune* said of her dancing, 'Miss Garbo's current attempt to trip the light fantastic is one of the awkward exhibitions of the season.' The *New York Times* observed:

> This is clearly one of the less propitious assignments of her career. Though she is her cool and immaculate self in the role of the clean-limbed ski instructress, she is as gauche and stilted as the script when playing the lady of profane love. No doubt her obvious posturings, her appallingly unflattering clothes and make-up were intended as a satire on the vamps of history – instead, her performance misses the satire and looks like something straight out of the movies of 1922. Mr. Douglas, who probably spends more time in pyjamas than any other male lead in history, continues to look as though a brisk walk in the open air in street clothes would refresh him. Apply that rule to the whole film, Messrs Cukor, Behrman, Oppenheimer et al: this is 1942, and Theda Bara's golden age is gone.

Hedda Hopper inadvertently glimpsed into the future, writing in *The Los Angeles Times*:

> Her pictures are so far apart that Metro starts off each publicity campaign with a broadside, as if she'd been buried and dug up for

the occasion. We've had 'Garbo Talks', 'Garbo Sings' [sic], 'Garbo Dances' and 'Garbo Laughs'. No doubt her ultimate picture will be 'Garbo Retires' – and do terrible business from a public expecting a bedroom farce.

Hedda was not alone. Six years earlier, the British novelist Eleanor Glin – the creator of the 'It' girl immortalised by Clara Bow – had uncannily predicted what would happen if Garbo ever had the misfortune to appear in a picture like this:

> If Greta Garbo were to play two parts in the same talkie, no matter how marvellous everyone found her acting, that magic fascination which she puts forth would immediately go. The public unconsciously would know it was 'art' and all illusion of her mysterious personality would vanish.[351]

Contrary to what has been written, *Two-Faced Woman* was *not* a flop at the box-office, and recovered its cost twice over. Neither did any of the reviews attack Garbo especially – the fans would have been content to leave the story just as it was, as had happened with almost all of her previous films. Adultery was her theme, the one she had made her own. Reading the reviews, and reflecting on the most miserable period of her career, Garbo concluded enough was enough at least until the war was over and she could return to making the sort of films *she* wanted to make. According to Mercedes, her exact words were, 'I will never act in another film.'

Word of this got back to Mayer, who reacted with typical Machiavellian aplomb. Hedda Hopper wrote that he had told her, 'As long as I'm head of this studio, Greta Garbo can go on making films here.' Salka Viertel claimed that he had informed her, having boasted that all of his other female stars were made to do as they were told, 'Only Garbo is difficult. I am her best friend. I want her to be happy. She should come and *tell* me what she wants. Then I'd talk her out of it.' In fact, Mayer neither gave her the chance to go and see him, nor went out of his way to thank her for her years of dedication to the studio, or for the fortune she had earned him: at the end of the month he gave orders for her dressing room at MGM to be refurbished for Lana Turner – Garbo's belongings were packed into cardboard boxes and dumped outside for her to collect.[352] [353]

Much of 1942 saw Garbo 'drifting'. Hollywood no longer appealed to her – indeed, it rarely had – and in the New Year she, Gayelord Hauser and Frey Brown travelled to New York. She was here on 16 January when news came in that Carole Lombard's plane had crashed into Mount Potosi, thirty miles south-west of Las Vegas, killing all twenty-two people on board. Lombard was in the middle of a phenomenally successful tour selling war-bonds – in one day alone she raised over $2 million for the war-effort. Garbo sent a message of condolence to Clark Gable and secretly gave $10,000 to Lombard's fund. She was also contacted personally by Eleanor Roosevelt, and invited to appear alongside Bob Hope, Marlene Dietrich and Ronald Colman in *March of the Dimes*, a radio show scheduled to be broadcast on 24 January and to raise funds for the First Lady's anti-polio campaign.[354]

Here, we come across another great Garbo mystery. Some sources claim that Garbo actually made the broadcast, but no recorded evidence has ever surfaced; others say a stand-in was substituted at the very last minute (possibly Geraldine Dvorak) because she had to leave New York unexpectedly. This tied in with at least one certified (as near as is possible) report that she was actually in England at the time, having flown to London around 18 January.

The Wheatsheaf Hotel, at Caperby in North Yorkshire, claimed that Garbo stayed there from 21 January 1942, while 'making appearances' with Henry Hall at the nearby Catterick Garrison. One soldier, Norman Taylor, recalled, 'It was definitely *the* Greta Garbo, not that she did much. She walked on to the stage between numbers, mumbled a few words of encouragement from a piece of paper, bowed politely and walked off again. But it was very definitely her, and I think she was staying somewhere nearby.' The hotel register certainly bears what looks like an authentic signature. But, one asks, what exactly was she doing in this part of the country, albeit this *was* Britain's biggest Army base? Was she, as Norman Taylor suggests, merely offering the servicemen morale? Or was she in pursuit of someone in particular? It is now quite likely that we will never know.[355]

There were also two male spies operating in Europe under the name 'Garbo' during the war, which has given rise to some critics believing that *Greta* Garbo, spy, was no more than a myth. The first, Luis Calvo, was interned in February 1942, during Garbo's visit to Britain. The second, a double-agent named Joan Pujol Garcia (1912–88), instrumental during the D-Day landings, was employed by MI5. Sir William Stephenson takes great pains to name her as 'that beautiful Swedish actress', and with his impeccable track record for honesty and detail, that *she* was the one hired by him.

Upon her return to New York during the late spring of 1942, Garbo alternated for a little while between staying with Jessica Dragonette and S. R. Behrman, by day reading scripts she probably had no intention of accepting, taking in a show or play most evenings. She rejected *The Paradine Case*, the story of the lawyer who falls in love with the proprietress of a Swedish barber's shop he is defending on a murder rap. Then, when she announced that she was putting down roots in New York and when in the autumn Bernie Hyman, the only MGM executive she had really got along with since Thalberg, died suddenly, aged just forty-five, Mayer gave up all hope of her ever returning to the screen. She rented an apartment at the Ritz Tower, on Park Avenue. Mercedes de Acosta had an apartment nearby. Having heard that Garbo might be staying in New York for the duration, she had moved one step ahead of her, using her influence to wangle a job working for *Victory*, the armed forces propaganda magazine based in the city.

For once, Garbo did not have to try too hard to evade her troublesome frangine: she received word that two of her old Weimar friends, Valeska Gert and Marianne Oswald, had recently arrived from Europe, having fled from the Nazis. They opened a Sapphic nightclub in Greenwich Village: Valeska the Beggars Bar, where most people on the scene would end up, while Marianne entertained her clients with what Albert Camus described as her 'songs of soot and flame', largely the works of Bertolt Brecht and Kurt

Weill, her interpretation of which was only rivalled at the time by Weill's wife, Lotte Lenya, who also sometimes performed there.

At around this time, Garbo showed interest in an English-language version of *The Girl from Leningrad*, the story of a Russian resistance fighter, set against the Russia-Finland conflict. Mayer gave the project his seal of approval and Garbo signed the contract: she would be paid $70,000 immediately and $80,000 when the film wrapped. No one knows who Mayer commissioned to write the script – since the *Two-Faced Woman* debacle, Salka Viertel was no longer 'representing' Garbo and had left MGM to work as an uncontracted writer for Warner Brothers with a considerable drop in salary. Harry Edington was gone too, replaced by Leland Hayward, then married to Margaret Sullavan. Soon after and without warning, MGM announced that Garbo had dropped out of the production. She had almost certainly been advised to do so by Alexander Korda or Sir William Stephenson, who may have believed that portraying such a heroine on the screen might compromise her position in real life. By the terms of her contract, Garbo could have retained the $70,000 MGM had paid her. Now she returned the money, her proviso being that Mayer should donate this to the war-bonds fund. Mayer may even have known or suspected that she was working for British Intelligence. Earlier in the year, when questioned about her 'mysterious and suspicious activities' in New York by the US State Department, he responded with a personal letter, 'Miss Garbo is a person of fine character and a thoroughly reliable and responsible individual.'[356]

Garbo was still working for MI6, reporting back to Korda or Stephenson anything suspicious she saw or heard while socialising. She liaised on a secret intelligence operation with future United Nations Secretary-General Dag Hammarskjold, a man who had intimate knowledge of MI6 operations in Scandinavia, providing him with the names of suspected Nazi sympathisers working in Stockholm, information she had gathered during that last trip home. 'There were some things that happened a long time ago that we had to talk about,' she told her friend Raymond Daum, though she was letting on no more than this, concluding, 'It was very painful for me – but I can't tell you that story.'[357] The film historian

Kevin Brownlow, speaking at a 2005 conference in Dublin to honour Garbo's centenary, claimed to have been told by her family, who said they had proof, that she very definitely had worked for Intelligence, though curiously none of this was included in *Garbo*, Brownlow's celebratory documentary – he claimed because he believed audiences would find such revelations 'incredulous'.

Garbo's biggest ambition, it would appear – the one, as previously mentioned, she spoke about to Roger Normand – was to perpetrate the 'big one', the assassination of Hitler. She later told Sam Green:

> Mr Hitler was big on me. He kept writing and inviting me to come to Germany, and if the war hadn't started when it did, I would have gone and I would have taken a gun out of my purse and shot him, because I'm the only person who would not have been searched.[358]

It was during this sojourn in New York that Garbo developed a passion for collecting paintings and antiques. In the past, she had frowned upon such 'ornaments' – the only 'artwork' in her possession being a pair of worthless flower vases and the framed picture of Mauritz Stiller on her piano. Now, with the help of Barbara MacLean – formerly Barbara Barondess who played the chambermaid in *Queen Christina*, and who had retired from the movies to take up antiques broking and interior design – Garbo began building an impressive collection. During her visit to a salesroom, so cautious where expenditure was concerned that even close friends sometimes dismissed her as a 'tight-wad', she bought a dozen canvasses – including two Renoirs which set her back almost $35,000. She made a point of *never* signing a document or delivery note, declaring the vendor would only end up making a great deal of money by selling this to collectors. By the end of the year, she had around thirty paintings in storage, declaring that once she relocated to New York, these would be hung on the walls of the apartment she was planning to buy.[359]

Garbo also appears to have been planning another trip to England, under the pretence that she was interested in making a film there. Hedda Hopper, who would not have known about the first trip, somehow got to learn about this one, though she got the date wrong, writing in her *Los Angeles Times'* column, 'Greta Garbo has finally got the role she's been waiting for. She'll sail sometime in September for England to play Joan of Arc in George Bernard Shaw's *Saint Joan*, under the direction of Clarence Brown.' This was picked up by the British press, who added that the film would be produced by J. R. Rank at the Pinewood Studios. Shaw, however, appears to have known nothing about the project – quite possibly because this was another espionage mission arranged by Alexander Korda who, upon hearing that Hedda had somehow got wind that Garbo was travelling *somewhere*, had 'leaked' news of the non-existent film to help cover her tracks. The trip was, however, aborted at the last minute.[360]

In August, Garbo put a call through to Stockholm from Alexander Korda's office, where she spoke at some length to Niels Bohr (1885–1962), the Danish physicist she had met while working with Mauritz Stiller, and again with Max Gumpel. Bohr had for some time been smuggling Jewish physicists out of Germany and sending them to safe-houses in Copenhagen, from where they were transported to Britain or the USA. In September, Garbo went to the very top, calling Gustav of Sweden himself and begging him to grant Bohr an audience, wherein the King was persuaded to offer asylum to Danish Jews, resulting in a massive operation by the Danish resistance movement, which rescued over 8,000 from under the Nazis' noses. Official figures reveal that over 95 per cent of Denmark's Jewish population survived the Holocaust because of their combined effort. Capturing Bohr would have been an immense scoop for Hitler; because of Garbo he failed, for it was she, liaising with Sir William Stephenson, who personally arranged for friends to get him out of the country. Before contacting Gustav, however, Garbo is even known to have checked out the royal family, with the help of Gumpel – also helping the Allies to locate and destroy important munitions sites in Germany – and the Swedish Consul-General, Axel Johnson. Gustav's Queen was German and with Norway and Denmark already under the jackboot, many believed Sweden might declare itself pro-German at any moment.

Later this year, Garbo was claimed to have had a fling with the actor Gilbert Roland, though as with many of her 'affairs', the physical aspect of this may have been the figment of an over-worked imagination, as had almost certainly been the case with Erich Maria Remarque. Roland (1905–94) was serving in the US Air Force and was involved with aerial reconnaissance. He was also married to Constance Bennett, so in getting involved with him, Garbo may have been exacting her revenge for her dreadful behaviour on the set of *Two-Faced Woman*. In November 1995, *The Los Angeles Times* ran the headline, 'If Underpants Could Only Talk', and described how, as a kinky going-away present when he had been returning to his base from leave, Garbo presented him with a pair of her cream-coloured, monogrammed silk knickers, which had now been put up for auction by his estate, along with a clutch of letters. The last of these, dated 4 December 1943 and ending their relationship, explained that there were many reasons why she would be unable to see him again, begged him to forgive her, to 'leave it all to fate', and above all, not to be sad. Oddly, none bore her signature – in most of them she refers to him as 'Little Soldier Boy' and herself as 'Eleanor', 'Harriet' or 'Mountain Boy' – but this did not prevent them from fetching over $150,000 at auction.

In his unpublished memoirs, Roland claimed to have bumped into Garbo in the street but while he had acknowledged her, she carried on walking. Then, a few days later, while visiting his Beverly Hills tailor, he was shown a pair of slacks the tailor had made for her, and offered to deliver them personally. Garbo refused to see him then but later called at his house when he was alone to thank him. According to the actor, she had stayed for dinner and:

> We sat there on the patio in silence. I went close to her, and found the lips of my desire. We went upstairs. The moon was full, the windows opened. I could see her shadow by the moon, and mine, then the two met. So it was, and [the next morning after he had given her his mother's gold ring and she had given him her under-wear] ... we kissed goodbye. I boarded the Army Transport plane back to the field, her panties inside my coat pocket.[361]

Roland claimed to have kept Garbo's panties in his knapsack for two years, and that they saw each other each time he came home on leave, before eventually going their separate ways, in March 1944. This was the month she bought Loretta Young's former house at 904 Bedford Drive, and hired Barbara MacLean to decorate, her first task being the removal of Loretta's overtly strong 'religious presence', the shrines and holy water-stoups installed in almost every room.

In June, there was no comment from Garbo when journalists tried to interview her, as she was pulling into her drive, in the wake of the D-Day landings. Neither did she have much to say about Salka's Viertel's divorce from Bertholt, or of the event a few weeks later when she woke up in the middle of the night to find a man standing outside her bedroom door. Calmly, according to the report in *The Los Angeles Times*, she locked the door from the inside, called the police, then opened the window and shinned down the drainpipe. The man, a fan searching for keepsakes and not interested in the $500,000 worth of paintings in the sitting room, fled and in his haste dropped his stolen treasures – a few jewels and Garbo's ration book with her signature on it – in the front garden. She specifically asked the police not to look for him.

Garbo was similarly unfazed on 18 October, when her mother died of a heart-attack in Scarsdale, New York, aged seventy-four. Indeed, even some of her closest friends never learned of Anna Gustaffson's death until several years after the event. The dutiful daughter, she had brought Anna over from Sweden to spare her the possible danger of the war, but after those preliminary months in Los Angeles had little to do with her or the rest of her family. Greta Garbo, mysterious movie star, had nothing in common with the Greta Gustaffson they had known. Indeed, for the remaining months of the war she kept a low profile, her only notable excursion an invitation to an artists' party, which would not have appealed to her had she not learned that Salvador Dalí had also been asked to attend. He turned up in a white suit, she in white slacks and tennis shoes. Walking up to the eccentric painter, Garbo looked him in the face and pronounced, 'One of us has got it wrong,' – and promptly left.[362]

CHAPTER FOURTEEN

STILL DRIFTING

'I keep getting these frightening thoughts about the future. Still, each to his own. Maybe it wouldn't be much fun if everything was easy.'

During the spring of 1946, Garbo was 'reunited' with the photographer Cecil Beaton – like Mercedes, Stokowski and Hauser another egotistical 'star-fucker' who took advantage of her naivety and increasing moments of weakness to further his own aims. Like this unscrupulous trio, Beaton (1904–80) claimed to have had a physical relationship with Garbo, one which almost certainly never progressed beyond his overworked imagination and the frequently exaggerated pages of his diaries, six of which were published during his lifetime. Beaton was gay, the great love of his life being the art collector Peter Watson, no less a reprobate than he and an aficionado of rough-trade and male prostitutes. Of his sexuality, Beaton observed in 1923:

> My attitude to women is this. I adore to dance with them and take them to theatres and private views and talk about dresses and plays and women, but I'm really much more fond of men ... I'm really a terrible, terrible homosexualist, and try so hard not to be.[363]

The chronicler Martin Greif hit the nail on the head some years later:

> In these post-Stonewall days of macho gay males in matching *ensembles* of bulging muscles and hairy chests, it's hard to know what to make of Cecil Beaton. Photographer, costumier, writer and raconteur, he was a snob, a man about town, a wit and a bit of a shit.[364]

Neither were Beaton's diaries entirely authentic. Before they were published, he 'spruced up' much of their content (sometimes to remove libel) and many entries which had been written years earlier were doctored. His biographer, Hugo Vickers, observed: 'An historian should always mistrust a diary edited by the diarist himself. In *The Wandering Years*, the first volume, entries were rewritten with hindsight, some extracts were added that do not exist in the original manuscript diaries, events were kaleidoscoped and even dates were tampered with.'[365]

Born in Hampstead, the son of a wealthy timber merchant, Beaton studied drama at Harrow and Cambridge, but failed to graduate. A member of the Bright Young Things, London's young and carefree aristocratic and bohemian set, he was taken on by *Vogue* in 1927. Beaton snapped most of the great personalities of the day, along with royalty, most notably the wedding pictures of the Duke and Duchess of Windsor. During the early days of World War II he accepted a commission from the Ministry of Information, which resulted in one of the most potent images of the day: a three-year-old Blitz victim, clutching her teddy bear while recovering in hospital. This was one of the images which, when syndicated in the American press, helped encourage the US public to pressurise their government into helping Britain in its darkest hour.

Beaton claimed to have first met Garbo in 1932 at Edmund Goulding's home. Initially, he said, she was reluctant to have anything to do with him, having heard what he had said about her during his first visit to Hollywood, two years earlier. He had asked Howard Strickling to sweet-talk her into participating in a photoshoot. She had said no, and in the published, sanitised version of his diary Beaton observes: 'No advice or pressure would be of avail – she could never be won by flattery.' In the original diary he had written words not dissimilar to his outburst back then: 'Hell. Damn. Blast the bitch ... Bloody Hell to Garbo, the independent and foolish bitch. Perhaps someday she may wish she *had* been photographed by me.' Of this meeting he had also gushed in his diary: 'She pervaded the scent of new-mown hay and of freshly-washed children', adding that, though he had detected an instant rapport, Garbo was unable to get away fast enough – making her excuses, she told him she never wanted to see him again, and left.[366]

Now, fourteen years on, on 15 March 1946, Garbo bumped into

this catty, unpleasant man at the New York apartment of a mutual friend, *Vogue*'s society author, Margaret Case. Again, Beaton goes over the top in recalling the event:

> As if someone had opened a furnace door on me, I had to almost gasp for the next breath. Then she had been like a large apricot in the first fullness of its perfection. Now the apricot quality had given place to vellum. Her eyes were still like an eagle's – blue-mauve and brilliant, the lids the colour of a mushroom – but there were a few delicate lines at the corners.[367]

Of course, she failed to recognise him after all this time, not that this prevented him from pestering her to step out on to the roof garden, determined that she should remain there 'until I struck a chord of intimacy ... by touching the knobbles of her spine.' Bunkum, for sure. Once again Garbo disappeared into the night, though not before promising to stay in touch with the camp photographer.

During the first week of April she turned up unannounced at his apartment and they went walking in Central Park. From then on, Beaton's story gets even more nonsensical: Garbo confessed that she had always regretted being a spinster, and he popped the question. Her response is not on record, but it is not that hard to imagine. She did not however reject Beaton's request to photograph her: her passport was due for renewal, and having him do the job was preferable to going elsewhere. Curiously, when applying for this she gave her address as Tistad and this appears on the document. Beaton recalled, 'At first she stood stiffly to attention, facing my Rolleiflex full face as if it were a firing-squad.' Those early shots are remarkable. Garbo wears no make-up, plain clothes – a biscuit-coloured two-piece and white crew-neck sweater – and looks pensive, reclining on the couch with a cigarette-holder, or with her now-longer hair cascading over the cushions. She was so thrilled with the results, Beaton claimed, that after choosing one for her passport she gave Margaret Case permission to publish them in *Vogue*.[368]

Beaton found himself faced with competition for Garbo's affection when Gayelord Hauser introduced her to the fashion designer Valentina and her partner, George Schlee, whose pasts were suitably interesting and enshrouded in enough mystery to capture her attention. According to their story, which may or may not be entirely true, Valentina (Valentina Nicholaevna Sanina, 1899–1989) was born and raised in Kiev, in the Ukraine. A drama student in Kharkov when the Revolution broke out in 1917, she is supposed to have met George Schlee (1900–74) at the railway station in Sebastopol while fleeing the country with the family jewels. There has always been doubt as to whether they were legally married. After living in Athens, Rome and Paris, they arrived in New York in 1923, where Valentina soon became a prominent member of the city's café society. Five years later, she opened her first couturier's on Madison Avenue.

One of Schlee's first moves as Garbo's *chevalier servant* was to oust Leland Hayward as her manager and appoint himself as her financial adviser, suggesting how and where she should invest her vast wealth – in the summer of 1946, she was already worth in excess of $5 million. Gayelord Hauser was still dictating how she should eat and think, while Mercedes and Salka were still engaged in a battle royal over the direction they believed her career should have been taking. Bounced back and forth between these four, who were constantly at loggerheads with each other, Garbo was a confused woman. And now she had Valentina, telling her what to wear, while Cecil Beaton was fussing in the background, serving little purpose other than using her, as others had done before, as a lavender crutch, and never missing out on a 'bitch-fest' with Mercedes to pull her to pieces behind her back.

Like Hauser, Valentina had amassed a Who's Who of New York and Hollywood A-list clients: currently singing her praises and paying over the odds for her creations in these austere times were Marlene Dietrich, the Duchess of Windsor, Vivien Leigh, Norma Shearer, Paulette Goddard, Joan Crawford and Gloria Swanson. Valentina also designed for top Broadway productions, most notably those starring Lynn Fontanne.

Since 1940, the Schlees had held court at Valentina Gowns, a four-storey building off Fifth Avenue. According to George's rather incredulous account, he first fell in love with Garbo when he saw her standing stark naked in one of Valentina's workrooms. As with Stokowski, Hauser, Beaton and Mercedes, the relationship which developed between them, though close, almost certainly never progressed beyond the platonic. On 6 July, they boarded the *Gripsholm*, where they would occupy separate staterooms. For the first time since arriving in New York with Mauritz Stiller, Garbo paused for photographs on the deck of a ship, some journalists taking this as an indication that they were probably seeing her for the last time, particularly as she had booked the passage in her own name. After a brief stopover in Liverpool, the ship reached Stockholm on 17 July. The usual throng awaited her at the pier, composed of fans who had also never expected to see her again. She and Schlee were collected from the lounge by Consul-General Axel Johnson, who drove them into the city, where they joined Max Gumpel.

Though the war had been over for almost a year, renegade Nazi sympathisers still infiltrated Stockholm society. Leaving Schlee to explore the city, Garbo, Johnson and Gumpel headed for the latter's summer retreat at Baggensnas, where 'matters of war' were discussed. After this, Garbo spent time with Mimi Pollak and her husband, then she headed for Tistad where, face to face, she ended her friendship with Horke Wachtmeister. Though there seemed no reason at the time why she should have done this, her confidant Sven Broman later speculated that Garbo had fallen for Horke's husband, Nils, and had needed to distance herself from the couple to prevent anything coming of this.

There was more drama when she received a call from Alexander Liberman, *Vogue*'s artistic editor, thanking her for the Beaton pictures. Garbo was livid, declaring that she had never given permission for them to be published. There was more: in February 1938, Beaton had published a sketch in the magazine, to which he had added an anti-Semitic caption, which included the offensive word 'kike'. This resulted in Condé Nast having to withdraw 130,000 copies of *Vogue* from the newsstands. Summoned to their offices, Beaton had offered the lame excuse that the 'gaffe' had occurred because he had been tired and suffering from a cold, but they fired him on the spot. The Garbo photographs had been his method of worming his way back into their good books.

Perhaps on account of the rift with Horke, Garbo cut short her visit to Sweden. She and Schlee boarded the *Gripsholm* during the last week of August, arriving back in New York on 4 September, where she granted an on-deck press conference, lasting all of sixty seconds, just long enough to tell reporters, 'I hate to be stared at. I know how animals in the zoo feel when they poke them with little sticks,' and to respond when asked about her plans for the future: 'I *have* no plans, not for the movies, not for the stage, not for anything. I haven't even got a place to live; I'm sort of drifting.'

No sooner had she settled in at the Ritz Tower than she was bombarded with calls from Cecil Beaton. These got no further than the reception desk as Garbo had given explicit instructions that no calls from Beaton be put through to her suite, although she was accepting others. Not to be outdone, Beaton trailed her to Hollywood, where he claimed he cornered her, only to be told, 'By your action, you have deprived me of a friend,' and that she never wanted to see or hear from him again. For over a year, she would stick to her guns.[369]

At the end of the month, Garbo was again approached with *The Paradine Case*, scheduled to begin shooting in December. The script had been revised by Alma Neville, whose husband Alfred Hitchcock would direct. She seriously considered the project, only to back out again. The part went to Alida Valli, who was supported by Gregory Peck and Ann Todd.

During the first half of 1947, with no work offers coming in, Garbo socialised with friends but was rarely seen in public. There was a flurry of excitement among the media when it emerged that she and George Schlee had booked to sail on the *Queen Mary*. One rumour declared that he was about to divorce Valentina and marry Garbo in Europe, another that this time, when she visited Sweden, she would stay put. By the time the ship docked in Southampton on 16 August, the story had changed: she had 'business meetings' to attend to in London, but refused to say what these were about, only that afterwards she would *not* be travelling on to Sweden. Upon their arrival in the capital, the couple were driven to Claridge's, where they had booked adjacent suites. The next morning, Schlee went sightseeing, while Garbo was collected from the hotel by

Winston Churchill's private chauffeur. After lunching with Prime Minister Clement Attlee at 10 Downing Street, she was driven to the Cabinet War Rooms, where she spent several hours in conversation with Churchill himself. This was almost certainly a debriefing, the minutes of which are currently housed in a vault at the Imperial War Museum.

Garbo's next assignment in London, after tying up these loose ends regarding her work with MI6, was a visit to the offices of a well-known law firm. The previous October one of her most fervent fans, seventy-year-old Edgar H. Donne, had died, bequeathing her his fortune. His will proclaimed, 'I hereby give my entire estate to Greta Lovisa Gustaffson, whose stage name is Greta Garbo, to her and no other. If Greta Garbo becomes my wife, then it goes to Greta Lovisa Donne.' An Englishman and reportedly a descendant of the poet, John Donne, Edgar had emigrated to America at the turn of the century, apparently banished by his family for some misdeed. A Howard Hughes-style recluse, he spent his last years in a tumbledown house in Michigan, from where he had written to Garbo, on one occasion asking her to marry him. The *Los Angeles Examiner* reported her as saying:

> I do not know Mr Donne. I vaguely recall that he sent me a letter some years ago which was returned to him. I don't recall anything he said in it. I'm told that he once made a trip to Los Angeles to see me. I didn't see him, nor did I talk to him.[370]

Garbo was probably being coy. It is a well-known fact that she *never* opened fan letters, therefore an admission that she vaguely recalled the one sent by Donne, among the thousands she received each week suggests there was more to this than she was letting on. Subsequently, she had become $75,000 richer, and the legal owner of 160 acres of oil-rich land in Michigan worth in excess of $120,000. Donne's only stipulation was that she would have to travel to London to collect her inheritance. Hedda, Louella and other columnist hacks hinted that Garbo, who had done 'so little' for the war effort, was little more than a money-grabber, though they were slow in reporting what happened next. Meeting with

Donne's lawyers in London, once she discharged the requisite
probate and inheritance taxes, she donated every penny of her
windfall to the Sister Mary Kenny Polio Foundation.

From London, Garbo and Schlee flew to Paris, where there was
yet another uneasy reunion with Mercedes de Acosta, who had
taken the liberty of booking three suites at the Hotel Crillon –
Garbo's under the name 'Mademoiselle Hanson'. Mercedes did
not get to see much of Garbo, though, as most of her time was
spent with Jean Cocteau, whose play, *L'Aigle À Deux Têtes*, she was
interested in bringing to the screen. In March she had seen the
English adaptation at New York's Plymouth Theatre, with Tallulah
Bankhead in the role of the Bavarian queen who falls in love with
Stanislas, the young man sent to assassinate her (played by German
actor Helmut Dantine, who had replaced a mumbling, troublesome Marlon Brando). Cocteau's lover, Jean Marais, had appeared
alongside Edwige Feuillère in the original French production and
Cocteau was currently directing the film version on location at the
Chateau de Pierrefonds, where Garbo visited the set to watch them
rehearse the final scene. The longest monologue in movie history,
this saw the queen enacting a twenty-minute, 20,000-word speech
before plunging head first down a huge staircase with a bullet in
her heart, while her killer drinks a cup of poison.[371]

Upon her return to New York, while the scriptwriters were working on *The Eagle Has Two Heads*, George Cukor introduced Garbo
to Tennessee Williams, who never found her less than daunting:

> She goes by the name of Harriet Brown and sneaks around like the
> assassin of Bugsy Siegel ... In appearance she is really hermaphro-
> ditic, almost as flat as a boy, very thin, the eyes and voice extraordi-
> narily pure and beautiful. But she has the cold quality of a mermaid
> ... She scares me to death.[372]

Williams' *A Streetcar Named Desire* was scheduled to open at the
Eleanor Roosevelt Theatre at the end of the year, with Jessica
Tandy in the central role of Blanche Du Bois and Marlon Brando
as the rough-and-ready, sweaty Stanley Kowalski. Williams was
being serious when he asked Garbo if she was interested in playing

Blanche in the screen version and one may only shudder to think what she would have sounded like, playing a Southern belle, or how she would have got along with someone as difficult as Brando. She declined, declaring that she was 'too masculine' for the part. Williams tried to tempt her with another role: that of The Mistress in a script he was currently working on titled *The Pink Bedroom*. A difficult, noisy and argumentative piece, this sees an actress and her older mentor-lover slugging it out in the bedroom where they have been conducting an affair for the last ten years, each blaming the other for its failure, while the younger lover, waiting to take his place, waits in the next room. Garbo was interested, and kept in touch with Williams; she even agreed to be his 'date' for the premiere of *Streetcar*. She balked however at the completed script, when she saw that he had named the older lover Michael Stiller and had him commit suicide in the final scene, in the pink bedroom, after the actress has left him for his rival.

Early in 1948, Alexander Korda announced that he wanted to direct *The Eagle Has Two Heads* at Shepperton Studios, with Cecil Beaton designing Garbo's wardrobe and assisting with the sets. When the deal inexplicably fell through, Korda offered her a London stage production of Chekhov's *Three Sisters*, which, with her horror of appearing in public, was out of the question. Much of the spring and summer was taken up with other hoped-for projects, all amounting to nothing. Billy Wilder approached her with *L'Inconnue de la Seine*, which centred around the celebrated death-mask in the Louvre of an unidentified young woman whose body had been fished out of the river during the 1880s. Wilder had for the purpose of this film 'identified' her as a banker's wife with a controversial past. 'No wives of bankers,' was Garbo's sharp response. Wilder is said to have been furious, but still paid tribute to her two years later when he wrote and directed *Sunset Boulevard* for Gloria Swanson. In one scene, faded siren Norma Desmond enthuses while watching the silent screen, '*We* didn't need dialogue. We had faces. There just aren't any faces like that anymore. Only one – Garbo!'

Next, Garbo herself came up with the notion of playing a female *Pagliacci*, and even had Cecil Beaton photograph her dressed as a clown. No one was interested, or in her subsequent suggestion that she might play Francis of Assisi! Then, on 26 August, there was considerable excitement when news broke that Garbo's seven-year hiatus from the movies was about to end: she had signed a one-film deal with Walter Wanger, who had produced *Queen Christina* and had been trying to purloin her from MGM for years.

The proposed film was *The Lost Moment*, recounting the love affair between feminist novelist George Sand and Frederic Chopin. Sand (Amandine Dupin, 1804–76) caused a sensation by smoking a pipe in public – which many believed was as low as a woman could sink – and by wearing men's clothes, for no other reason, she claimed, than that they were cheaper and more practical than the voluptuous gowns of the day. This attire gained her admittance to society venues usually prohibited to women. In this respect, she and Garbo had much in common. Wanger had yet to find an actor to portray Chopin, but he settled on Robert Cummings to play another of Sand's lovers, Alfred de Musset. Her sanitised story had been told three years earlier in *A Song to Remember*, starring Merle Oberon and Cornel Wilde; this one promised to remain as close to history as the Breen Office would permit. Wanger commissioned Salka Viertel to write the script, and Cecil Beaton for the costumes and sets, hoping this might make Garbo easier to handle, and unaware that they were not speaking.

Garbo had other ideas. She had recently seen G. W. Pabst's recent drama about anti-Semitism, *Der Prozess* (The Trial) and was so impressed that she announced only he should direct *The Lost Moment*. Neither did she want Robert Cummings in the film. Back in March, she had seen Montgomery Clift's new film, *The Search*, directed by Fred Zinnemann. This was set in post-war Berlin and tells the story of a sensitive American soldier helping a little boy search for his mother, last seen in Auschwitz. Salka knew Monty and effected an introduction. He and Garbo hit it off at once and would remain friends until Monty's early death in 1966. Pabst had not seen Garbo since *Die Freudlose Gasse* and was only interested in having her play the dual roles of Circe and Penelope in his adaptation of Homer's *Odyssey*, with Orson Welles approached to play Ulysses. As Wanger wanted neither Pabst nor Monty involved with his film, the project was abandoned.

The rift between Garbo and Cecil Beaton ended not long afterwards, when he waylaid her in the lobby at the Ritz Tower. Whatever was said is not known, save that she appears to have forgiven him for the *Vogue* incident. With typical Beaton hokum, he claimed that just hours later they were in bed, recording in the fantasy world of his diary: 'She said firmly that she wanted to make a man out of me.' According to him, they spent most of the festive season together: 'I gave a toast to our marriage, our life together, but Greta did not elaborate on this theme and smiled a little diffidently,' he observed of their New Year's Eve 'tryst', adding their subsequent lovemaking had been 'wild and tender'. In January, Garbo returned to Hollywood, Beaton following in hot pursuit. He claimed to have stayed at her house for twelve days, something that virtually no one would ever do, the only exceptions having been Borg, Nils Asther and Garbo's family. He also invented an even more ridiculous scenario of seeing Garbo working stark naked in her garden, manuring her roses and mending the broken fence. At the end of the month he returned to New York, though Garbo would never learn: like Mercedes, Beaton would turn up time and time again and always find himself welcomed back with open arms.[373]

On 10 March 1949, Harry Edington suffered a stroke and died while Garbo was on her way to visit him in hospital. She had refused to travel to New York when Anna Gustaffson had died but she visited Edington's widow, *Flesh and the Devil* co-star Barbara Kent, helped out with the arrangements and was one of the chief mourners at his funeral. Though he had stopped representing her, they had remained good friends and his death had come as a tremendous shock.

A few days later, Garbo was somewhat cheered when Walter Wanger proposed a film version of *La Duchesse de Langeais*, the second part of Honoré de Balzac's trilogy, *Histoire des Treize*. Published in 1834, it tells the story of Antoinette de Langeais, the noblewoman-coquette who jilts her lover and gives up on the high life to become a nun, only to die at twenty-nine. First filmed by André Calmettes in 1910, there had been a thirty-five minute American version, *The Eternal Flame* (1922) by Frank Lloyd, starring Norma Talmadge and

Adolphe Menjou, and four years later a German adaptation, *Liebe*, with Elisabeth Bergner. More recently (1942), it had been filmed with the much-revered Edwige Feuillère, the actress Garbo had admired in *L'Aigle À Deux Têtes* and, she was the first to admit, not an easy act to follow.

Max Ophuls was pencilled in to direct the film and Sally Benson – most famous for *Meet Me In St Louis* (1944) – was hired for the script. Garbo had met Ophuls (1902–57) in Paris and attended a private screening of his 1939 classic, *Sans Lendemain*. Ophuls also scored a massive scoop in persuading the only star of Garbo's magnitude ever to agree to appear in one of her films, Edith Piaf, to perform 'Pour Moi Toute Seule'. In a café-concert sequence inspired by Garbo's visit to the Concert-Damia some years earlier, while Antoinette sits feeling dejected, Piaf was to sing, 'Faded walls, joyless days ... For me, all alone, a dream begins. It will end tomorrow, but for now I am fine.' British actor James Mason was expected to co-star.

Garbo's fee was the lowest it had ever been: $25,000 upon signing the contract, and a further $25,000 on completion of the film, but she would pocket a percentage of the box-office takings. The film was to be a joint Italo-American production, shot mostly on location in Rome and largely financed by Angelo Rizzoli and Giuseppe Amato. The former was Italy's leading magazine publisher, the latter a producer of some distinction; their most famous film would be *La Dolce Vita* in 1960. They were a finicky pair who, before giving the go-ahead to release capital for the project, asked that Garbo submit to a screen test. The thought of asking her to do this filled Walter Wanger with dread, yet she was the first to admit that Rizzoli was within his rights to make such a demand since it had been a long time since Garbo had faced a camera. 'If I disliked it all then, what would I feel about it now?' Cecil Beaton claimed she asked him.[374]

In fact, three tests were made, running to a combined total of between twenty and forty minutes, depending on which account one reads. The released test, discovered in 1990, lasts less than five minutes. Because the footage has been mixed, it is not easy to distinguish one test from another. Garbo is seen wearing a checked shirt and scarf, sometimes against a plain backdrop, sometimes with props: a Grecian column, a table, a hood, a jacket, a cigarette. A wind-machine is switched on and she fidgets with her hair as her facial expressions alternate in rapid succession: frowning, pondering, anxious, arching one brow then the other, smiling, laughing, sniggering, turning aside to joke with the crew. And, at forty-three, still looking flawlessly gorgeous throughout.

Garbo had wanted William Daniels to test her, but Walter Wanger brought in Joseph Valentine, who had just photographed Ingrid Bergman in *Joan of Arc*. Valentine made the test at the Chaplin Studio on 5 May. No sooner was this in the can than he collapsed on the set, and on 18 May he died. Garbo was satisfied with the test, and declared it her personal tribute to Valentine's memory, but Wanger declared it null and void and commissioned a second test from James Wong Howe for 25 May. Garbo protested and as a compromise two tests were made on this day, Howe's during the morning, Daniels' later in the day. These were done at the Universal Studios, where both photographers were currently working. Both tests, Garbo declared, would be submitted to the Italian backers.

Early in August, Garbo and George Schlee sailed for Cherbourg and from the ship cabled Walter Wanger to say that she no longer wanted Max Ophuls to direct. While in New York she had caught a performance of *South Pacific*, produced by Joshua Logan, and had been so impressed that she wanted him to direct her in *La Duchesse*. There was another more potent connection between Garbo and Logan: drafted into the US Army in 1942, he too had worked as an intelligence officer. Wanger cabled back to say that he would think about it. He and his business partner Gene Frenke, with whom he had set up International Productions to finance the film, were starting to tire of Garbo's 'finicky ways', declaring that she was driving them to bankruptcy.

The previous August, the company had assigned a $250,000 budget to whatever project might have taken her fancy: a sizeable portion of this had already been wasted on the aborted George Sand movie, and besides financing Garbo and Schlee's trip to Europe, the company had advanced Sally Benson $15,000 for the script of *La Duchesse*. Additionally, there were problems with James

Mason, who was demanding $150,000 – three times what Wanger was paying Garbo – as well as top-billing in the film. Eventually, he would be persuaded to drop this to $75,000, which Garbo did not mind as Mason would not be netting a share of the profits, but there was no way that she or anyone else would have submitted to his name appearing above hers in the credits.

In Rome, despite her elaborate disguise, Garbo was recognised leaving the studio with Schlee by one pesky journalist, who spent the entire day trailing her:

There was a swish of revolving doors, and a figure that looks like a devotee of some less austere monastic order emerges. An enormous straw hat covers four-fifths of her face; there are sunglasses unseen beneath the brim. There is a loose one-piece dress, caught at the middle with a simple girdle. On the feet there are sandals. In one stride she is in the car. A man following takes one stride and is beside her. The high-powered roadster roars off, followed by three cars, two jeeps and a motorcycle ... and [when she returned to her hotel] now Miss Harriet Brown sweeps through the swing-doors, and like a shot from a gun is in the lift, leaving the great bunch of flowers from her Italian producer where it has been since the morning, on the porter's desk.[375]

In Italy, Garbo's paranoia of meeting strangers worked against her, whereas in Hollywood, she had got most of her own way by using her quest for solitude, going into hiding, or threatening to go home as a bargaining counter. MGM had played her game because, as their most bankable star, they had needed her more than she needed them. Now, whenever she retreated into her shell, she was heartlessly forced out of it as Angelo Rizzoli and his team alerted the paparazzi to her every movement, forcing her to change her hotel three times within the space of a week. The 'secret' meeting she was supposed to have with Rizzoli and his project partner, Giuseppe Amato of Scalera Films, turned into a nightmare when she found herself surrounded by hundreds of reporters who blocked her entrance to the building until she smiled and pronounced, 'I want to be alone!'

At a subsequent meeting she wore a veil over her face through-out the entire ordeal, like the mysterious character at the end of *As You Desire Me*, and was accused of mocking the backers. News next arrived that the Breen Office had condemned Sally Benson's script as, 'Obscene – a story of adultery, without any voice for moral-ity.' Rizzoli demanded a rewrite, at Wanger's expense. By now the budget had risen to almost $500,000 and Wanger saw little point in throwing good money after bad. Rizzoli refused to compromise by injecting more of his own cash into the project and the plug was pulled on the project, the backers and Wanger screaming at each other over the phone, while Garbo and George Schlee slipped out of the city and headed for Paris. Here they retreated as best they could from the public spotlight, and on 2 October took the train to Le Havre. The next day they boarded the *Ile-de-France* for New York. James Mason never forgave Garbo for what had happened, though it was not her fault, arrogantly declaring, 'They probably cancelled it because they just couldn't deal with this crazy dame.'[376]

On 9 February 1951, Garbo finally became an American citizen. Her reason for doing so, bearing in mind that she had spent most of her career threatening to go home, owed more to her wanting to hold on to her Swedish investments than to any loyalty she might have felt towards the country. This was the Cold War, and with Russia posing a threat to Scandinavia, lawyers and friends such as Sir William Stephenson advised her that as a legalised American, such investments would remain protected. As part of the process she was questioned about her association with 'known Communist' Salka Viertel, whose name had recently been added to the Communist List compiled by the FBI. In fact, the 'reds under the bed' appear to have been Salka's ex-husband Berthold and their son Peter (1920–2007) and, without a doubt Peter's wife, Virginia Ray Schulberg, who, in the 1930s was publicly acknowledged as a major force in the Communist Party. Garbo confessed that she *had* known Salka while she had been working in the movies but that, since retiring almost ten years ago, they had gone their separate ways. Untrue,

of course, but denouncing Salka allowed Garbo's application to go through without further challenge. She signed the document and even allowed a photographer to record the event. Unable to shield her face with a newspaper or hat, she wore the veil she had worn for her last meeting with Angelo Rizzoli.

There would be few serious offers of work from now on, with those making the offers knowing full well what the answer would be. Garbo had devoted her entire career to MGM. She had tolerated their unscrupulous and conniving ways, they her threats to leave and multitude of mood-swings. She had felt it preferable to put up with two-faced executives that she knew how to cope with, rather than up sticks and move to another studio, where she would have to start all over again. For a little while, there was talk of remaking *Flesh and the Devil*, with Clarence Brown at the helm and even an American-Swedish co-production of *Lady Chatterley's Lover*, to be filmed in Stockholm by her old Academy friend, Gustaf Molander, to avoid censorship issues but neither project ever materialised. Garbo also turned down $45,000 for five-minute spots on two television shows: CBS' *This Is Show Business* and NBC's *The Kate Smith Hour*.

For several years, Cecil Beaton had been trying to tempt Garbo to visit Reddish House, his home near Salisbury, in Wiltshire. His greatest ambition, he said, was to photograph her within the secluded grounds, to chaperone her around the beautiful neighbouring English countryside and, of course, to show her off to his snooty friends. Another ambition was to be the first to photograph her in colour, but she gave this commission to his rival, Anthony Beauchamp, the British society photographer married to Winston Churchill's daughter, Sarah. Garbo and Beauchamp, who committed suicide six years later, met during one of her visits to 10 Downing Street. He took just six shots of her, one of which appeared on the cover of the June 1951 issue of *McCall's* magazine. The commission was her way of exacting revenge on Beaton for selling her passport picture to *Vogue*.

Beaton was furious, but kept on pestering Garbo all the same, and in October, after selling her Hollywood home, her way of saying goodbye to 'Tinseltown' forever, she gave in. Even so, she never completely forgave Beaton for what he had done, and in her suitcase packed a copy of *Cecil Beaton's Scrapbook*, which she would read aloud to whoever happened to be present whenever he started getting on her nerves, which appears to have been often. Compiled and published in 1937, after he had met her, the section of the book devoted to Garbo starts off well enough. He describes her as 'as beautiful as the aurora borealis', applies over-syrupy praise to her acting abilities, goes into great detail when discussing every aspect of her physique, then spoils it all by launching a savage attack on her personality:

> She has a sense of humour, a sense of fun, but she is unhappy, neurasthenic, morbid ... She is not interested in anything or anybody in particular, and she has become as difficult as an invalid and as selfish, quite unprepared to put herself out for anyone ... She is superstitious, suspicious and does not know the meaning of friendship. She is incapable of love.[377]

Through Beaton, Garbo met an upper-crust fop even more insufferable than he was: his neighbour, Stephen Tennant (1906–87). Tennant was a former Bright Young Thing, a poet, painter, novelist, agoraphobic, hypochondriac and arch snob. This peculiar man had spent most of his long life 'retreating from society' and had spent the last fifteen years in bed, for no other reason than he was lazy and wished to be waited on hand and foot. Terrified of leaving his home, yet eager to meet Hollywood's most illustrious star, Tennant called Beaton and demanded that he drive her over for dinner, whether Garbo wanted to see him or not. Such was her curiosity that she agreed, her only stipulation being that no one else should be there. The two got along well, so much so that Tennant accepted an invitation to dine at Reddish House, the first time he had left his room in months. Beaton also introduced Garbo to his sisters and octogenarian mother, to Princess Margaret, the Marquis of Bath, and to one of the doyennes of British society, Diana Cooper. All took an instant dislike to her, a feeling which was mutual. Garbo and Beaton, sometimes accompanied by his on-off lover Peter Watson, visited Bath, Oxford, Eton and Cambridge, getting immense pleasure from meeting the students in their 'spiffing' uniforms, but always refusing to pose with them for photographs or sign autographs. According to Beaton, during this trip he once again asked Garbo to marry him, getting the same response as before. Alone, she lunched with Clement Attlee and Winston Churchill at 10 Downing Street, two weeks before the latter was elected to serve a second term. In 1952, Garbo came close to playing the central role of the contessa suspected of murdering her husband in the screen adaptation of Daphne du Maurier's best-selling novel, *My Cousin Rachel*. This would have seen her playing opposite Richard Burton in one of his early leads, had she not decided that she would never succeed in effecting a credible Cornish accent.

In the autumn of 1953, Garbo forked out $38,000 for a seven-room apartment on the fifth floor of The Campanile, a 14-storey, pre-war tower block situated at 450 East 52nd Street, in New York's Sutton Place area. This remained her home for the next thirty-seven years. It was not a mausoleum, like her previous residences, but an opulent, comfortable and well-furnished abode where she could relax, surrounded by her paintings and objets d'art, or lounge on her terrace and enjoy panoramic views of the East River and Manhattan. The musical-comedy star Mary Martin was a near neighbour and, more importantly, George and Valentina Schlee had an apartment on the ninth floor.

Initially, Garbo had the apartment refurbished by Barbara MacLean, but over the next few years she hired several interior designers, most notably Billy Baldwin (1903–83), one of the best – and costliest – in the business, who later worked for Jacqueline Kennedy and Aristotle Onassis. In his memoirs, Baldwin described the finished effect: 'All the colours were rosy and warm: there were beautiful curtains of eighteenth-century silk, a Louis XV Savonnerie carpet, the finest-quality *Régence* furniture and wonderful Impressionist paintings.' He recalled how Garbo had come up with the unusual colour-scheme for her bedroom. During a trip to Sweden, she was so taken with the mulberry-coloured lampshades in the dining-car on the train that she 'lifted' one, and now asked Baldwin to replicate it: 'She lit a candle and held it beneath the shade. Our job was to paint the room the colour that resulted from the candlelight shining through the silk.'[378]

The drifting and socialising continued. As happened with Marlene Dietrich when she retired – 'Address all letters to Mrs Sieber,' she told friends, this being her married name – Garbo very quickly 'put the star to bed', save that, while Marlene bowed out at almost eighty, Garbo had done so at thirty-six. And like the great stars who had died before their time – Valentino, Harlow, James Dean, Marilyn Monroe – to the world outside her intimate circle she was able to remain eternally young, while still alive. As the years passed, fans may have wondered what she looked and sounded like, extant of the blurred paparazzi photos which cropped up periodically, but all they really saw in their mind's eye were the beautiful images in *Camille* and *Queen Christina*.

In retirement, even Garbo's closest friends were told to address her as Harriet Brown. She never entertained at home, though she was a welcome if not communicative guest at others' social events, providing she knew everyone present: the slightest whiff of a stranger and she would flee into the night. She still saw a lot of Salka Viertel and she was hardly ever away from George Schlee, mindless of his wife Valentina's increasing chagrin. She grew close to David Niven and his Swedish wife, Hjordis, and often visited Montgomery Clift. Another intimate was Jane Gunther, the former editor of *Reader's Digest*, and every now and then, she enjoyed a reunion with Sven Hugo Borg. Then there were the *frangines*, usually defined as belonging to two categories: the 'butch' including Mercedes, Marianne Oswald and Valeska Gert, and the 'fems': Cecil Beaton, Gayelord Hauser and Frey Brown.

Because Garbo avoided public functions, she did not have to care how she looked and no longer bothered to keep up with the latest fashions, though she did own a collection of stunning Valentina gowns. When Harriet Brown showed up at a party, it was in slacks, sweater or shirt, flat shoes and, more often than not, with her hair unkempt and windblown. Friends have said that she rarely talked about her films or about Hollywood and that if she did, she spoke about herself in the third person. During the early to mid-Fifties, her mystique saved her from the unethical probings of slander mags like *Confidential* – their editors' opinions being there was no dirt to dish on Garbo because, away from Hollywood, she had never done anything.

In the spring of 1955, the Motion Picture Academy awarded Garbo an Honorary Oscar. No one expected her to turn up at the 30 March ceremony, though the Academy hoped that she would allow them to tape a brief acceptance speech. She refused: the Oscar was accepted on her behalf by actress Nancy Kelly, and handed over to her friend, Minna Wallis (sister of producer Hal), for safe keeping. It took Garbo another two years to enquire about the statuette, which she shoved into the back of a drawer and promptly forgot about.

There was also another *frangine* waiting in the wings for George Schlee to bow out, having heard all was not always well between him and Garbo. For some time, the Schlees had been going their separate ways, while refusing to divorce. The reason for this, according to some sources, was that they had never married in the first place. For once, the new 'guardian' was not out for all she could get by associating with her: Cécile de Rothschild was a member of the fabulously wealthy dynasty and owned several 'official' residences, including a house in Paris, on the rue Faubourg-St-Honoré, next to the Elysée Palace. Each year from 1955, Garbo spent several weeks here and several more at Le Roc Fleury, a sumptuous villa at Cap d'Ail, which Schlee purchased for $50,000, probably with Garbo's money. An early visitor here was Greek shipping tycoon Aristotle Onassis, who owned the casino at nearby Monte Carlo, and famously allowed Garbo to enter the establishment wearing slacks, just weeks after they turned away Marlene Dietrich and Edwige Feuillère for doing the same. That first summer, while the villa was being refurbished, Garbo and Schlee enjoyed a vacation on Onassis' sumptuous yacht, the *Christina*. In July, they visited Capri, and while everyone else stayed at one of the island's most exclusive hotels, Garbo stayed with Gracie Fields at her restaurant complex, not in a staff chalet this time, but at the singer's home. In September, off the coast of the island of Itáki, and with little fuss, Garbo celebrated her fiftieth birthday.

In New York at the end of 1958, there was yet another reconciliation with Mercedes de Acosta, who had fallen on bad times. The previous year she had been hospitalised with a serious eye infection, which resulted in her wearing a black patch and, to pay the medical bills, she had given up her Park Lane apartment and moved into a much smaller one. She was also adding the finishing touches to her memoirs, *Here Lies the Heart*, and was anxious to get everyone on side for when the explosion occurred. Marlene Dietrich and Cecil Beaton had, she declared, read and approved the unedited script and, terrified that she might die before the book was published, she now needed Garbo's blessing to let the world in on their 'more intimate' moments. But Garbo was horrified: even when told that Mercedes might have to sell her jewels to pay for an operation to remove a brain tumour, she declared that she neither wanted to see nor hear from her ever again. This time she meant it.

In October 1960, not wishing to be in America when Mercedes' book was published, Garbo flew to Switzerland, where she visited the ski resort of Klosters for the first time. Salka Viertel had moved there to be close to her son, Peter, who lived there with his new wife, British actress Deborah Kerr. Cécile de Rothschild had a chalet in St Moritz, a two-hour drive away. Garbo fell in love with the then largely uncommercialised retreat and returned here most years, always in summer, always leaving before mid-September when the tourist season began. Here, Salka ran a smaller version of the salon she had presided over in Hollywood, though few of her regular guests were household names: writers Irwin Shaw and Gore Vidal, actors Jack Larson, Yul Brynner, Brian Aherne and Richard Burton – the latter *never* with Elizabeth Taylor, who Salka disapproved of. Garbo never stayed with her friend, preferring her own space – a rented chalet or flat. She rose at dawn to go walking, covering four or five miles before breakfast, mostly alone and unhindered because the locals were less intrusive here than in New York.

Garbo had just returned to New York when on 18 September 1961 – her 56th birthday – news broke that her friend Dag Hammarskjöld, also fifty-six, had been killed with fifteen others in a plane crash in Northern Rhodesia (now Zambia). Since working with him on espionage missions during the war, they had kept in touch and she would always believe that his death had not been an accident. Others thought the same, though three subsequent Official Enquiries failed to prove otherwise.

In January 1962, Garbo returned to Sweden for the first time in sixteen years and there were rumours that she might have been about to make her movie comeback. The reason for this was her meeting with the country's most important director, Ingmar Bergman, at Stockholm's Grand Hotel. After dining together, they collected Mimi Pollak and Vera Schmiterlöw, and spent the morning 'discussing possible projects' in Mauritz Stiller's former office at the Svensk Filmindustri Studios before heading off for the locations where *Gösta Berlings Saga* had been filmed. Sadly, nothing ever came of this.

Only Garbo could have turned down three invitations to the White House and still be asked again, on 21 October 1963, when Jackie Kennedy 'twisted her arm' and she capitulated. Who she met there, apart from the President and First Lady, is not known – there were rumours that she took off her shoes and 'bounced' on Abraham Lincoln's bed and that she left early because she did not wish to become another notch on the infamous Jack Kennedy bedpost, but such stories may be speculation. What is known is that she was devastated when Kennedy was assassinated, just weeks later. Garbo wrote Jackie a letter of condolence and sent flowers to the funeral, and for a few years the two women stayed in touch – until Aristotle Onassis, the man who had once had designs on her, dumped Maria Callas and moved in on the President's widow.

Garbo had known television producer William Frye for over a decade as he sometimes escorted her around New York when Gayelord Hauser and Frey Brown were unavailable. Early in 1964, Frye asked her to appear in his first major film, *The Trouble With Angels*, a coming-of-age drama set in a convent. Garbo was to play the mother superior and Ida Lupino would direct. 'She would have been perfect,' Frye recalled. 'No hair problems, no costume changes and, best of all, no leading man to worry about.' The script was commissioned, Frye flew to New York, presented it to Garbo personally, and the next day they went out on a 'date' to a performance of *Funny Girl*, starring Barbra Streisand at the Winter Garden Theater. She spent several minutes chatting to Streisand in her dressing room and outside the theatre was mobbed by hundreds of fans. For whatever reason, she changed her mind about the film.[379]

On 3 October, Garbo suffered the first of a trio of tragedies which hit her hard. George Schlee had been ill for some time. In friendlier days when he had twice been hospitalised, she and Valentina had taken turns to sit at his bedside. She and George Schlee had just dined with Cécile de Rothschild and were taking a stroll before returning to their suite at the Hotel Crillon when he complained of chest pains. Minutes later, he suffered a heart attack. An ambulance was summoned, while Garbo fled back to Cécile's house. A few hours later, at the Hôpital Lariboisière, he died alone.

Valentina's treatment of the woman who had only ever been her partner's closest friend was abhorrent. The next day, she flew to Paris to collect her 'property', and on 7 October Garbo arrived back at New York's Idlewild Airport to learn that the funeral was taking place that day and that instructions had been given not to admit her to the ceremony. Valentina had also tried, but failed, to obtain an order prohibiting her from ever visiting his grave at the Ferncliffe Cemetery. Later, she collected every item of 'Garbo memorabilia' from the East 52nd Street apartment – including valuable antiques – had these crated up, driven to a patch of wasteland and incinerated. And as if that was not enough, she brought in a Russian Orthodox priest to have Garbo's 'presence' exorcised, a procedure which was repeated at Le Roc, in France. Over the next twenty-five years, bearing in mind they inhabited the same building, it was inevitable that the paths of the two women in George Schlee's life should cross. Whenever this happened, Valentina would make the sign of the Cross and hurried past the woman she had baptised 'The Vampire'. Schlee's place as Garbo's unofficial 'business manager' would be taken by her niece, Gray Reisfield, and Anthony Palermo, the director of Gayelord Hauser's Modern Products food company. Garbo is said to have been worth around $15 million in 1964, her investments steadily increasing with little active involvement from herself. She was netting an average of $20,000 a month from property rentals alone, much of which was ploughed back into her very impressive collection of paintings and antiques.

On 8 April 1965, Garbo received word that Lars Hanson had died after a short illness, aged seventy-eight. Though he had had numerous affairs, including the one with Garbo, he remained married to Karin Molander for over forty years. Despite numerous offers from Hollywood, he had refused to return there, preferring to work in his own language on the stage and screen, and was one of the earliest recipients of the prestigious Eugene O'Neill Award. Along with Mimi Pollak and Max Gumpel, Hanson was one of the few old flames she spent quality time with during her return trips to Sweden. He was buried at Skogskyrkogården (The Woodland Cemetery), which would eventually be chosen by her family as Garbo's final resting place. Gumpel and Pollak attended the funeral and took a wreath on her friend's behalf. Then, on 3 August, Garbo learned that Gumpel had also died, aged seventy-five.

As if she had not lost enough loved ones, 67-year-old Sven Gustaffson was next. Garbo's brother had been suffering from congestive heart disease for some time and on 27 January 1967, while undergoing treatment at the Desert Hospital, Palm Springs, suffered a fatal coronary. Sven left his entire estate to his widow, Marguerite, and did not even mention his sister in his will, mindless of the fact that she had paid his way most of his adult life. Neither did he (nor his estate) publicly acknowledge Sven Jr, his illegitimate son by Elsa Hagerman. Indeed, the young man was not informed of his father's death until 1971, when he legally changed his name to Gustaffson.

Inasmuch as *Here Lies the Heart* had ended her friendship with Mercedes, so Garbo – along with many others, including members of the British royal family – severed ties with Cecil Beaton towards the end of 1967 when he announced that he was compiling *The Happy Years*, the third volume of his diaries, covering the period 1940–48. Having heard of her tantrum over Mercedes' book, Beaton desperately wanted her blessing for this one, while making it clear that nothing he had written about her would be changed. He called her apartment, but Garbo refused to come to the phone. Salka Viertel, on the other hand, she helped and encouraged in writing *her* memoirs, *The Kindness of Strangers*, well aware that her best friend would never betray her confidences.

On 13 April 1968, at one of George Cukor's 'pink tea-parties', the host asked Garbo who in the whole world she would most like to meet. Never more serious she replied, 'Mae West!' Mae, arguably the most controversial Hollywood star of them all, was preparing her movie comeback. Her last film, *The Heat's On* (1943), had suffered the same critical panning as *Two-Faced Woman* and now, courtesy of Gore Vidal, she was to appear with Raquel Welch in the screen version of his novel, *Myra Breckinridge*. The sex-change subject fascinated Garbo. Cukor made the arrangements and the meeting took place a few weeks later. Also present were Gayelord Hauser and Frey Brown, Roddy McDowall, and Jayne Mansfield's muscleman ex-husband, Mickey Hargitay. Garbo recalled what appears to have been a boring evening to her producer friend, William Frye:

> During dinner, all Miss West discussed was monkeys. I don't know anything about monkeys, so I didn't talk ... After dinner all she talked about was musclemen. I don't know anything about musclemen, so I didn't talk then either. I was home at 10:30, and I didn't say a word all evening.[380]

On 9 May, Mercedes de Acosta died, aged 75. She had been ill for some time, and had never stopped believing that Garbo would drop by and all would be forgiven. Today, her lasting legacy is an exaggerated memoir which frequently sells for more than it may be worth over the internet, simply on account of its who-did-who curiosity value. In the original introduction, Mercedes offered her excuses for shopping her friend: 'To write of Greta and things connected with her is the most difficult task I have had ... No one knows better than I how much she dislikes being discussed, but I cannot write my life and have her out of it.' More controversial were a set of topless photographs taken of Garbo during their Silver Lake vacation. These were discovered among Mercedes' effects and soon winged their way into the sleazier tabloids and movie magazines. Garbo neither commented on her death, nor sent flowers to her funeral. So far as she was concerned, Mercedes had died in 1960 when she had published her book.[381]

CHAPTER FIFTEEN

ALONE AT LAST

'The story of my life is about back entrances and side doors and secret elevators and other ways of getting in and out of places so that people won't bother you.'

In March 1971, 'Harriet Brown' flew to Rome, and checked in at the Minerva Hotel. Over the next few days there were secret meetings with the director Luchino Visconti, who wanted her for a cameo in a proposed Franco-Italian production of Marcel Proust's *Remembrance of Things Past*. Much of this was made by the Italian press, not least of all how the 65-year-old Garbo would photograph in close-up. In America, *Time* magazine announced:

> Hardly since General Douglas MacArthur's 'I shall return' has so momentous a comeback loomed ... The role that caught her fancy: Maria Sophia, the sixtyish Queen of Naples, who will only have one scene. Nothing has been signed as yet, but Visconti sounded as if Garbo's reappearance was already a fait accompli. Said he, 'I am very pleased that this woman, with her severe authoritarian presence, should figure in the decadent and rarefied climate of the world described by Proust.'[382]

Sadly, the project was scrapped – not because Garbo backed out, but because the director's delusions of grandeur for a film he predicted would run to four hours resulted in the projected budget being so prohibitive, Cinécitta feared that it would bankrupt the studio. Therefore it was back to 'everyday' life. While Hollywood stars of a lesser stature were waited on hand and foot by a coterie of servants, Garbo employed a staff of just one: a Swiss woman called Claire Koger, around her own age, recommended to her by Valentina Schlee and utterly discreet. Koger's main duties were preparing her meals and answering the phone, which was unplugged when she went home at 4.30 on the dot. The cleaning duties they shared. Garbo had no use for a chauffeur: if one of her *chevalier-servants* was not available, she would call a cab.

In all weathers, she kept up her favourite pastime of walking. Her regular routine in New York was to rise at dawn, window-shop until the stores opened, then spend the afternoon at a gallery. Her three main walking companion-confidants were Robert Reud, Raymond Daum – a United Nations film producer who had lived next door to Gayelord Hauser and Frey Brown in Palm Springs, where he had seen her many times in the flesh (literally, from his bedroom window), but not been properly introduced until January 1963 – and Sam Green. Initially, though she asked for their telephone numbers to summon them whenever she wanted to go out, often at a moment's notice, none of them were given hers or allowed to meet each other, for fear they might 'swap' their Garbo stories.

Boston-born Sam Green (1941–2011) was for many years the confidant most trusted by Garbo. A college drop-out, handsome and bearded, he was a pioneer promoter of Pop Art, particularly the works of Andy Warhol, while managing the Green Gallery (name unrelated) on New York's 57th Street. In 1965 he was appointed director of Philadelphia's Institute of Contemporary Art, a tenure he held for three years before returning to New York as cultural adviser to the Mayor. A sucker for a sugar-daddy, in 1970 he 'retired' to become Cecil Beaton's *chevalier-servant*, accompanying him on his travels until tiring of his finicky ways and tantrums. Green was also a close friend of Cécile de Rothschild, and it was at her home in Saint-Raphael, in the South of France, that he first met Garbo on 18 September 1970, her 65th birthday. Green often stayed at Cécile's various abodes but if a visit from Garbo was expected, was always requested to leave before she arrived. This time he was invited to stay, and Green recalled how Garbo surprised him while he was alone in the living room, fixing drinks:

I heard a door open behind me. I assumed it was the butler. When I turned around, there was Garbo, about six inches away from me.

My jaw dropped and I stood there speechless. Garbo smiled. 'Mr Green, I've been so looking forward to meeting you,' she said, in that throaty voice of hers. 'I'm sure we're going to have the most wonderful time together.'[383]

The two apparently got along well, though it would take them several more months to meet again, at New York's Regency Hotel, and begin cementing the deep bond which formed between them. Garbo often stayed at Green's house in Cartagena, Colombia: alternatively they retreated to his cottage on Fire Island, the gay district. Green was one of the few allowed inside her apartment, yet despite their closeness they always addressed each other as 'Miss G' and 'Mr Green'. He was perhaps the nearest she had had to a factotum since Borg, although unlike Borg they were never amorously involved. Much of the time, when they were outdoors – on home territory and overseas – Green was there to protect her from 'customers', Garbo's term for intrusive fans and journalists.[384]

Garbo for her part would be close at hand to comfort Sam Green in November 1972, in the wake of the fallout from a rather messy affair when the heiress Barbara Baekeland was stabbed to death by her son, Antony, in her London apartment. A few years earlier, Green had had an affair with both Baekeland – an unbalanced, alcoholic former starlet – *and* her equally neurotic son, Antony, a gay man she had tried to 'cure' by procuring him prostitutes and, when this had failed, by having sex with him herself.[385]

In 1974, in what would be her final serious offer, Garbo's producer William Frye asked her to play herself in one of the first of a spate of so-called 'disaster' movies, *Airport 75*. The stars of the film were Charlton Heston and Karen Black. She considered the cameo for a few days, but the response was predictable and the part went to Gloria Swanson.

In fact, though she almost certainly never found out, Garbo *did* have a three-minute cameo in a film made that year. Though it may not be the regular Garbo fan's cup of tea, it is nevertheless important because it is her very last celluloid appearance. *Adam & Yves* was an XXX-rated gay pornographic feature, directed by Peter de Rome, and starring Marcus Giovanni and Michael Hardwick.

Obsessed with Garbo, de Rome's cameraman, Jack Devean, had filmed her through a telephoto lens on New York's First Avenue and this was incorporated into the story. The lovers are in a post-coital mood when Yves (Giovanni) recalls to Adam (Hardwick) the most thrilling moment of his life, apart from the sex which has just taken place, was bumping into his elusive icon. 'I saw *her*,' he says, 'I *really* saw her!' Then Garbo appears: wearing a trenchcoat and hat, she strides along pavement, pauses to chat to a passer-by, then crosses the street.

In February 1975, Garbo flew to Hollywood where she learned – before the news broke in the media – that Susan Hayward, who had always wanted to meet her, was dying of brain cancer. Garbo spent several hours at her bedside: Hayward died on 14 March. History repeated itself in 1984 with *Garbo Talks*, directed by Sidney Lumet. In this, a cantankerous matriarch (Anne Bancroft), obsessed with Garbo and also suffering an inoperable brain tumour, wants to meet her idol before she dies. Then there would be considerable speculation that the faceless woman who appears at the end of the film was Garbo herself, but in fact it was former silent star Betty Comden.

That July, Garbo visited Sweden for the last time. Her first outing here was a sombre one – to Lars Hansons' grave at Skogskyrkogården, accompanied by Mimi Pollak. She also spent a few days in Copenhagen, where she attended a recital at the Tivoli Gardens by the great Wagnerian soprano, Birgit Nilsson. Afterwards, she and Nilsson dined with friends and photographs of the event, taken against her will, were wired around the world and resulted in more offers of work, all turned down. There was also a brief reunion with Horke Wachtmeister, the last time Garbo would see or speak to her – she died in 1977.

Early in October, Sam Green's cousin, Henry McIlhenny, invited him to spend a week at his estate, Glenreagh Castle, in County Donegal, Ireland. Green took Garbo and Cécile de Rothschild with him, and some years later the playwright Frank McGuinness used the visit as a setting for his hit stage play, *Greta Garbo Came to Donegal*, which premiered at London's Tricycle Theatre in January 2010 with Caroline Lagerfelt in the role of Garbo.[386]

In the middle of the month, Garbo, Green and de Rothschild flew from Belfast to London, where they rented an apartment near Piccadilly for three weeks. While here, under extreme duress, Garbo agreed to pay Cecil Beaton a visit: the prissy photographer had suffered a stroke which left him confined to a wheelchair and virtually immobile and like Mercedes de Acosta, he was anxious to make his peace with her before he died. She and Green took the train from Waterloo, arriving at Salisbury just as it was getting dark, and continued the journey to Reddish House by taxi where, at the last moment she suffered a panic attack, believing this had been a set-up, and that Beaton had arranged for reporters to be hiding in the trees. Green calmed her down: the meeting with the man who duped her by selling her pictures to the press was emotional, and she agreed to stay the night, though she is said to have been 'repulsed' by watching him eat. The next morning, she paused in the hall and signed her name in his guestbook – one of the rare occasions when she actually *volunteered* her signature. Her sentiments, however, may have been questionable. The subject of her rejecting his marriage proposal must have been brought up at some time during the visit: according to Beaton's secretary, Eileen Hose, before leaving, Garbo turned to her and pronounced, 'Well, I couldn't have married him, could I? Him being like this!' Beaton lingered until 18 January 1980 when he died, shortly after his seventy-sixth birthday. As had happened with Mercedes, there were neither condolences nor flowers from Garbo.[387]

In the spring of 1976, Garbo flew to Antigua, where she stayed at the exclusive Gallery Bay Surf Club. The owner, Edee Holbert, took her request for 'intense security' literally, assigning a machete-wielding guard to stand outside her door at night and hiring her a jeep to drive around in. It was in Antigua that the press were introduced to her new *frangine*, her niece, Gray Reisfeld. Until this time, hardly any of Garbo's intimates had ever seen her and she is thought never to have spoken to anyone about her family. Similarly, Gray and her husband, Donald, had never let on that they were related to the most famous Hollywood star of them all. Sam Green later said that Garbo never expressed any great fondness for her family, which of course had been proved by her lack of response to the deaths of her mother and brother.[388]

The Antigua trip was manna from heaven for the photographer from *People* magazine who happened to be holidaying on the island, and who was less interested in the travelling companion than he was in training his telefoto lens on Garbo swimming and sunbathing in the nude and still looking good at seventy. This 'picture of health' was no longer evident later in the summer, however, when Garbo made her annual visit to Klosters and fell ill with bronchitis. Her doctors advised her to give up smoking – she was still getting through two packs a day, and trying to convince herself that they were doing her no harm because she had switched to a nicotine-free brand – but she refused. No sooner had she recovered than she developed a cancerous mole on her nose. This proved benign and was removed during a discreet trip to a clinic in Zurich.

In November 1977, Garbo was faced with a 'cancer' of another kind. Polish-born author Antoni Groniwicz (1913–85) had crossed swords with her in 1971 with the publication of his novel, *An Orange Full of Dreams*, which boasted a foreword by 'Greta Garbo'. She had had nothing to do with the book: therefore when she learned that Gronowicz had signed a contract with Simon & Schuster to publish her 'biography' – that he was claiming she had collaborated with him on this, Garbo declared him a fraud and hit him with an injunction, which he initially ignored. On 7 February 1978, she signed a sworn deposition before a judge, avowing that she had neither met nor spoken with Gronowicz, nor collaborated with or supplied the foreword to his book. Simon & Schuster opted not to publish the work during Garbo's lifetime.[389]

No sooner had Garbo recovered from this debacle than she learned that someone else was writing her life story – this time someone she *did* know. She had met British writer Frederick Sands by way of Salka Viertel during the summer of 1977. By his own admission, Sands was little more than an stalker and made no secret of the underhand method he adopted to con Garbo into confiding in him, using Salka and her rapidly declining health as a way of approaching the reclusive star. They met over afternoon tea at Salka's home, got along well, and when the time came to leave luck was on Sands' side – it was pouring with rain, he did not have an umbrella, and shared Garbo's while he escorted her across the road to her house. She loaned him the umbrella because his car was parked several streets away. Sands asked her if they could meet again, and the next morning he accompanied her on her walk.[390]

What Garbo did not know was that Sands had hired a photographer, Ekhard Nitsche, to trail them, and snap them discreetly through a telephoto lens. This way, the public would be given the impression – no matter how much Garbo denied this – that she and Sands were genuine friends. By the time of the pair's first of what would be several walks, Nitsche had already 'cased' the layout of the village, *and* Garbo's house. He subsequently photographed them at Lake Davos then, when Sands returned to his hotel room, he wrote down everything they had discussed. The writer also had a cohort, operating in Sweden: Sven Broman was a journalist and the editor of *Aret Runt* (Year Round), one of the country's biggest magazines. The result was *The Divine Garbo*, and she was all the more horrified because Sands and Broman had researched her largely undocumented childhood and youth by interviewing people she had known then. According to Irwin Shaw, Garbo acquired a copy of the book, showed it to a few friends, then burned it.[391]

Another pest who entered Garbo's life at this time was a Hawaiian-born paparazzi photographer named Ted Leyson, who began stepping out of the shadows only occasionally to snap her when she was least expecting it. Over the years, however, he became a nuisance – lingering outside her New York apartment for hours, sometimes days, waiting for her to emerge. 'That poor little man who's always lurking,' was how she referred to him. After being caught out a few times, she would always be ready for him, shielding her face with a newspaper, hat or tissue. As such, Leyson never took a single picture which was not blurred and at best mediocre. There were times when he made her life such an absolute misery that friends implored her to report him to the police, but she never did. Once, Leyson followed her for over an hour and to escape him she fled into a fruit store, where the owner asked her, 'Do you want me to cripple him with a baseball bat?' In 1987, Leyson boasted in an interview that she actually liked him, which one finds hard to believe:

Greta is my biggest challenge. I have to take care because if she sees me, she covers her face. She even tries to spot me in the reflection of shop windows. She's very smart. What I like is that no other photographer is following her as intensely as I. I always say this may be my last picture of Garbo because she's so old ... I love her. Some celebrities wither so soon as I catch their image in my lens, but not Greta. She's all mine.[392]

On 20 October 1978, Salka Viertel died at her home in Klosters, aged eighty-nine. She had been ill for some time, virtually uncommunicative during her final years, and almost certainly suffering from dementia when Garbo had last visited her. Even so, she had spent several hours of each day at Salka's bedside, reminiscing over times past, even though her friend had no longer been aware of her surroundings. There was another shock on 19 February 1981, when Garbo received a call informing her of the death of Sven Hugo Borg, aged eighty-four. Exactly seven months later, on 19 October, word came to her that Nils Asther had died, also aged eighty-four. 'Who knows, maybe I'll be the one to make it three in a row,' she told Roger Normand over the phone. 'Eighty-four is such a good age to go, don't you think?'[393]

In Paris, during the early eighties, Garbo discovered the delights of the Marais – the city's elegant gay quarter, where she and her escort could stroll the streets 'unmolested'. Sam Green recalls her saying the first time he accompanied her to the French capital, 'Let's go where the queens are. Someone once took me there – oh-la-la!' That 'someone' was Roger Normand, who one day took her to the Marché aux Puces, at Clignancourt. Here they visited the antiques market, where Garbo purchased a genuine Louis XV wardrobe. Roger explained:

I told her how hideous I thought it was, and that she would have to pay the same again to get the thing shipped out to America. Then she said, 'Oh, I didn't buy it for me. I saw the little cupboard you had in your place, so I bought it for you!' The last time I went to see my godfather, in 1999 just before he died, 'Garbo's wardrobe' was still taking up almost an entire wall in his tiny Avenue Rachel apartment.

Garbo liked to visit because it was just yards from the Montmartre Cemetery, where she sometimes liked to go walking.[394] [395]

On 2 November 1983, King Carl XVI Gustav of Sweden awarded Garbo the *Nordstjärneorden* (Commander of the Order of the Polar Star), one of the country's most prestigious titles, created by Frederick I in 1748, and largely restricted to members of the royal family. The award was presented to her at the New York apartment of her friend, Jane Gunther, by Wilhelm Wachtmeister, the Swedish Ambassador to the United States and a distant relative of Horke.

In January 1984, a routine hospital check-up revealed breast cancer and a partial mastectomy was performed at a New York clinic. Three months later and after further treatment, doctors gave Garbo the all-clear. She had few ambitions left in her last years, apart from living as long and in as reasonably good health as was possible, and without being a burden to others. Most of the retainers, good and bad, were gone and towards the end of the year she learned that 89-year-old Gayelord Hauser was seriously ill with pneumonia. Frey Brown had died in 1977, since which time Hauser had deteriorated rapidly. Garbo spent Christmas with him, and she was at his bedside when he died on Boxing Day. Though she did not attend his funeral in Beverly Hills, it was she who organised it.

In Klosters during the summer of 1985, Garbo met her very last 'confidant'. Sven Broman, holidaying in the resort with his wife, had co-authored *The Divine Garbo* with Frederick Sands, which makes her wanting anything to do with him all the more bizarre. According to Broman, after getting to know him better she forgave him for what he called 'this mistake of my youth'. Broman was also her last link with her homeland – much of the time they spoke only Swedish. Over the next five years they met as often as her failing health permitted – when she stopped visiting Klosters, they 'hooked up' in New York.

Though it did not end completely, Garbo's friendship with Cécile de Rothschild took a tumble on 18 September of that year, the occasion being her eightieth birthday and the party thrown by Cécile at her brother's vineyard home, the Château Mouton in France's Médoc region. Garbo was told this was to be a quiet, intimate affair – just a handful of friends. As she entered the salon, to the cries of 'Surprise!', to her horror she discovered over a hundred people, all complete strangers, and over fifty members of the press. Rather than flee, she 'suffered a martyrdom through nine courses' – Cécile's one redeeming act having been that no cameras were allowed in the room. The incident destroyed Garbo's trust: though she spoke every now and then to Cécile on the phone, she refused ever to see her again.

Garbo was therefore in no mood for what happened next with Sam Green, who during the space of a brief telephone conversation found himself transformed from best friend to treacherous foe. There had been a 'scare' in 1978 when, after a trip to Green's house in Colombia, a piece appeared in the *New York Post*'s 'Suzy's Column' hinting that she and Green were more than just friends. Garbo had taken much convincing by Green that he had not spoken about her to the press. The feature penned by Leon Wagener in the 29 October issue of the *Globe* convinced her otherwise:

> GARBO TO WED AT 80! Sources close to the couple say that the aging screen legend and Sam Green, thirty years her junior and who has been her constant companion for over a decade, will be wed at Christmas in Paris – at the home of Baroness Cecil [sic] de Rothschild, an old friend ... When she is with Sam, she has no fear of the photographers who have hounded her since her retirement [sic] in 1928. She's terrified if she's alone, but with him, it's a joke. They laugh and run like kids. Also, she has decided that she does not want to spend the rest of her years alone, sad and lonely.[396]

Green maintained that the news of their 'engagement' had been leaked by a disgruntled former secretary, Bart Gorin. Not that it made much difference for Garbo found out that Green had been recording their telephone conversations – worse than this, that he had played a tape of one of these to friends at a party. Green called her and attempted to explain, and when he asked her what he should do next, she responded abruptly, 'Hang up!' They never spoke again.

It was at around this time that I met Garbo for the one and only time: under an awning outside a Paris theatre in the pouring rain. The occasion was a performance of *Lily Passion*, an intense musical drama featuring Barbara (Monique Serf, 1930–97), France's most famous singer after Edith Piaf, and one of my closest friends. Indeed, because of her mystique and intensely private life, Barbara was known as '*La Garbo de la Chanson*'. The piece told the story of the singer who falls for the Ripper-style thug, David (Gérard Depardieu) who, each time he hears her sing, stabs a woman to death! The piece ended with her achieving her greatest ambition – being killed by David after giving the greatest performance of her career.

After the show, Barbara came up to us in her dressing room and whispered in my ear, 'There's an old lady standing outside the side-door. It's Greta Garbo and she wants to talk to you. Whatever you do, don't breathe a word to anyone!' Though it was dark outside, Garbo was wearing shades. She had on a trench coat, men's brogues, a purple scarf was wrapped several times around her neck – and she was wearing gloves of different colours. I smoked in those days, and offered her a *Gitane*, which she politely refused. Then she indicated my camera, which I instinctively shoved into the bag I was carrying. This seemed to relax her. Looking me in the eye, she pronounced in a voice almost a whole octave lower than the one I had heard in her films, 'You don't *look* like a killer to me!' To explain, Barbara had used me as a basis for her knife-mad thug in the play because, she said, David was not a name one usually associates with killers, and because the psychopaths she had read about were invariably dark-haired, never blond! It was a back-handed compliment, which I proudly accepted. Throughout our ten-minute conversation, Garbo and I talked only about Barbara – how much she admired her, how she loved her theme-song, 'Ma Plus Belle Histoire D'Amour', what a 'strapping fellow' Depardieu was. Then she extended her hand, signalling that it was time to say goodbye: 'Well, mister, it was good meeting you!' I kissed her on both cheeks, and that was that. My wife and I went back into the theatre, and ten minutes later, the news of Garbo's presence having been leaked, I was approached by one of the reporters who had been there to interview Barbara. What had Garbo's face looked like? How had she sounded? What kind of a handshake did she have? Had she talked about her movies? On and on he went – and I said nothing. It had been our moment, one I did not wish to share.

In March 1987, Garbo tripped over a vacuum cleaner in her apartment, and badly sprained her ankle. This put paid to her daily walks for a while, and she never really recovered – henceforth she would almost always walk with a cane. In April 1988, Sweden's King Gustav XVI and Queen Sofia made a state visit to New York, and naturally wanted to meet their country's most famous export. The meeting took place at Garbo's apartment, with no press present. Soon afterwards she 'severed her ties' with her homeland in a letter to Mimi Pollak, now eighty-seven and herself ailing. Pollak never revealed what her friend had written, only that the tone of the letter was loving, and closed with the promise that there would be no more.

That August, at Klosters, Garbo suffered what is thought to have been a mild heart attack, which she laughed off as acute indigestion. There would be no more trips to Switzerland. On 5 January 1989, she was admitted to the New York Hospital, in severe pain. Doctors diagnosed kidney failure, but she refused further treatment and after an overnight stay returned to her apartment, where over the next few months she received twice-daily visits from a private nurse. Her condition worsened: she developed diverticulitis and became so ill that she could barely keep anything down. In May she began a thrice-weekly course of dialysis at the Rogin Institute. Claire Koger, who until now had adhered to a strict nine-till-five routine, began spending the night at the apartment – if she could not stay, Gray Reisfield took her place.

On 14 September, four days before what would be Garbo's last birthday, Valentina Schlee died of Parkinson's Disease in 'the apartment upstairs', aged ninety. Surprisingly, considering they had avoided each other for years, extant of the hard stares if they crossed paths in the foyer, Garbo was upset. Acutely aware of her own mortality, she told Sven Broman,

People learn to accept death. If you live in good health, then you have not been trained nor made ready for death ... I often think about death. I really wish I could believe, but I can't. For me, it's over when it ends. Maybe I am too prosaic. And yet I do feel that life has been good in my old age.[397]

On 9 February 1990, in tremendous pain though desperately trying not to show it, Garbo spent the afternoon at Katharine Hepburn's house, reminiscing over old times with the actress who had had a crush on her all those years ago. There were few outings after this. She was last seen walking, leaning heavily on Gray Reisfield's arm, on 1 April. Ten days later, with a raging fever, she was admitted to the New York Hospital. The pesky Ted Leyson was lurking in the shadows opposite her apartment when she left for the last time – he reached the hospital before she did, and his last pictures prove what a reprehensible human being he was. In each shot, Garbo positively glares at him.

No sooner had Garbo been settled into her private suite than her condition worsened and she developed pneumonia. She, who had longed for solitude almost her whole life, was not left alone for a single moment as the Reisfields kept a vigil at her bedside. The end came peacefully. At 11.30 on the morning of 15 April, Easter Sunday, the greatest movie star the world has ever known slipped away.

EPILOGUE

Garbo was eighty-four. Just how her 'rival' Marlene Dietrich found out before the news made the press, I shall never know. At 12.15 a.m. I received a call from Paris. 'That other woman is dead!' Marlene boomed, and promptly hung up.

Within hours of her death, Garbo's body was taken to the Garden State Crematorium in New Jersey, cremated at once, and her ashes placed in storage until the Reisfields decided what to do with them. (After a lengthy legal battle, in 1999 they would be interred at Skogskyrkogården, not far from Lars Hanson's final resting place.) On 17 April, a memorial service was held at Campbell's Funeral Home, in New York, attended by family and close friends.

Garbo had signed her will on 2 March 1984. Aside from a few small bequests – these included the doormen at the apartment block who had escorted her to and from the elevator and kept unwelcome intruders at bay, and the faithful Claire Koger, who was also left an annuity – she left her entire fortune to Gray Reisfield. As much of her real estate – including several shops along the fashionable Rodeo Drive – had been sold off years before, this mostly amounted to paintings and antiques. The sale which took place at Sotheby's on 13 November raised just under $20 million – her two Renoirs alone fetching over half of this. Garbo's 'nick-nacks' brought in over $1 million – candlesticks, ornaments, lamps and clocks and other paraphernalia probably worth only a few hundred dollars each sold for several thousand simply because they had belonged to her. Additionally there was a wealth of stocks and shares – Time Warner, Texaco, General Motors, Eastman Kodak, and the Federal Farm Credit Bank figured among her major holdings, but there were many more, bringing the total to around $8 million. Garbo's bank accounts contained around $650,000. She had set up a number of trust funds, but to whom and for how much has never been revealed by her estate.[398]

Some resented Garbo leaving everything to a niece she appeared to have grown close to only later in life – though it must be said that Gray Reisfield had been her rock during her last years. Anthony Palermo, Gayelord Hauser's former business partner who handled her financial affairs, and who claimed that *he* had been the one to persuade her to have dialysis treatment, was peeved not to have been left one cent and complained, 'I worked for her for fourteen years, for nothing because I was promised to be in the will.'[399]

A clause in Garbo's will stipulated that no claims would be considered by relatives extant of Gray and her children. In March 1984 she was thinking specifically of Sven Gustaffson Jr, but he died in 1988 and a subsequent codicil was added citing a new name, Ake Fredriksson, her brother Sven's love-child, the result of a liaison with a maid at Stockholm's Grand Hotel in 1926. Frederiksson, who lived in Oxelösund, contested the will in the most hostile manner, declaring Garbo had been 'unsound of mind' and 'prone to alcohol-related episodes' when she had signed it – also, that Gray Reisfield had manipulated her aunt into bequeathing everything to her. His claim was quickly dismissed.

The tributes and eulogies were legion. Some were syrupy and long-winded, others offered retrospectives of Garbo's long life and comparatively brief career – extant of the early Swedish shorts and *Peter the Tramp*, just sixteen of her eighty-four years. The *New York Times* called her, 'The Screen's Greatest Sufferer'. *The Sun*, more used to reporting the more scandalous episodes in a deceased star's life, made an exception with Garbo. Their headline ran, 'GOD, SHE WAS GORGEOUS!' – and accompanying the moving script was a cartoon, Garbo floating on a cloud outside the gates of heaven. The caption was, 'SHE STILL VANTS TO BE ALONE!'

The *Daily News* observed, 'Hers was a myth made by machine, but man's imagination took it from there to dizzying heights.' Bette Davis, who regretted never having worked with Garbo, despite the fact that she would have eclipsed even her on the screen, said, 'Her instinct, her mastery over the machine was pure witchcraft. I cannot analyse this woman's acting. I only know that no one else so effectively worked in front of a camera.'

Garbo is unique, and will never be replaced. Not one actress has come close to surpassing her, nor ever will. Such was the depth of emotion within her performances that cinema-goers could see into her soul, a power that the years and modern movie techniques, where special effects all too frequently replace acting ability, have not diminished whether one is watching Garbo on a fifty-foot screen, a front room television set, or one's laptop computer.

For many who did not witness her clomping through the streets of New York, or one of her social gatherings, Garbo is not dead: she simply disappeared from view in 1941, vanishing into a cloud of mystery to leave an electrifying spirit that will live on forever.

NOTES

Chapter One

1 The family name. Some biographers insist this was spelt 'Gustafson'. In early Swedish playbills it is frequently printed 'Gustavson'. However, it is spelt 'Gustaffson' on Garbo's birth certificate and employment contract for PUB (which she signed) and on her father's death certificate – therefore it is spelt thus throughout this book.

2 This photograph of Karl Alfred Gustaffson appears in Alexander Walker, *Garbo* (Weidenfeld & Nicolson: 1980).

3 'I was born…': Garbo interview (unedited), Ruth Biery, 31 December 1927.

4 'When just a baby…': Biery, ibid.

5 'I found my greatest…':Garbo interview, Lars Saxon, March 1931.

6 'In a small courtyard…': Peter Joel, 'The First True Story Of Greta Garbo's Childhood', *Screen Book*, 1933.

7 John Bainbridge, *Garbo* (Doubleday: 1955).

8 'I hated school…': Saxon, ibid.

9 'I would smell the greasepaint…': Biery, ibid.

10 'We are on a sandy beach…': Elizabeth Malcolm, *Motion Picture*, June 1932.

11 'My father would be sitting…': Saxon, ibid.

12 'Before the whole class…': Kaj Gynt, to Adela Rogers St Johns (unedited), *Liberty*, summer 1934.

13 'I saw two men fighting…': Biery, ibid.

14 'Unless the studios…': Elizabeth Malcolm, ibid.

15 Quoted in Barry Paris, *Garbo: A Biography* (Sidgwick & Jackson: 1995).

16 'It was a slip of a girl…': Garbo to Roger Normand, 1970.

17 'There was only sobbing…': Saxon, ibid.

18 'I was the youngest…': Saxon, ibid.

19 'One thing you must tell me…': Fritiof Billquist, *Garbo* (Putman: 1960).

20 'Well, so you promise…': Billquist, ibid.

21 Tin Andersén Axell, *Djavla Alskade Unge!*, 2005.

22 *Hatter For Dammer Och Flickor*, PUB Catalogue, March 1921, p.109.

23 'I was really…': Ake Sundborg, 'That Gustafsson Girl', *Photoplay*, April–May 1930.

24 Though Garbo appeared in the Brunius films *before* the PUB short, this was the first to be released.

25 Paris, ibid., p.28, footnote. There may have been a short, English title, *From Top to Toe*, made to celebrate PUB's 40th anniversary. This had Greta 'as one of the daughters in the story of a family whose house burned down and then who visit PUB to replace their lost clothing'.

26 As related to Vera Schmiterlow, quoted in Sven Broman, *Garbo on Garbo* (Bloomsbury: 1990).

27 'As beautiful as…': Billquist, ibid.

28 'They look…': Billquist, ibid.

29 Saxon, ibid.

30 Billquist, ibid.

31 'As we others…': Billquist, ibid.

32 'She was a very…': Bainbridge, ibid.

33 'The fact that her…': Enwall, speaking with reference to Greta's in-house interpretation of *Madame Sans-Géne*, quoted in Walker, ibid.

34 'All I could see was…': Biery, ibid.

35 'To read some of…': Walker, ibid.

36 'Though I do not…': Normand, ibid.

37 Andersén Axell, ibid.

38 This photograph appears in Sven Broman & Frederick Sands, *The Divine Garbo* (Grosset & Dunlap: 1969).

39 Mimi Pollak, Swedish TV interview, 1993.

40 'In the classroom…': Bainbridge, ibid.

41 'Though American bathing…': *Swing*, December 1922.

Chapter Two

42 'Stiller was ugly…': Sven Hugo Borg, 'The Private Life Of Greta Garbo' (unedited), *Film Pictorial* 1933.

43 'Stiller's subtextual coming-out…': Mark Finch, *European Gay Review*.

44 'Then I knew…': Garbo interview (unedited), Ruth Biery, 31 December 1927.

45 'My dear Miss Gustafsson…': Robert Payne, *The Great Garbo* (WH Allen: 1976).

46 'Greta had a beautiful…': Sven Broman & Frederick Sands, *The Divine Garbo* (Grosset & Dunlap: 1969).

47 Fritiof Billquist, *Garbo* (Putman: 1960).

48 'She's shy…': Payne, ibid.

49 John Bainbridge, *Garbo* (Doubleday: 1955).

50 The new 'husband', Paris, 250, quoted by David Diamond.

51 'She's still inexperienced…': Alexander Walker, *Garbo* (Weidenfeld & Nicolson: 1980).

52 'Acting in front of…': Inga Gaate, *Filmjournalen*.
53 'I'm finding it…': Ibid.
54 'She has the most amazing…': Biery, ibid.
55 'I'm burning…': Payne, ibid.
56 'There he was, roaring…': Gaate, ibid.
57 'I went away…': Biery, ibid.
58 'What are these…': Ake Sundborg, 'That Gustafsson Girl' (unedited), *Photoplay*, 1930.
59 'The smell of…': Biery, ibid.
60 'She would walk…': Roger Normand to author.
61 'Berlin received us…': Sundborg, ibid.
62 In 2003, Gustaf Sobin penned a fictitious account of Garbo and Stiller's trip to Constantinople, *In Pursuit of a Vanishing Star*.
63 'Look at that girl…': Leatrice Gilbert Fountain & John R. Maxim, *The Dark Star* (St Martin's Press: 1985).
64 'Mr Mayer hardly…': Sundborg, ibid.
65 'The Turks…': Biery, ibid.
66 'I was terribly…': Mercedes de Acosta, *Here Lies the Heart* (André Deutsch: 1960).
67 Hugo Vickers, *Loving Garbo* (Jonathan Cape: 1994).
68 Marlene Dietrich and Roger Normand to author.
69 'In two days…': Billquist, ibid.
70 'Gentlemen, in consideration…': MGM archives, dated 31 January 1925, in Walker, ibid.
71 Axel Dotti and Fernand Lumbruso to author.
72 Gideon Bachman & Marc Sorkin, 'G. W. Pabst', *Cinemages*, 1955.
73 Walker, ibid.; Michael Conway, Dion McGregor & Mark Ricci, *The Films Of Greta Garbo* (Citadel Press: 1968); Diana McLellan, *The Girls: Sappho Goes To Hollywood* (St Martin's Press: 2000); and most importantly, Marlene Dietrich herself – all maintain she was in the film, though studying the two scenes should be proof enough.
74 'Of course…': Marlene Dietrich to author.
75 Paul Rotha & Richard Griffith, *The Film Till Now* (Spring Books: 1967).
76 'A pretty dingy lot…': *Variety*, 1927.

Chapter Three

77 'Both Mother…': Garbo interview, Lars Saxon, March 1931.
78 'Welcome to New York…': Hubert Voight, 'I Loved Garbo' (unedited) *New Movie Magazine*, 1934.
79 'I want to go…': Adele Whitely Fletcher, *Motion Picture*, July 1925.
80 'She was in…': Kaj Gynt to Adela Rogers St Johns (unedited), *Liberty*, summer 1934.
81 Rolf Laven to Sven Hugo Borg, 'The Private Life of Greta Garbo' (unedited), *Film Pictorial*, 1933.

82   'He no flamenco...': Darwin Porter, *The Secret Life of Humphrey Bogart* (Blood Moon), 2003.
83   Larry Engelmann, 'Little Garbo', *The American Way*, October 1988.
84   Rolf Laven to Sven Hugo Borg, ibid.
85   The full photograph, comprising Garbo and nineteen others, appears in Alexander Walker, *Garbo* (Weidenfeld & Nicolson: 1980). He describes it as 'more like a wedding party than a reception committee'.
86   'Her shoes...': Robert Payne, *The Great Garbo* (WH Allen: 1976).
87   'God, how I hate...': Letter to an unspecified recipient, possibly Pollak or Schmiterlow, in Fritiof Billquist, *Garbo* (Putman: 1960).
88   John Bainbridge, *Garbo* (Doubleday: 1955).
89   'They were a melancholy...': Bainbridge, ibid.
90   'Don't take...': Sven Broman, *Garbo on Garbo* (Bloomsbury: 1990).
91   Ake Sundborg, 'That Gustafsson Girl' (unedited), *Photoplay*, 1930.
92   *Photoplay*, November 1925.
93   'I was delighted...': Borg, ibid.
94   'Let him haff it, Borg...': Borg, ibid.
95   'I didn't create...': Charles Higham, *Hollywood Cameramen*, 1970.
96   'Miss Garbo...': Billquist, ibid.
97   'This girl has...': *Variety*, February 1926.
98   *Pictures*, February 1926.
99   *Motion Picture*, February 1926.
100 'The public...': Billquist, ibid.

Chapter Four

101 Alexander Walker, *Garbo* (Weidenfeld & Nicolson: 1980).
102 'It was the act...': Sven Hugo Borg, 'The Private Life of Greta Garbo' (unedited), *Film Pictorial*, 1933.
103 'It almost makes...': Fritiof Billquist, *Garbo* (Putman: 1960).
104 Barry Paris, *Garbo: A Biography* (Sidgwick & Jackson: 1995). According to Paris, Garbo's niece, Gray Reisfield, suggested cancer as a cause of death, but there is nothing to suggest this is anything other than hearsay – this also applies to Reisfield's claim that the cancer was 'aggravated by a blow to the chest from an abusive boyfriend'.
105 Ake Sundborg, 'That Gustafsson Girl' (unedited), *Photoplay*, 1930.
106 'Don't forget...': Garbo interview, Lars Saxon, March 1931.
107 'I think I should...': Letter of 12 July 1926, quoted in Walker, ibid.
108 'Borg, people...': Borg, ibid.
109 'She was still...': John Bainbridge, *Garbo* (Doubleday: 1955).
110 'Borg, that girl...': Borg, ibid.
111 'I am so tired...': Billquist, ibid.
112 'Terrible...': Saxon, ibid.
113 Press reviews, October 1926.

114   Kevin Brownlow, *The Parade's Gone By* (Ballantyne: 1969).
115   'Always the vamp…': Borg, ibid.
116   Leatrice Gilbert Fountain & John R. Maxim, *The Dark Star* (St Martin's Press: 1985).
117   'You are hereby…': Letter quoted in Walker, ibid.
118   'It was love…': Billquist, ibid.
119   'Some instant…': Borg, ibid.
120   'I don't know…': Sundborg, ibid.
121   'Garbo is marvellous…': Bainbridge, ibid.
122   'If I needed…': Adela Rogers St Johns (unedited), *Liberty*, summer 1934.
123   'Garbo was never…': Ibid.
124   'I suppose you have read…': Bainbridge, ibid., and Sven Broman, *Garbo on Garbo* (Bloomsbury: 1990). Bainbridge offers no date for the letter, part of a longer missive to Saxon; Broman includes more, but omits the section quoted by Bainbridge and offers November 1926, which in view of Garbo's reference to Christmas would appear correct. This confirms that, despite being jilted, the press were reporting that Gilbert still wanted to marry her.
125   Fountain, ibid. The earlier biographies (Payne, Bainbridge, Billquist) do not refer to the wedding or incident at all. One biographer (Mark A. Vieira, *Greta Garbo: A Cinematic Legacy* (Harry N. Abrams: 2005), p.274) suggests no double wedding was ever planned, and that Boardman's account of the incident remains 'questionable'. He further suggests Boardman was jealous of Garbo's success at a time when her own career was a standstill. He concludes, referring to Boardman's known anti-Semitism, 'Besides wanting to malign Garbo with her story, Boardman was also eager to get at Mayer, who had never been particularly helpful to her or Vidor … This might explain why a long-retired movie actress might have unkind stories to tell about the most successful Jewish executive in movie history.'
126   'She shows…': *National Board of Review Magazine*, 1927.
127   Walker, ibid.
128   'You can see…': Vitto Russo, *The Celluloid Closet: Homosexuality in the Movies* (Harper & Row: 1981).
129   'Here is a picture…': *Variety*, February 1927.
130   'Never before…': *New York Herald Tribune*, February 1927.
131   'In *The Flesh and the Devil*…': Jim Tully, *Vanity Fair*, May 1928.
132   'What do you do…': Billquist, ibid.

Chapter Five
133   'Jack wanted…': John Bainbridge, *Garbo* (Doubleday: 1955).
134   *Women Love Diamonds*, directed by Edmund Golding, was re-cast with Pauline Starke, Douglas Fairbanks Jr and Lionel Barrymore. It proved a costly flop.

135 'You have disobeyed…': Alexander Walker, *Garbo* (Weidenfeld & Nicolson: 1980).

136 'The difficulties…': Walker, ibid.

137 'Had I been employed…': Sven Hugo Borg, 'The Private Life of Greta Garbo' (unedited), *Film Pictorial*, 1933.

138 'An author…': Norman Zierold, *Garbo* (Stein & Day: 1969).

139 'She hates…': Zierold, quoting Adela Rogers St Johns, ibid.

140 'Garbo's face…': Borg, ibid.

141 'He became convinced…': Ake Sundborg, 'That Gustafsson Girl' (unedited), *Photoplay*, 1930.

142 'Gott…': Rilla Page Palmborg, *The Private Life of Greta Garbo* (Doubleday: 1931).

143 Agnes Smith, 'Up Speaks A Gallant Loser!', *Photoplay*, February 1927.

144 'When in sheer...' Adela Rogers St Johns, ibid.

145 Leatrice Gilbert Fountain & John R. Maxim, *The Dark Star* (St Martin's Press: 1985).

146 Howard Dietz, *Dancing in the Dark* (Quadrangle: 1974).

147 'I know you are not acting…': Borg, ibid.

148 'When I first…': *Liberty*.

149 Karen Swenson, *Greta Garbo: A Life Apart* (Simon & Schuster: 1997).

150 'Mr Behrman said…': Mark A. Vieira, *Greta Garbo: A Cinematic Legacy* (Harry N. Abrams: 2005), Source Notes, p.275, 'Notes between Mr Behrman and Mr Davidson,' unpublished transcript.

151 'Pre-Raphaelite sensuality…': Richard Corliss, *Garbo* (Pyramid: 1974).

152 Walker, ibid.

153 'Miss Garbo may lift…': Mordaunt Hall, *New York Times*, December 1927.

154 'Lovers of Tolstoy…': *Motion Picture*, January 1928.

155 'Peculiar combination…': *Variety*, January 1928.

Chapter Six

156 'I will be very frank…': Rilla Page Palmborg, *The Private Life of Greta Garbo* (Doubleday: 1931).

157 'We insist…': Harriette Underhill, *New York Times*, September 1927.

158 'This picture is a huge…': Delight Evans, *Screenland*, October 1927.

159 'I am leaving…': Letter quoted in Karen Swenson, *Greta Garbo: A Life Apart* (Simon & Schuster: 1997).

160 'Let's not talk…': Garbo interview (unedited), Ruth Biery, 31 December 1927.

161 Biery, ibid.

162 'I do not like…': Biery, Ruth: *The Greta Garbo Story*, *Photoplay*, 3 segments, April–June 1928.

163 Biery, ibid.

164 'Her natural aloofness…': Howard Gutner, *Gowns by Adrian* (Abrams: 2000).

165 Press reviews, August 1928.

166 Thalberg's first choice was *The Woman of Affairs*, but the single word change was forced when a scriptwriter named Maxine Alton submitted a treatment bearing this title to a rival studio, who then threatened MGM with legal action.

167 Jerry Vermilye, *Films of the Twenties* (Citadel: 1985).

168 Press reviews, January 1929.

169 'She puts in…': Palmborg, ibid. Lilyan Tashman's affairs are detailed in Lillian Faderman & Stuart Timmons, *Gay LA: A History of Sexual Outlaws, Power Politics & Lipstick Lesbians* (Basic Books: 2006).

170 Swenson, ibid.

171 'Sex is the meat…': *Variety*, April 1929.

172 Victor Sjöström, *Classics of the Swedish Cinema*, SFI, 1951.

173 'Dear Greta…': Alexander Walker, *Garbo* (Weidenfeld & Nicolson: 1980).

174 'After Moje died…': Ake Sundborg, 'That Gustafsson Girl' (unedited), *Photoplay*, 1930.

175 'Stiller's death…': *Liberty*, ibid.

176 'I just think how…': Fritiof Billquist, *Garbo* (Putman: 1960).

177 'Oh, Miss Garbo…': Mark A. Vieira, *Greta Garbo: A Cinematic Legacy* (Harry N. Abrams: 2005).

178 'Return, or great loss…': Walker, ibid.

179 Prince Sigvard. In 1934, upon his marriage to a commoner, he lost his title and right to succession. Later a successful industrial designer, he became Count Bernadotte of Wisborg in 1951.

180 Interview on board the *Kungsholm*, 16 December 1928. The order of the questions is not known: this account is taken from Billquist and various newspaper reports.

181 'I am unspeakably…': Sundborg, ibid.

182 'Look, Lucretia…': Billquist, ibid.

183 'What kind of sailor…': John Bainbridge, *Garbo* (Doubleday: 1955).

184 'After this, Greta would…': Bainbridge, ibid.

185 'I am so popular…': Hubert Voight, 'I Loved Garbo' (unedited), *New Movie Magazine*, 1934.

186 'I saw a new…': Voight, ibid.

Chapter Seven

187 'You are a very foolish…': St Johns, ibid.

188 Leatrice Gilbert Fountain & John R. Maxim, *The Dark Star* (St Martin's Press: 1985).

189 'For the first time…': Pare Lorenz, *Judge*, July 1929.

190 'What some girls…': *Variety*, August 1929.

191 John Bainbridge, *Garbo* (Doubleday: 1955).

192 Lenore Coffee, *Confessions of a Hollywood Screenwriter* (Cassell: 1973).

193 'I am rather like…': *Picture Show*, October 1935.

194 Karen Swenson, *Greta Garbo: A Life Apart* (Simon & Schuster: 1997).

195 'I didn't want…': Barry Paris, *Garbo: A Biography* (Sidgwick & Jackson: 1995).

196 'Why are people…' Garbo, writing for *Liberty*, ibid.

197 'Just the thing…': John Bainbridge, *Garbo* (Doubleday: 1955).

198 'Fruit juice…': Alexander Walker, *Garbo* (Weidenfeld & Nicolson: 1980).

199 'There is no doubt…': Rilla Page Palmborg, *The Private Life of Greta Garbo* (Doubleday: 1931).

200 Press reviews, November 1929.

201 'As she rose…': Clarence Sinclair Bull & Raymond Lee, *Faces of Hollywood* (A. S. Barnes: 1968).

202 'If you really…': Sven Broman & Frederick Sands, *The Divine Garbo* (Grosset & Dunlap: 1969).

203 'You know…': Bainbridge, ibid.

204 Fritiof Billquist, *Garbo* (Putman: 1960).

205 'I must sit…': Bainbridge, ibid.

206 'Gaily…': Salka Viertel, *The Kindness of Strangers* (Holt, Rinehart & Winston: 1969).

207 'If any voice…': Mordaunt Hall, *New York Times*, December 1927.

208 'Greta works almost…': Paul Hawkins, 'A New Slant On Garbo', *Screenland*, June 1931.

209 'Suddenly it…': Anon, 'The Day That Garbo Dreaded', *Sunday Express*, June 1955.

210 'Her voice is…': *New York Herald Tribune*, January 1930.

211 'Whether she is dealing…': *New York Times*, January 1930.

212 'The voice that shook the world!', *Picture Play*, February 1930.

Chapter Eight

213 'She knew…': Dietrich to author.

214 'If I had the dynamic…': Fritiof Billquist, *Garbo* (Putman: 1960).

215 'Garbo is lonely…': Marie Dressler, *My Own Story* (Little Brown: 1934).

216 'Greta Garbo and Fifi d'Orsay…': *Los Angeles Record*, February 1930. Some sources suggest that the piece was 'planted' by someone at MGM who wanted the too-talkative Fifi out of Garbo's hair so that her future career would be unblighted by such rumours; others (Diana McLellan, *The Girls: Sappho Goes To Hollywood*, St Martin's Press: 2000) that it was the work of a jealous Salka Viertel, who wanted Garbo all to herself. The latter may be unlikely, since most Americans were aware of what lesbians did in private – following the

     recent (1928) publication of Radclyffe Hall's *The Well of Loneliness* – that any studio would wish to 'out' one of its major stars.

217 'Fifi was young…': Biery, Ruth: 'Hollywood's Cruelty to Greta Garbo', *Photoplay*, January 1932.

218 'Most of ze…': *Los Angeles Record*, June 1930.

219 Press reviews, August 1930.

220 'She was always…': Gustav Norin quoted in Rilla Page Palmborg, *The Private Life of Greta Garbo* (Doubleday: 1931).

221 'I'm not interested in…': Norman Zierold, *Garbo* (Stein & Day: 1969).

222 'I'd have the…': Katherine Albert, 'Did Brown And Garbo Fight?' *Photoplay*, March 1931.

223 Press reviews, February 1931.

224 'It is as if the…': Norbert Lusk, *Playbill*, November 1930.

225 'There is a definite…': Louella Parsons, *Herald Examiner*, November 1930.

226 'If Garbo retires…': *Motion Picture Classic*, April 1931.

227 Marlene Dietrich to author.

228 'He's a tall, limp…': *Photoplay*, April 1931.

229 'Brown is through…': *Los Angeles Record*, March 1931.

230 'Said Clarence Brown…': Katherine Albert, *Photoplay*, March 1931.

231 'Why does she always…': Hannen Swaffer, 'Hannen Swaffer indicts Garbo', *Picturegoer*, February 1932; other press reviews, October 1931.

232 'The smug…': Ruth Morris, *Variety*, December 1931.

233 'Women love dirt…': *Variety*, June 1931.

234 'If that woman…': Marlene Dietrich to author.

235 'What is one…': Martin Greif, *Gay Book of Days* (Main Street Press: 1982).

236 'As we shook…': Mercedes de Acosta, *Here Lies the Heart* (André Deutsch: 1960).

237 Ibid.

238 'That's how he got…': Mistinguett to Roger Normand.

239 'Her emotional…': Ralph Wheelright, 'When Nordic Met Latin', *Photoplay*, February 1932.

240 'She needed…': Ibid.

241 Press reviews, December 1931 and January 1932.

Chapter Nine

242 'I just wanted…': Joan Crawford to John Springer, April 1973.

243 'I was on the top…': Joan Crawford, *My Way of Life* (Simon & Schuster: 1971).

244 'Is Garbo Going Home…': *Movie Mirror*, December 1931.

245 'One day in April…': Rilla Page Palmborg, *The Private Life of Greta Garbo* (Doubleday: 1931).

246 'Would Miss Cornell…': Katharine Cornell, *I Wanted to Be an Actress* (Random House: 1938).

247 'Garbo will be forgotten...': Clare Boothe Luce, *Vanity Fair*, February 1932.

248 'My wife and I...': Gene Fowler: *Good Night, Sweet Prince* (Viking: 1944).

249 Press reviews, April 1932.

250 'Miss Leontovich...': Canfield, ibid.

251 'I never knew...': Robert Payne, *The Great Garbo* (WH Allen: 1976).

252 'I was very surprised...': Thomas Quinn Curtiss, *Von Stroheim* (Farrar, Straus & Giroux: 1971).

253 Marianne Oswald was the singer with whom Garbo had an affair while in Berlin. Damia (Marie-Louise Damien, 1889–1978) was generally regarded as the greatest of all the *chanteuse-réalistes*, pre-Piaf. The bell-necked top that Garbo wears in *As You Desire Me* was later adopted by Piaf's successor, Barbara (Monique Serf, 1930–97). Zarah Leander (1907–81) remains Sweden's greatest all-round entertainer.

254 'Miss Garbo has not...': *Hollywood Reporter*, July 1932.

255 'Why speak...': *Los Angeles Herald*, July 1932.

256 'From aboard...': *Daily News*, July 1932.

257 'President Hoover...': Unknown quote, August 1932, in Fritiof Billquist, *Garbo* (Putman: 1960).

258 'I don't dislike...': Gotheberg Customs House, August 1932.

259 'Isn't there some neat...': Billquist, ibid.

260 'She came...': Damia to author, 1974.

261 'One of the most lurid...': From a clipping in the Kevin Brownlow Collection.

Chapter Ten

262 The names of the major characters – Kristina, Karl Gustav, etc. – were anglicised for the film.

263 'I am unable...': Henry Woodhead, *Memoirs of Queen Christina*, (BiblioBazaar: 2008).

264 'A Chinese...': Tallulah Bankhead, *Tallulah: My Autobiography* (Harper & Brothers: 1952).

265 'I thought...': Sven Hugo Borg, 'The Private Life of Greta Garbo' (unedited), *Film Pictorial* 1933.

266 'In place of...': Borg, ibid.

267 'From a critical...': Larry Carr, *Four Fabulous Faces* (Galahad: 1970).

268 'This may have...': Dietrich to author.

269 'I was too nervous...': Laurence Olivier: *Confessions of an Actor* (Simon & Schuster: 1982).

270 Leatrice Gilbert Fountain & John R. Maxim, *The Dark Star* (St Martin's Press: 1985).

271 'Garbo's face...': Fountain, ibid.

272 'Three years ago...': Fritiof Billquist, *Garbo* (Putman: 1960).

273 'The one persistent…': *New York Herald Tribune*, 1933.
274 'It's really bad…': Sven Broman, *Garbo on Garbo* (Bloomsbury: 1990).
275 Press reviews, January 1934.
276 'There are two…': *Hollywood Citizen-News*, December 1933.
277 'I'd hardly opened…': Fountain, ibid.
278 'Can you think…': Broman, ibid
279 'For the life of me…': *Hollywood Citizen-News*, February 1934.
280 'Oh, it's such a pity…': Broman, ibid.
281 Press reviews, December 1934.

Chapter Eleven
282 'We would bounce…': Norman Zierold, *Garbo* (Stein & Day: 1969).
283 'Before each…': Zierold, ibid.
284 Peter Hanning, *The Legend of Garbo* (W H Allen: 1990).
285 Press reviews, September 1935.
286 'Sven is a…': Letter from Lawrence to MGM in Alexander Walker, *Garbo* (Weidenfeld & Nicolson: 1980).
287 'I have been…': Letter from Garbo to Salka in Barry Paris, *Garbo: A Biography* (Sidgwick & Jackson: 1995).
288 'In my opinion…': Dietrich to author.
289 'Poor Mercedes…': Sven Broman, *Garbo on Garbo* (Bloomsbury: 1990).
290 'I don't know why…': Interview on ship, various syndicated columns, May 1936.
291 'It has been…': Kay Proctor, *Screen Guide*.
292 'So beautiful…': Paris, ibid.
293 'She has a…': quote subsequently included in the feature, 'The Truth About & Garbo Me', *Picturegoer Supplement: Camille*, September 1937.
294 'When Stanwyck…': Jane Ellen Wayne, *Barbara Stanwyck* (JR Books: 2009).
295 'Ask me…': Wayne, ibid.
296 'Men marry…': Thalberg, quoted in Karen Swenson, *Greta Garbo: A Life Apart* (Simon & Schuster: 1997).
297 Katharine Hepburn, *Me: Stories of My Life* (Alfred Knopf: 1991).
298 'I expected…': Swenson, ibid.
299 'If I hadn't…': Broman, ibid.
300 'It really didn't…': Broman, ibid.
301 Press reviews, February 1937; anonymous British review, in John Bainbridge, *Garbo* (Doubleday: 1955).
302 'How I would have…': Roger Normand to author.
303 'I liked him…': Broman, ibid.
304 'A little hunchbacked…': Broman, ibid.
305 'The sacrifice…': quoted in Frederic Masson, *Marie Walewska* (Ed. Guillaume: Paris, 1897).

306 Other rejected titles included: *The Road To Waterloo*, *The Woman Before Waterloo*, *The Great Surrender*, *The Captains & The King*, *Man Without A Country*, *The Gods & The Flesh*, *Less Than The Dust*, *Symphony Without Music* and *A World Is Born*.

307 'I would have been…': Larry Swindell, *Charles Boyer: The Reluctant Lover* (Doubleday: 1983).

308 'I have a great…': Letter to Horke Wachtmeister, July 1935, quoted in Paris, ibid.

309 Press reviews, November 1937.

Chapter Twelve

310 'G.G. What do…': Norman Zierold, *Garbo* (Stein & Day: 1969).

311 'Stoky didn't…': John Bainbridge, *Garbo* (Doubleday: 1955).

312 Jim Simmons, 'I Won't Marry Stokowski, Says Greta Garbo', *Photoplay*, January 1938.

313 Emilie Danielson, 'The Swedish Home Of Greta Garbo', *Movie Mirror*, April 1938.

314 'I live in…': quoted in Barry Paris, *Garbo: A Biography* (Sidgwick & Jackson: 1995).

315 Hettie Grimstead, 'With Garbo At Home', *Screenland*, April 1938.

316 'Don't you think…': Grimstead, ibid.

317 'Greta Garbo? Oh…': Various Italian tabloids, March 1938.

318 Martha Kerr, 'Garbo Finds Love', *Modern Screen*, June 1938.

319 'I never…': Various Italian tabloids; Bainbridge, ibid.

320 *Hollywood Reporter*, March 1938.

321 Press-conference: the questions and responses, in no particular order, as detailed in various syndicated columns.

322 'Garbo Goes Cruisin'…': *Daily News*, October 1938.

323 'It is wholly…': *New York Times*, October 1938.

324 'It may be…': Zierold, ibid.

325 Nancy Nelson, *Evenings with Cary Grant* (William Morrow: 1991).

326 'And damn you…': Zierold, ibid.

327 'She was unable…': Melvyn Douglas & Tom Arthur, *Melvyn Douglas: See You at the Movies*, (University Press of America: 1986).

328 'My film is…': Sven Broman, *Garbo on Garbo* (Bloomsbury: 1990).

329 Press reviews, November 1939

330 'Famous names…': Fritiof Billquist, *Garbo* (Putman: 1960).

331 'She was at…': Gayelord Hauser, *Gayelord Hauser's Treasury of Secrets* (Farrar, Straus & Giroux: 1963).

Chapter Thirteen

332 'In some mysterious…': William Stevenson: *A Man Called Intrepid: The Secret War* (Harcourt Brace Jovanovich: 1976).

333 'If peace…': Sven Broman, *Garbo on Garbo* (Bloomsbury: 1990).

334 'FDR's voice…': Norman Zierold, *Garbo* (Stein & Day: 1969).

335 'Garbo met…': Wenner-Gren main file, Charles Higham Collection, USC.

336 'Just now I'm lying…': Broman, ibid.

337 'My guess…': Leiland, 1993, quoted in Karen Swenson, *Greta Garbo: A Life Apart* (Simon & Schuster: 1997).

338 Among those titles rejected were: *Turns, The Gay Twin, Naughty Today & Nice Tomorrow, Anna & Anita, Her Weekend Sister, One-Day Bride* and *I Love Your Sister.*

339 'He was the type…': Patrick McGilligan, *George Cukor: A Double Life* (St Martin's Press: 1991).

340 'I'm serving…': Zierold, ibid.

341 Constance Bennett shared top-billing with Gracie Fields in the 1945 wartime drama *Paris Underground*, and recalled, 'That woman was a devil. She tried to make me face the opposite way, so the camera didn't get my best profile. There was never any compromise – she *always* had to be the centre of attention.' David Bret, *Gracie Fields* (Robson Books: 1995).

342 'In her last…': John Bainbridge, *Garbo* (Doubleday: 1955).

343 'I'm very sorry…': Barry Paris, *Garbo: A Biography* (Sidgwick & Jackson: 1995).

344 'She entered…': Julie Gilbert: *Opposite Attraction: The Loves of Erich Maria Remarque & Paulette Goddard* (Pantheon: 1993).

345 'One of the most…': 'Cardinal Spellman's Dark Legacy', *New York Press*, May 1902.

346 John Cooney, *The American Pope: The Life and Times of Francis Cardinal Spellman*, Dell, 1984.

347 'They've dug…': Bainbridge, ibid.

348 'This prince…': Gottfried Reinhardt, *The Genius: A Memoir of Max Reinhardt* (Knopf: 1979).

349 'Learned it would…': *INSTCD Ledger*, November 1941.

350 Press releases, January 1941.

351 'If Greta Garbo…': *Motion Picture*, January 1933.

352 'As long as…': *The Los Angeles Times*, January 1942.

353 'Only Garbo…': Salka Viertel, *The Kindness of Strangers* (Holt, Rinehart & Winston: 1969).

354 Marlene Dietrich stressed that the *only* time that she and Garbo had ever shared the bill had been in *Die Freudlose Gasse*.

355 'It was definitely…': Norman Taylor to author, July 1995.

356 'Miss Garbo is…': Mayer's letter, March 1942, quoted in Alexander Walker, *Garbo* (Weidenfeld & Nicolson: 1980).

357 'It was very painful…': Broman, ibid.

358 'Mr Hitler…': Sam Green, quoted in Paris, ibid.

359 In 1990 'L'enfant en Robe Bleue' sold at Sotheby's for over $7 million.

360 Greta Garbo has finally…': *The Los Angeles Times*, May 1943.

361 'We sat…': Gilbert Roland, unpublished memoirs, quoted in Kathleen O'Steen, 'Commitments: A Brief Affair, Greta Garbo & Fellow Actor Gilbert Roland', *The Los Angeles Times*, November 1995.

362 'One of us…': Meredith Etherington-Smith: *Salvador Dalí: A Biography* (Sinclair-Stevenson: 1992).

Chapter Fourteen

363 'My attitude…': Cecil Beaton, *Self-Portrait With Friends: The Selected Diaries of Cecil Beaton, 1926–1974* (Times Books: 1979).

364 'In these post…': Martin Greif, *Gay Book of Days* (Main Street Press: 1982).

365 'An historian…': Hugo Vickers, *Loving Garbo* (Jonathan Cape: 1994).

366 'No advice or…': Cecil Beaton, *Diaries*, published and unpublished; Vickers, ibid.

367 'As if someone…': Beaton, ibid.

368 'At first she stood…': Beaton, ibid.

369 'I *have* no plans…': Croswell Bowen, *New York Herald Tribune*, September 1946.

370 'I do not know…': *Los Angeles Examiner*, March 1947.

371 Chateau de Pierrefonds, near Compiègne, best-known for the *Merlin* television series.

372 'She goes…': Tennessee Williams, *Letters To Donald Windham, 1940–1965* (Holt, Rinehart & Winston: 1977).

373 'She said firmly…': Beaton, ibid.

374 'If I disliked…': Beaton, ibid.

375 'There was a swish…': Walter Lucas, *Sunday Express*, September 1949.

376 'They probably cancelled…': quoted in Barry Paris, *Garbo: A Biography* (Sidgwick & Jackson: 1995).

377 'She has a sense…': Cecil Beaton, *Cecil Beaton's Scrapbook* (Batsford: 1937).

378 'All the colours…': Billy Baldwin, *Billy Baldwin Remembers* (Harcourt, Brace, Jovanovich: 1974).

379 'She would have been perfect…': William Frye, 'Classic Hollywood: The Garbo Next Door', *Vanity Fair*, April 2000.

380 'During dinner…': Frye, ibid.

381 'To write of Greta…': Mercedes de Acosta, *Here Lies the Heart*, (André Deutsch: 1960).

Chapter Fifteen

382 'Hardly since General…': *Time*, March 1971.

383 'I heard…': Sam Green, 'I Wasn't To Blame For Heiress Murder', *Daily Mirror*, July 2008.

384   More of his friendship with Garbo, with verbatim accounts of some of their (one assumes recorded) conversations can be found in Barry Paris, *Garbo: A Biography* (Sidgwick & Jackson: 1995), pp.473–83.

385   Antony Baekeland was defended by *Rumpole of the Bailey* writer John Mortimer and sent to Broadmoor for eight years. Days after his release, he returned to New York, stabbed his grandmother, into whose care he had been discharged (she survived) and, while awaiting trial, self-suffocated, aged thirty-five. The tragedy was brought to the screen in 2007. In *Savage Grace* Hugh Dancy played Green, described in the publicity as 'a homosexual walker who spends his time tending to the needs of very rich women'. Green sued the studio, but died before the matter was resolved.

386   McGuinness moved the scenario back to 1967, the year homosexuality was legalised in Britain, and a time when Ireland was on the cusp of violent change. The action is set in the house of a gay artist and deals with problems encountered by his household, into the midst of which Garbo appears, effecting a calming influence.

387   'Well, I couldn't…': Hugo Vickers, *Loving Garbo* (Jonathan Cape: 1994).

388   Paris, ibid.

389   In 1984 Gronowicz ran into trouble with the publication of *God's Brother*, an 'autobiography' of fellow countryman Pope John Paul II, who he claimed to have interviewed. Condemned as 'totally fraudulent' by the Vatican, this was withdrawn from sale and all remaining copies destroyed. His equally fictitious *Garbo, Her Own Story* was published shortly after her death in 1990, and five years after his own death.

390   Sands' conning of Garbo is explained by himself in his book, *The Divine Garbo* (Grosset & Dunlap: 1969).

391   Karen Swenson, *Greta Garbo: A Life Apart* (Simon & Schuster: 1997).

392   'Greta is my…': Lisa Braestrup, 'The Man Who Stalks Garbo', unpublished, 1987.

393   'Who knows…': Garbo to Roger Normand.

394   'Let's go…': Green, quoted in Paris, ibid.

395   'I told her how…': Roger Normand to author.

396   'GARBO TO WED…': Leon Wagener, *Globe*, October 1985.

397   'People learn…': Sven Broman, *Garbo on Garbo* (Bloomsbury: 1990).

Epilogue

398   For more details regarding the sale and estate see Barry Paris, *Garbo: A Biography* (Sidgwick & Jackson: 1995), pp.414, 540–1.

399   'I worked for her…': Michael Cross, 'Garbo's Last Days', *New York*, May 1990.

FILMOGRAPHY

En Lyckoriddare (Soldier of Fortune), Skanda Film Company, 1921
Director & Script: John W. Brunius. With Gösta Ekman, Mary
Johnson. Greta and Alva Gustaffson were extras. No other details. No
print of this film survives.

Kärlekens ögon (Scarlet Angel), Skanda Film Company, 1922
Director & Script: John W. Brunius. With Gösta Ekman, Pauline
Brunius, Karen Winther. Greta Gustaffson was an extra. No other
details. No print of this film survives.

Herr och fru Stockholm (How Not to Dress), Tullberg Productions, 1922
Director & Script: Ragnar Lasse Ring. With Olga Andersson, Erick
Fröander, Ragnar Widestedt. In this advertising short for the PUB
department store Greta Gustaffson played 'A Mannequin'. (7 mins.)

Konsum Stockholm Promo (Our Daily Bread), Fribergs Filmbrya
Productions, 1922
Director & Script: Ragnar Lasse Ring. With Lars Hanson. In this
advertising short for a local bakery, Greta Gustaffson played 'A Cake
Eater'. (8 mins.)

Luffar-Petter (Peter the Tramp), Petschler Productions, 1922
Director & Script: Erik Arthur Petschler. Photography: Oscar Norberg.
With Erik Arthur Petschler, Helmer Larsson, Fredrik Olsson, Gucken
Cederborg; Tyra Ryman, Anná Brandt. Greta Gustaffson (2nd billing)
played Greta Nordberg. (75 mins or 35–40 mins, depending on sources.)

Gösta Berlings Saga, Svensk Filmindustri, 1924
Director: Mauritz Stiller. Script: Ragnar Hyltén-Cavallius, Mauritz
Stiller, Selma Lagerlöf. Photography: Julius Jaenzon. Artistic Director:
Vilhelm Bryde. Special Effects: Olaf Äs, Nils Elffors. With Lars Hanson,
Sven Scholander, Ellen Hartman-Cederström, Mona Mårtenson,
Torsten Hammarén, Gerda Lundequist; Jenny Hasselqvist, Sixten
Malmerfelt. Garbo (originally 5th billing) played Countess Elisabeth
Dohna. (Original print, part one: 94 mins; part two: 91 mins; 1934
condensed version: 91 mins; 1975 restored version: 180 mins.)

Die Odaliske von Smolny, Trianon-Film AG (aborted), 1925
Director: Mauritz Stiller. Script: Ragnar Hyltén-Cavallius, Vladimir Semitjov, Mauritz Stiller. Photography: Julius Jaenzon. Artistic Director: Stefan Lhotha. With Einar Hansson, Conrad Veidt, Mouschin Bey. Garbo (top-billing) was to have played Maria Ivanovna. No film is believed to have been shot: the production was cancelled when Trianon went into liquidation.

Die Freudlose Gasse (Joyless Street), So-Far Film, 1925
Director: Georg Wilhelm Pabst. Script: Willy Haas, Hugo Bettauer, Georg Wilhelm Pabst. Photography: Guido Seeber, Robert Lach, Curt Oertel. Artistic Directors: Otto Erdmann, Hans Sohnle. With Werner Krauss, Valeska Gert, Asta Nielsen, Jaro Fürth, Henry Stuart, Einar Hanson, Marlene Dietrich, Tamara Geva. Garbo (4th billing) played Greta Rumfort. (Original print: 175 mins approx.; 1981 restored version: 94 mins.)

Torrent, MGM, 1926
Director: Monta Bell. Script: Dorothy Farnum, Vicente Blasco Ibáñez. Photography: William H. Daniels. Sets: Cedric Gibbons. Costumes: Kathleen Kay, Maude Marsh, Max Rée. With Ricardo Cortez, Gertrude Olmstead, Edward Connelly, Martha Mattox, Lucy Beaumont, Arthur Edmund Carewe, Mario Carillo, Joel McCrea. Garbo (2nd billing) played Leonora Moreno. (87 mins.)

The Temptress, MGM, 1926
Director: Fred Niblo (replacing Mauritz Stiller). Script: Dorothy Farnum (replacing Stiller), Vicente Blasco Ibáñez. Photography: William H. Daniels (replacing Tony Gaudio). Stills: Buddy Longworth. Sets: Cedric Gibbons, James Basevi. Costumes: Max Rée, André-ani (Clement Andreani). With Antonio Moreno, Marc McDermott (replacing H. B. Warner), Lionel Barrymore, Armand Kaliz, Roy D'Arcy, Robert Anderson. Garbo (top-billing) played Elena of Torre Bianca. (Original version one: 117 mins; version two: 112 mins. 2005 restored version one: 106 mins; version two: 101 mins.)

Flesh and the Devil, MGM, 1926
Director: Clarence Brown. Script: Benjamin Glazer, Hermann Sudermann. Photography: William H. Daniels. Sets: Cedric Gibbons, Fredric Hope. Costumes: André-ani. With John Gilbert, Lars Hanson, Barbara Kent, George Fawcett, Eugenie Besserer, Marc McDermott, Philippe De Lacy, Polly Moran. Garbo (2nd billing) played Felicitas. (Original print: 112 mins; revised print: 117 mins.)

Anna Karenina, MGM, 1927
> Director: Dimitri Buchowetzki. Photography: Merritt Gerstad. With Ricardo Cortez*, Lionel Barrymore, Dorothy Sebastian. * replaced by Norman Kerry. The film was aborted. See below.

Love (Anna Karenina), MGM, 1927
> Director: Edmund Goulding. Script: Frances Marion, based on Tolstoy's *Anna Karenina*. Photography: William H. Daniels. Sets: Cedric Gibbons, Alexander Toluboff. Costumes: Gilbert Clark. With John Gilbert, George Fawcett, Emily Fitzroy, Brandon Hurst, Philippe De Lacy, Mathilde Comont, Jacques Tourneur. Garbo (2nd billing) played Anna. (82 mins.)

The Divine Woman, MGM, 1928
> Director: Victor Sjöström. Script: Dorothy Farnum; Gladys Unger, based on her play, *Starlight*. Photography: Oliver T. Marsh. Sets: Cedric Gibbons, A. Arnold Gillespie. Costumes: Gilbert Clark. With Lars Hanson, Lowell Sherman, Polly Moran, Dorothy Cumming, Johnny Mack Brown, Paulette Duval. Garbo (top-billing) played Marianne. (Original production: 80 mins; surviving one-reel section: 9 mins.)

The Mysterious Lady, MGM, 1928
> Director: Fred Niblo. Script: Bess Meredyth, Ludwig Wolff. Photography: William H. Daniels. Sets: Cedric Gibbons. Costumes: Gilbert Clark. With Conrad Nagel, Gustav vo Seyffertitz, Albert Pollet, Edward Connelly, Geraldine Dvorak. Garbo (top-billing) played Tania Fedorova. (96 mins.)

A Woman of Affairs, MGM, 1929
> Director: Clarence Brown. Script: Bess Meredyth, Michael Arlen (based on his novel, *The Green Hat*). Photography: William H. Daniels. Sets: Cedric Gibbons. Costumes: Adrian. With John Gilbert, Johnny Mack Brown, Douglas Fairbanks Jr, Lewis Stone, Hobart Bosworth, Dorothy Sebastian, Anita Louise. Garbo (top-billing) played Diana Merrick Furness. (88 mins.)

A Man's Man, MGM, 1929
> Director: James Cruze. Script: Forrest Halsey, Patrick Kearney. Photography: Merritt B. Gerstad. Sets: Cedric Gibbons. With William Haines, Josephine Dunn, Sam Hardy, Mae Busch. Garbo and Gilbert appear as themselves, attending a film premiere with Fred Niblo. (80 mins.)

Wild Orchids, MGM, 1929
> Director: Sidney Franklin. Script: John Colton, Willis Goldbleck, Hans Kräly, Richard Schayer. Photography: William H. Daniels. Sets:

Cedric Gibbons. Costumes: Adrian. With Lewis Stone, Nils Asther. Garbo (top-billing) played Lillie Sterling. (98 mins.)

The Single Standard, MGM, 1929
Director: John S. Robertson. Script: Josephine Lovett, Adela Rogers St Johns. Photography: Oliver T. Marsh. Sets: Cedric Gibbons. With Nils Asther, Johnny Mack Brown, Dorothy Sebastian, Lane Chandler, Fred Solm (billed as Robert Castle), Wally Albright, Zeffie Tilbury. Garbo (top-billing) played Arden Stuart Hewlett. (71 mins.)

The Kiss, MGM, 1929
Director: Jacques Feyder. Script: Hanns Kräly, George M. Saville. Photography: William H. Daniels. Sets: Cedric Gibbons. Costumes: Adrian. With Conrad Nagel, Anders Randolf, Lew Ayres, Holmes Herbert, George Davis, André Cheron. Garbo (top-billing) played Irene Guarry. (62 mins.)

Anna Christie, MGM, 1930 (English-language version)
Director: Clarence Brown. Script: Frances Marion, Eugene O'Neill. Photography: William H. Daniels. Sets: Cedric Gibbons. Costumes: Adrian. Music: William Axt. With Charles Bickford, George F. Marion, Marie Dressler, James T. Mack, Lee Phelps, Jack Baxley, William H. O'Brien. Garbo (top-billing) played Anna Christopherson (aka Christie). (86 mins.)

Romance, MGM, 1930
Director: Clarence Brown. Script: Bess Meredyth, Edward Sheldon, Edwin Justus Mayer. Photography: William H. Daniels. Sets: Cedric Gibbons. Costumes: Adrian. Music: William Axt. Musical pieces: 'The Last Rose Of Summer'; 'Una voce poco fa' performed by Diana Gaylen; 'Annie Laurie', performed by Gavin Gordon. With Gavin Gordon, Lewis Stone, Elliott Nugent, Florence Lake, Clara Blandick, Mathilde Comont, Geraldine Dvorak. Garbo (top billing) played Rita Cavallini. (76 mins.)

Anna Christie, MGM, 1931 (German-language version)
Director: Jacques Feyder. Script: Walter Hasenclever, Frank Reicher, Eugene O'Neill. Photography, sets, costumes, music as original film. With Theo Shall, Hans Junkermann, Salka Viertel (billed Salka Steuermann), Herman Bing, Leo White. Garbo (top-billing) played Anna Christopherson (aka Christie). (85 mins.)

Inspiration, MGM, 1931
Director: Clarence Brown. Script: Gene Markey, James Forbes, Alphonse Daudet. Photography: William H. Daniels. Sets: Cedric

Gibbons. Costumes: Adrian. Music: William Axt. Song: 'Inspiration' (Gordon, Nils-Georg). With Robert Montgomery, Lewis Stone, Marjorie Rambeau, Judith Vosselli, Beryl Mercer, John Miljan, Karen Morley. Garbo (top-billing) played Yvonne Valbret. (75 mins.)

Susan Lenox: Her Fall & Rise (The Rise of Helga), MGM, 1931
Director: Robert Z. Leonard. Script: Leon Gordon, David Graham Phillips, Edith Fitzgerald, Zelda Sears. Photography: William H. Daniels. Sets: Cedric Gibbons, Alexander Toluboff. Costumes: Adrian. Music: William Axt. With Clark Gable, Jean Hersholt, John Miljan, Alan Hale, Hale Hamilton. Garbo (top-billing) played Helga/Susan Lenox. (73 mins.)

Mata Hari, MGM, 1931
Director: George Fitzmaurice. Script: Benjamin Glazer, Leo Birinsky, Gilbert Emery, Doris Anderson. Photography: William H. Daniels. Sets: Cedric Gibbons. Costumes: Adrian, based on original designs by Paul Poiret. Music: William Axt. With Ramon Novarro, Lionel Barrymore, Lewis Stone, C. Henry Gordon, Karen Morley, Mischa Auer. Garbo (equal-billing with Novarro) played Mata Hari. Original version, 90 mins. 1939 re-released version (with cuts), (85 mins.)

Grand Hotel, MGM, 1931
Director: Edmund Goulding. Script: William A. Drake, Vicki Baum, Béla Balázs. Photography: William H. Daniels. Sets: Cedric Gibbons. Costumes: Adrian. Music: Charles Maxwell, William Axt. With John Barrymore, Joan Crawford, Wallace Beery, Lionel Barryome, Lewis Stone, Jean Hersholt, Ferdinand Gottschalk, Rafaela Ottiano. Garbo (top-billing) played Elisaveta Grusinskaya. (108 mins.)

As You Desire Me, MGM, 1932
Director: George Fitzmaurice. Script: Gene Markey, Luigi Pirandello. Photography: William H. Daniels. Sets: Cedric Gibbons. Costumes: Adrian. Music: William Axt. With Melvin Douglas, Erich von Stroheim, Owen Moore, Hedda Hopper, Rafaela Ottiano, William Ricciardi, Roland Varno, Nella Walker. Garbo (top-billing) played Zara/Countess Maria Vanelli. (70 mins.)

Queen Christina, MGM, 1933
Director: Rouben Mamoulian. Script: Salka Viertel, H. M. Harwood, Margaret P. Levino, S. N. Behrman (dialogue). Photography: William H. Daniels. Sets: Edwin B. Willis, Alexander Tolubuff, Greta Garbo. Costumes: Adrian. Music: Maurice de Packh, Herbert Stothart. With John Gilbert, Ian Keith, Lewis Stone, Elizabeth Young, C. Aubrey Smith, Reginald Owen, Cora Sue Collins, Barbara Barondess, Akim

Tamiroff, Audrey Scott. Garbo (top-billing) played Queen Christina. (97 mins.)

The Painted Veil, MGM, 1934
Director: Richard Boleslawski. Script: Salka Viertel, Edith Fitzgerald, John Meehan, William Somerset Maugham. Photography: William H. Daniels. Sets: Cedric Gibbons, Hubert Stowitts. Costumes: Adrian. Music: Herbert Stothart. With Herbert Marshall, George Brent, Warner Oland, Jean Hersholt, Bodil Rosing, Katharine Alexander, Soo Yong. Garbo (top-billing) played Katrin Koerber Fane. (84 mins.)

Anna Karenina, MGM, 1935
Director: Clarence Brown. Script: Salka Viertel, Clemence Dane, Leo Tolstoy, S. N. Behrman. Photography: William H. Daniels. Sets: Cedric Gibbons. Costumes: Adrian. Music: Herbert Stothart, Count Andrey Tolstoy. Dance arrangers: Chester Hale, Margarete Wallman. With Fredric March, Freddie Bartholomew, Maureen O'Sullivan, May Robson, Basil Rathbone, Reginald Owen, Phoebe Foster, Gyles Isham, Constance Collier. Garbo (top-billing) played Anna Karenina. (95 mins.)

Camille, MGM, 1937
Director: George Cukor. Script: Zoe Akins, Frances Marion, James Hilton, Alexandre Dumas Fils. Photography: William H. Daniels, Hal Rosson, Karl Freund. Sets: Cedric Gibbons, Henry Grace, Jack D. Moore. Costumes: Adrian. Music: Herbert Stothart, Milton Benjamin. Dance sequences: Val Rasset. With Robert Taylor, Lionel Barrymore, Elizabeth Allan, Jessie Ralph, Henry Daniell, Lenore Uric, Laura Hope Crews, Rex O'Malley. Garbo (top-billing) played Marguerite Gautier. (108 mins.)

Marie Walewska (*Conquest*), MGM, 1937
Director: Clarence Brown. Script: Salka Viertel, Samuel Hoffenstein, S. N. Behrman, Helen Jerome, Talbot Jennings, Waclaw Gasiorowski. Photography: Karl Freund. Sets: Cedric Gibbons, William A. Horning. Costumes: Adrian. Music: Herbert Stothart. With Charles Boyer, Reginald Owen, Alan Marshal, Henry Stephenson, Leif Erickson, Dame May Whitty, Maria Ouspenskaya, George Houston, Scotty Beckett. Garbo (top-billing) played Coutness Marie Walewska. (107 mins.)

Ninotchka, MGM, 1939
Director: Ernst Lubitsch. Script: Walter Reisch, Billy Wilder, Charles Brackett, Melchior Lengyel. Photography: William H. Daniels. Sets: Cedric Gibbons, Edwin B. Willis. Costumes: Adrian. Music: Werner

R. Heymann. With Melvyn Douglas, Ina Claire, Bela Lugosi, Sig Ruman, Felix Bressart, Alexander Granach, Rolfe Sedan, Edwin Maxwell, Richard Carle, Albert Pollett. Garbo (top-billing) played Nina Ivanovna Yakushova, aka Ninotchka. (110 mins.)

Two-Faced Woman, MGM, 1941
Director: George Cukor. Script: Salka Viertel, George Oppenheimer, S. N. Behrman, Ludwig Fulda. Photography: Joseph Ruttenberg, Charles Dorian, Andrew Marton. Sets: Cedric Gibbons, Edwin B. Willis. Costumes: Adrian. Music: Bronislau Kaper, Leo Arnaud. Choreographer: Robert Alton. With Melvyn Douglas, Constance Bennett, Roland Young, Robert Sterling, Ruth Gordon, Robert Alton, Gloria de Haven. Garbo (top-billing) played Karin Borg Lake. (92 mins.)

Adam & Yves, Hand-In-Hand Productions, 1974
Director & Script: Peter De Rome. Photography: Jack Deveau. With Marcus Giovanni, Michael Hardwick, Kirk Luna, Bobby Jones. Garbo's final celluloid appearance lasts around three minutes and was incorporated into this pornographic gay feature, set in Paris. Filmed without her knowledge she is actually seen in a New York Street as Yves (Giovanni) recalls how he once bumped into his elusive idol. (90 mins.)

SOURCES

Books and Articles

Anonymous, 'Dirt Craze Due To Women', *Variety*, June 1931.

Asther, Nils, *Narrens vag* (The Road of the Jester), Sweden, 1988.

Axell, Tin Andersén, *Djavla Alskade Unge!* (*Bloody Beloved Kid!*), 2005.

Bachman, Gideon & Sorkin, Marc, 'G. W. Pabst', *Cinemages*, 1955.

Bainbridge, John, *Garbo*, Doubleday, 1955

Baldwin, Billy, *Billy Baldwin Remembers*, Harcourt, Brace, Jovanovich, 1974.

Bankhead, Tallulah, *Tallulah: My Autobiography*, Harper & Brothers, 1952.

Beaton, Cecil, *Cecil Beaton's Scrapbook*, Batsford, 1937.

Beaton, Cecil, *Self-Portrait with Friends: The Selected Diaries of Cecil Beaton, 1926–1974*, Times Books, 1979.

Biery, Ruth, *The Greta Garbo Story* (unedited version of the interview conducted 31 December 1927, *Photoplay*, 3 segments, April–June 1928.

Biery, Ruth, 'Hollywood's Cruelty to Greta Garbo', *Photoplay*, January 1932.

Billquist, Fritiof, *Garbo*, Putman, 1960. Translated by Maurice Michael & Arthur Baker.

Borg, Sven Hugo, 'The Private Life of Greta Garbo' (unedited), *Film Pictorial*, 1933.

Bret, David, *Marlene, My Friend*, Robson Books, 1993.

Bret, David, *Tallulah Bankhead: A Scandalous Life*, Robson Books, 1996.

Broman, Sven, *Garbo on Garbo*, Bloomsbury, 1990.

Broman, Sven & Sands, Frederick, *The Divine Garbo*, Grosset & Dunlap, 1969.

Brownlow, Kevin, *The Parade's Gone By*, Ballantyne, 1969.

Bull, Clarence Sinclair & Lee, Raymond, *Faces Of Hollywood*, A. S. Barnes, 1968.

Calhoun, Dorothy, 'Why Garbo's Friends Dare Not Talk', *Motion Picture*, July 1935.

Carr, Larry, *Four Fabulous Faces*, Galahad, 1970.

Coffee, Lenore, *Confessions of a Hollywood Screenwriter*, Cassell, 1973.

Combs, 'Mauritz Stiller' in *Cinema: A Critical Dictionary*, Secker & Warburg, 1980.

Conway, Michael, McGregor, Dion & Ricci, Mark, *The Films of Greta Garbo*, Citadel Press, 1968.

Cooney, John, *The American Pope: The Life & Times of Cardinal Spellman*, New York Books, 1984.

Corliss, Richard, *Garbo*, Pyramid, 1974.

Cornell, Katharine, *I Wanted to be an Actress*, Random House, 1938.

Crawford, Joan, *My Way of Life*, Simon & Schuster, 1971.

Curtiss, Thomas Quinn, *Von Stroheim*, Farrar, Straus & Giroux, 1971.

Daum, Raymond, *Walking with Garbo*, HarperCollins, 1991.

Davies, Marion, *The Times We Had: Life With William Randolph Hearst*, Bobbs-Merrill, 1975. De Acosta, Mercedes, *Here Lies the Heart*, André Deutsch, 1960.

Dietz, Howard, *Dancing in the Dark*, Quadrangle, 1974.

Douglas, Melvyn & Arthur, Tom, *Melvyn Douglas: See You at the Movies*, University Press of America, 1986.

Dragonette, Jessica, *Life is a Song*, St Anthony's Guild Press, 1967.

Dressler, Marie, *My Own Story*, Little Brown, 1934.

Engelmann, Larry, 'Little Garbo', *The American Way*, October 1988.

Etherington-Smith, Meredith, *Dalí: A Biography*, Sinclair-Stevenson, 1992.

Eyman, Scott, 'Clarence Brown: Garbo & Beyond', *Velvet Light Trap*, University of Wisconsin, 1978.

Eyman, Scott, *Lion of Hollywood: The Life & Legend of Louis B. Mayer*, Robson Books, 2005.

Faderman, Lillian & Timmons, Stuart, *Gay LA: A History of Sexual Outlaws, Power Politics & Lipstick Lesbians*, Basic Books, 2006.

Finch, Mark, *European Gay Review*, 2001.

Fountain, Leatrice Gilbert & Maxim, John R., *The Dark Star* (John Gilbert), St Martin's Press, 1985.

Fowler, Gene, *Good Night, Sweet Prince*, Viking, 1944.

Gaate, Inga, Garbo & Stiller Interview, *Filmjournalen*, September 1933.

Garbo, Greta, 'Why I Shall Not Marry' (unedited), subheaded 'In Which The Celebrated Sphinx of the Screen Breaks Her Silence and Tells What Is In Her Heart', *Liberty*, 22 October 1932.

Gilbert, Julie, *Opposite Attraction: The Loves of Erich Maria Remarque & Paulette Goddard*, Pantheon, 1993.

Greif, Martin, *The Gay Book of Days*, Main Street Press, 1982.

Gutner, Howard, *Gowns by Adrian*, Abrams, 2000.

Gynt, Kaj, *Greta Garbo's Life By Her Friend From Childhood*, (unedited) as told to Adela Rogers St Johns, *Liberty*, August 1934.

Hall, Mordaunt, Interview with Garbo, *New York Times*, March 1929.

Hamann, G. D., *Greta Garbo in the 30s*, Filming Today Press, 2003.

Hanning, Peter, *The Legend of Garbo*, WH Allen, 1990.

Hauser, Gayelord, *Gayelord Hauser's Treasury of Secrets*, Farrar, Straus & Giroux, 1963.

Hepburn, Katharine, *Me: Stories of My Life*, Alfred Knopf, 1991.

Higham, Charles, *Hollywood Cameramen*, 1970.

Higham, Charles, *Merchant of Dreams: Louis B. Mayer, MGM & The Secret Hollywood*, Sidgwick & Jackson, 1993.

Joel, Peter, 'The First True Story of Garbo's Childhood' (unedited), *Screen Book*, 1933.

Lindroth, Orjan, 'The True Story of Axel Wenner-Gren', Swedish Press, 2006.

Masson, Frederic, *Marie Walewska*, Ed. Guillaume, Paris, 1897.

McGilligan, Patrick, *George Cukor: A Double Life*, St Martin's Press, 1991.

McLellan, Diana, *The Girls: Sappho Goes to Hollywood*, St Martin's Press, 2000.

Morris, Ruth, 'Sinful Girls Lead In 1931', *Variety*, December 1931.

Nelson, Nancy, *Evenings with Cary Grant*, William Morrow, 1991.

Olivier, Laurence, *Confessions of an Actor*, Simon & Schuster, 1982.

Olson-Buckner, *The Epic Tradition in Gösta Berlings Saga*, Theodore Gaus, 1978.

Osborne, Robert (editor), *Hollywood Legends: The Life & Films of Humphrey Bogart & Greta Garbo*, Marvin Miller, 1968.

Palmborg, Rilla Page, *The Private Life of Greta Garbo*, Doubleday, 1931.

Paris, Barry, *Garbo: A Biography*, Sidgwick & Jackson, 1995

Payne, Robert, *The Great Garbo*, WH Allen, 1976.

Porter, Darwin, *The Secret Life of Humphrey Bogart*, Blood Moon, 2003.

Reinhardt, Gottfried, *The Genius: A Memoir of Max Reinhardt*, Knopf, 1979.

Roberts, W. Adolphe, 'Greta Garbo', *Motion Picture*, November 1925.

Rotha, Paul & Griffith, Richard, *The Film Till Now*, Spring Books, 1967.

Russo, Vito, *The Celluloid Closet: Homosexuality in the Movies*, Harper & Row, 1981.

Saxon, Lars, 'Garbo Ungdomsminnen' (Youth Memories), unedited, *Lektyr* magazine, Sweden, 1931.

Sjöström, Victor, *Classics of the Swedish Cinema*, SFI, 1951.

Smith, Agnes, 'Up Speaks A Gallant Loser!', *Photoplay*, February 1927.

Stevenson, William, *A Man Called Intrepid: The Secret War*, Harcourt Brace Jovanovich, 1976.

St Johns, Adela Rogers, 'Garbo: The Mystery of Hollywood, *Liberty*, 1929.

St Johns, Adela Rogers, *Love, Laughter & Tears: My Hollywood Story*, Doubleday, 1978.

Streichen, Edward: *A Life in Photography*, WH Allen, 1963.

Sundborg, Ake, 'That Gustafsson Girl' (unedited), *Photoplay*, 1930.

Swenson, Karen, *Greta Garbo: A Life Apart*, Simon & Schuster, 1997.

Swindell, Larry, *Charles Boyer: The Reluctant Lover*, Doubleday, 1983.

Various, *Who's Who in Gay & Lesbian Literature from Antiquity to World War II*, Routledge, 2002.

Vermilye, Jerry, *Films of the Twenties*, Citadel, 1985.

Vickers, Hugo, *Cecil Beaton*, Little, Brown & Co., 1985.

Vickers, Hugo, *Loving Garbo*, Jonathan Cape, 1994.

Vieira, Mark A., *Greta Garbo: A Cinematic Legacy*, Harry N. Abrams, 2005.

Viertel, Salka, *The Kindness of Strangers*, Holt, Rinehart & Winston, 1969.

Voight, Hubert, 'I Loved Garbo', *New Movie Magazine*, unedited, 1934.

Wakerman, John, *World Film Directors 1890–1945*, H. W. Wilson, 1987.

Walker, Alexander, *Garbo*, Weidenfeld & Nicolson, 1980.

Wayne, Jane Ellen, *The Lives & Loves of Barbara Stanwyck*, JR Books, 2009.

Williams, Tennessee, *Letters to Donald Windham, 1940–1965*, Holt, Rinehart & Winston, 1977.

Williams, Tennessee, *Memoirs*, Doubleday, 1975.

Woodhead, Henry, *Memoirs of Queen Christina*, BiblioBazaar, 2008.

Zierold, Norman, *Garbo*, Stein & Day, 1969.

Documentaries

Garbo, BBC Productions, 1969

Producer: Fred Burnley. Script: Alexander Walker. Hosted and narrated by Joan Crawford who insisted that she should share equal screen time with Garbo. With George Cukor and Rouben Mamoulian – the lack of other contributors is compensated by longer than usual film extracts, and the Garbo story ends abruptly with *Two Faced Woman*. This is also believed to have been the first time that Mauritz Stiller's homosexuality was publicly revealed. (60 mins.)

The Divine Garbo, Turner Pictures, 1990

Director: Susan F. Walker. Script: David Ansen. Narrated and hosted by Glenn Close. A quickly made tribute, released shortly after Garbo's death, with no participants. (45 mins.)

Garbo & Gilbert, BBC/Nugus/Martin Productions, 1997

Director: Jonathan Martin. Narrator: Robert Powell. Part of the *Great Romances of the Twentieth Century* series. With Eleanor Boardman, King Vidor. (30 mins.)

Greta Garbo: A Lone Star, London Weekend Television/Iambic Productions, 2001

Director: Steve Cole. Script/Narrator: Melvin Bragg (US: Lauren Bacall). With Molly Haskell, Karen Swenson, Kitty Carlisle Hart, Sam Green, Hugo Vickers, Signe Hasso, Karen Morley, Leatrice Gilbert Fountain, Ty Burr, George Sidney, Peter Viertel, Diana McLellan, Luise Rainer, Jack Larson. (53 mins.)

Garbo, Turner Classic Movies, 2005

Director/Script: Kevin Brownlow, Christopher Bird. Music: Carl Davis. Narrator: Julie Christie. With Charles Busch, Barry Paris, Daniel Selznick, Karen Swenson, Mimi Pollak, James Karen, Gray Reisfield, Clarence Brown, Mark Vieira, Leatrice Gilbert Fountain, Gavin Lambert, Gore Vidal, Joseph Newman, Adela Rogers St Johns, Cari Beauchamp, George Cukor, Sam Green, James Lax, Scott Reisfield. (90 mins.)

INDEX

Paterson, Pat 275
Pavlova, Anna 63
Pedersen, Kalle 4, 11–12, 35, 37
Peter The Tramp (film) 22–3, 29
Petschler, Erik Arthur 22–3, 24
Photoplay (magazine) 5, 69, 121–2, 130, 186, 188, 194, 242, 257, 259
Piaf, Edith 338
Pickford, Mary 7, 85, 130–1, 176
Picture Play (magazine) 173, 181–2, 186, 252
Pictures (magazine) 75
Pitts, Zasu 65
Pollak, Mimi 27–9, 34, 35, 36, 37, 75, 84, 139, 141, 143, 144, 224, 225, 258, 284, 331, 355
Pollet, Alfred 125
Poole, Abram 195
Proctor, Kay 262
PUB department store 15–17, 18–19, 22

Queen Christina (film) 224, 228–45
Quigley, Martin 243

Ralph, Jessie 268
Rambeau, Marjorie 185
Rambova, Natacha 124
Ramsey, Walter 242
Randall, Rae 216, 248, 255
Randolf, Anders 160
Rathbone, Basil 254–5
Red Dust (film) 198
Redemption (film) 166
Rée, Max 80, 81
Reid, Laurence 75
Reinhardt, Gottfried 282, 310, 311
Reinhardt, Max 166
Reisch, Walter 291, 308
Reisfield, Gray (GG's niece) 283, 299, 349, 356–7, 363, 364, 365, 366
Remarque, Erich Maria 314–15
Reud, Robert 99, 290, 353
Ring, Ragnar Lasse 18–19, 140
Roberts, W. Adolphe 63
Robertson, John S. 148
Robinson, Grace 222, 223, 224
Robson, May 256
Rogers, Adela 90–1, 106, 147

Roland, Gilbert 325–6
Romain, Jules 44
Romance (film) 175–6, 179–82
Roosevelt, Eleanor 320
Rosay, Françoise 158, 166
Rose Marie (film) 132
Rosing, Bodil 252
Rosson, Hal 272
Rothstock, Otto 58
Royal Dramatic Academy 23–9, 42, 44
Rubens, Alma 69, 131
Rubin, Robert 105
Rumann, Sig 293, 294
Rumfort, Greta 54, 56–7
Ruttenberg, Joseph 311
Ryman, Tyra 22, 23

Sands, Frederick 357–8
Sanina, Valentina 330, 349
Saratoga (film) 103
Sartov, Hendrik 69
Saville, Victor 308
Saxon, Lars 3, 7, 13, 78, 84, 91
Scarlet Angel (film) 18
Scarlet Letter, The (film) 47, 67, 69
Schenck, Nicholas 145
Schlatter, David 43, 46, 51
Shlee, George 330–4, 339, 340, 346, 349
Schmiterlow, Vera 26–7, 34–5
Scott, Audrey 248
Screenland 120
Seastrom, Victor 31, 33, 36, 47, 65, 103, 116, 117–18, 120, 131, 134, 137
Sebastian, Dorothy 129, 176
Seeber, Guido 55, 56
Seenwald, André 252
Selsey, E. W. 285–6
Selznick, David O. 253, 254, 255
Semitjov, Vladimir 44, 45
Seyfferitz, Gustav von 124–5, 126
Shall, Theo 184
Shaw, George Bernard 324
Shearer, Norma 91, 92, 118, 131, 182, 272
Sheldon, Edward 175
Sherman, Lowell 118
Sherwood, Robert E. 84–5